reign of caspian the navigator

SEVEN ISLES

ISLE OF MUIL

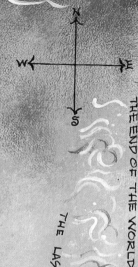

N
W E
S

THE END OF THE WORLD

LONE ISLANDS

TEREBINTHIA

DRAGON ISLAND

DEATH WATER ISLAND

BURNT ISLAND

CORIAKIN AND DUFFLEPUDS

THE DARKNESS

THE LAST WAVE

RAMANDU'S ISLAND

ASLAN'S COUNTRY

EASTERN SEA

UNDERWATER CIVILIZATION

SEA OF LILIES

CALORMEN SHIPS PLY THESE WATERS

FIRE

ASLAN AS LAMB

BEACHAM'S SOURCEBOOKS

EXPLORING C.S. LEWIS'
THE CHRONICLES OF NARNIA

by Kirk H. Beetz

BEACHAM PUBLISHING CORP.

For my friend Walton

Kay Curtis, illustrator of Kirk H. Beetz' maps of Narnia

Kay Curtis majored in art at the University of Oklahoma, and has exhibited throughout the U.S. and in Mexico and Australia. She says of her paintings: "We are part of the natural resource system on this planet, and the quality of human life is directly related to the diversity of other life. My paintings explore the complex and integrated relationship between animals, humans and other living things." Ms. Curtis lives and paints in Sarasota, Florida.

Library of Congress
    Cataloging-in-Publication Data
Beetz, Kirk H., 1952
    Exploring C. S. Lewis' The Chronicles of Narnia/ by Kirk H. Beetz.—1st American ed.
    (Beacham's Sourcebooks)
    Includes bibliographical references and index.
    Soft cover ISBN 0-933833-58-X   Hardcover ISBN 0-933833-63-6
    1. Lewis, C. S. (Clive Staples), 1898-1963. Chronicles of Narnia. 2. Lewis, C. S. (Clive Staples), 1898-1963.—Study and teaching. 3. Children's stories, English—History and criticism. 4. Christian fiction—History and criticism. 5. Fantasy fiction, English—History and criticism. I. Title. II. Series.

PR6023.E926 C532 2000
823'.912–dc21
    00-062175

Printed in Canada
First Printing, February 2001
First Edition

WHAT THE REVIEWERS ARE SAYING ABOUT

Beacham's Sourcebooks:Exploring Harry Potter

Public News Service, October 3, 2000. Today's Books. 5 star (highest rating) MUST READ!

Grand Rapids Press. Beacham's Sourcebooks: Exploring Harry Potter will be the most valuable of the tie-ins to the Hogwart's world. Author Elizabeth D. Schafer has compiled a complete compendium of all things Potter to both enhance the reading of the Harry Potter series. The meat of the guide traces complicated relationships between characters, helping children understand the formative boarding school experience and the mythology upon which many of the sub-plots are based. This book is a very useful tool to harness the excitement the Harry Potter books have generated and use it to jumpstart other scholastic pursuits.

Orange County (CA) Register. Parents and teachers interested in helping their children get a deeper understanding of the world of the boy wizard will want to check out *"Exploring Harry Potter,"* which includes everything from historical and literary references in the Potter series to discussion questions, educational activities, and reading recommendations to enrich the Harry Potter experience.

The Commercial Appeal (Memphis, TN). This book gives readers a fact-filled, fascinating look at the literary roots of Rowling's series. It is a wonderful source book for teachers and librarians, as well as parents and other adults who enjoy the Harry Potter books.

The Baltimore Sun. Schafer fills in holes and provides doors that open other doors, laying out information, activities, discussion questions and reading recommendations that encompass the range of subjects upon which the series touches. The result is a comprehensive compendium where chapters on characters and themes, geography, food, sports, history, science and (of course) magic and witchcraft help readers peer behind the scenes.

The Washington Post. If you like the [Harry Potter] books and think you might want to study them one day, this is a good introduction to the way teachers and critics think and talk about literature. It is also filled with interesting background information, like the fact that Nicholas Flamel, a name from the Potter books, was a real person (a 14th-century alchemist).

Los Angeles Times. "Exploring Harry Potter," by historian and children's literary expert Elizabeth D. Schafer, is a 478-page compendium of everything you could ever want to know about Harry Potter, and more.

Seattle Post-Intelligencer. One of the sourcebook's most intriguing features is a historical timeline in which Schafer shows what was happening in the real world as the novel's fictional events unfolded. For instance, sandwiched in between the death of King James II during the siege of Roxburgh Castle (Aug. 3, 1460) and the beginning of the Spanish Inquisition (1478) is the entry "1473: World Cup Quidditch match in which all 700 fouls occurred."

CONTENTS

EDITOR'S INTRODUCTION

O n this, the fiftieth anniversary of the publication of the *The Lion, the Witch and the Wardrobe,* we present the second in the series of *Beacham's Sourcebooks: C. S. Lewis' The Chronicles of Narnia,* soon to be followed by L. Frank Baum's *[The Wizard of] Oz* novels. Our sourcebooks are intended to expand readers' enjoyment and knowledge of the novels by providing insights into the creative process that have made them unique. There are many projects, discussion questions, and research topics that teachers and parents can use to further children's excitement for the novels and provide opportunities to study the layers of meaning and to admire *The Chronicles of Narnia* and its creator.

Although Lewis said that he did not write the Narnia series to explain his views of Christianity, the seven novels are, in essence, the story of the Creation, God's involvement with humankind, and Christ's role in the redemption and salvation of individuals on Judgment Day. Therefore, this sourcebook contains much discussion of Christian ideas and ideals, and each chapter devoted to the novels presents quotes from the Bible that Lewis incorporates into his narrative. As a result, this sourcebook is an excellent resource for exploring religion, particularly Christianity, with children.

Sourcebooks are not generally intended to be read cover to cover but to provide answers to questions as a reader becomes more involved in the novel. The extensive index helps locate chapters that may answer your questions about the parallels between the novels and mythology; religious symbols and allusions; specific references to the Bible; the geography of the adventure in each of the seven novels; and many other features, including websites for internet exploration; a timeline; an interpretative biography of C. S. Lewis; and resources for further reading and research.

Of special significance are the ten original maps, which Dr. Beetz has created to help readers specifically locate events that are discussed in the analysis of each novel. Although some editions of the Narnia novels have included a few maps, they are primarily decorative, while the maps that Dr. Beetz has compiled are instructional and are integral to understanding his analysis. The color map across the end pages depicts the known world at the end of the reign of Caspian the Navigator. The other nine maps are located in the "Geography" section of each chapter analyzing the novels. They depict:

1. The beginning of the world of Narnia (*The Magician's Nephew*)
2. The world of Shasta, King Cor, and Aravis (*The Horse and His Boy*)
3. Narnia during the long winter of the White Witch (*The Lion, the Witch and the Wardrobe*)
4. Prince Caspian's Rebellion (*Prince Caspian*)
5. The Voyage of the Dawn Treader in the fourth year of King Caspian (*The Voyage of the Dawn Treader*)
6. The Voyage of the Dawn Treader: Felimath, Doorn, and Avra islands
7. The Voyage of the Dawn Treader: Dragon, Deathwater, and Dufflepuds islands
8. The search for Prince Rilian (*The Silver Chair*)
9. The end of the world (*The Last Battle*)

Each of the maps contains a legend explaining events that occurred on the map.

How Parents Can Use the Sourcebook

There is much more to *The Chronicles of Narnia* than most student readers will recognize, and readers who have enjoyed the novels can be easily stimulated to explore related learning ideas, especially Christianity, world religions, and mythology. Parents can also use the predicaments of the children in the Narnia novels to open discussions with their own children about religion, moral values, fears, behavior, principles, government, and society.

How Teachers Can Use the Sourcebook

For teachers, we have provided chapter-by-chapter discussion questions (Section III) that develop analytical thinking and vocabulary expansion. These questions can be used to create lesson plans or to construct activities that students enjoy with each other. There are many, many projects and discussion ideas suggested, which teachers can turn into classroom activities or school projects.

How Student Readers Can Use the Sourcebook

Many of the questions are appropriate for students to use as a game to test each other's knowledge of the novels. There are also activities that students can perform without adult supervision. Students with internet access can search our recommended websites for fascinating facts and images related to Narnia's mystical world.

How Librarians Can Use the Sourcebook

For librarians who are helping students or entire classes locate information related to Narnia, or giving them ideas for research or reports, the sourcebook provides hundreds of suggestions, including websites.

Visit our own website at www.beachampublishing.com for extensive information about our first sourcebook, *Exploring Harry Potter,* to contact us by e-mail, and to keep abreast of forthcoming sourcebooks in this series.

WALTON BEACHAM

AUTHOR'S INTRODUCTION

One of the passages of literature that has stuck with me ever since I first read it is:

> She [Lucy] spent a good deal of time sitting on the little bench in the stern playing chess with Reepicheep. It was amusing to see him lifting the pieces, which were far too big for him, with both paws and standing on tiptoes if he made a move near the centre of the board. He was a good player and when he remembered what he was doing he usually won. But every now and then Lucy won because the Mouse did something quite ridiculous like sending a knight into the danger of a queen and castle combined. This happened because he had momentarily forgotten it was a game of chess and was thinking of a real battle and making the knight do what he would certainly have done in its place. For his mind was full of forlorn hopes, death or glory charges, and last stands.

How like Reepicheep! I first read this passage from *The Voyage of the "Dawn Treader"* when I was a child. C. S. Lewis was alive, then, and the book had been published perhaps five years before I read it. The memory of this passage lasted me all through school, through high school, college, and graduate school. It stuck with me as I wrote books and articles and as I taught English to college students. I loved Reepicheep and still do; I suspect that millions of the youngsters who have read *The Chronicles of Narnia* loved him, as well. It is a sign of the brilliance of characterization in *The Chronicles of Narnia* that Reepicheep and many other characters seem alive; one knows them, just as one knows that the gallant Reepicheep would forget himself and sometimes place a knight in danger of a queen just as he would place himself in the spot of greatest danger in battle.

This sourcebook closely examines each of the seven novels in the Narnia series. The discussion of each novel is divided into "Overview," "Geography," "Themes and Characters," "Chapter-by-Chapter Development of Themes and Characters," "Vocabulary," "References to the Bible," and " Discussion Questions and Projects." The "Development of Themes of Characters" examines each individual chapter, noting its focus and themes as well as how it advances the characterizations and themes of the entire novel. "Vocabulary" is also organized chapter-by-chapter and offers definitions for difficult words and phases. "References to the Bible" is organized chapter-by-chapter and lists the passages in *The Chronicles of Narnia* that parallel Biblical ones; each passage is presented in full, followed by comments on how the Biblical passage illuminates the events in the books. Of great help to me has been the "Biblical Allusions" section of Paul F. Ford's *Companion to Narnia*. In this section, Ford offers a list of allusions for each novel. I do not use all of his allusions, and I have added many of my own, but his listing suggests avenues of research that were of value to me, especially for *The Last Battle*.

The Discussion and Projects sections are divided into two parts: ideas for the novel as a whole and ideas for each individual chapter. If you are presenting one of the novels to a young audience, these ideas may help you generate a discussion about each chapter as your presentation progresses, especially if you are reading the novel aloud to your audience.

While the chapters on the seven books about Narnia are the heart of the present volume, there are other substantial sections. There is an interpretative "Life of C. S. Lewis" with an emphasis on his religious conversion, writing of the Narnia books, and his late-in-life romance with Joy Gresham. The Life is followed by Ideas for Book Reports and Projects and Topics for Discussion, both of which are geared to the biography of Lewis. Whatever his imperfections, Lewis was a great man, and how he lived his life offers many opportunities for discussing what makes for living a good life, as well as for discussing the context in which he wrote his books.

In addition to these sections, the present book offers chapters on The Theology of C. S. Lewis and His Writings for Young People, An Introduction to the Lands of Narnia, A Short History of Narnia, Thematic Development through Characters, Mythology, Historical Background, The Foods of Narnia, Geography, and Maps.

Lewis' theology is very complex; he read several different languages and was knowledgeable of the Bible in its original tongues and of the theological writings in languages as diverse as French and Latin. Rather than repeat his views in their entirety (something that would require a book all by itself), I focus on those aspects of his theology that are most evident in *The Chronicles of Narnia*. One of the techniques Lewis uses to bind the individual novels together is that of recurring characters. For instance, the valorous Reepicheep appears in *Prince Caspian, The Voyage of the "Dawn Treader,"* and *The Last Battle,* in each case providing some continuity among the books. In the "Recurring Characters" section, I offer an account of where the recurring figures appear, of how Lewis develops each, and of the significance of each in *The Chronicles of Narnia*. Finally, come Resources for Young Readers and Resources for Adults, where I note the biographies and autobiographical resources currently available; there are bound to be readers who will wish to read about Lewis's life in detail.

This book is not intended to substitute for reading the actual novels of *The Chronicles of Narnia,* and it cannot do so. Instead, it enhances the enjoyment of reading the novels and to aid in fully understanding what the novels are about and what Lewis achieves in them. As I discuss the novels chapter by chapter, you may want to follow along in the novels themselves. I point out some passages of special significance that you may wish to read in their entirety, and I recommend that you do so if you can.

KIRK H. BEETZ, PH.D.

SECTION I

~

THE LIFE AND
THEOLOGY OF
C. S. LEWIS

CHAPTER 1

HIS LIFE

OVERVIEW

C. S. Lewis lived most of his life as a college teacher, mostly in the college town of Oxford, England. Yet, he lived one of the most extraordinary lives of the twentieth century. It was marked by war, terror, and heroism; by terrible tragedy and noble sacrifice; by a shouted defiance of tyranny; by a romantic tragedy that ranks with the greatest romantic tragedies of fiction and history. For these aspects alone, Lewis' life story provides gripping drama and captivating reading.

Even so, it must be fairly said that other people have fought in terrible wars and been heroic; that others have endured awful tragedies and made great sacrifices; that many a marriage has had its moments of great romance, and that many have ended in tragedy. But Lewis' life offers more: His is a remarkable case of a life of the mind that has captured the imaginations of millions of people. The accounts of the intellectual lives of authors can be dull, of interest primarily to scholars, but in Lewis' case, many people have debated his writings and the significance of the life he lived.

Although an eminent scholar himself, Lewis wrote in plain English so that he could reach a wide audience. Whether he was writing a study of Renaissance literature or a book about the meaning of pain in everyday life, he wrote as if everyone should be interested in his subject, and he supplied numerous reasons to his audience for why the poet Edmund Spenser or the sufferings of a soldier should matter to them. Because he believed that both literature and theology belonged to ordinary people as well as college professors, he developed a hard-driving prose style that made history come alive and which drove through his nonfiction and fiction like a pile-driver on a railroad track.

His style is very personal, with the tone of a storyteller sitting in the room with the individual reader, telling him or her a wonderful story, sometimes in confidential whispers and other times in shouts with waving arms. Further, his best subject was very often himself. Particularly when explaining his theology, he would draw examples from his own experiences, as well as from the Bible and from history. In *Surprised by Joy,* he offers a history of his intellectual life that reads like a novel, bluntly explaining his atheism and how he once devoted his great intellectual and speaking talents to mock the religious beliefs of others, and then just as bluntly explaining his years-long climb out of darkness and into faith. This book, as well as others such as *The Meaning of Pain* and *Mere Christianity* invite examinations of his life, and some people study his work and life as if he were a modern saint, someone on a level with Augustine.

EARLY LIFE

Lewis was born into a Protestant Irish family on November 29, 1898, in Belfast. He was christened Clive Staples Lewis, but while still very young and on a holiday at the beach with his family, he announced that he wanted to be called "Jack," perhaps in honor of a friend's dog by that name. Throughout his life, C. S. Lewis was known as Jack to all his family and acquaintances, and for the sake of clarity, that is what I shall call him, here.

His father Albert was a solicitor (lawyer) in Belfast and was noted for his gift with words, often using his exceptional eloquence to win cases. Albert was a great reader and had a house full of books. Jack's mother, Flora Hamilton Lewis, was the daughter of a rector, and her family took pride in their long-standing association with the Anglican Church. Jack remembered her as being somewhat remote from her children, as Victorian mothers tended to be.

On April 21, 1905, the Lewises moved to a large country house called "Little Lea." It is the house on which Digory Kirke's country house is based in *The Magician's Nephew, The Lion, the Witch and the Wardrobe,* and *The Last Battle.* Little Lea was badly designed; its interior walls, floors, and ceilings rarely joined the exterior walls, leaving odd gaps between the walls, floors, and ceilings throughout the house. Jack and his brother Warren Hamilton Lewis (called "Warnie") found ways into these odd spaces, turning them into places of refuge and more importantly into places where they lived fantasy lives, creating imaginary lands and kingdoms.

It was at Little Lea that Jack developed his habit of reading. He would select several books that interested him (although he later complained that authors such as Coleridge and Shelley were missing) and would make several sandwiches. Little Lea had a multitude of rooms, and several, especially upstairs, were not used. Jack would take his books and sandwiches, plant himself in the middle of a room that was unlikely to be disturbed, and spend a day reading one book after another while munching his way through his sandwiches, which he stacked at his side. Throughout his life, he would associate food, reading, and pleasure with each other.

Life at Little Lea was not all games, reading, and sandwiches. Jack's mother had cancer, but by the time it was correctly diag-

nosed, the cancer was too advanced to treat. Surgery was tried, but in those days there were not the chemical treatments and radiation therapies available today and there was little that could be done for her. On August 23, 1908, Jack was sick in bed himself and wondering why his mother did not come to look in on him, but she lay dying and passed away that evening.

Jack's father Albert was overcome by grief; he never truly recovered from his wife's death and he mourned Flora all his life. This resulted in an emotional distance between himself and his two sons. Each boy wanted desperately to be comforted, but while Jack and Warnie comforted each other, Albert could not let go of his own misery enough to help his sons. As years passed, the estrangement between father and sons worsened, with Jack believing that his father did not truly care about the welfare of himself and Warnie.

In September 1908, Jack was sent to Wynyard House, a private school for boys. It was intended to prepare young men for college, but it was run by a madman who took pains to savagely beat his students not only for breaking rules but simply because they were in reach and he wanted to beat someone. Jack later called Wynyard a "concentration camp," and it began his outright hatred for schools. His experience at Wynyard House is one of the reasons why schools are disparaged in *The Chronicles of Narnia*.

In a letter to a young correspondent, Francine, Lewis wrote, "I was at three schools (all boarding schools) of which two were very horrid. I never hated anything so much, not even the front line trenches in World War I." (C. S. Lewis, *Letters to Children*, ed. Lyle W. Dorsett and Marjorie Lamp Mead, New York,

Simon and Schuster, 1985, p. 102.) The other two schools were Cherbourg School and Malvern College.

In 1910, when he was twelve, Jack returned to Ireland and Little Lea. He was frequently ill, and it is possible that these illnesses began the weakening of his heart that would vex him in the last years of his life. Next door to Jack lived a boy about his own age, Arthur Greeves. Aside from Warnie, Arthur may have been Jack's closest lifelong friend. When Lewis was away, they wrote to each other constantly and were very open about their lives and feelings. For instance, Arthur wrote about his homosexuality bluntly, even after Jack became a famous author of books about Christianity. Jack believed that the love of God meant salvation, just as greeting Aslan with love gains entry into Heaven in *The Last Battle.* It is possible that he saw such salvation for Arthur, although he did not seem to make any judgments about Arthur's sexuality.

During this period, Jack briefly attended a day school in Belfast, which he remembered primarily for its cruel bullies. In 1911, he was sent to Cherbourg School in Malvern, England. He loved Malvern but despised the school, where bullying was constant and the adults in charge did nothing to protect victims. Aside from learning how to take a beating, Jack regarded attending schools up to this moment a waste of time.

This changed in 1913, when he attended Malvern College, a place where violence was minimized and he could actually enjoy himself sometimes. It was the custom among the English of Jack's era to send their sons away to school at about the age of eight, a tradition that extended back to the early 1700s; parents would often only see their sons during school holidays from age eight until age eighteen. They often would not know their own sons. That this was so did nothing to alleviate Lewis' anger toward his father; he felt that Albert had abandoned him to evil people.

But in 1914, Albert Lewis did Jack a very good turn. One of Albert's favorite teachers, then living in retirement, agreed at Albert's request to take Jack in and tutor him. This tutor was a formidable logician named William Kirkpatrick, who appears as Digory Kirke in *The Chronicles of Narnia*. In the novels, the grownup Professor Digory mutters in exasperation about what schools seemed not to be teaching children. This is drawn from Kirkpatrick, who taught Jack how to be ruthlessly logical; this logic leads Digory Kirke to conclude that Lucy is telling the truth about Narnia in *The Lion, the Witch and the Wardrobe*, and in real life it taught Jack how to present his thoughts plainly and how to strip away fallacies in arguments. This made him one of the most formidable debaters of his time (although he did not win *every* debate) and a very intimidating college instructor.

In 1916, Jack read *Phantastes* by George MacDonald, an author who used fantasy to depict religious ideas; Jack later credited MacDonald with influencing his own fantasies. Yet MacDonald's deeper insights regarding religion seemed to have had no immediate effect on Jack's own religious attitudes. At about age thirteen, Jack had decided that there was no God, not of any kind. When he attended University College at Oxford University, he used his immense talents for language and argument to defy religious people; when he debated religion, he debated in favor of atheism, and he was very good at it.

World War I had begun in 1914, and by 1917 it had resulted in many millions of deaths. England lost a multitude of its young men in the trenches and wastelands of the war. As an Irishman, Jack was exempt from the military draft in England, but in 1917, he volunteered for the army, anyway, and he underwent a brief period of training to be an officer. At this time he made friends with Paddy Moore; before being sent to fight, they made a pact with each other. If Jack died but Paddy lived, Paddy would see to the welfare of Jack's father; if Paddy died but Jack lived, Jack would see to the welfare of Paddy's mother Janie Moore. Paddy was killed, and Jack took Janie, who was called "Minto," and Paddy's sister Maureen into his home. Although Jack selflessly cared for mother and daughter for many years, his brother Warnie believed them to be ungrateful burdens on Jack.

Jack fought at the front in World War I. He remembered the horrors of sudden death, as well as misery in rat-infested, disease ridden trenches (although he would later declare that life in the trenches was much more pleasant than life in school). In 1918, he and his sergeant were standing together talking when the sergeant was blown to pieces, his body fragments sticking to Jack. Jack himself was badly injured in combat and he spent the rest of the war recovering in hospitals. He was a robustly built, tough young man, and he eventually overcame his physical injuries.

RELIGIOUS CONVERSION

Jack returned to Oxford University to complete his studies. In 1925, he received a fellowship in English at Oxford's Magdalen College, whose duties included teaching. That same year, he met J. R. R. Tolkien, who was already working on the stories that would tell of Middle Earth and the lives of such figures as Bilbo and Frodo Baggins. Tolkien was a Roman Catholic and very devoted to his faith. Jack remained steadfast in his atheism, although Tolkien's writings for *The Lord of the Rings* would eventually have a profound effect on him.

Throughout his twenties, Jack was a ruthless advocate of atheism. He ridiculed religious faith and argued down those who defied his views. Even so, Tolkien stood his ground and still became Jack's closest friend during those years. In the meantime, Jack studied literature with ferocity, teaching himself to read in foreign languages so he could read literary works in their original tongues. When not studying, he was teaching. As a junior faculty member, he had a heavy load of students and classes. He was expected to meet with each of his students individually to discuss their papers; some disliked him for his pugnacious style of debating their papers, but most loved him and admired how he helped them to become better thinkers. In this, Jack drew on the techniques Kirkpatrick had used to tutor him.

Jack was past thirty years old before his religious views changed. Influenced heavily by the writings of Plato, as well as Aristotle and other philosophers, Lewis had what he described as a religious experience, or an epiphany when he was riding a bus: He realized that God was a fact. He did not at that time believe that God was necessarily the deity that Christians accept or the deity of any other religion, but suddenly believed that there was indisputable evidence that there had to be a Supreme Being. It was at this time that he concluded that human thinking was a metaphysical act, meaning that the ability to think in abstractions had to occur apart from the human body, which could allow only for concrete thought. Abstract ideas such as honor, love, and truth therefore had a supernatural element to them. This implies that every person, even atheists, like it or not, touch on the divine when they think.

In 1930, Jack moved to a house at Oxford called "The Kilns." It had a pond in back for swimming, a spacious yard, and was a big, rambling house reminiscent of but better constructed than Little Lea. It would be his home for the rest of his life. In it, he installed Minto and Maureen, and when his older brother Warnie retired from the navy, he lived there as well. Minto was a sad, difficult person, and she frequently called Jack away from his work to help with household chores. These Jack did cheerfully; it is possible that washing dishes was a good break from the difficult mind work that writing requires. Warnie, on the other hand, was very helpful to Jack. When Jack became famous (he was not famous quite yet), Warnie served as his secretary, sorting the huge volume of mail Jack received, and helping prepare Jack's manuscripts for publication. Although not the genius Jack was, through hard studying, Warnie made himself an expert on French literature and published books of his own on the subject.

Minto hired an eccentric gardener, Fred Paxford, to work at The Kilns. He regarded the property's greenhouse as his own private place, and even Jack had to ask his permission to enter. He frequently spouted strange pronouncements on life, politics, and philosophy, which Minto quoted as if they were brilliant insights, and which Jack tolerated with good cheer. Paxford appears as Puddleglum, the Marsh-wiggle in *The Silver Chair*.

In his studies, which included the literatures of cultures as far away as China and India, Lewis noted the constant theme of the divine in the effort of people to explain their metaphysical

lives through myths. The myths could be very elaborate and beautiful, but there seemed little doubt that while all mythologies recognized a supernatural god, they were all untrue. This had been at bottom of some of his arguments in favor of atheism—not all mythologies could be true, therefore all must be false. By 1931, Jack knew that this was an insipid argument that could scarcely be called reasoning.

In the late summer of 1931, while exploring a country town with friends, including Tolkien, he had his most momentous religious experience. He had, as Jack recalled the time, been long resisting the inevitable consequences of his research into cultures and myths in particular. Tolkien had been reading aloud portions of *The Hobbit, The Silmarillion,* and *The Lord of the Rings* to gatherings at The Kilns, and Jack was very impressed at how Tolkien was able to express complex, important ideas about spiritual lives in his invented mythology of Middle Earth. While walking with Tolkien and discussing mythology, Jack came to the conclusion that all his thought and research seemed to aim toward Christianity as a "true myth." That is, like other mythologies, Christianity offers explanations for the spiritual aspects of human life and accounts of the relationship of humanity to the supernatural universe; the difference between them and Christianity was that Christianity could be proven to be true.

This conclusion on Jack's part changed his life dramatically. He joined the Anglican church and attended services regularly. He saw himself as a prodigal son who has returned home to God. He had been a very closed-minded atheist; now he was a very open-minded Christian. Perhaps because of his memories of the religious antagonism between Protestants and Roman Catholics in Belfast, he rejected the notion that any one denomination was the one true Christian denomination, and he began developing his concept of "mere Christianity," the elements of Christianity that unite all Christians, regardless of their differences.

In 1935, Jack met Charles Williams. Although at first put off by Williams's rough behavior, Jack and he became good friends. Like George MacDonald and J. R. R. Tolkien, Williams tried to express his views on religion and culture in the form of fantasy novels such as *Descent into Hell*. By then, Jack was well on his way to establishing himself as a great Christian theologian, but with MacDonald, Tolkien, and Williams in mind, he undertook the writing of fantasies, producing *Out of the Silent Planet* in 1938.

Tolkien's success with creating a mythology inspired Jack to try creating his own and he began the most famous of his chronicles of Narnia, *The Lion, the Witch and the Wardrobe* in 1939. That year, World War II began with Germany and the Soviet Union's joint invasion of Poland. The evils of the war find their way into *The Chronicles of Narnia,* although they are not as important as the changes in Jack's household that the war brought on. Jack and Minto volunteered to take in London children during the war because Germany was bombing the city night and day. In *The Lion, the Witch and the Wardrobe* the Pevensie children are sent to Professor Kirke's house to escape the bombing. During the war, Jack had many children come and go in his household, mostly girls, and he entertained them with stories of Narnia. Thus, by the end of World War II all, except possibly *The Last Battle,* of the Narnian stories were in progress.

EARLY WORKS

The 1940s were very busy for Jack. In 1940, his book *The Problem of Pain* was published. In it, he tries to explain why there is suffering in a world created by God. In 1941, he began a series of radio lectures on Christianity. These enormously popular lectures were published in three volumes, and later gathered into *Mere Christianity*. These made him world famous. In 1942, he published the classic *The Screwtape Letters,* about a demon's efforts to corrupt a good man. This expanded the audience of fiction readers that Jack had reached with his *Out of the Silent Planet*. In 1943, he published *Perelandra,* a sequel to *Out of the Silent Planet*. When World War II ended in 1945, Jack's foster children returned to their parents and his household became quiet again. He missed them, and his private life was dealt a second blow when Charles Williams died that same year.

In 1947, Jack published *Miracles* in which he tries to answer common questions about miracles. He maintains that miracles occur only at important moments when history, religious faith, and movements in the universe coincide to create a crisis. This idea is seen throughout *The Chronicles of Narnia*. The miracles of the children being transported to Narnia occur at critical periods in the history of Narnia's world. The centaurs, who are very learned and study astronomy, assert that Aslan only comes to Narnia when the stars and planets are themselves in critical positions. *Miracles* was the source of one of Jack's most humiliating defeats as a debater, when he tried to defend his view that miracles occurred only at special times against someone who believed miracles to be much more common. In the late 1950s, Jack drifted to a moderate position, accepting that miracles may be more common than he supposed, but still not everyday events.

HIS LIFE WHILE WRITING NARNIA

In the late 1940s and early 1950s, Jack was immersed in his Narnia books. There is much disagreement among scholars about the order in which they were written. Jack helps a little in a letter to a young reader named Laurence: "When I wrote *The Lion,* I did not know I was going to write any more. Then I wrote *P. Caspian* as a sequel and still didn't think there would be any more, and when I had done *The Voyage* I felt quite sure it would be the last. But I found I was wrong." (C. S. Lewis, *Letters to Children*, 1985, p. 68.) I think we should take Jack at his word about *The Lion, the Witch and the Wardrobe*; *Prince Caspian*; and *The Voyage of the "Dawn Treader"* being the first three books he wrote in the series; they were published in that order. But after these, Jack says the books were published in an order of his publisher's choosing, not his own. This would suggest that all the books were completed or nearly completed when *The Lion, the Witch and the Wardrobe* was published in 1950. The internal references in each novel to events that occur in later novels also suggest that Jack knew what he was putting into all the books before the publication of each. Further, it is plain that the publisher issued one book per year not because Jack wrote one per year, but to maximize sales of each volume.

Lewis seems to have revised his books up until publication. Thus, all the novels may have been written by the end of 1949, but Jack continued to tinker with them. There is evidence that he was still making minor revision to *The Voyage of the "Dawn Treader"* in February 1950 and to *The Horse and His Boy* in the summer of 1950.

The entire *Chronicles of Narnia* seems to have been written primarily in an explosion of creative energy that lasted three to five years, so that he had finished revising *The Last Battle* (the seventh book of the series) by March 1953. This helps to explain why, even as volumes were still being published in the mid-1950s, Jack was telling young fans that there would be no more books in the series. He had finished with them except for revising phrases here and there. They were already part of his past.

In 1950, the year *The Lion, the Witch and the Wardrobe* was published, Jack began his correspondence with Joy (Davidman) Gresham. She was a poet and married to an abusive, alcoholic husband. She was short, slim, and had a face that was all points and angles. Jack found her beautiful. By 1952, the year *The Voyage of the "Dawn Treader"* was published, she and Jack had exchanged several letters. Desperate to get away from her husband, she took her two sons, David and Douglas, with her to London. Minto had died on January 12, 1951, the year *Prince Caspian* was published. Jack mourned her greatly, although Warnie saw her passing as a liberation for his brother. Thus, when Joy visited Jack during Christmas time in 1951, the Kilns had not known a woman resident for almost two years. Joy was not like Minto; she fended for herself and did not impose on Jack. Further, she could swear as well as Jack, who relished good swearing, and she shared Jack's love of tobacco and strong drink. When among Jack's men friends, she held her own. She was smart, quick witted, and outspoken.

In 1953, the year *The Silver Chair* was published, Joy divorced William Gresham and moved with David and Douglas to England, to stay. As an American, she associated America with the miseries and brutality of her marriage. In England there was the kindest man she had ever known, Jack. (Almost everyone who knew Jack and has written about him says that he was remarkably kind.)

In 1954, *The Horse and His Boy* was published, and in 1955, the same year *The Magician's Nephew* was published, Lewis became a professor at Magdalene College, Cambridge University. He had long been denied promotions at Oxford University. Atheist faculty members detested his writings about Christianity and strove mightily to deny him any honors, and they were by-and-large successful. Colleagues were suspicious of his popularity; even his most scholarly works seemed to be written with a clarity that appealed to general readers. Their belief was that popular works could not be deep works, as if *Hamlet* were shallow. Other faculty members were jealous of Jack's popularity, not only as a writer but as a teacher. Further, Jack was a pugnacious man who loved a good argument. Some of his colleagues resented how he had bested them in debates. On the other hand, the faculty and administration at Cambridge University by-and-large thought they had done well to attract a distinguished man of letters whose books on literature had become standard readings for students and professors. Jack remained living at The Kilns after he took the Cambridge position; a train ran directly between Oxford and Cambridge, and he rode it almost daily.

His autobiography *Surprised by Joy* (1955) is mostly about his spiritual life, and the joy came when he recognized God as God.

To him, his life had been dreary and sad until his religious conversion. Thereafter, he thought himself a happy man. Later, his "joy" would be severely tried as he lost the woman he loved.

THE RECEPTION OF THE NARNIA BOOKS

When *The Chronicles of Narnia* were first published, they were snubbed as too trivial for book reviewers to write about, but then, in the 1950s, most literary critics routinely ridiculed children's books and their writers. In Jack's case, they thought that a great writer had greatly lowered his reputation by writing *The Chronicles of Narnia*. Although there were respectful discussion of *The Chronicles of Narnia* here and there during the 1960s and 1970s, it was not until the 1980s that *The Chronicles of Narnia* began to receive its due. This corresponded with expanding academic studies of children's literature and the creation of college courses in children's literature throughout much of the United States. Jack himself never accepted the idea that he had in any way lowered himself by writing seven children's books instead of more theological studies or novels for adults. When challenged, he bluntly defended his children's books.

More difficult for Jack to bear were J. R. R. Tolkien's disparagements of the Narnia books, especially *The Lion, the Witch and the Wardrobe*. Tolkien insisted that for a modern mythology to succeed, it must be consistent in its sources and background. For instance, his own *The Lord of the Rings,* even then recognized as a masterpiece, stuck with medieval northern European sources. Its monsters and magical beings all are consistent with a particular culture. In *The Lion, the Witch and the Wardrobe*, Tolkien complained that Lewis had mixed myths from Ancient Greek culture, medieval northern European culture, and from modern popular culture. Further, the fauns and dwarfs were from pagan myths and therefore incompatible with the Christian Father Christmas, who seems to be utterly out of place when he appears in *The Lion, the Witch and the Wardrobe*. Lewis was striving for a universal mythology, one in which every culture may find a place in God's world, but he apparently was never able to get this point across to Tolkien. In the great universe of Aslan, as Aslan notes at the end of *The Last Battle,* all good people are welcome, even if they had not known Aslan.

On the other hand, the reaction of children to *The Chronicles of Narnia* was powerful. While reviewers were prattling nonsense about books they plainly did not understand, children were devouring the stories. In *The Chronicles of Narnia,* the story is more important than the themes, and children may merrily read the wondrous adventures without worrying about moralistic endings or deep, long disquisitions on good and evil. Further, the characterizations are brilliant. It was, and still is, easy for youngsters to love Puddleglum and Reepicheep and to admire and love Lucy, Peter, Susan, Edmund, and the other visitors to Narnia. I first read *The Lion, the Witch and the Wardrobe* around 1961 or 1962, and I did not come across it forlorn on a dusty library bookshelf. My classmates were all a-buzz about it; I must have heard a dozen different young readers recommend it to their friends. Therefore, I sought it out. It was hard to find in the library, as were the other volumes in *The Chronicles of Narnia*; people kept checking them out, and even three or four copies of each volume did not seem enough to meet the demand—and this was a decade

after the first publication of *The Lion, the Witch and the Wardrobe*!

Around 1959, someone, a friend of children and a friend of Narnia, coined the phrase *The Chronicles of Narnia*. It was a term that Jack did not use. They seem like chronicles because of their personal tone; their narrator sometimes breaks in with an "I don't know what happened to them" or other personal remarks. This makes the narrator seem like a storyteller, speaking to us in front of a warm fire on a cold night, telling us the *history* of a another time and place—a chronicler. As we have grown up, some of us have written about *The Chronicles of Narnia* and Jack, out of love and respect. Even as I write, the critical view is changing and I hope the wiser views of children will prevail, with *The Chronicles of Narnia* standing as a masterpiece of literature.

LEWIS' GREAT ROMANCE

By 1956, the year *The Last Battle* was published, Joy Gresham and Jack were in love. They enjoyed a robust, active relationship, but Joy was diagnosed with cancer. Under English law, she could not receive the free medical attention that British subjects were entitled to; she had to be a British subject or be married to one, but she was an American citizen and she and Jack seem to have given little thought to marriage, although Joy was now single. Jack had paid her rent and for schooling for her sons, and he was willing to pay for her cancer treatment, but the financial burden would be great. After much thought and discussion, Jack and Joy decided to be married in a civil ceremony in order that she might receive medical care under English law. Thus, they were married on April 23, 1956 at the Oxford Registry Office. Their marriage was very private, and few people, including friends, realized that it had happened.

The event was an unhappy affair. Joy's cancer was spreading through much of her body, and she seemed certain to die within weeks. The wedding troubled Jack's friends as they slowly learned of it. They wondered why it was held in near secrecy, and they were hurt that they had not been informed at the time the wedding took place. Other people, from that day to the present, wondered why Jack and Joy chose a civil ceremony rather than a church ceremony: after all, they were both outspoken Christians. One explanation that has been offered is that Jack and Joy were friends but not in love, and that the civil ceremony was no more than a way to get Joy care she needed. This is utterly false; testimony from those who knew, Joy's son Douglas in particular, makes it clear that Jack and Joy were in love and were virtually inseparable. A more probable explanation is that both Jack and Joy were independent spirits who wished to maintain an air of independence; Jack was a lifelong bachelor, so the explanation goes, and he preferred the company of men to women, so he wanted no public, religiously binding ceremony. This is a poor explanation that runs counter to what is known of Jack's personality and beliefs. The whole "devoted bachelor" idea fails to take into account the history of his life; his home at The Kilns had Minto and Maureen in it for many years, and during World War II, it was alive with the shouts and playing of children, which Jack enjoyed.

Troubling to some Christians is the fact that the wedding was civil. Many Christian denominations hold that any wedding, civil as well as church, is binding before God, and they have a

thousand years full of precedents that they can cite to support their belief. Thus, that Jack regarded a civil wedding as something apart from a wedding before God disturbs them. Jack and some Christian denominations, for instance the Roman Catholic church, see a difference between civil, or legal weddings and religious ones; the former is bound by earthly laws, the latter by God's Law. Thus, a better explanation is that Jack and Joy held a hasty, almost desperate civil wedding in order to secure her medical treatment while intending to have a Christian wedding later, God willing.

They were not to have a church wedding, in the company of friends and with the celebrations of wedding cake and honeymoon. On March 21, 1957, Jack and Joy were married in a Christian ceremony as she lay near death in Wingfield Hospital. It had been difficult to persuade a minister to conduct the rites, but before God as well as the law they were married. The ceremony in the hospital was a way of declaring to each other their enduring love; each hoped for a reunion after death, in what in *The Chronicles of Narnia* Jack called "Aslan's country." Indeed, Jack hoped that Joy would be present at his own death, to greet him in his new life.

Both of them regarded it as a miracle when Joy's cancer went into remission. The cancer had riddled her bones, making them very weak and prone to snapping. Now they regained calcium and returned to what they should be. The metastasized cancer abandoned the rest of her body, and Joy was free from pain. She and her sons moved in with Jack at The Kilns, but the happiness occasioned by her coming to live with her husband was tempered somewhat by his failing health.

Jack had long had a weak heart. Before he and Joy were married he had consulted with his physician about whether his heart could tolerate sexual activity; his physician said that he would be okay. Even so, his heart was a matter of anxiety. Further, he was suffering from osteoporosis—the loss of calcium from his bones. As Joy's bones had strengthened, his had weakened.

Still, life at The Kilns seems to have been happy. David and Douglas came to live there as Jack's sons. Warnie remembered David as being bitter and resentful, an unpleasant house mate. On the other hand, Douglas bonded deeply with his stepfather. He remembers discovering a wardrobe in the house and asking whether it was *the wardrobe* and being told that indeed it was the wardrobe from Little Lea that became the entry to Narnia in *The Lion, the Witch and the Wardrobe*. Douglas would not peek into it for years after learning this.

In 1959, Joy's cancer returned. Much of her ill health (and that of Jack, as well) may be attributable to their smoking. Jack smoked sixty-six cigarettes a day for decades, and when not puffing on a cigarette, he was inhaling his pipe. By 1959, medical science had long known (since the mid-1880s) that tobacco smoke was poisonous, but the general public, people like Jack and Joy, were not so well informed.

Jack and Joy traveled to Greece with some friends in 1960. Jack did not like to travel; he said that he preferred to imagine other places. He had had his fill of seeing the world during World War I when he lived in a France torn and blown apart by war. Even so, the trip to Greece was fun. Everyone knew that Joy was dying, and she had difficulty walking and needed much rest, but she took pleasure in visiting the historical sights. They

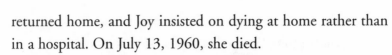

returned home, and Joy insisted on dying at home rather than in a hospital. On July 13, 1960, she died.

This occasioned Jack's greatest crisis of faith since his religious conversion in 1931. Romantic love had come late to him, but he loved with all the passion of a young man, and Joy's death crushed him. He wondered whether God was nothing more than an observer of life who took pleasure in the many difficulties people got into, or whether God was a sort of puppet master who played with human lives without regard to their feelings.

In 1961, his book *A Grief Observed* was published. It is a short book that discusses how Jack came to terms with the loss of his wife. He insisted that it be published under a pen name, not wanting it to be a popular work because he had written it, but to be a helpful work that was important by itself. It did not sell well until after his own death, when his heirs gave the publisher permission to put his name on the book; it then sold millions of copies.

David and Douglas remained with Jack after Joy's death. In her last few years, Minto had become querulous and unpleasant, but Jack took care of her with cheerful forbearance; although others regarded David as a problem, Jack regarded him with the same honest patience that he gave to others he loved. When David insisted that he wanted to follow the faith of his mother's ancestors, Judaism, Jack inquired of a rabbi about how to raise David in that faith and found places where he could buy kosher foods for the teenager. When Joy died, Jack and Douglas stood in the middle of a room and hugged each other and cried together. Douglas has always written about Jack as his father, and although he had many pressures on him as a youngster in early adolescence, he proved to be a great help and comfort to Jack. Their family unit in the last days of Jack's life was filled out by Warnie, who enjoyed better health than his younger brother. Warnie undertook to relieve the ailing Jack of as many burdens as he could, but even on his last day, Jack, as he had for many years, arose before dawn to read and reply to letters, many from children. He made sure to read every child's letter and to reply to it, although Warnie often had to do the actual writing. On November 22, 1963, Jack collapsed in his bedroom and died, probably of heart failure, perhaps of a stroke. Warnie remembered that earlier Jack had remarked that he had done all that God had set for him to do.

IDEAS FOR REPORTS AND PROJECTS

1. C. S. Lewis was born in Belfast in 1898, during a period in which religious strife seemed to have abated. Even so, there was friction between Protestants and Roman Catholics. What was the religious state of affairs in Ireland in 1898? Compare the situation then to the situation in 1998.

2. Lewis hated the schools he attended as a child. What were "public schools" (Americans would call them private) like in Lewis' era? What would make them hateful to him?

3. What are the origins of the custom of sending children off to boarding schools in England? Why would parents continue to do it when they themselves hated the schools?

4. What did science know about breast cancer in 1908, when Flora Lewis died? What treatments were there? How would Lewis' wife Joy have been treated in the late 1950s?

5. Where is Malvern in England? What aspects of the town did Lewis like? What did it look like when he went to school there? What does it look like now?

6. Who was Arthur Greeves? Why was he important to Lewis?

7. Who was William Kirkpatrick? What is the history of his life? How did he help Lewis? How closely does Professor Kirke of *The Chronicles of Narnia* resemble him?

8. Who was George MacDonald? Why would his *Phantastes* be of special interest to Lewis?

9. What would life have been like for Lewis at the front in World War I in 1917?

10. Lewis became a fellow in English at Magdalen College, Oxford University, in 1925. What were the duties of a fellow at Magdalen College in those days?

11. Who was J. R. R. Tolkien? What about his writings might have encouraged Lewis' religious conversion? What about those writings might have inspired Lewis to write *The Lion, the Witch and the Wardrobe*?

12. Lewis believed that the act of thinking is a metaphysical experience. In this belief, he was influenced by Plato's views on concrete and abstract thought. What were Plato's views on the matter?

13. Who was Charles Williams? What books did he write, and what were they about? Why would Lewis especially admire Williams?

14. Why were children often lodged in the homes of strangers in England during World War II? What were their experiences during the war?

15. Why would the children who lived with Lewis at The Kilns during World War II not know that he was famous?

16. What were Joy Gresham's qualities that would have attracted Lewis to her?

17. What role has Lewis' stepson Douglas Gresham played in the history of Lewis' publications? (You might do well to begin your research with Douglas' *Lenten Lands,* 1994.)

18. Why would the faculty and administration at Oxford University keep Lewis in a junior faculty position rather than promoting him and honoring him for his immense body of good work?

19. Why do some literary critics regard children's literature as inferior? Why would they regard *The Chronicles of Narnia* as a waste of Lewis' time?

20. What were Tolkien's objections to *The Chronicles of Narnia*? How did Lewis respond to them?

21. Find the passages in which the narrator mentions himself in one of the novels in *The Chronicles of Narnia*. What are the effects of his personal comments on events?

22. Why would people have been disturbed by Jack and Joy's civil wedding on April 23, 1956? Why would some Christian observers be bothered by it, even now?

23. How did Lewis come to terms with Joy's death? How did her death affect his views of God?

24. Why would Lewis want his book *A Grief Observed* to be published under a pen name rather than his real name? Were his reasons sound?

25. What happened to David Gresham after Lewis' death?

26. What were Warren Lewis' publications? What were his most significant achievements?

TOPICS FOR DISCUSSION

1. Why would Lewis refuse to write any more Narnian books after *The Last Battle,* even though children asked him for more?

2. Are Lewis' writings for adults more important than his writings for young people?

3. If Lewis had defended his Narnian books against his critics, what might have he said?

4. Why did Tolkien disapprove of *The Lion, the Witch and the Wardrobe*? Was he right?

5. Why was Lewis more interested in telling good stories than in promoting Christian ideas in *The Chronicles of Narnia*?

6. Lewis remarked that children usually understood the deeper ideas of *The Chronicles of Narnia* better than adults. Why would this be so?

7. Lewis was noted as an aggressive, fierce debater and a tough, demanding teacher, yet also as a very kind man. How could he be aggressive, fierce, tough, and demanding, yet very kind?

8. Why would Lewis, a scholar and theologian, enjoy telling stories to children?

9. Why did Lewis still love God after the horrible death of his wife Joy?

10. Why is Lewis' life of interest to people? Lewis himself thought that his life had little relevance for understanding his writings, yet readers persistently look at his life while studying his publications. Why would they do this?

CHAPTER 2

HIS THEOLOGY AND
HIS WRITINGS FOR
YOUNG PEOPLE

There are three aspects of Lewis' religious life and theology that are particularly important for understanding what he achieved in *The Chronicles of Narnia*. First is his belief that the supernatural was a part of everyday life. For him and many of his friends, angels were always busy among people; the battle for the souls of people continued everyday, everywhere, even among people who did not recognize what was happening; and God's Presence was there for every person. What many people would call *extraordinary*, the supernatural world, was for Lewis *ordinary*. Miracles, lost souls, saved souls were all part of his world. They and especially angels could be in his home, at the market, or in the classroom.

As one consequence of the daily presence of supernatural beings and events, lost souls or souls on the verge of being lost could be saved anywhere. Lewis himself had important religious experiences on a bus and during a walk along a street. As a result of his belief that people's souls could be saved anywhere, Lewis wrote books on religion that gave people great hope for salvation. Although he did not originally intend *The Chronicles of Narnia* to speak of religious matters, they were from the first concerned with the supernatural and with making supernatural events part of the lives of the characters in *The Lion, the Witch and the Wardrobe*.

The idea that there is not only a supernatural world, but that it is really just an ordinary part of life may be hard for some people to accept, but it is not necessary for the enjoyment of *The Chronicles of Narnia*. Nor is it necessary for readers to accept Lewis' belief that there are *universal moral laws* that transcend religious beliefs, although it is a concept that helps with

understanding *The Chronicles of Narnia*. Remember, Lewis was exceptionally well read in the histories of other cultures; he was conversant in ancient Chinese and Hindu theology as well as ancient Norse religious beliefs and many other mythologies. He also was well-schooled in philosophy, including the philosophical views of atheists such as David Hume and Voltaire; he had been, after all, an outspoken atheist into his thirties. Lewis incorporate ideas from all these sources into *The Chronicles of Narnia*, and although it is not necessary that readers recognize or accept these allusions in order to enjoy the novels, understanding the diversity of myths and religions Lewis draws upon will deepen the reader's appreciation of his accomplishment.

What Lewis discovered were rules that he regarded as the foundations for moral behavior. An individual person might reject the moral rules, but a culture as a whole would embrace them. Among these universal moral codes were abhorrence of murder, respect for the elderly, and despising cruelty to children, each a subject in *The Chronicles of Narnia*. Lewis argued that the existence of these *universal moral laws* were valid evidence for his religious beliefs. He maintained that the cross-cultural moral laws meant that there was a source of moral thinking that was not dependent on culture, place, or era. It seemed to him reasonable to suppose that the ancient Egyptians, Chinese, and Australian Aborigines, existing far apart both in location and historical era, would have had moral codes that would have been utterly different. Their environments were different; their needs for survival were different; yet they shared in common with Vikings, Indians, and Englishmen certain moral standards against which the behavior of people could measured.

For instance, a man who protected children from harm would be considered good in the context of the *universal moral law* prohibiting cruelty to children.

This concept was especially important to Lewis because it was one of the reasons for his developing a belief in God. That such laws existed was something he was sure he could prove. If they existed, then they implied a unifying force in human affairs. Psychoanalyst Carl Jung would have suggested that the *universal moral laws* were evidence of the "universal unconscious," in which people all over the world shared ideas in common. Jung suggested that events and moral views shared in different cultural mythologies were evidence of the sharing of ideas through the universal unconscious. Lewis argued that there was more to shared values than a universal unconscious mind; he insisted that the universality of certain moral views had to have a source and that the source had to be outside of human beings, not within them. To him, this meant proof of a supernatural world and proof of the existence of God. That most people in most cultures would recognize certain moral laws in common also meant that God was active in the everyday lives of people, that He was present in their homes, at work, on streets—everywhere there are people, there is God.

The third aspect of Lewis' religious life and theology that is particularly important for understanding *The Chronicles of Narnia* is his concept of *mere Christianity,* a phrase he used for a collection of his World War II radio speeches. By *mere Christianity,* Lewis meant the essential tenets of Christianity—tenets so basic that every Christian denomination could agree on them.

Although some Christian denominations may claim Lewis as particularly their own, Lewis detested the divisions among Christians. After all, he was from Ulster, where Protestants and Roman Catholics seemed to be perpetually at odds over minor religious differences. The conflicts among Irish Christians, especially the killings, sickened him; Christians killing Christians could not be what Christ Himself wanted. In vast research that served as the foundation for his theology, Lewis found what he considered to be fundamental agreements among all Christian denominations everywhere, such as Christ's divinity, a belief in God, and the idea that Christ made a sacrifice for all human beings, for all time.

Lewis' effort to find common ground among all Christian denominations is called *ecumenism*; ecumenism is not unique to Lewis and has been an ideal aspired to by many Christians for several centuries. On the other hand, Lewis' thinking about *mere Christianity* has been broadly influential—perhaps more influential than the ecumenical arguments of anyone else. Even Pope John Paul II, while still living in Poland before he became pope, read the books of the rough-spoken Lewis, perhaps passing over Lewis' injudicious use a few times of the word *papists*, a word describing Roman Catholics that many find offensive.

Pope John may also recognize the powerful essence of Lewis' ecumenical arguments as explained in everyday language. In his personal life, Lewis was equally comfortable discussing religion with Roman Catholics such as J. R. R. Tolkien, Anglicans, and Methodists. In his arguments for *mere Christianity*, he speaks to everyone in his audience as if he or she is every bit as capable of understanding what he means as he is; their differing rituals and disagreements over religious behavior need not stand between them and an understanding of the core beliefs of their religious faith. This aspect of his theology is part of what makes *The Chronicles of Narnia* so emotionally moving—the events played out in them overlay a small set of Christian beliefs that young as well as old readers can understand and appreciate. They help make the killing of Aslan one of the most emotional, most terrible passages in literature—any literature, not just literature intended for young people.

SECTION II

BACKGROUND TO
THE CHRONICLES
OF NARNIA

CHAPTER 3

INTRODUCTION
AND HISTORY

AN INTRODUCTION TO THE LANDS OF NARNIA

In a letter to some fifth graders, Lewis says, "I said 'Let us *suppose* that there were a land like Narnia and that the Son of God, as He became a Man in our world, became a Lion there, and then imagine what would happen.'" (C. S. Lewis, *Letters to Children,* p. 45, to Fifth Graders.) Lewis had long believed that intelligent life could exist on other worlds, and he believed that such life would be as much a creation of God as life on earth is. He enjoyed toying with the idea of different beings in alien cultures trying to come to terms with their divine origins, and he thought that each world made by God would have its own special strengths and weaknesses. For instance, the first man and first woman on another world might have obeyed God and never eaten the forbidden fruit. Something like this happens in *The Magician's Nephew* when Digory obeys Aslan and defies the severe temptation to eat the fruit of the tree of life.

But Lewis makes clear in other letters that what became *The Chronicles of Narnia* did not begin with religious themes. It began with images, as he says his fiction always did: "With me all fiction *begins with* pictures in my head. But where the pictures come from I couldn't say." (C. S. Lewis, *Letters to Children,* p. 95, to Meredith.) The inspirations for *The Lion, the Witch and the Wardrobe,* the first novel he wrote for the series, were images from his teens, such as that of an eccentric faun who became Mr. Tumnus. Other images were of a lamp standing out-of-place in a forest and a lion, fierce, large, and golden. He pulled together these and other images when he was inspired by his friend J. R. R. Tolkien, who in the late 1930s

was working on the novels that would establish him as one of the titans of English literature. Tolkien was pulling together the myths of ancient Celts and Germanic peoples and weaving out of them the original stories of Bilbo and Frodo, the heroes of *The Hobbit* and *The Lord of the Rings*. Tolkien read his latest chapters to gatherings at Lewis' home, and Lewis' imagination was fired by the adventures Tolkien recounted.

Thus, *The Chronicles of Narnia* was begun in the late 1930s, inspired by but not similar to Tolkien's works. *The Lion, the Witch and the Wardrobe* was meant to be much shorter than Tolkien's novels, and perhaps for a younger audience. Further, Lewis intended to mix in modern as well as ancient myths, and he chose to be more varied in the mythological sources for his characters, drawing on Ancient Greek and Roman myths and on Arabian folklore, as well as Nordic myths. The religious themes worked their way into *The Lion, the Witch and the Wardrobe* as it slowly evolved over a period of ten to twelve years. *The Chronicles of Narnia* as a whole was heavily influenced by the London children who stayed at Lewis' home during World War II, to escape Germany's bombing of the city. Most of them had no idea that Lewis was famous, but they responded well to his storytelling, and they helped Lewis find out what youngsters really wanted to read.

During the same period, Lewis' fame as a Christian thinker grew far beyond the bounds of the English-speaking world. During World War II, he made regular radio broadcasts about religion and faith. Thus, religion was constantly in the back of his mind while he worked on *The Lion, the Witch and the Wardrobe,* and, he says, the religious allegory worked its way into the Narnia stories after he had already created characters and their adventures. This may explain why readers not of the Christian faith enjoy the books—and likely explains why *anybody* likes the books—for they are not lectures or religious tracts; they are firstly adventures filled with excitement, danger, and derring-do. Further, the characters are vivid, well-rounded figures who seem very plausible. Lewis knew the potential courage and good sense in children well because he had observed them when their lives were endangered by the war, and his young characters seem entirely capable of the great deeds they perform.

Once he decided that Aslan would be the son of the Emperor-over-the-sea, that is Christ in the form He would take in Narnia, Lewis managed to work in his religious themes seamlessly; he never forgot that his first objective was to tell a good story. To one of his young correspondents, Ruth, he writes, "I'm so thankful that you realized [the] 'hidden story' in the Narnian books. It is odd, children nearly *always* do, grown-ups hardly ever." (C. S. Lewis, *Letters to Children*, p. 111, to Ruth.) And that is how he viewed his Christian allegory in *The Chronicles of Narnia*—as the hidden story, the story behind the action that is there for those who care to see it. In *The Magician's Nephew*, he notes that some people refuse to hear or understand God, as is the case with Uncle Andrew, and it is possible that he expected that some adults would miss the "hidden story" of *The Chronicles of Narnia* because of this.

A SHORT HISTORY OF NARNIA

The land of Narnia is but a part of a much larger world, most of which does not directly figure in *The Chronicles of Narnia*, although the world-shaping events in the books certainly involve

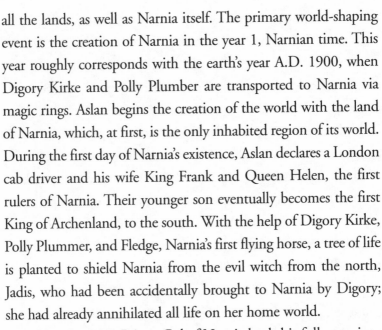

all the lands, as well as Narnia itself. The primary world-shaping event is the creation of Narnia in the year 1, Narnian time. This year roughly corresponds with the earth's year A.D. 1900, when Digory Kirke and Polly Plumber are transported to Narnia via magic rings. Aslan begins the creation of the world with the land of Narnia, which, at first, is the only inhabited region of its world. During the first day of Narnia's existence, Aslan declares a London cab driver and his wife King Frank and Queen Helen, the first rulers of Narnia. Their younger son eventually becomes the first King of Archenland, to the south. With the help of Digory Kirke, Polly Plummer, and Fledge, Narnia's first flying horse, a tree of life is planted to shield Narnia from the evil witch from the north, Jadis, who had been accidentally brought to Narnia by Digory; she had already annihilated all life on her home world.

In Narnian 180, Prince Col of Narnia leads his followers into Archenland and establishes a new kingdom there. In 204, refugees from Archenland set up a new kingdom of Calormen. This kingdom will reject Aslan and the Emperor-over-the-sea in order to establish a false religion. They will worship the demon Tash, sacrifice humans on Tash's altars, and become a source of evil that will plague their neighbors. By the end of Narnian 300, they will have expanded their territory through conquest and will establish a colony in Telmar.

Those in Telmar give themselves wholly over to evil, causing Aslan to transform them into dumb beasts in 302. Also in 302, King Gale of Narnia frees the Lone Islands of their dragon, and the grateful people of the Lone Islands declare King Gale their emperor, thus establishing Narnia's claim to the islands. In Narnian 460, pirates from the South Seas of earth establish themselves in Telmar. Their descendants will eventually rule Narnia, and become the ancestors of Caspian X.

The events that will lead to *The Lion, the Witch and the Wardrobe* begin in Narnian 898, when Jadis, the White Witch, returns to Narnia to seek revenge on her enemies. Aslan had predicted that this would happen. By 900, she has seized control of Narnia, and rules by terror. Her spies seem to be everywhere; she turns her enemies to stone. This marks the beginning of the endless winter in which Christmas never comes. Narnia is buried in snow, symbol of the cold cruelty of the White Witch.

After a hundred years, in 1000 (about 1940 earth time), Lucy, Edmund, Peter, and Susan Pevensie walk through an old wardrobe and find themselves in the snows of Narnia. Edmund betrays his brother and sisters to the White Witch in exchange for Turkish delights (sugared fruit candies). Aslan makes the great sacrifice, exchanging Himself for Edmund, whom the White Witch intends to kill. The witch gleefully murders Aslan and leaves Him for dead. He is revived by the Deep Magic that is older than the world, thus symbolically perishing for the sins of His people and then offering new life to all people. Under the command of Peter, Aslan's army defeats the forces of the White Witch, and Peter, Lucy, Susan, and Edmund become the rulers of Narnia. This marks the beginning of the brief golden age of Narnia.

Near the end of this golden age, Peter, the High King, defeats the Northern Giants in battle. With the help of Narnian forces led by King Edmund, Queen Lucy, and Queen Susan, Archenland's King Lune repels an attack by forces led by Prince Rabadash of Calormen. Aslan turns Rabadash into an ass and sends him on his way back to Calormen with the warning that he never venture far

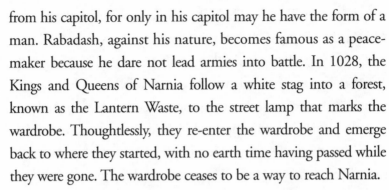

from his capitol, for only in his capitol may he have the form of a man. Rabadash, against his nature, becomes famous as a peace-maker because he dare not lead armies into battle. In 1028, the Kings and Queens of Narnia follow a white stag into a forest, known as the Lantern Waste, to the street lamp that marks the wardrobe. Thoughtlessly, they re-enter the wardrobe and emerge back to where they started, with no earth time having passed while they were gone. The wardrobe ceases to be a way to reach Narnia.

Ram the Great becomes King of Archenland in Narnian 1050. About fifty years later, Queen Swanwhite rules Narnia. *The Chronicles of Narnia* record little of what happens until Narnian 1998, when the Telmarines conquer Narnia, although there are hints in *The Last Battle* that many years of peace and happiness mark hundreds of years of uneventful history. It is in Narnian 1998 that Caspian I makes himself king of Narnia. His descendant Caspian X will figure prominently in *The Chronicles of Narnia* and Narnia's last great age, depicted in *Prince Caspian, The Voyage of the "Dawn Treader,"* and *The Silver Chair.*

Prince Miraz, brother of Caspian IX, murders his brother Caspian and declares himself king in 2290. In 2303 (perhaps 1941, earth time), Lucy, Peter, Susan, and Edmund are recalled to Narnia when Caspian X, son of Caspian IX, blows on Queen Susan's horn, but they reappear still as children, not as the grownup kings and queens they had been. Even so, their reap-pearance heralds the beginning of a great new era, and Caspian X rules almost as well as Kings Peter and Edmund and Queens Lucy and Susan had. In 2304, Caspian X repeats one of King Peter's feats by defeating the giants of the north in battle.

In 2306, Lucy, Edmund, and Eustace return to Narnia and

join Caspian X's voyage on the *Dawn Treader* to the ends of the world. In 2310, Caspian X marries the daughter of Ramandu, a retired star. Prince Rilian is born in 2325. In 2345, a serpent kills the queen and Prince Rilian vanishes. King Caspian is unable to find his son, and many of his kingdom's greatest heroes perish in their attempts to find Rilian. Eustace and Jill find their way to Narnia in 2356; they thought they had called to Aslan, but Aslan says that He inspired them to call Him. They rescue Rilian from a witch who may be related to Jadis, but King Caspian dies just after seeing that his son was safe.

Narnia, a mighty kingdom, builds fortifications in the Lantern Waste to fend off outlaws that plague the region in 2534. Twenty-one years later, in 2555, Shift the Ape leads a revolt in Narnia, deceiving Narnians with clever lies. Eustace and Jill help to rescue King Tirian, but Narnia is overrun by the Calormenes. The Final Battle is cataclysmic; Aslan awakens Father Time, marking the beginning of the end of Narnia's time. Eventually the great dragons and lizards of the world arise and lay waste to Narnia. Everything dies. Those willing to see the wonderful lands beyond the barn and to greet Aslan with love, even those who had fought of the wrong side of the Final Battle, walk into a new and beautiful world, a copy of Narnia that is the true Narnia, with the now dead Narnia having been a shadow-land in comparison. It is about 1949, earth time, and the children, except for Susan, have died in a train accident. But Aslan gives them everlasting life in what Lewis said would be the first chapter of the great book, in which people will have adventures more wonderful than anything they have experienced before.

TIMELINE COMPARING EVENTS ON NARNIA WITH EVENTS ON EARTH

EVENTS ON NARNIA	YEAR	YEAR	EVENTS ON EARTH
The world of Narnia is created by Aslan. Evil is introduced into the world in the form of the witch Jadis. Aslan appoints King Frank and Queen Helen to be the first rulers of Narnia.	1	1900	Digory and Polly visit the Wood Between the World, Charn, and Narnia. Digory's mother is healed by a fruit given to Digory by Aslan.
		1914	World War I
Prince Col of Narnia, younger son of King Frank and Queen Helen, founds the kingdom of Archenland.	180	1917	Lewis is critically wounded in battle
		1918	World War I ends
Unhappy subjects of Archenland migrate south across the desert to found the Kingdom of Calormen.	204		
Calormen has become a despotic empire, conquering its neighbors and colonizing Telmar.	300		
The Calormenes in Telmar give themselves entirely over to evil and are then transformed by Aslan into dumb beasts. King Gale of Narnia frees the Lone Islands from the tyranny of a dragon, and the islanders declare him and all his successors Emperor of the Lone Islands.	302	1929	Worldwide economic depression begins
		1933	Lewis converts to Christianity

EVENTS ON NARNIA	YEAR	YEAR	EVENTS ON EARTH
South Seas pirates from earth colonize Telmar.	460		
Jadis, the White Witch, enters Narnia.	898		
		1937	Lewis begins writing *The Lion, the Witch, and the Wardrobe.*
Jadis seizes control of Narnia, declaring herself its queen. The One Hundred Year Winter without Christmas begins.	900		
		1939	World War II begins; the Depression wanes.
Lucy, Edmund, Peter and Susan Pevensie walk through a wardrobe and into Narnia. Aslan gives His life in exchange for the traitor Edmund's. Aslan is resurrected by the Deeper Magic of His Father, thus making death run backwards. Aslan's army, led by Peter, defeats the army of the White Witch, who is killed. All four Pevensie children are crowned the kings and queens of Narnia, and the Golden Age begins.	1000	1940	The Pevensie children are sent to Prof. Digory Kirke's country house to escape the German bombing of London. They have adventures in Narnia, which takes many years, with almost no time elapsing on earth. Lewis, himself, tells Narnian stories to the children who stay at his home to escape the bombing.
Peter, Lucy, Edmund, and Susan disappear during a hunt, ending Narnia's Golden Age.	1028		
Ram the Great, son of King Cor and Queen Aravis, becomes King of Archenland.	1050		

Events on Narnia	Year	Year	Events on Earth
Circa 1100, Queen Swanwhite begins her rule of Narnia. Peace reigns in Narnia for almost 900 years.	1100		
The Telemarine humans invade Narnia and Caspian I declares himself king. This begins the Telemarine repression of the Old Narnians.	1998		
The usurper Miraz murders his brother Caspian IX and declares himself king within a year.	2290		
Caspian X leads the Old Narnians in a revolt against Miraz. With the help of the Pevensie children and Aslan, the Old Narnians defeat the Tememarine humans at the Second Battle of Beruna. Caspian X is declared King of Narnia and reestablishes the true religion of Aslan.	2303	1941	While waiting at a train station, Peter, Lucy, Edmund and Susan are transported to Narnia.
Caspian defeats the northern giants.	2304		
Lucy, Edmund, and Eustace return to Narnia and join Caspian X's voyage on the *Dawn Treader*	2306		
Caspian marries Ramandu's daughter.	2310		

EVENTS ON NARNIA	YEAR	YEAR	EVENTS ON EARTH
Prince Rilian is born.	2325		
The Queen of Narnia is murdered and Rilian is kidnapped.	2345		
Aslan summons Eustace and Jill to rescue Rilian. Rilian kills the Queen of the Underworld, freeing the Earthmen. Caspian the Navigator dies. This begins another long period of peace and prosperity for Narnia, although they must fight to preserve their freedoms.	2356	1945	World War II ends.
Narnia builds fortified towers in the Lantern Waste to help fend off outlaws from the northwest.	2534	1947	Lewis begins working on another novel about Narnia.
Shift the Ape creates the Anti-Aslan and subverts the faith of many Narnians. Calormene soldiers, followers of the demon Tash, seize control of Narnia. Aided by Narnian traitors, they defeat King Tirian's forces in *The Last Battle*. Aslan then commands the end of the world.	2555	1949	Peter, Lucy, Edmund, their parents, Eustace and Jill are killed in a train accident. Eustace and Jill are transported to Narnia to aid King Titian. All worthy creatures enter into Aslan's Country and begin the first chapter of the Great Book.

CHAPTER 4

CHARACTERS

THEMATIC DEVELOPMENT THROUGH THE RECURRING CHARACTERS

Aslan is the Lion, the Lord of the Wood. According to Lewis, His name was derived from an Arabic word for *lion*. The Lion is also a representation Christ as He might appear in another world. Lewis' reasoning was that Narnia was a land of Talking Animals and therefore Aslan would take the form of a lion, the traditional king of beasts. Aslan can change shape and appears briefly as a lamb. The children from earth notice that He grows larger each time they see Him; He explains that He grows as they grow. In *The Magician's Nephew* He is the Creator of Narnia. He sings with a voice that is not like a lion's or a human's, and His songs generate stars and seas and the sun and land and plants and animals. He is angry at Digory's bringing Jadis to Narnia, but he forgives the boy. In *The Lion, the Witch and the Wardrobe,* He has enabled the Pevensies to venture into Narnia so that they may fulfill the prophecy that two Sons of Adams and two Daughters of Eve will put an end to Jadis' reign and then reign themselves as kings and queens at Cair Paravel. Aslan repeats Christ's sacrifice by giving His own life to redeem a sinner, Edmund.

His very name brings joy to the hearts of good people, even ones who had never before heard of Him, and it brings dread to evildoers. In *The Horse and His Boy,* He appears in various forms, such as a domesticated cat, to Shasta in the graveyard. He proves Himself to be both mysterious and a tough friend, even scratching the back of Aravis as part of His plan for Archenland. In *Prince Caspian,* He helps the Pevensies in their effort to rescue Caspian X, even though the Pevensies seem determined to ignore Him.

Lucy knows He is present, but the others are much slower to recognize Him. At the end of *Prince Caspian,* He is a healer of the wounds of war, as represented by His healing Reepicheep. In *The Voyage of the "Dawn Treader,"* His presence is felt, especially by Lucy, His closest friend in *The Chronicles of Narnia.* Having told Peter and Susan that they are too old to return to Narnia again at the end of *Prince Caspian,* Aslan, taking the form of a lamb, tells Lucy and Edmund the same thing at the end of *The Voyage of the "Dawn Treader."* In *The Silver Chair,* He appears to Jill Pole, telling her the four signs she and Eustace must follow in order to help Caspian X find his son Rilian. He is not One for explaining Himself, and much of the novel is a lesson for Jill and Eustace in trusting Aslan's commandments. In *The Last Battle,* Narnia seems bereft of Aslan. Evil overthrows good, and even good Narnians believe utter nonsense; much of the novel is about recognizing evil and good by their works. The murdering of the dryads should have been clue enough that Aslan was not commanding the ape Shift. In the end, Aslan praises King Tirian for his spirited defense of Narnia, then calls forth Father Time to end the world. He then calls forth all the humans and Talking Animals animals of the world of Narnia by the millions; those who greet Him with love pass into Aslan's country, but those who greet Him with hatred pass into shadow, their fates, says the narrator, unknown. He then becomes playful, cheerfully inviting everyone "further up, and further in," an amazing journey into Aslan's beautiful worlds.

Caspian X is the true king of Narnia in *Prince Caspian,* although his uncle Miraz has illegally claimed the throne. His nurse has captivated him with stories of a past Narnia that was full of Talking Animals and great wonders; his interest in the stories increases when his nurse is sent away and he is forbidden to hear such tales. With courage and honor he leads a band of Narnians against the army of King Miraz, and he proves a crafty, stubborn leader. Even so, his small force of Talking Animals and Dwarfs seems sure to lose before the kings and queens of Narnia's Golden Age arrive to help him. High King Peter challenges Miraz to mortal combat and then leads a successful fight against Miraz's forces. Descended from pirates who had entered the Narnian world through a portal on a South Sea island of earth, Caspian's ancestors conquered Narnia and suppressed the native Narnians to such a degree that most humans in Narnia have never seen a Talking Animal in Caspian's time. Even so, Caspian X makes good on his promises to the nonhuman Narnians and quickly creates a benevolent kingdom in which everyone lives in harmony.

Leaving a trusted Dwarf in charge while he is gone, Caspian seeks the seven faithful men sent on a suicide mission to the east by Miraz in *The Voyage of the "Dawn Treader."* Only four years after the events in *Prince Caspian,* Caspian has become larger, stronger, and more impressive. His followers love him and risk their lives to do as he wishes. His discovery of what became of the seven faithful men, putting an end to slavery in the Lone Islands, and sailing right up to the last wave before Aslan's Country earn him the titles Caspian the Seafarer and Caspian the Navigator. In *The Silver Chair,* he is seen only briefly twice. The first time, he is an old man sailing away to search for his missing son. The second time he is near death and only has a moment with his son before he passes on.

D.L.F. stands for Dear Little Friend, the nickname the Pevensie children give the Dwarf Trumpkin in *Prince Caspian*. Trumpkin does not care for the nickname. See "**Trumpkin.**"

Lord Drinian is the captain of the *Dawn Treader* and later on is Caspian X's closest friend at Cair Paravel in *The Silver Chair*. He is sober minded, faithful, smart, and courageous. There is no doubt of his determination to sail to the end of the world if Caspian wants to go there. In *The Silver Chair*, he sees the woman in green, who may be Queen Jadis' witch sister, but he does not tell Caspian. When Caspian learns of this he nearly cuts Drinian's head off with an axe, but thinks better of it and declares Drinian to be his friend.

The Emperor-over-sea (aka the Emperor-beyond-the-sea and the Emperor-over-the-sea, and other variations involving fewer hyphens or additional capitalizations) is never seen in *The Chronicles of Narnia* but is always present as a power behind the scenes. He is the Father of Aslan and therefore the Father of Jesus on earth. He is the author of the Deeper Magic that existed even before time itself existed; it is the source of miraculous events, most importantly Aslan's resurrection from the dead in *The Lion, the Witch and the Wardrobe*. Aslan uses His Father's powers to create the world of Narnia, and to work miracles, although He Himself is bound by His Father's laws and may not transgress them. It is to His Father the Emperor-over-sea that Aslan attributes the good in the world, and it is in the Emperor-over-sea that He finds reassurance that the universe of Narnia is well made. In the worst or most confusing of times, the Emperor-over-sea offers security and a purpose for the world of Narnia. He is Joy.

Jadis the White Witch is the first source of evil in the world of Narnia. In *The Magician's Nephew,* Digory Kirke awakens her from a centuries old sleep. Rather than surrender her throne to her sister, Queen Jadis spoke the Deplorable Word with all the proper ceremonies and thereby murdered everyone in the world known as Charn; she preferred to rule a world in which everyone was dead than not be a ruler. Thus, she is a monstrous being, a source of unending evil. Seven feet tall, utterly white except for her red lips, Jadis is a striking, even commanding figure, yet the people of London find her outrageous ambition comical. She tricks Kirke into hesitating long enough for her to grasp part of his clothing when he transports himself with Jill Pole and Uncle Andrew to the new world of Narnia. There, the offspring of the Tree of Life keeps her out of Narnia for several hundred years. While trapped in the icy north, she becomes ever more proficient in evil magic and eventually seizes control of Narnia, apparently putting an end to the line of kings that began with King Frank and Queen Helen in the Narnian year 1.

In *The Lion, the Witch and the Wardrobe,* Jadis confronts the greatest threat to herself, the children Lucy, Peter, Susan, and Edmund, and she manages to subvert Edmund, who is attracted to her evil magic. By accepting the offer of Aslan's life in exchange for Edmund's, she believes she will secure the whole world of Narnia for herself for all time. Yet, as knowledgeable as she is in Deep Magic, she does not reckon with the miraculous, the Deeper Magic of Aslan and the Emperor-over-sea, and does not realize that Aslan's death means redemption for Edmund and Narnia. She seems to be killed in battle as High King Peter and the forces of Aslan overcome her, but a hag in

Prince Caspian insists that a witch such as Jadis can never truly die and can be brought back to Narnia in all her evil; in *The Silver Chair*, there are hints that the green witch is a sister to or a manifestation of Jadis.

Digory Kirke is probably based on W. T. Kirkpatrick, Lewis' beloved tutor. He appears in *The Magician's Nephew* as a boy who brings evil into the newly created world of Narnia, in *The Lion, the Witch and the Wardrobe* as the wise Professor who believes Lucy's story about the wardrobe, and in *The Last Battle* as one of the saved. Although he brings evil into the world of Narnia just as Aslan is creating the world, he, unlike Adam and Eve, brings Aslan an apple from the tree of life without eating any of the tree's fruit, in spite of temptation, with Jadis filling the role of the serpent. In so doing, he helps guarantee the land of Narnia hundreds of years of peace before the White Witch can harm it. It is Digory who plants an apple core that becomes a great tree, which, after it falls, is made into the *wardrobe* that the Pevensies walk through into Narnia.

Edmund Pevensie appears in *The Lion, the Witch and the Wardrobe*; *The Horse and His Boy*; *Prince Caspian*; *The Voyage of the "Dawn Treader"*; and *The Last Battle*. Lewis wrote to young Laurence that "Edmund is like Judas, a sneak and a traitor. But unlike Judas he repents and is forgiven (as Judas no doubt [would] have been if he'd repented)." (C. S. Lewis, *Letters to Children*, p. 68.) For most of *The Lion, the Witch and the Wardrobe*, Edmund is a rat; he torments Lucy, sides with the White Witch, and betrays his brother and sisters, all so that he may indulge his greed for sweets and have revenge on them for imagined wrongs. It is his evil behavior that occasions Aslan's death in *The Lion, the Witch and the Wardrobe*. In order to save Edmund from the White Witch, who intends to kill him, Aslan offers His life for Edmund's. In this act, Aslan parallels the sacrifice of Christ.

Redeemed by Aslan, Edmund becomes famous for his wisdom and justice. In *The Horse and His Boy*, he proves himself not only to be compassionate, but a fine, courageous leader. While High King Peter battles giants to the north, Edmund leads Narnian forces to the aid of Archenland's King Lune. It is very interesting to see the sort of man he became. In *Prince Caspian*, he is a boy again, but is still possessed of wisdom and courage. When Lucy sees that Aslan and the others do not believe her, Edmund backs her, noting as Professor Kirke did in *The Chronicles of Narnia* that Lucy does not lie; it turns out that he was right to do so. In *The Voyage of the "Dawn Treader,"* he joins Lucy and Eustace in King Caspian's quest to find the lost friends of his father, who had been sent on a suicide mission to the east by false King Miraz. In *The Last Battle*, he appears in Aslan's Country looking as he did when he was King Edmund who ruled with High King Peter and his sisters during Narnia's Golden Age.

Lucy Pevensie appears in *The Lion, the Witch and the Wardrobe*; *The Horse and His Boy*; *Prince Caspian*; *The Voyage of the "Dawn Treader"*; and *The Last Battle*. She is the most important of the children who visit Narnia because she comes the closest of anyone to understanding Aslan. She embodies many of Aslan's virtues such as compassion, honesty, a loving attitude, and

courage. This last quality often goes unremarked in writings about *The Chronicles of Narnia,* but she is known as Lucy the Valiant for good reason. In *The Horse and His Boy,* she leads a contingent of Narnian archers at the battle against Rabadash and acquits herself heroically. In *Prince Caspian,* she is in tune with what Aslan wants her and her companions to do, but is frustrated by their refusal, with the exception of Edmund, to accept her guidance when she sees Aslan. If Edmund can get it through his thick head that she is in tune with Aslan, why can't the others? In *The Voyage of the "Dawn Treader,"* she is much quicker to understand most events than other characters, and she makes friends with the equally valiant High Mouse Reepicheep. Throughout these books, Lucy is stouthearted, scrappy, and willing to undertake great challenges. In *The Last Battle,* she sees Aslan's Country more fully and deeply than anyone else and is the most reliable source of information about Aslan's intentions.

Peter Pevensie is the High King of Narnia; all of Narnia's monarchs are second to him, even when he reappears in Narnia in the form of a boy. In *The Lion, the Witch and the Wardrobe,* he leads Aslan's forces into a terrible battle against the forces of the White Witch. Such is his courage and intelligence, that every time he reappears in Narnia, his great leadership and fighting skills make him an attractive leader and formidable opponent. The era in which he reigned at Cair Paravel as the High King is Narnia's Golden Age. In *The Horse and His Boy,* he is offstage, leading his army into battle against the northern giants. In *Prince Caspian,* he with his brother and sisters is summoned to Narnia when Caspian blows on Susan's horn, by then an almost sacred artifact from the Golden Age. It is Peter who battles the false King Miraz in single combat; when Miraz is betrayed by his own followers, Peter, already wounded, proves to be a thoroughly deadly warrior, lopping off the head of one of the conspirators. At the end of *Prince Caspian,* Aslan tells him, as well as his sister Susan, that he and she are too old to return again to Narnia. He takes the disappointing news stoutheartedly. He reappears in *The Last Battle* at the train station, at the dinner where King Tirian appears, and in Aslan's Country, where he is again the High King and the most respected of Narnia's leaders.

Susan Pevensie passes through the wardrobe into Narnia, accompanying her brothers and sister. In all of her appearances in *The Chronicles of Narnia,* she is bossy and pretends to be more mature than she is. Even so, she is courageous and stands watch with Lucy while Aslan is sacrificed on the Stone Table. A master with the bow and arrow, she finds ways to disable enemies with her shots without harming them. In *The Horse and His Boy,* she foolishly agrees to visit a Calormen suitor, Prince Rabadash, in his home city, Tashbaan. When she flees from Rabadash, he leads a small army of skilled horsemen to invade Archenland, Narnia's southern neighbor, as a prelude to invading Narnia itself. In *Prince Caspian,* she is sometimes a nuisance because of her wish to avoid trouble, but she is nonetheless Queen Susan who sat beside High King Peter during Narnia's Golden Age; she behaves as a queen should. Many readers have been troubled by her being excluded from Aslan's Country in *The Last Battle.* Lewis wrote to a young correspondent, Martin, "The books don't tell us what happened to Susan. She is left

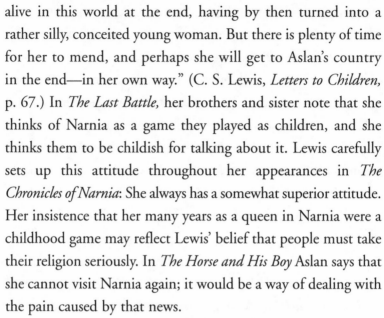

alive in this world at the end, having by then turned into a rather silly, conceited young woman. But there is plenty of time for her to mend, and perhaps she will get to Aslan's country in the end—in her own way." (C. S. Lewis, *Letters to Children,* p. 67.) In *The Last Battle,* her brothers and sister note that she thinks of Narnia as a game they played as children, and she thinks them to be childish for talking about it. Lewis carefully sets up this attitude throughout her appearances in *The Chronicles of Narnia*: She always has a somewhat superior attitude. Her insistence that her many years as a queen in Narnia were a childhood game may reflect Lewis' belief that people must take their religion seriously. In *The Horse and His Boy* Aslan says that she cannot visit Narnia again; it would be a way of dealing with the pain caused by that news.

Some critics have suggested that Susan represents a young friend of Lewis', and that Susan's absence (not *exclusion,* for Aslan makes it plain that she can still get in) from Aslan's Country is Lewis' expression of disapproval of his young friend drifting away from religion after her marriage. Lewis himself said, when writing to young Marcia, "No, I didn't start with four real children in mind: I just made them up." (C. S. Lewis, *Letters to Children,* p. 51.) There is much internal evidence to suggest that Susan's behavior was well developed throughout her appearances, so I am inclined to take Lewis at his word.

Polly Plumber appears in *The Magician's Nephew* and *The Last Battle*. In *The Magician's Nephew,* she is the common-sense companion of Digory Kirke, who is impulsive. She also has the virtue of forgiveness, which Aslan values. She is blessed by Aslan and eventually is to be found in Aslan's Country; having grown old on earth, in Aslan's Country she is young and vigorous. She was present at the meal when King Tirian appeared to plead for help.

Jill Pole is a tough person to figure out. As a victim of bullies and a cruel school administration, she is at first a sympathetic figure worthy of Eustace's comforting in *The Silver Chair*. Yet, she returns Eustace's sympathy with contempt and nearly kills the boy in the process, flinging him off a cliff in Aslan's Country. Through several perilous adventures she learns to be compassionate and understanding, as well as learning that the seemingly weak Eustace has courage and intelligence. Given plain instructions by Aslan about what needs to be done, she botches them, which makes for a thrilling adventure as she, Eustace, and Puddleglum try to find Prince Rilian. She arrives in Narnia with Eustace in *The Last Battle,* and her cleverness and courage prove to be very helpful in the nearly hopeless battle of King Tirian to protect his realm. When she enters Aslan's Country through the stable door, she is surprised by a joyous land.

Reepicheep is the High Mouse, also called the Chief Mouse, in *Prince Caspian* and *The Voyage of the "Dawn Treader."* When the mice gnawed through Aslan's bonds in *The Lion, the Witch and the Wardrobe,* Aslan granted them speech and made them somewhat bigger, one to two feet tall. (One foot in *Prince Caspian* and two feet in *The Voyage of the "Dawn Treader."*) Reepicheep and his followers were among the first to volunteer to fight for Caspian X against the false King Miraz. They distinguished themselves by their very honorable conduct toward everyone

and their immense courage. When Reepicheep lost his tail in battle, his followers prepared to lop off theirs, too, so that they would not dishonor their leader by having tails that would call attention to his having none. Aslan gave Reepicheep a new tail, saving much discomfort for the other Talking Mice. When a youngster, Reepicheep heard a prophesy that he would sail to the east, to Aslan's Country. In *The Voyage of the "Dawn Treader,"* he fulfills the prophesy. During the voyage he is the source of much good cheer, and he challenges every danger. For Caspian X and the other voyagers, Reepicheep's honor becomes the honor against which they measure their own, and they trust him to do what is right. In the end, he paddles in a little boat over the last wave and is last seen making his way toward a land that could be Aslan's country. Reepicheep appears again in *The Last Battle,* having fulfilled his destiny by entering into Aslan's Country.

Eustace Scrubb has some first rate adventures. At the beginning of *The Voyage of the "Dawn Treader,"* he is a nasty brat who loves the misery of others; he is about as detestable as a person can be. Yet, like Edmund, he can be redeemed. In *The Voyage of the "Dawn Treader,"* he learns to value friendship; when he is turned into a dragon, a monstrous form suited to his monstrous self, he undergoes a reformation, becoming a true friend, although he still remains a grouchy person. In *The Silver Chair,* he and his schoolmate Jill Pole flee bullies and end up in Aslan's Country when they step through a doorway in a wall. Eustace, still a complainer although a much better person than he had been, is outdone by Jill, who has a very superior attitude. In *The Last Battle,* he and Jill feel a jerk on the train they are riding and land in Narnia at a time when the forces of evil are beginning to destroy the land and its inhabitants. Having learned how to face his fears in *The Voyage of the "Dawn Treader"* and *The Silver Chair,* Eustace courageously helps King Tirian in Narnia's version of Armageddon, in which evil masquerades as good and the evil Calormen demon Tash seems to have supplanted Aslan. Eustace eventually enters Aslan's Country to stay, his life having ended in a train wreck on earth.

Trumpkin is a Red Dwarf (called that because he has red hair) in *Prince Caspian* and *The Silver Chair,* and he is mentioned in *The Voyage of the "Dawn Treader."* After Caspian blows Susan's horn in *Prince Caspian,* he is sent to search for the Pevensie children in the area where Cair Paravel once stood, but he is captured by the usurper Miraz's forces and is carried off to be murdered by drowning. Susan saves him by well-placed arrow shots that bang the helmets of the soldiers, sending the soldiers fleeing and leaving Trumpkin to be pulled to safety by the children.

He is willing enough to believe that the youngsters Peter, Lucy, Edmund, and Susan are the four fabulous rulers of Narnia's Golden Age, but he doubts that as children they can help Caspian. After Edmund knocks him around in mock combat, Trumpkin changes his mind. The Pevensies take a quick liking to him because of his good humor and courage; he also has valuable skills such as cooking and catching fish. The children had grown tired of eating only apples. They call him their Dear Little Friend, which he does not like, probably because he is sensitive about his size, so the youngsters use the abbreviation D.L.F., even after they have forgotten what the letters stand for.

Although he is very good to have around, he contributes to one of the major miscues of the children's adventure: When Lucy says she saw Aslan atop a trail leading up along a hillside beside the gorge of the Great River, Trumpkin votes with Peter and Susan and against Lucy and Edmund in choosing to go down into the gorge instead of going to where Lucy says Aslan was. This results in Lucy being reprimanded by Aslan for not following Him in spite of what others said. Trumpkin has more of an excuse than Peter and Susan, who should know to trust Lucy, but he is nonetheless the crucial third vote that results in the group turning from Aslan's path.

Trumpkin is a doughty fighter when it comes to battle in *Prince Caspian*. In *The Voyage of the "Dawn Treader,"* he is mentioned as the regent Caspian has left behind to run Narnia until the king returns from fulfilling his vow to Aslan to find the Seven Noble Lords Miraz had sent on a voyage to the far east. He appears briefly in *The Silver Chair*. He is again the regent for Narnia when Caspian sails to the Lone Islands, where Aslan has reportedly been seen. When Jill and Eustace fail to fulfill the first of Aslan's signs—to greet King Caspian—they find themselves under Trumpkin's care. Glimfeather the Talking Owl tells Jill that Caspian has left orders that no one be allowed to search for his missing son Rilian because too many of Narnia's bravest heroes have disappeared while looking for him; this means, Glimfeather explains, that Trumpkin would lock them in prison to keep them from fulfilling the quest given to them by Aslan. Thus, Jill and Eustace leave Trumpkin's care without telling the noble Dwarf what they are doing.

Trumpkin is a humorous character, creating strange curses, and in *The Silver Chair,* he is so deaf that what is said to him must be repeated, to comic effect. Among the most endearing characters in *The Chronicles of Narnia,* his faithfulness, honesty, and courage are some of the qualities that bring him into Aslan's Country at the end of *The Last Battle.*

Mr. Tumnus is a faun and the first Narnian that Lucy meets in *The Lion, the Witch and the Wardrobe.* He quickly recognizes her as a Daughter of Eve, someone he has promised to report to the White Witch. In spite of his promise, his good heart will not allow him to tell the White Witch about Lucy. The White Witch's secret police discover what he has done, invade his home, and take him to the White Witch, who turns him to stone. Aslan reverses the witch's spell. Lewis said that he had had a picture of the eccentric faun in his head for years, perhaps since his teens, and that he wrote a story, *The Lion, the Witch and the Wardrobe,* around that image. In *The Horse and His Boy,* Mr. Tumnus is a graying counselor to Queen Lucy and her sister and brothers.

The White Witch is the name in *The Lion, the Witch and the Wardrobe* of Jadis, onetime ruler and destroyer of the world of Charn. See **Jadis the White Witch.**

THEMATIC DEVELOPMENT THROUGH THE OTHER MAJOR CHARACTERS

Aravis Tarkeena, later **Princess then Queen of Archenland**, is a teenaged daughter of Kidrash Tarkaan, ruler of Calavar, a province of Calormen, and a descendant of Ardeeb Tisroc, her great-great-great-grandfather, giving her royal ancestry. A cruel stepmother persuades Kidrash to arrange for Aravis to marry

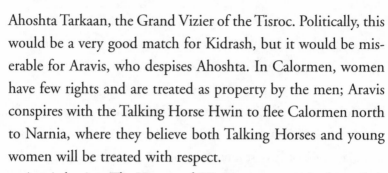

Ahoshta Tarkaan, the Grand Vizier of the Tisroc. Politically, this would be a very good match for Kidrash, but it would be miserable for Aravis, who despises Ahoshta. In Calormen, women have few rights and are treated as property by the men; Aravis conspires with the Talking Horse Hwin to flee Calormen north to Narnia, where they believe both Talking Horses and young women will be treated with respect.

Aravis begins *The Horse and His Boy* as a conceited, spoiled, condescending young woman, but her adventures with Hwin, Shasta, and Bree teach her that her prejudices are foolish, and she learns to respect bravery and intelligence instead of social class. Her behavior makes Shasta suspect that she would abandon him at the Tombs of Ancient Kings, but beneath her hauty exterior is a courageous, honorable person who keeps her word (highly valued by Aslan) and would never willingly abandon Shasta or anyone else to whom she had made a promise.

After fleeing her father's home—riding Hwin north through the Calormen countryside, being chased by lions (actually Aslan) until she meets Shasta and Bree (also chased by lions), making a harrowing journey through the city of Tashbaan, trekking across a hot desert, being chased by another lion (also Aslan) who scratches her—she is able to rest in the Hermit's enclave. She is a more humble person than she was by the time she meets Aslan, and she has developed much respect for Shasta, the slave boy who turns out to be the heir to the throne of Archenland. She and Cor, Shasta's original name, marry, and she becomes Queen of Archenland. Lewis does not say much about her conduct as queen, although he implies that she was a fine ruler. She and Cor have at least one child, a son, Ram the Great.

Mr. and Mrs. Beaver are Talking Animals in *The Lion, the Witch and the Wardrobe*. They maintain a home on the Great River, where they take in Lucy, Edmund, Susan, and Peter. Mr. Beaver explains to the children what the situation is with the White Witch and that Aslan has been seen to the east, down river. When it is discovered that Edmund has sneaked away, probably to warn the White Witch, Mr. and Mrs. Beaver flee with the remaining children. In a scene that may have been inspired by the "Noah" pageants (plays) of medieval mystery cycles (a series of plays all based on Biblical stories that lead up to Christ's crucifixion), in which Noah's wife always bustles about while the flood waters rise, Mrs. Beaver seems to take her time to be sure that she and the others take everything they may need, even while the White Witch's secret police may be racing to her home.

The Beavers manage to take good care of Lucy, Susan, and Peter, hiding them in a hole along the bank of the Great River, and eventually getting them to Aslan. By the time of *Prince Caspian* Talking Beavers have sadly disappeared from Narnia, and they apparently never reappear.

Bern is one of the seven lords sent on a suicide mission across the Eastern Sea by the usurper Miraz in *Prince Caspian*. When he and the others reached the Lone Islands, he fell in love with a local woman and decided to settle on Avra, where he founded Bernstead, an estate populated by free people (no slaves). In *The Voyage of the "Dawn Treader,"* he buys Caspian's freedom and helps Caspian put an end to the slave trade and slavery, as well as to replace the corrupt government of the Lone Islands.

Caspian declares Bern the Duke of the Lone Islands, giving him a hereditary title to govern the Lone Islands in the king's absence. Bern is notable for his honesty and his honor; his placing his hands between those of Caspian is representative of the medieval gesture of fealty and honor.

Bree is short for Breehy-hinny-brinny-hoohy-hah, but Shasta is unable to pronounce the full name and says just "Bree." At the start of *The Horse and His Boy*, Bree is the warhorse of Anradin Tarkaan, a nobleman and warrior. The horse was kidnapped from Narnia when very young and has kept his ability to think and speak secret all the time he has been in Calormen. He is very proud of his deeds in battle against Calormen's many enemies. During *The Horse and His Boy*, he learns humility and wins the love of Hwin, the Talking Horse who escapes Calormen with Aravis. He is frightened to discover that Aslan really is a lion; he has believed that *lion* was a metaphor. It is Bree who gives *The Horse and His Boy* its title: When it is suggested that he may be called Shasta's horse, he points out that he was made the human's equal by Aslan and that he may as well be called Shasta's owner.

Cor is the name given to Shasta when he becomes the crown prince of Archenland in *The Horse and His Boy*. See **Shasta** for more details.

Doctor Cornelius is made Caspian's tutor in *Prince Caspian* after Miraz dismisses Caspian's nurse for telling the boy stories about Old Narnia. While pretending to teach Caspian astronomy,

Doctor Cornelius takes the prince to a balcony on a high tower several nights a week and tells him the true history of Narnia, including stories about Aslan and the Talking Animals and Trees. The night Miraz's son is born he helps Caspian to flee before the prince is murdered. Eventually, he rejoins Caspian at the Great Council.

Emeth (meaning *faithful* in Hebrew) is a young Calormene warrior who has searched for the god Tash all of his life. He was born in Tehishbaan, a town in northwestern Calormen, bordering on the desert that lies between Calormen and Archenland to the north. In *The Last Battle,* he has doubts about the veracity of his commanding officer Rishda Tarkaan and Shift and steps through the stable door to see for himself whether Tash, Aslan, or Tashlan actually are to be found within. He overpowers a guard who was lurking behind the door and who was under orders to kill whoever came through the door. To Emeth's amazement, a beautiful country surrounds the door. He sets out to find Tash in the country but is greeted by Aslan, instead. A man of noble heart, Emeth immediately recognizes Aslan for who He is and is amazed that Alsan embraces him, even though he had followed Tash. Emeth is important because his story explains some of Lewis' thoughts about what would happen to good people who die without having worshiped Christ. Aslan explains that whenever Emeth sought to do good, he served Aslan; Emeth's instant recognition of Aslan and his willingness to honor Aslan even though he thinks Aslan will kill him show the Emeth has a true heart that has always yearned for Aslan, even without Emeth realizing it.

Fledge is the name given to the London cab horse Strawberry after Aslan gives him wings in *The Magician's Nephew*. He carries Digory and Polly through the air into the Western Mountains to find the garden surrounded by a wall with golden gates. Although he seems meant to father more winged horses, by Caspian X's time winged horses are unknown. He is reunited with Digory and Polly in Aslan's Country in *The Last Battle*.

Hwin is a Talking Horse who spent most of her early life in the stables of Kidrash Tarkaan in southern Calormen. Tarkaan's second wife, who is jealous of his daughter Aravis, persuades him to marry her to an old, unpleasant man. Aravis decides to commit suicide rather than submit to a forced marriage, but Hwin persuades her not to do so, suggesting they both run away to Narnia, instead. Hwin has, like Bree, refrained from speaking while in Calormen, fearing that she would be subjected to abuse if it were discovered that she could talk. Although *The Horse and His Boy* begins with Shasta and Bree, when Hwin and Aravis meet them, they quickly become partners in the novel's action. Hwin shows much determination and good sense. Further, when she sees Aslan, she recognizes Him for Who He is and immediately declares that she would rather be eaten by Him than fed by anyone else. Aslan kisses her, a form of blessing. She eventually settles in Narnia, always an independent spirit, and lives a good and happy life.

Andrew Ketterley, Digory Kirke's Uncle Andrew, is a magician who has given himself over to evil in *The Magician's Nephew*. Dabbling in magic is always dangerous in *The Chronicles of Narnia* because it often takes its users into evil; it tends to be contrary to the salvation offered by Christ or the Deeper Magic of Aslan. Uncle Andrew sees nothing wrong in risking the lives of Polly and Digory in order to avoid risking his own. He had been given magical rings in the will of a witch, Mrs. Lefay (an allusion to King Arthur's sister, Morgan LeFey, a witch in Arthurian tales), and he had discovered that they could take someone to another world just by touching them. He does not realize that the touch of the rings could lead to several different worlds until Digory forces him to come along on a journey to the Wood between the Worlds.

Andrew is a witness to the creation of Narnia, but he is terrified by Aslan. All evil people feel fear and loathing in their hearts when they see Aslan. He refuses to believe all that he witnesses, making him seem to be an incoherent babbler to the newly created Talking Animals of Narnia, who try to plant him like a tree to see what he might grow into. Because of his abuse of the magical rings, which the terms of the will said he should dispose of, he is indirectly responsible for bringing evil in the form of Jadis the White Witch into Narnia's world. In spite of his evil, self-righteous behavior, he is somewhat reformed by his experiences in Narnia and behaves fairly well once he returns to earth.

Lady of the Green Kirtle is the Queen of Underworld (also Underland). See **Queen of Underworld**.

Miraz is the murderer of his brother Caspian IX and the usurper of the throne that rightfully belongs to Caspian X in *Prince Caspian*. He tries to keep knowledge of Old Narnians from young Caspian, but fails. When his son is born, he tries to have

Caspian murdered, but the prince is warned in time to flee Miraz's great castle. It is Miraz who sent the Seven Noble Lords to explore the Eastern Sea as a way of getting rid of them.

When he learns of Caspian's whereabouts, he brings a great army of his own to confront Caspian's army of Old Narnians, and he and his army are successful in battle, forcing Caspian and his followers to flee. When Caspian sets up headquarters in Aslan's How, the mound that covers the Stone Table, Miraz brings his army to a camp across the Great River from the village of Berunda to lay siege.

Although probably middle-aged, Miraz is a robust man and an exceptional warrior. He is goaded by two of his lieutenants into accepting High King Peter's challenge to single combat, and those same lieutenants betray him in an effort to seize power for themselves. He dies a traitor's death, being stabbed in the back by another traitor.

Nikabrik is a Black Dwarf (because he has black hair) in *Prince Caspian*. He hates humans and sides with Caspian against Miraz because he hates Miraz and his Telmarine followers more than he hates Caspian and Caspian's Old Narnian followers. He remarks that while others may have detested the White Witch, Dwarfs did fairly well under her rule, and he would be happy to have her rule again. This foreshadows the "Dwarfs are for the Dwarfs" attitude of the ungrateful Dwarfs in *The Last Battle*. Eventually, Nikabrik brings a hag and a wer-wolf to a war council at the Stone Table and is killed in the fight that results when Caspian objects to the use of evil magic. Nikabrik is an example of someone who has been soured by hatred.

Puddleglum is a Marsh-Wiggle in *The Silver Chair*. Marsh-Wiggles live in a marsh north of Cair Paravel, near the Narnian border with Ettinsmoor, a land of evil giants. Marsh-Wiggles are somewhat solitary, living individually on square patches of land surrounded by marshy water. They fish for eels and try to think philosophically; they value seriousness. Puddleglum is very serious, but tells Jill and Eustace that he is considered by other Marsh-Wiggles to be far too cheerful.

Altogether, he is one of Lewis' most delightful creations, which makes him a source of comedy for much *The Silver Chair*, with his dour comments reflecting an effort to find the seriousness in everything. His comic highpoint comes when he pretends to be gay and carefree so that the giants of Harfang will not suspect that he knows they intend to cook and eat the children and him. Although Puddleglum is the source of comedy, his is not a comic figure; his courage, good sense, and most of all faith make him a major force in the events in *The Silver Chair*.

For instance, it is he who finds effective ways to defy the enchantments of the Queen of Underworld, from pointing out that if Alsan were only a dream, then He is still better than the queen's pallid, miserable world, and he even steps his feet in fire to shock himself into reality. Where Jill and Eustace complain and argue, he keeps himself and them focused on their quest.

Puzzle is one of the strangest characters in *The Chronicles of Narnia*. He is a donkey who lives near Shift the Ape, doing chores for Shift because Shift is smarter than he is. He often fetches things for Shift from a nearby village. When Shift sees a lion skin splash down the Great Waterfall, he devises a scheme, with Puzzle at the heart of it. In a conspiracy with Calormen, he ties the skin onto Puzzle and claims that Puzzle is actually Aslan.

Believing that he should do as the supposedly smarter Ape tells him to do, Puzzle carries out his part of the fraud. Many Narnians are fooled by what would seem to be an obvious deception, but Aslan has not been seen in Narnia for many (perhaps hundreds) of years, and the faith of some Narnians has grown weak to the point that they are not sure exactly what Aslan should be like.

When he is liberated from Shift and the Calormenes, King Tirian wishes to kill Puzzle, who has posed as Aslan, roughly fulfilling part of the role of the Antichrist, but Jill begs for his life and Tirian relents. In traditional Christian theology, the Antichrist comes to earth to deceive people into believing that he is Christ, thus leading them away from faith. In *The Last Battle*, this figure is split into two: Shift and Puzzle. Although Puzzle wears the lion skin, it is Shift who devises the lies and figures out how to mislead Narnians. He is one of those who declares that the demon Tash, who is the opposite of Aslan, is actually Aslan in another form, and it is for this that Shift is taken by Tash.

On the other hand, Puzzle declares himself truly sorry and unhappy with what he has endured, and it appears that Shift and the other conspirators treated Puzzle very cruelly. Perhaps it is Puzzle's true repentance that redeems him, because he appears in Aslan's Country as a magnificent, beautiful donkey, although he is still not sure he understands what is happening.

Queen of Underworld (also Underland) is a witch who has the ability to transform into a serpent. Her serpent form has green skin, and she wears green clothing, which is why she is called the Lady of the Green Kirtle. In *The Silver Chair,* she has murdered the Queen of Narnia, the daughter of Ramandu from *The Voyage of the "Dawn Treader."* In addition, she has kidnapped Prince Rilian, son of Caspian the Navigator and heir to Narnia's throne. Having cast an enchantment on Rilian, she parades him above ground in black armor; she has taken away his former memory and has no idea who he really is.

The Queen has made him part of her scheme to conquer Narnia. She has created an army of Earthmen who will storm out of Underworld into Narnia, defeat Narnia's army, and seize control of the country. Prince Rilian, the legitimate heir to the throne, will then become king and through him she will rule Narnia. Her fixation on conquering Narnia, to which she has devoted at least ten years of effort (that is how long Rilian has been her prisoner), is reminiscent of that of the White Witch in *The Lion, the Witch and the Wardrobe,* who also wanted to control Narnia and make its people her subjects. *The Magician's Nephew* suggests that the White Witch wanted revenge on Aslan and took it by subjecting the country that Aslan first created in the world, Narnia itself. Like the White Witch, the Queen of Underworld is beautiful, tall, and imposing. Unlike the White Witch, she is able to speak subtly and beguilingly.

Another link to the White Witch is the Queen's serpent form. In *The Magician's Nephew,* Jadis, who becomes the White Witch, is in the walled garden when Digory picks a fruit from a tree, and like the Biblical serpent tempting Eve, she tempts Digory. The Queen of Underworld is the embodiment of the evil tempting serpent, speaking with honeyed words to beguile people into doing deeds that are against their better natures such as making the enchanted Rilian look forward to conquering an above-ground kingdom. In *Prince Caspian,* a hag asserts that a witch never truly dies, and even wishes to use magic to summon the White Witch. It is possible that the Queen of Underworld is a manifestation of the White Witch. You may recall that in *The Magician's Nephew,* Jadis is the first evil in the world of Narnia, which suggests that the Queen of Underworld represents that original evil is still at work, trying to ruin Aslan's creation.

Rabadash is the heir to the Tisroc of Calormen and suitor to Queen Susan in *The Horse and His Boy.* A courageous fighter, he has impressed Susan with his gallantry during games at Cair Paravel, but when she is a guest in Tashbaan, she discovers that he is cruel and selfish, and she learns that women are little more than property in Calormen society. She and her companions are captives of Rabadash, who presses her to marry him, but she and the others escape by devising a plan to get to their ship and cast off before Rabadash realizes what is happening.

Furious at Susan's escape, Rabadash forms an army of two hundred horsemen and sets out to invade Archenland, which along with the desert is between Calormen and Narnia, and from there launch an attack on Cair Paravel, where he will force Susan to marry him, and where he plainly intends to rape her. Rabadash is motivated by lust and by anger at having something he wants denied to him, and he is motivated by a desire for power that makes even his father distrust him. Indeed, the Tisroc would not mind if Rabadash were killed because Rabadash may choose to take the Calomene throne early by assassinating his father.

When he gives orders to his troops at Anvard, Rabadash shows the depth of his desire for power as well as his great villainy. He tells his men (no women allowed) that they may keep for themselves all the riches of Anvard, gold, jewels, and women (who are to his mind property) if they murder every male inhabitant, from the oldest to the baby who is but a day old. For him, controlling Archenland matters more than riches. From Archenland he can launch an invasion of Narnia before High King Peter can return from fighting the giants of the north.

Rabadash has much physical courage, and he fights until he is disarmed. When he meets Aslan, he responds with loathing, defying the Lion, who gives him a chance to redeem himself. Refusing the opportunity, he is transformed into an ass. This is reminiscent of Aslan's warning in *The Magician's Nephew* that Talking Animals may become dumb animals if they fall into evil ways. Aslan tells the ass that he may return to human form at Tash's altar in a temple in Tashbaan, but that he will become an ass permanently if he ever ventures more than ten miles from the city.

This creates an odd turnaround for Rabadash. He cannot lead his armies into war, and he fears that any generals who were successful in war would threaten his life and throne, so conquering Calormen's neighbors is not an option for him. He must be intelligent, because he finds ways to keep the peace throughout his reign. Even so, out of his hearing and after his death he is known in Calormen as Rabadash the Ridiculous, because thousands of people saw him transform from ass to man in the Temple. He is not mentioned in the passages about Aslan's country in *The Last Battle,* so perhaps his heart remained evil in spite of the good he achieved. That Aslan found a way to make such a vile person a positive force is remarkable.

Prince Rilian has been missing for ten years when Aslan sends Jill Pole and Eustace Scrubb to look for him in *The Silver Chair*. He is the son of King Caspian and Ramandu's daughter, so he has star ancestry as well as human ancestry because Ramandu is a star. (See **Ramandu** in **Minor Characters**.) While on an outing on grounds around a fountain, Rilian's mother is killed by the bite of a large green serpent, and Rilian devotes most of his time to hunting for the snake in order to kill it. Lord Drinian suggests that Rilian give up the hunt because the snake was merely a dumb animal; he is wrong about this, because the serpent also takes the form of a beautiful woman (Queen of Underworld) dressed in green. Eventually, this woman enchants Rilian and kidnaps him, taking him to Underworld.

After many adventures, Jill, Eustace, and Puddleglum find Rilian in the Queen of Underworld's palace, but they do not recognize him, and he has no idea who he is. When the travelers first see him, he has a strange twist to his face, implying a mental problem, which becomes more evident in his unstable manner of speaking. He becomes himself only for a short period, and during that period he is tied to a silver chair; while tied to the chair he calls frantically for help, telling the travelers that he is only in his right mind while tied to the chair. Although we readers may feel sure that he must be Rilian, Jill, Eustace, and Puddleglum are frightened by Rilian's frantic cries for help, which sound to them like the ravings of a madman. When Rilian calls upon Aslan's name for help, he fulfills one of the signs given to Jill by Aslan.

Once freed, he proves to be a formidable personality, both commanding and courageous. Even so, the Queen of Underworld nearly manages to enchant him again, but Puddleglum's faith and determination thwart her efforts. In a frightening battle, she turns herself into a serpent and attacks the others, but Rilian manages to grab hold of her and cut her down with his sword. When in his right mind, Rilian is a true follower of Aslan; only while insane does he do the bidding of evil. His sword, like that of High King Peter, represents the Holy Spirit, and the slaying of the serpent represents the victory of the sanity of Rilian's faith over the insanity of the Queen of Underworld's fundamental evil.

Rishda Tarkaan is the commanding officer of the Calormenes at the stable in *The Last Battle*. He has no faith in any god, and conspires with Shift the Ape and others to create a fake god he calls "Tashlan," a combination of Tash and Aslan. When he calls upon Tash, the demon Tash actually comes to the stable. Devious, cruel, and arrogant, Rishda murders many Narnians. As it dawns on him that there may really be a Tash inside the stable, he becomes afraid and hopes the people he tosses into the stable will be accepted as offerings. Although he is a tough warrior, Tash terrifies him, and it is he whom Tash carries away when he is ordered to leave (probably by High King Peter). He is an example of what may happen to someone who calls upon evil; he belongs to evil.

Shasta is the name by which Prince Cor of Archenland is known through nearly all of *The Horse and His Boy*. A govern-

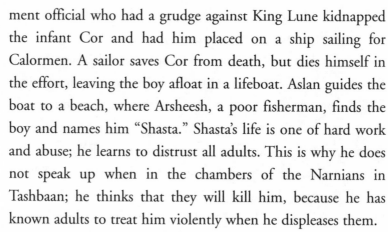

ment official who had a grudge against King Lune kidnapped the infant Cor and had him placed on a ship sailing for Calormen. A sailor saves Cor from death, but dies himself in the effort, leaving the boy afloat in a lifeboat. Aslan guides the boat to a beach, where Arsheesh, a poor fisherman, finds the boy and names him "Shasta." Shasta's life is one of hard work and abuse; he learns to distrust all adults. This is why he does not speak up when in the chambers of the Narnians in Tashbaan; he thinks that they will kill him, because he has known adults to treat him violently when he displeases them.

Much of what happens to him seems to be coincidences; in fact, the coincidences pile up one upon another. For instance, he and his "father" Arsheesh live near an isolated beach; the nearby road is more a path than a throughway, and it is infrequently traveled. Even so, a great Calormene lord, Anradin Tarkaan, rides by the fisherman's home, and he happens to see Shasta and to realize that the boy must come from a northern country, not Calormen. Further, he is riding his great warhorse rather than an ordinary horse; still further, the horse turns out to have been kidnapped from Narnia and can talk. This is a long string of coincidences, but these and the others in *The Horse and His Boy* turn out to be no coincidences at all, but divine providence. All are part of Aslan's plans for Shasta.

While they are headed north, Shasta and the horse Bree are chased by lions in the direction of Aravis and Hwin, who were themselves are chased by lions to the horse and his boy. This encounter begins Shasta's process of learning to respect girls; at first he shares the Calormene male's attitude that women are inferior to men. Among the tombs outside Tashbaan, a large golden cat keeps Shasta company and protects him from danger. When a lion chases the horses, and Shasta and Aravis toward the Hermit's enclosure in Archenland, Shasta seems to recognize the lion as one that chased them in Calormen. Eventually, Shasta is lost on horseback in a dense fog along treacherous mountain trails, yet his horse remains calm; a giant lion appears out of the mist, walking alongside the horse. The great lion is plainly Aslan, and His appearance reveals that Shasta has been progressing by divine influence, not mere coincidences. The stay in the tombs helped him learn not to fear the dark and to treat animals kindly, rather than the harsh way he had learned from Arsheesh. Crossing the desert taught him how to endure prolonged hardship and how to stick to achieving a goal, rather than quitting. When the lion chases the travelers in Archenland, Shasta makes a breakthrough into maturity by thinking of the welfare of others ahead of himself, and he races back to protect Aravis and Hwin from the lion, rather than run away. His running to warn King Lune and then riding a horse while lost teaches him how to push himself, how to press on when he wants to rest. Finally, Aslan's making Himself known to the boy teaches Shasta not only about divine providence but about the terror and joy to be found in knowing Aslan.

By the time Shasta is unhorsed during the battle at Anvard, he has earned the respect of others and has learned how to deserve respect. In fact, his selflessness and courage become lessons to others. For instance, through knowing Shasta and seeing how he behaves when the going gets tough, Aravis learns not only to respect him but to drop her notions of superiority over others. By the end of *The Horse and His Boy*, Shasta has become an example of how the least of people, a slave boy, can through divine providence not only persevere but be exalted. When King Lune declares Shasta to be the long lost Prince Cor, Shasta has had lessons in humility, thoughtfulness, determination, and courage that are beyond the normal education for a prince or noble.

Shasta, now Prince Cor, and Aravis fall in love, and when they are grown up, they marry. They may have more than one child, the text is not clear about this, but they have at least a son, Ham, who will become Ham the Great for deeds Lewis does not explain.

Shift the Ape devises the deception of having Puzzle the Donkey pose as Aslan. He conspires with the Calormenes to overthrow Narnia's government and to make Narnia a Calormene possession. He does this primarily to satisfy his desire or luxuries, mostly expensive food and drink. He gives himself wholly over to his desires and becomes a drunkard who can barely think. When Tirian tosses him into the stable, Tash eats him whole. It is Shift who establishes a camp at the Lantern Waste and begins the murdering of the Talking Trees for lumber to be sold for profit, and his lies are those that deceive many Narnians into believing that he speaks for Aslan. Although it is Puzzle who actually wears the lion skin, it is Shift who more fully fills the role of the antichrist, someone who through lies and tricks will deceive others into believing God is cruel and evil. In Christian theology, the antichrist's deceptions will mark the beginning of the end of the world. In *The Last Battle*, Shift's deceptions provoke the cataclysmic battle that will mark the end of Narnia.

Strawberry is the name of a 1900 London cab horse who is transformed into the winged horse **Fledge** in *The Magician's Nephew*. See **Fledge**.

Tirian is the king of Narnia in *The Last Battle*. At first confused by the deceptions of Shift, he soon realizes that Shift is lying and cannot speak for Aslan. He knows this because: 1) There is only one Aslan and there can be no others, hence Tash cannot be Aslan; 2) No one can speak for Aslan as Shift pretends to do; 3) Aslan is good and would never ask people to do evil such as commit murder or sell people into slavery; 4) Aslan would not hide because He has no fear. Once certain that Tashlan is a fraud, Tirian tries to rally Narnia's forces to resist Shift and the Calormene invaders, but too many Narnians have been fooled enough by Shift to have doubts about right and wrong and therefore do not help Tirian fight. Atheists, in the form of the ungrateful Dwarfs, further complicate Tirian's efforts by attacking anyone of any religious faith, murdering many good Narnians who would have helped Tirian. Outnumbered, already aware that "Narnia is no more," Tirian nonetheless uses all his leadership skills and considerable intelligence to resist the false god and the great evil that has been unleashed on Narnia. He is rewarded by the great compliment of "Well done" by Aslan, the highest praise anyone can receive. He enters Aslan's Country bodily (that is, he does not die first) and is joyously reunited with his father.

Uncle Andrew: See **Andrew Ketterley**.

THEMATIC DEVELOPMENT THROUGH THE MINOR CHARACTERS

Ahoshta Tarkaan is the elderly man to whom Aravis is to be given in marriage in *The Horse and His Boy*. He is small, humpbacked, and obsequious. In *The Horse and His Boy*, he is seen groveling at the feet of the Tisroc of Calormen, but he is supposedly a shrewd manipulator who has worked his way to the inner circles of his nation's powers. Aravis is contemptuous of him.

Anradin Tarkaan is the owner of the Talking Horse Bree at the start of *The Horse and His Boy*. While riding along an infrequently traveled path, he sees Shasta and realizes that the boy cannot be of Calormene descent; he bargains with the boy's owner to purchase Shasta. Later, he is among the horsemen who join Rabadash in the invasion of Archenland.

Argoz is one of the seven lords sent on a suicide mission across the Eastern Sea by the usurper Miraz in *Prince Caspian*. He is found sleeping at Aslan's Table on Ramandu's island in *The Voyage of the "Dawn Treader."*

Arsheesh is a fisherman who found the infant Shasta on a beach. He has raised Shasta but made the boy his slave in *The Horse and His Boy*. When Anradin Tarkaan offers to buy Shasta, he is interested, although he would lose a valuable worker. He is cruel to Shasta, making the boy very reluctant to trust adults, all of whom seem at first to be like Arsheesh. It is for this reason that Shasta keeps silent while in a room with the

Narnians in Tashbaan; he expects abuse from the adults if he says who he really is.

Bacchus accompanies Aslan through Berunda and to the field of battle near the end of *Prince Caspian*. He and his followers are merry people who invite people to dance for joy as Aslan passes. He is able to make water into wine, a power probably given him by Aslan. He also frees the River God when Aslan tells him to.

Brickelthumb is one of the Dwarfs with whom Shasta shares breakfast near the end of *The Horse and His Boy*.

Bullies who terrorize other children at the school Experiment House in *The Silver Chair* include Bannister, Carter (notable for his brutal cruelty toward animals), Garrett twins, Edith Jackle, Cholmondely (pronounced "chumley") Major, Adela Pennyfeather, Spotty Sorner, and Edith Winterblot.

Camillo is a Talking Rabbit who joins Caspian's forces in *Prince Caspian*. It is he who realizes that a man who turns out to be Doctor Cornelius is near the Great Council of Old Narnians.

Chervy (*chervus* is *deer* in Latin) is a stag who upon hearing Shasta's story about Rabadash invading Archenland races to Cair Paravel to warn Lucy, Edmund, Susan, and Prince Corin, newly returned from Calormen in *The Horse and His Boy*.

Chief Duffer is the leader of the Dufflepuds in *The Voyage of the "Dawn Treader."* Like all the Dufflepuds, he is silly and

sometimes stupid, and he is afraid of the magician Coriakin, who in reality is a kind ruler. No matter what he says, all the other Dufflepuds agree with him. He is vain, and not liking his appearance decides to have his daughter Clipsie recite Coriakin's spell of invisiblity, so that what he supposes are the bad looks of himself and the other Dufflepuds cannot be seen. He eventually decides that he does not like being invisible and pressures Lucy into climbing the stairs up to Coriakin's rooms and reciting the visibility spell she finds in the magician's books.

Clipsie is the daughter of the Chief Duffer in *The Voyage of the "Dawn Treader."* It was she who recited the spell of invisibility in Coriakin's book of magic, making everyone on their island invisible. Because Clipsie seems to be about Lucy's age, the Dufflepuds want Lucy to find and recite the visibility spell.

Cloudbirth is a centaur who applies medicine to Puddleglum's burned foot near the end of *The Silver Chair*.

Coalblack is Prince Rilian's horse in *The Silver Chair*.

Coriakin is the magician that Aslan has put in charge of the Dufflepuds in *The Voyage of the "Dawn Treader."* He is a generous and kind man who tells Aslan that he is content to rule such silly people. He is a star who committed some unspecified transgression and as a result has been forced to live on an island in the world of Narnia rather than live in the firmament; he shows no signs of resentment over his punishment. He knows of the existence of Lucy, Edmund, and Eustace's world of earth and even magically creates an English teatime for Lucy.

Corin is a prince of Archenland, the second son by twenty minutes of King Lune; his older twin is Cor, who is known as Shasta for most of *The Horse and His Boy*. He and Cor are identical twins, which is why the Narnians in Tashbaan mistake Shasta for Corin. In *The Horse and His Boy*, he has formed a close friendship with Queen Susan of Narnia and defends her honor while in the Calormene capital. He has a short temper and loves to fight; because of this, he thoughtlessly injures Thornbut before the battle at Anvard. Ordered by King Edmund to stay out of the battle, he thoughtlessly charges into the fight, bringing Shasta (Cor) with him with nearly catastrophic results when Shasta is unhorsed. A superior boxer, he becomes known as Corin Thunder-Fist after defeating the Lapsed Bear of Stormness in a thirty-three round contest. In *The Silver Chair*, Lord Rilian sings a song about him.

Dar is the brother of Lord Darrin in *The Horse and His Boy* and fights in the battle at Anvard.

Lord Darrin is part of King Lune's hunting party when Shasta runs to it in *The Horse and His Boy*. He questions Shasta's warning about the invasion of Archenland by the Calomenes, but appreciates Shasta's fine horsemanship and wonders whether Shasta may be more than he seems. In the battle at Anvard, he fights courageously. Later, he points out to King Lune that the king might be more unhappy with Prince Corin if the boy had not shown courage by joining the battle than he is for the boy's having disobeyed orders to stay out of the battle.

Daughter of Ramandu greets the crew of the *Dawn Treader* on Ramandu's Island. Ramandu is a star, but whether the daughter is a star, too, is not explained; her mother seems to be absent. She is very beautiful, graceful, dignified, and blonde. She meets Caspian the Navigator in *The Voyage of the "Dawn Treader,"* and they later marry. They have a son, Rilian, and she seems to have a good life until she is murdered by a serpent who is a witch, the Queen of Underworld, in *The Silver Chair.* After her death, Rilian returns often to the fountain where she died, seeking to find and kill the serpent. Her murder is not avenged until at least ten years later, when Rilian—aided by Puddleglum, Jill Pole, and Eustace Scrubb—kills the Queen of Underworld while she is in her serpent form.

Destrier is the horse Caspian rides when he flees the usurper Miraz. Destrier is not a Talking Horse but a dumb beast.

Diggle is the spokesman for the ungrateful Dwarfs after they have been tossed into the stable in *The Last Battle.* He refuses to look around him and insists that he is in a dark, smelly place. When Lucy offers him some violets to smell, he tries to hit her with his fist. No matter what Lucy, King Tirian, or even Aslan says to him, he refuses to believe, to see, or to smell. He insists on keeping his existence bleak.

Duffle is a Red Dwarf (meaning he has red hair) who takes Shasta to a good breakfast near the end of *The Horse and His Boy.*

Erlian is the second-to-last King of Narnia and the father of King

Tirian. He appears in Aslan's Country in *The Last Battle*. Tirian remembers him as a fine father, and their reunion is joyful.

Farsight is the eagle who brings King Tirian the bad news of Roonwit's murder and the invasion of Cair Paravel by Calormenes in *The Last Battle*. He is a shrewd observer of people and realizes before the Last Battle that Rishda Tarkaan is frightened by what seems to be happening in the stable. Further, he is a great warrior who intimidates his Calormene adversaries, and he does them much harm. Because he knows right from wrong and which side he should be on, he is not seduced by Shift and Rishda's nonsensical lies. He is among the multitude who enter Aslan's Country at the end of the world.

Father Christmas is a mystical being in *The Lion, the Witch and the Wardrobe*. Although plainly a parallel of the Father Christmas, Santa Claus, or Kris Kringle of earth's Christmases, which we can tell by his large size and red clothing, he is more of a partner of Aslan in *The Lion, the Witch and the Wardrobe*. It is he who brings the magical gifts for Lucy, Susan, and Peter, including the sword (the Holy Spirit) and shield (Faith) he gives Peter, which means he is closely tied to both Aslan and Aslan's Father, the Emperor-over-sea, who is the source of both the Holy Spirit and Faith. He comes across as a tough, reassuring man—as someone the White Witch would find very formidable as an opponent.

Father Time is seen asleep in Underworld in *The Silver Chair*. When he is awakened by Aslan, he blows the trumpet that

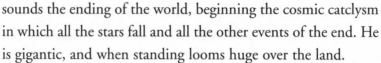

sounds the ending of the world, beginning the cosmic catclysm in which all the stars fall and all the other events of the end. He is gigantic, and when standing looms huge over the land.

Anne Featherstone is a schoolmate of Lucy. When in the magician's tower on the island of the Dufflepuds in *The Voyage of the "Dawn Treader,"* Lucy magically eavesdrops on Anne and Lucy's friend Marjorie Preston, and she overhears Anne saying bad things about her to Marjorie.

Fenris Ulf is the chief of the White Witch's secret police. He is a big grey wolf who may be based on the Fenris Ulf of Norse mythology, a wolf created by the god Loki. He is slain by Peter in *The Lion, the Witch and the Wardrobe,* which is why Aslan gives Peter the name Sir Peter Fenris-Bane when He knights the boy.

Frank I is a 1900 London cab driver who is made the first king of Narnia by Aslan in *The Magician's Nephew.* He promises Aslan to treat everyone in Narnia fairly, and he seems to live up to his promise. He also may have lived to very great age, since his second son Col establishes the kingdom of Archenland in the Narnian year 180, which would be 180 years after the events in *The Magician's Nephew.*

Ginger is an orange Talking Cat in *The Last Battle.* He figures out that Shift and Rishda are deceiving Narnians about Aslan, and he joins forces with them to promote the deception. Knowing the truth but choosing to serve evil anyway, he is apparently very surprised to actually find the demon Tash behind the stable door, rushing out and racing up a tree before disappearing. He loses his ability to speak and to reason, becoming a dumb animal, in front of the gathered Narnians at the stable. It is this which leads Rishda to suspect that there may be some reality to Tash, and to toss people into the stable to appease Tash. The event has the sad effect on some Narnian witnesses of affirming that Aslan is angry with them and means to punish them.

Glenstorm is a centaur who joins Caspian's forces in *Prince Caspian.* Like most centaurs in *The Chronicles of Narnia,* he is an expert on cosmic signs and knows in advance what Caspian will try to do. A very honorable fellow, he is one of the marshalls of the lists during High King Peter's contest against the usurper Miraz. He reappears in Aslan's Country in *The Last Battle.*

Glimfeather is a Talking Owl in *The Silver Chair.* He witnesses Eustace and then Jill fly over the Eastern Sea into Narnia, which is why he seeks them out. When he learns of their quest to find Prince Rilian, he warns them not to tell the regent Trumpkin, who may have them thrown in prison in order to prevent them from leaving Cair Paravel, because King Caspian has ordered that no more people search for his lost son (all the previous searchers have never returned). He carries Jill to the Parliament of Owls. He appears at the end of *Prince Caspian,* sleepy after bringing a message to Prince Rilian, and he reappears in Aslan's Country in *The Last Battle.*

Glozelle is a Telmarine lord who believes that he was not properly rewarded for helping Miraz seize Narnia's throne. In *Prince Caspian,* he goads Miraz into accepting High King Peter's challenge to single combat by implying that Miraz might appear cowardly if he did not accept, hoping that Peter will kill Miraz and that he and Sopespian will then lead Telmarine forces to victory over the poorly trained and armed forces of Caspian. During the fight between Miraz and Peter, Miraz slips and falls face down. On that instant, Glozelle and Sopespian begin a cry of treachery that creates a stampede of Telmarines toward the Old Narnians. During this charge, Glozelle stabs the fallen Miraz in the back as revenge for a perceived insult, killing the usurper. Thus one traitor murders another.

Golg is an Earthman (a dweller in Underworld, not someone from planet earth) in *The Silver Chair.* He is short, stout, with small pink eyes. When captured by Prince Rilian, Jill, Eustace, and Puddleglum, he explains to them that Earthmen would be their friends because they killed the Queen. She had forced Glog and other Earthmen out of their home in Bism, deeper below Underworld, and made them serve her plans to invade the surface world and seize control of Narnia. He hated the idea of going out into sunlight and is delighted to be able to return to Bism.

Griffle is a leader of the ungrateful Dwarfs in *The Last Battle.* He is an atheist who mocks Jill for saying she has actually seen Aslan, which those who have read *The Silver Chair* know is true. An opportunist, he tries to prevent either Calormene forces or King Tirian's forces from winning the last battle, hoping the Dwarfs will emerge as rulers of the land after the rival forces have destroyed each other. He and his followers are fools; they easily enough murder the horses who rush to aid King Tirian, but are much less successful against armed and well-trained Calormene soldiers, who capture them and toss them into the stable as offerings to Tash (no more pretense about "Tashlan," by then).

Gumpas is the Governor of the Lone Islands in *The Voyage of the "Dawn Treader."* When King Caspian confronts him, he spouts clichéd political nonsense about forms and procedures; he has secured his power by surrounding it with red tape. He is as infuriating as any petty-minded bureaucrat can be, but King Caspian is not fooled by any of Gumpas' pompous efforts to bury issues of right and wrong in mounds of excess verbiage. He forcefully ejects Gumpas from power, replacing him with Lord Bern.

Gwendolen is a schoolgirl in Beruna when Aslan walks through the small town. While in class, she sees Aslan, calls attention to Him, and then is delighted when He invites her to join Him. She happily dances with the maenads, who help her remove her restrictive school clothing. Lewis disliked school uniforms, and Gwendolen's removing them probably not only makes her much more comfortable, but may represent her being liberated from an oppressive school system.

Hardbiters are three badgers that attend the Great Council in *Prince Caspian,* two of whom are sent to investigate the human who turns out to be Doctor Cornelius.

The Head runs Experiment House, the horrible school that Jill Pole and Eustace Scrubb attend in *The Silver Chair*. Part of the experiment of Experiment House is a lack of discipline that allows very nasty bullies to beat up and otherwise molest everyone smaller and weaker than they. They are utter cowards, the sort that in *Prince Caspian,* in Beruna, might have found them reduced to dumb animals like the piggy boys. The Head thinks the bullying is marvelous and studies it. Terrified by the sight of Jill, Eustace, and Caspian swatting the bullies at the end of *The Silver Chair,* she babbles nonsense about an otherworldly attack and is removed from being Head. She eventually is elected to Parliament, where she stupidly interferes with government. At the time *The Silver Chair* was written, Lewis blamed the Labor Party, then the ruling party, for the sharp economic downturn in England after World War II. As someone who as Head of a school created an undisciplined, cruel, supposedly experimental environment, she would have been a "liberal" and probably a Laborite.

Queen Helen is the first queen of Narnia, having been appointed by Aslan Himself in *The Magician's Nephew*. She was the wife of a cabby who was brought by Digory to the world of Narnia before it was formed. Aslan, who can intersect any of His worlds at will, brings her to Narnia to be with her husband, who becomes King Frank. She and her husband have children, at least two of whom explore much of the rest of the world. The time line for the history of Narnia implies that she and King Frank lived very long lives, because their second son establishes Archenland in the Narnian year 180, which is 180 years after she was made queen. Her long reign was apparently a happy one, with Narnia untroubled by evil.

The Hermit in *The Horse and His Boy* takes Hwin, Aravis, Bree, and Shasta into his circular walled enclosure after they have been chased by a lion in southern Archenland. It is the Hermit who tells Shasta that he must run to tell King Lune about the invasion of Archenland by Calormenes. The hermit does not seem to have any symbolic aspect: he is bearded and tall, with a kingly commanding presence. He is also very old. His enclosure is populated by goats, as well as himself, and he takes good care of animals, giving Bree and Hwin rubdowns. A magician of limited power, he can see faraway events by looking into a pool; this allows him to act like a radio reporter, telling his guests what is happening at Anvard.

Hogglestock is a Talking Hedgehog at the Great Council in *Prince Caspian*.

Jackdaw makes the "first joke" in the history of Narnia's world in *The Magician's Nephew*. He is a good-natured Talking Bird, who enjoys jokes, even at his own expense.

Jewel, a unicorn, is King Tirian's best friend in *The Last Battle*. He is vacationing with Tirian when Tirian learns that the Talking Trees of the Lantern Waste are being murdered. Jewel never wavers in his faith to Tirian and to Aslan, although, like Tirian, he is at first a bit confused by Shift the Ape's deceptions. He is a fearsome warrior who slays many enemies before he himself is slain in *The Last Battle*. He is reunited with King Tirian in Aslan's Country.

Mabel Kirke, Digory's mother in *The Magician's Nephew*, has been seriously ill for an undefined amount of time, probably many months. She and Digory have been taken into the home of her sister Letitia Ketterley. As a parent should be, she is a moral force in Digory's life, teaching virtues such as keeping promises that serve the boy well when Aslan assigns him the task of retrieving a special fruit without eating it. Aslan eventually gives Digory an apple to take to his mother that cures her when she eats it. This is a sign that Aslan's power is as great on earth as it is in Narnia. Her husband, away in India, inherits a country estate, retires, comes home, and takes Mabel and Digory to live in the country house where the Pevensie children begin *The Lion, the Witch and the Wardrobe*.

Letitia Ketterley (Aunt Letty) is Digory Kirke's aunt in *The Magician's Nephew*. Digory's mother is dying, and Aunt Letty has taken her and Digory into her own home in London. There, she has also taken in her brother Andrew. At first she seems like a bossy stick-in-the-mud, because she tries to prevent Uncle Andrew from talking to Digory, but it turns out that she was doing what she could to protect Digory and that she was right to dislike Uncle Andrew's activities. Just as it would do the Narnians in *The Last Battle* good to judge the behavior of the fake Aslan against what would be good behavior, so it would do Digory good to judge Aunt Letty by her behavior; if he would, he would notice that she is kind to his mother, manages her household well, and is generous with her time and money. Very important for Digory, she remarks within his hearing that fruit of youth is all that may save Digory's mother; this remark is transformed by events into the apple Aslan gives to Digory to feed to his mother. It cures her, and Aunt Letty's response to the happy event is to cheer up.

Kidrash Tarkaan is Aravis' father in *The Horse and His Boy*. He is the ruler of the Calormene province of Calavar and lives in a palace. He decides to give Aravis in marriage to Ahoshta Tarkaan, the Grand Vizier to the Tisroc, ruler of Calormen, thus compelling Aravis to flee to Narnia, where girls cannot be forced to marry.

Lasaraleen Tarkeena is the friend who aids Aravis in *The Horse and His Boy*. She does not fully understand why Aravis, or any Calormene, would want to go to live in Narnia, a place that she imagines to be horrible. Further, she thinks that Aravis is foolish to pass up an excellent marriage with one of the most powerful men in Calormen. Often viewed as shallow and disspated, Lasarleen must have more to her, because in the end, in spite of being very frightened, she helps Aravis escape Tashbaan. She has ample opportunity to give both Aravis and herself away but manages to keep her wits sufficiently to avoid being suspected. She chooses to honor her friendship with Aravis over her own prejudices and misgivings.

King Lune of Archenland wisely heeds Shasta's warning in *The Horse and His Boy* and locks the gates of Anvard before Rabadash's small army arrives. When his Narnian friends attack the Calormenes outside the main gates to Anvard, he leads a spirited sortie into the ranks of the enemy, causing much confusion

among them, eventually helping to trap Rabadash himself against one of Anvard's walls. When he first sees Shasta, he gives the boy a hard look; later he has Shasta and Prince Corin stand together and invites others to look at them and see for themselves that they are identical. He realizes that Shasta is actually Prince Cor, stolen away by a disgraced bureaucrat many years before.

Mrs. Macready (called "the Macready" by the Pevensie children) is a servant in Professor Kirke's big country house in *The Lion, the Witch and the Wardrobe*. She sometimes leads tourists through the historic house, and during one such tour the Pevensie children hide in the Wardrobe to get out of her way, because she is very bossy and probably would be annoyed if they interrupted her tour. This is when all four children find themselves walking through the wardrobe and into Narnia.

Man-headed Bull is part of Aslan's army in *The Lion, the Witch and the Wardrobe*.

The Master Bowman, in *The Voyage of the "Dawn Treader,"* worries that the ship may be unable to return home because it is becalmed, a worry Lord Drinian attributes to his inexperience with sailing.

Maugrim is the name given **Fenris Ulf** in some editions of *The Lion, the Witch and the Wardrobe*.

Mavramorn is one of the seven good lords who was sent to explore the eastern seas by the usurper Miraz. In *The Voyage of the*

"Dawn Treader," he is found sleeping at Aslan's table on Ramandu's Island. He is probably the one of the three lords sleeping at the table who during a brief moment of near wakefulness asks Caspian for the mustard, and he is likely to have been the one who just wanted to eat while the other two bickered.

Mullugutherum is one of two guards who receive Jill, Eustace, and Puddleglum at the palace of the Queen of Underworld in *The Silver Chair.* Although he wants to imprison the travelers, the mysterious prince (later proven to be Rilian under an enchantment) overrules him. He may be the chamberlain who helps strap Rilian to the silver chair.

Old Raven of Ravenscaur talks too much at the Great Council in *Prince Caspian.*

Orruns is a faun who greets Jill after she wakes up in Narnia after having emerged from Underworld near the end of *The Silver Chair.* He explains some of the facts about centaurs.

Pattertwig is a red Talking Squirrel who attends the Great Council in *Prince Caspian.* After Caspian blows Susan's horn, Pattertwig is sent to the Lantern Waste to see whether the Pevensies have appeared there.

Peepiceek is a gallant Talking Mouse who after the battle in *Prince Caspian* tells Aslan that he and the other Talking Mice will cut off their tails rather than dishonor the High Mouse Reepicheep by having tails while he has none. This convinces Aslan to give

Reepicheep a new tail. In *The Voyage of the "Dawn Treader,"* Reepicheek designates Peepiceek his successor as High Mouse.

Peridan is in the service of the Kings and Queens of Narnia in *The Horse and His Boy* and is probably a knight. In Tashbaan, he takes Shasta to the quarters of Edmund, Lucy, and Susan. Later, he is a horseman carrying a banner with the Narnian forces that attack the Calormenes at the gates to Anvard. After the battle, he notes that King Lune has the right to execute Rabadash.

Mr. and Mrs. Pevensie are the parents of Lucy, Edmund, Susan, and Peter. He is a college professor, but little else is told about him. During World War II, they send their children to Digory Kirke's country house to keep them away from the Germans' bombing of London. In 1942, he lectures in America, leaving Edmund and Lucy in the care of the Scrubbs. Later, he and his wife are in the same train wreck that kills Jill, Eustace, Lucy, Edmund, Peter, Digory, and Polly; he appears in Aslan's Country in *The Last Battle.*

Marjorie Preston is Lucy's friend from school. While leafing through a book of magic in the magician's tower in *The Voyage of the "Dawn Treader,"* Lucy casts a spell that allows her to eavesdrop on Majorie and another schoolmate, Anne Featherstone, while the two ride together on a train. Anne says bad things about Lucy, and Marjorie, being a weak spirit, agrees. The dangers of using magic are illustrated by the evil that comes of Lucy having listened to a conversation that she had no business knowing about. Aslan implies that a potentially great friendship with Marjorie was lost because Lucy had spied on her. Lucy will be unable to forget Marjorie's words, spoken in weakness and not truly representing her kind regard for Lucy.

The Phoenix appears in *The Magician's Nephew*. In Ancient Egyptian mythology, it is a bird that lives for a thousand years, is consumed in flames, and then is reborn in the remaining ashes. It is often used as a symbol of resurrection, although its function in *The Magician's Nephew* seems to be simply an observer.

Pittencream is the only sailor left behind on Ramandu's Island when the *Dawn Treader* sails to the End of the World. Although almost all of the crew was fearful of sailing farther east, he is the last to volunteer to go and is too late. He is unhappy at being left behind, even more unhappy when the returning *Dawn Treader* picks him up. Finding himself regarded as a coward, he deserts the ship in the Lone Islands. From there, he voyages to Calormen, where he tells outrageous tales about his sailing to the east. Calormenes in general love good stories, and Pittencream's storytelling earns him a good life in Calormen.

Poggin is the only Dwarf liberated by King Tirian from the Calormene slave traders to join the king's cause, the others proving ungrateful and declaring that the "Dwarfs are for the Dwarfs" in *The Last Battle*. He has many skills, shooting and then cooking a rabbit and making soap, but his best trait may be his optimism. In the face of great danger, he lifts spirits and keeps calm; his intelligence and good sense help Tirian's plan-

ning. His faithfulness and honesty contrast him with the ungrateful Dwarfs, and although some of them (not all) refuse to see the glories of Aslan's Country, he meets the Seven Friends of Narnia and shares in the wonders of the land.

Miss Prizzle is teaching in a girl's school in Beruna when one of her students, **Gwendolen** (see above), declares that she sees a lion outside. After reprimanding Gwendolen, Miss Prizzle sees Aslan herself and runs away, a sign that evil has hold of her heart, because evil people are universally frightened by Aslan.

Prunaprismia is the wife of the usurper Miraz in *Prince Caspian*. Offstage, she gives birth to a son, which leads to Miraz wanting to murder Caspian, a rival heir to Narnia's throne.

Pug is the slave trader who kidnaps King Caspian and others in *The Voyage of the "Dawn Treader."* When Caspian, having been rescued by Lord Bern, confronts him in Narrowhaven's slave market, Caspian seems merciful when he allows Pug to live. Forced to free his captives and return the money from slaves already sold, Pug complains that he will be ruined, but Caspian points out that it will be better than being a slave.

Ramandu is a retired star living with his daughter on an island in the far east of the Eastern Sea in *The Voyage of the "Dawn Treader."* Everyday his life is reinvigorated by a fire-berry that a bird sets in his mouth. On his island is Aslan's Table, set daily at Aslan's behest with a royal repast for anyone who ventures to the island. Ramandu's beautiful daughter (see **Daughter of**

Ramandu) marries Caspian and becomes the mother of Rilian.

Restimar is probably the golden statue of a man diving, found in the pond on Deathwater Island in *The Voyage of the "Dawn Treader."* He was one of the Seven Noble Lords sent to explore the far east by the usurper Miraz in hopes that they would never return.

Revilian, like Restimar, was one of the Seven Noble Lords sent to explore the Eastern Sea by the usurper Miraz. He is found by King Caspian and his crew asleep at Aslan's Table on Ramandu's Island in *The Voyage of the "Dawn Treader."* He is likely to be the one of the three sleeping lords who wished to turn around and return to Narnia.

Rhince is Lord Drinian's second in command on the *Dawn Treader* in *The Voyage of the "Dawn Treader."* He is often acts as the spokesman for the crew and has a common sense attitude toward his adventures. His concern for the welfare of the ship's crew is evident in bits and snatches throughout the novel, and his concerns tend to be homey ones. For instance, he hopes the adventure ends before his tobacco runs out.

Rhoop is one of the seven lords sent on a suicide mission across the Eastern Sea by the usurper Miraz in *Prince Caspian*. He is found in the Darkness that surrounds Dark Island, where sleeping dreams come alive. He is nearly insane by the time he is rescued in *The Voyage of the "Dawn Treader."* Unable to sleep because of his experiences on Dark Island, he is able to sleep

without dreaming at Aslan's Table on Ramandu's island, where he takes a seat next to Lord Argoz.

The River-god is one of the first beings created by Aslan in *The Magician's Nephew*. He is large and bearded, with water plants in his hair. In *The Magician's Nephew,* he is part of Aslan's First Council. In *Prince Caspian,* he asks Aslan to free him from the bridge at Beruna, because the bridge is to him like chains, and at Aslan's command Bacchus destroys the bridge. In both *The Magician's Nephew* and *Prince Caspian,* the River-god represents the divine powers of water; for instance, Aslan uses water to help cleanse Eustace Scrubb of his sins in *The Voyage of the "Dawn Treader."* In *The Last Battle,* bathing in the river refreshes King Tirian and his followers before their final confrontation against evil.

Rogan is one of the Dwarfs with whom Shasta shares breakfast near the end of *The Horse and His Boy.*

Roonwit is a centaur in *The Last Battle* who has seen the approaching evil by reading the heavenly bodies in Narnia's sky. His readings tell him that the figure at the stable cannot be Aslan. King Tirian sends him to warn Narnians at Cair Paravel of the invasion by Calormenes, but he is murdered along the way. At his death, he tells the Eagle Farsight that "noble death is a treasure which no one is too poor to buy," which suggests that he dies while in a courageous frame of mind. His name is from Old Norse, roughly meaning someone who can read sacred writing (*roon* meaning written symbols and *wit* meaning knowledge).

Rumblebuffin is a Narnian giant. The giants of Narnia tend to be good, as opposed to the giants to the north in Ettinsmoor, who tend to be bad. He had been turned into stone by the White Witch, but in *The Lion, the Witch and the Wardrobe,* Aslan breathes on him, bringing him back to life. Earlier in the novel, Aslan had been sacrificed and then resurrected, thus turning death backwards; that is, turning death into life, so Rumblebuffin's revival is part of the theme of resurrection in *The Lion, the Witch and the Wardrobe.* He has a sweet attitude toward Lucy, but is dangerous in battle. He is happy to do whatever Aslan asks him to do such as knock down the gates to the White Witch's castle.

Rynelf is a particularly courageous sailor in *The Voyage of the "Dawn Treader,"* and he is helpful throughout the novel, as when he feeds Lucy, Edmund, and Eustace after they are freed from the slaver Pug. When crew members are reluctant to continue sailing eastward from Ramandu's Island, he from the start is for continuing and requires no persuasion; indeed, he tries to persuade the rest of the crew to continue.

Sallowpad (meaning "yellow foot") is a Talking Raven in the chambers of the Narnian visitors to Tashbaan in *The Horse and His Boy.* He seems to be a senior counselor and is well-informed about doings in Tashbaan.

Sarah is a maid in Letitia Ketterley's house in *The Magician's Nephew.*

The Sea Serpent is a monster that attacks the voyagers in *The Voyage of the "Dawn Treader."* It is a witless beast that the voyagers escape from partly because it does not understand that it has failed to destroy the *Dawn Treader*.

The Seven Brothers of the Shuddering Wood are Red Dwarfs (called that because of the color of their hair) and blacksmiths who give armor to Caspian in *Prince Caspian*. They make the best armor of anyone. They attend the Great Council and fight against the army of the usurper Miraz.

Alberta Scrubb is the aunt of the Pevensie children and the mother of Eustace. She dislikes art and places the beautiful painting of a ship at sea on the wall of room into which she seldom ventures. It is through this painting that Eustace, Edmund, and Lucy enter Narnia in *The Voyage of the "Dawn Treader."* Alberta Scrubb has insisted that Eustace read only nonfiction books that are full of statistics about economics and shipping trade and the like. Because of her, Eustace has no idea what an adventure is and has never read a book that might expand his mind and encourage his creativity. Further, she encourages Eustace to view himself as superior to others because he is ignorant of anything but supposedly useful knowledge. As a consequence, he is not only unable to cope with life on his own, but he is a miserable monster who delights in tormenting his supposed inferiors such as Edmund and Lucy. Alberta Scrubb has many weird notions about how to live well, keeping her house almost bare of anything decorative, maintaining a reserved relationship with her husband, and abstaining from tobacco, alcoholic beverages, and meat. This would place her among the fallen, in Lewis' view, partly because he liked smoking, drinking wine and beer, and eating meat, but additionally because her abstaining from meat would be an insult to God, Who according to the Apostle Paul included livestock for eating among the bounty God created for human beings to enjoy.

Harold Scrubb is Eustace's father. He apparently tolerates Eustace calling him by his first name "Harold," a sign of disrespect of a child toward a parent, but he otherwise comes across as intolerant. From him Eustace has picked up the notion that people should look directly at facts, however unpleasant they may be. In both Harold's and Eustace's cases, this actually is a cover for their ignorance; the insistence that facts should be viewed without embellishment means that they understand neither the context of the facts nor the richness of life that may underlie the facts. Even after his religious conversion, Eustace likes to annoy people by expressing facts, expecially obvious ones, without thought to the feeling of others, or even to deliberately annoy them. This makes him a sometimes unpleasant companion in *The Silver Chair* and *The Last Battle,* and we have Harold Scrubb to thank for it.

Clodsley Shovel (probably named for seventeenth-century British admiral Cloudsley Shovel) is a mole who joins Caspian's forces in *Prince Caspian.* It is not clear whether he is the Chief Mole or not, but it is he who suggests building earthen defenses. Later, after the triumph of the Old Narnians, he tells the moles to prepare the earth for the trees to feast on.

Silenus is a follower of Bacchus in *Prince Caspian*. His name appears on a book in the home of Mr. Tumnus in *The Lion, the Witch and the Wardrobe*. In Ancient Greek mythology, Silenus is usually drunk, often riding and falling off of a donkey. In *Prince Caspian*, he seems to have the ability to promote the growth of vines.

Slinkey is a fox who sides with the Calormenes in *The Last Battle*, and who is killed by Eustace in battle.

Snowflake is the horse of the Queen of Underworld in *The Silver Chair*.

Sopespian is a Telmarine lord and follower of the usurper Miraz who conspires with Glozelle to contrive Miraz's death and then to seize control of Narnia for themselves. Sopespian badly overestimates his own abilities and badly underestimates those of High King Peter. When he and Glozelle cry foul and lead a charge across the spot where Peter and Miraz are duelling, Peter quickly lops off Sopespian's head.

Tash is the chief god of Calormen, and his greatest temple is in Tashbaan, the capital city named for him. Human sacrifices are made on his altars. He has the torso of a man, four humanlike arms with talons instead of fingernails, and the head of a bird, with a sharp, curved beak. When first seen in *The Last Battle*, he floats above the ground as he moves, and the grass beneath him withers then dies as he passes over it. In the stable, he eats Shift whole, and he snatches Rishda Tarkaan in his arms, carrying the man away when someone, probably High King Peter, banishes him to his own realm, probably hell.

Tashlan is a name given by Shift and Rishda Tarkaan to Puzzle the donkey's impersonation of Aslan. It is the combining of "Tash" plus "Aslan," and is the product of the claim that Tash and Aslan are one and the same. See **Puzzle**.

Thornbut is a dwarf assigned by King Edmund to look after Prince Corin of Archenland during the battle at Anvard in *The Horse and His Boy*. Corin picks a fight with Thornbut, and the dwarf falls and injures his ankle. Edmund is furious at Corin's injuring Thornbut, a good warrior who will not be able to fight.

The Three Bulgy Bears attend the Great Council in *Prince Caspian*. They claim a hereditary right to have a bear made a Marshal of the Lists during High King Peter's duel against the usurper Miraz, and Peter makes the eldest of them a marshal. They seem to be slow witted, and they are prone to sucking their paws while their minds wander.

The Three Sleepers are the three Noble Lords who are discovered sleeping at Aslan's Table on Ramandu's Island in *The Voyage of the "Dawn Treader."* See **Argoz**, **Mavramorn**, and **Revilian**.

Tisroc is the title of a king of Calormen. In *The Horse and His Boy*, the Tisroc is a scheming, heartless man, who lets his son Rabadash lead an attack on Archenland and Narnia partly in the hope that Rabadash will be killed, because ambitious sons

have been known to murder their fathers in order to become tisrocs. Both Aravis and her friend Lasaraleen are terrified of the Tisroc, because he would not hesitate to murder them both.

Trufflehunter is a Talking Badger in *Prince Caspian* and appears in Aslan's Country in *The Last Battle*. It is he who rescues Caspian after the boy has been knocked from his horse while trying to flee to Archenland, and he prevents others, particularly the Dwarf Nikabrik, from doing him harm. Trufflehunter is honest, true to his word, and courageous. He is also faithful. He regards *remembering* to be one of the essential duties of a Talking Badger, and it is he who reminds others that the White Witch was an enemy to Narnia, and he points out that Aslan is Narnia's friend. He and Nikabrik argue over whether they should have the help of evil. Nikabrik tries to kill him, but is himself killed. Caspian comes to trust Trufflehunter's faithfulness and good sense.

Urnus is a faun who carries Trumpkin's ear-trumpet in *The Silver Chair*.

The Warden of the Marches of Underland (also Underworld) is an Earthman (someone who lives underground in Narnia's world, not someone from the planet earth) and the first person to speak to Jill, Eustace, and Puddleglum in Underland in *The Silver Chair*. They have just escaped the dogs of the giants of Harfang and slid down a steep, long slope of stones. "Warden of the marches" means "guardian of the borders," which in Underworld's case would primarily be places where Overworld and Underworld are near each other, although the borders with

Bism and other lower places might be included. The Warden warns the travelers that he has one hundred armed Earthmen with him, and when light is provided, they see he leads spear-carrying earthmen. His catch phrase is "Many fall down, and few return to the sunlit lands," which he says, as he says everything, in an utter monotone. His flat voice and sad demeanor are shared by the other earthmen, and his catch phrase is like a password; when at the Queen of Underworld's palace, he says to the guards, "Many sink down to the Underworld," and they reply, "And few return to the sunlit lands."

The Water Rat pilots a raft of logs from Talking Trees downriver past King Tirian and Jewel early in *The Last Battle*. He believes Aslan has ordered him to do so.

The White Stag is said to grant wishes to any who catch it in *The Lion, the Witch and the Wardrobe*. By chasing the White Stag in the Lantern Waste, Kings Peter and Edmund, as well as Queens Lucy and Susan end up in the portal to earth in the wardrobe and fall out its doorway into Professor Digory's house. Although in medieval writings a white stag would sometimes represent Christ, Lewis is working with Eastern European folklore, here. Many folktales survive in Hungary and the Czech Republic about the elusive, magnificent white stag, the pursuit of which leads people into great adventures or to their deaths. In the sacred Hindu book *Ramayana*, the killing of such a stag leads to a tragic conflict among both humans and gods that affects entire nations. The loss of the Pevensie kings and queens puts an end to Narnia's twenty-eight-year golden age, and their pursuit of the stag results in great tragedy for the nation they ruled.

Wimbleweather is a good Narnian giant who joins Caspian's army of Old Narnians in *Prince Caspian*. Courageous and strong, he is somewhat slow to understand what is happening around him, and he therefore attacks at the wrong time in a battle, ruining it for the Old Narnians. For this, he is ashamed and cries. Even so, he is one of the Marshals of the Lists for Peter for the High King's duel against the usurper Miraz. In the Second Battle of Beruna, he acquits himself well.

Wraggle is a satyr in *The Last Battle* who sides with the Calormenes during the final battle. Jill kills him with an arrow.

THEMATIC DEVELOPMENT THROUGH FIGURES MENTIONED BUT NOT SEEN

Adam is often mentioned in *The Chronicles of Narnia,* and human males are referred to by Aslan as Sons of Adam. This refers to the Biblical Adam who in Genesis ate the forbidden fruit and was cast out of Paradise. By Aslan's command, only Sons of Adam can be rightful kings of Narnia.

Alimash is a Calormene lord mentioned in *The Horse and His Boy* as having fought in the war against Teebeth.

Ardeeb Tisroc was ruler of Calormen and the great-great-great-grandfather of Aravis, making her and her father of royal descent.

Axartha Tarkaan was the man who preceded Ahosta Tarkaan as Grand Vizier of Calormen in *The Horse and His Boy.*

Azaroth is a Calormene goddess mentioned by Aravis in *The Horse and His Boy.*

The Bastables appear in novels by Edith Nesbit and are mentioned in *The Magician's Nephew.*

Belisar is a lord who is murdered by Miraz in a fake hunting accident.

Betty is a servant of Professor Kirke in *The Lion, the Witch and the Wardrobe.*

Caspian I was a Telmarine human who declared himself king of Narnia in 1998, and he is mentioned in *Prince Caspian.* Then Telmarine humans settled Narnia, building towns along its rivers and turning much of the land into farms. A period of repression of the original Narnian population and superstitious fear followed, ended by Caspian X, also known as Caspian the Navigator.

Caspian VIII is the father of Caspian IX and is mentioned briefly in *Prince Caspian.*

Caspian IX was murdered by his brother Miraz, who eventually declared himself King of Narnia, before the beginning of events covered in *Prince Caspian.* His son was Caspian the Navigator.

Prince Col is the second son of King Frank and Queen Helen, whom Aslan appointed the first king and queen of Narnia. They may have lived an extraordinarily long time, because 180 years later their son Col leads his followers south to found the kingdom of Archenland. It seems likely that his descendants form an unbroken line of monarchs for Archenland from the Narnian year 180 until Caspian the Navigator's era in the first half of the 2300s; the line may well have extended unbroken all the way to the end of the world.

Erimon is a lord who was executed by the usurper Miraz before the outset of *Prince Caspian*.

Eve is often mentioned in *The Chronicles of Narnia,* and human females are referred to by Aslan as Daughters of Eve. This refers to the Biblical Eve who in Genesis ate the forbidden fruit and was cast out of Paradise. By Aslan's command, only Daughters of Eve can be rightful queens of Narnia. This is somewhat confusing, because Caspian the Navigator's wife is the daughter of a star, Ramandu. Perhaps the command applies only to rulers of Narnia and not to the wives of ruling kings. Or perhaps her mother was a Daughter of Eve, which would make her one, too.

King Gale was ruler of Narnia in the Narnian year 302, when he slew the dragon that was plaguing the Lone Islands. The people of the Lone Islands declared him and all future kings of Narnia their emperor. It is this that gives Caspian the Navigator the authority to depose the governor Gumpas and end slavery in the Lone Islands.

Harpha is the father of Emeth in *The Last Battle*.

Sherlock Holmes is a fictional detective created by Arthur Conan Doyle. He is mentioned in *The Magician's Nephew*.

Ilsombreh Tisroc was ruler of Calormen and is the great-great-grandfather of Aravis in *The Horse and His Boy*.

Ivy is a servant of Professor Kirke in *The Lion, the Witch and the Wardrobe*.

Kidrash Tarkaan is the name of Aravis' great-grandfather as well as her father in *The Horse and His Boy*.

Kraken is a sea monster from Ancient Norse Mythology and in *The Voyage of the "Dawn Treader,"* is mentioned as a source of fear for the sea people.

The Lapsed Bear of Stormness was a Talking Bear who had gone wild. He is defeated in a long boxing match by Prince Corin of Archenland, and he then returns to behaving like a civilized creature.

Mrs. Lefay was a descendant of fairies and practiced magic. She was Andrew Ketterley's god mother in *The Magician's Nephew*, and left him her magic box when she died. Her last name is intended to call to mind the evil Morgan LeFay, who helps destroy King Arthur's kingdom in Arthurian tales.

Lilith is the demonic mother of the White Witch in *The Lion, the Witch and the Wardrobe*. In Jewish folklore, she is a demon, whose name means "Night Monster," who is variously depicted as the mother of Adam's demonic offspring following his separation from Eve.

Lilygloves was a Talking Mole who, during Narnia's golden age, planted an apple orchard near Cair Paravel and told High King Peter that he would someday be grateful for the trees. When called to Cair Paravel in *Prince Caspian*, Peter has cause to be glad of the old, overgrown orchard because apples are all he has to eat.

Lady Liln married King Olvin of Archenland, according to songs in *The Horse and His Boy*.

Margaret is a servant of Professor Kirke in *The Lion, the Witch and the Wardrobe*.

Moonwood was a Talking Hare who could hear what people were saying in Cair Paravel even though he was all the was across Narnia near the Great Waterfall, according to *The Last Battle*.

Nain is the King of Archenland in *Prince Caspian*. Doctor Cornelius tells Prince Caspian that Nain will protect him from the usurper Miraz, but Caspian does not make it to Archenland.

Octesian was one of the seven lords sent to explore the Eastern Sea by the usurper Miraz. In *The Voyage of the "Dawn Treader,"* he seems to have been killed on Dragon Island.

Olvin who, according to *The Horse and His Boy,* was an Archenland king who turned into stone the two-headed giant Pire in the Narnian year 407.

Pire was a two-headed giant that according to songs in *The Horse and His Boy* was turned into stone by King Olvin of Archenland in the Narnian year 407.

Plato is mentioned by Professor Digory Kirke in *The Lion, the Witch and the Wardrobe* and *The Last Battle.* Plato argued that the human mind existed separate from the body, an idea Lewis found very appealing.

Pomely is Glozelle's horse in *Prince Caspian.*

Pomona is drawn from Ancient Roman Mythology. According to Peter in *Prince Caspian,* she blessed the apple orchard near Cair Paravel when it was first planted by Lilygloves during the reign of Peter, Lucy, Edmund, and Susan.

Ram the Great is mentioned in *The Horse and His Boy* as the son of King Cor and Queen Aravis. He became the king of Archenland in 1050. Lewis does not indicate what made Ram great.

Restimar was one of the seven lords sent to explore the Eastern Sea by the usurper Miraz. The golden statue found on Deathwater Island is probably him.

Rishti Tarkaan is the grandfather of Aravis in *The Horse and His Boy*.

The sister of Jadis led a revolt in the world or Charn against Jadis, according to Jadis in *The Magician's Nephew*. Just as she was about to defeat Jadis, Jadis invoked the Deplorable Word and thereby killed everyone in the world except herself.

Spivvins was helped by Eustace when persecuted by the bullies at Experiment House in *The Silver Chair*.

Stonefoot is a giant the King Tirian tries to summon for help in *The Last Battle*.

Queen Swanwhite rules Narnia around Narnian year 1100, which is seventy-two years after Kings Peter and Edmund and Queens Lucy and Susan disappear. Her primary significance is that her being queen suggests a little about what happened after the disappearance of the Pevensie monarchs. Apparently, by 1100, Narnia had established a government and a line of royal succession.

The two brothers of Beaversdam are lords imprisoned by the usurper Miraz in *Prince Caspian*.

Uvilas is a lord who is murdered by Miraz in a fake hunting accident in *Prince Caspian*.

Zardeenah is a Calormene moon goddess who is supposed to help young women in *The Horse and His Boy*.

THEMATIC DEVELOPMENT THROUGH THE MYTHICAL BEINGS AND BEASTS

Bacchus is the Roman god of grapes and wine. He is often associated with the Greek god Dionysus, who in addition to loving to party was a protector of women. Thus Bacchus is accompanied by female followers called *Bacchae* who enjoy his protection as well as his love of fun.

Centaurs, in Roman mythology, are characterized by the head, arms, and torso of a man and the body and legs of a horse. In *The Chronicles of Narnia* they tend to be very learned, knowing much about Narnia's Cosmos. Lewis' centaurs have two digestive systems and eat human meals and horse meals (grass and the like); they are not often invited to visit people because they eat so much that they can be heavy burdens on their hosts. They are passionate followers of Aslan.

Dragons are reptilian beasts that breathe fire and can fly. Lewis takes his images of dragons from medieval European traditions in which dragons are enemies to humans and love to fill their dens with loot such as precious gems and metals. Dragons typ-

ical of these are to be found in *Beowulf* and *The Hobbit.* The Lone Islands make the Narnian king their emperor after Narnians free them of a dragon. Eustace witnesses the sad end of an old, lonely dragon and then turns into a dragon himself in *The Voyage of the "Dawn Treader."*

Dryads are wood nymphs from Greek mythology and are protectors of forests. In *The Chronicles of Narnia,* they are the spirits of living trees and can walk about in human form. In *The Lion, the Witch and the Wardrobe,* Mr. Tumnus says that some trees have joined the White Witch's side, but most dryads in *The Chronicles of Narnia* are benevolent and side with Aslan and good in conflicts. Their march in the form of trees against the forces of Miraz in *Prince Caspian* is a highlight of that novel.

Dwarfs have many antecedents. In European folklore, they are short, stout, and live or work in caves. They are traditionally great diggers and fearsome warriors. The Dwarfs in *The Chronicles of Narnia* have many human qualities and can even mate with human beings: Caspian's tutor Cornelius is an offspring of a union between a dwarf and a human. Like humans, their loyalties vary widely among individual dwarfs, with many serving Aslan and Narnia with great good will as in *The Silver Chair,* and with others happily serving evil as in *The Lion, the Witch and the Wardrobe* and *The Last Battle.* It is important to note that Dwarfs are admitted to Aslan's Country.

Fauns come from Roman Mythology and typically have the head, arms, and body of a human and the horns, ears, tail and legs of a goat. They walk upright. They usually live in forests and tend to be fun-loving creatures.

Giants in *The Chronicles of Narnia* are based on the ones in Norse mythology, and like the ice giants of Norse mythology, they live in the far north where the land is often barren. Some giants choose good over evil and are welcomed in Narnia; their courage in facing Narnia's enemies is evident in *The Lion, the Witch and the Wardrobe* and *The Horse and His Boy*. Many, probably most, northern giants are dangers to Narnia, and Narnian kings periodically must fight wars against them to keep them from pillaging Narnia. Some giants eat humans and Marsh-Wiggles, as we learn in *The Silver Chair*.

Hamadryads are wood nymphs from Greek and Roman mythology. They are very dependent on their personal trees in order to stay alive and cannot move about as freely as dryads can. The female who dies in front of King Tirian early in *The Last Battle* may be a hamadryad, because she perishes when her tree is cut down.

Kraken is a monster from Norse mythology. It lives in deep waters and is large, dark, fearsome and mysterious. It may attack ships.

Maenads, from Greek and Roman mythology, are Bacchae (see **Bacchus** above), and in *Prince Caspian* they are happy, dancing women whose good spirits add life to wherever they travel.

Minotaurs are Ancient Greek monsters with the bodies of men and the heads of bulls. In *The Chronicles of Narnia,* they are enemies of Aslan.

Naiads come from Greek mythology and are female spirits who live in water, usually streams. In *Prince Caspian,* they are daughters of the river-god.

Nymphs come from Greek and Roman mythology and are female nature spirits. In Greek and Roman myths they can be seductive and dangerous; water nymphs can lure people into drowning, but in *The Chronicles of Narnia* they tend to be benign and faithful to Aslan.

Ogres are man-eating monsters of great strength and often are much bigger than human beings. They probably have their origins in Roman mythology, stemming from Orcus, an underworld deity. In *Prince Caspian,* Caspian is shocked to learn that such evil beings still exist in Narnia.

Pomona is a Roman goddess for fruit trees mentioned in *Prince Caspian.*

River-god may be based on very early Greek mythology in which gods inhabited rivers, mountains, and other natural places. On the other hand, he may be drawn from ancient Celtic mythology, whose water gods populated lakes (for example, the Lady of the Lake in Arthurian tales), rivers, mountains and other natural landmarks. In *The Magician's Nephew,* he is among the nature spirits called forth by Aslan, and in *Prince Caspian* he needs the bridge at Beruna to be destroyed in order that he may be free.

Satyrs are often mistaken for fauns but are actually different creatures in Greek mythology. They are woodland deities in Greek mythology and are much more goatlike than faunlike; they also tend to be lecherous. In *The Chronicles of Narnia*, they are woodland people and most of the time they are on the side of the Narnian monarchs.

Silenus is sometimes mistaken for Bacchus but he is actually Bacchus' foster father, and he is usually portrayed as a satyr and woodland deity in Roman mythology. He drinks to excess and rides a donkey.

Silvans are minor forest gods in Roman mythology. In *The Lion, the Witch and the Wardrobe*, they are woodland spirits.

Unicorns are among the most popular creatures in folklore. They are usually depicted as Lewis depicts them: beautiful, with the bodies of horses and a single spiral horn in their foreheads. In *The Last Battle*, the unicorn Jewel is a very dangerous warrior and the veteran of many battles. In folklore and the Bible (Isaiah 34:7) they are sometimes portrayed as warlike.

Wer-Wolves (werewolves) come from medieval European folklore and are humans who can turn into wolves. In medieval folklore the transformation would be complete, with the werewolf dropping to all fours and looking exactly like a wolf. In *Prince Caspian*, the Wer-Wolf is on the side of evil magic.

Chapter 5

I am Truth

MYTHOLOGY

OVERVIEW

Mythology became a passion for Lewis when he was a boy and found an account of the mythology of the Ancient Norse. He was captivated by the outsized heroes and heroines, the great drama, and the profound tragedy of the stories. This passion for Norse mythology eventually grew into a passion for the mythologies of the world, and Lewis was probably one of the most knowledgeable experts of his time in world mythology.

It is important for understanding Lewis and for understanding how mythology fits into *The Chronicles of Narnia* to understand what he meant by the word *myth*. The word often is used derisively in everyday speech, meaning a story that is a lie. This was not Lewis' view. During his long period of atheism, he studied mythology avidly, but reading and thinking about myths led him to ideas about religion. Eventually, after many years of research, he concluded that the world's myths were all in varying degrees humanity's recognition that there was more to life than the material world. That is, many people in many cultures realized that there was a divine influence at work, and they created stories that would account for where the divine influence came from. Thus, *myths* were not lies but efforts to find a truth that was not fully comprehended by the people who believed the myths. This view of mythology contributed to Lewis' religious revelation that there was a God, although he did not at first believe that any mythology was factual.

This is why he treated Christianity as a mythology, much as many anthropologists did in his day and still do. He considered the accounts in the Old Testament to be mythological,

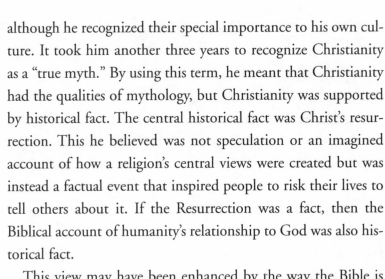

although he recognized their special importance to his own culture. It took him another three years to recognize Christianity as a "true myth." By using this term, he meant that Christianity had the qualities of mythology, but Christianity was supported by historical fact. The central historical fact was Christ's resurrection. This he believed was not speculation or an imagined account of how a religion's central views were created but was instead a factual event that inspired people to risk their lives to tell others about it. If the Resurrection was a fact, then the Biblical account of humanity's relationship to God was also historical fact.

This view may have been enhanced by the way the Bible is organized and by how those who wrote it composed their passages as if part of a great history. Judaism, Christianity, and Islam, more than other religions (or as Lewis might say, "mythologies") emphasize a historical structure, with events falling in a particular order in recorded time. When Lewis was a young man, much of the Old Testament was regarded as fantasy by scholars. This stemmed from a trend begun in the nineteenth century in which the mythological aspects of the Bible were taken as indications that it was the same as Norse or Greek mythology: tales created by people to explain aspects of nature that they did not understand. By the time Lewis was writing *The Chronicles of Narnia,* this trend was dying. It received its last great expression in *The Masks of God* by Joseph Campbell (four volumes, 1959). What had happened during the twentieth century is that archeologists found almost all of the places and peoples mentioned in the Old Testament. Jericho, long thought to be a "myth," became a well-known, real site.

Similarly, the Assyrians were believed to be inventions of the writers of the Bible, but they are now known to be a historical people. Even the very ancient legends, such as the Hebrew migration into Egypt, have been shown to be historical and can even be dated. What this meant for Lewis' "true myth" is that the historical validity of the Bible's account of places and cultures was being proven true, year-by-year.

Contrary to what one might expect, Lewis was not entirely happy with the scientific evidence that was accumulating, proving the history but not the revelations of the Bible to be true. Part of the attraction of the Bible for Lewis was its mythological qualities, and he loved the great stories. It was his belief that modern Christians were losing their sense of the grandeur of God and of God's everyday presence in their lives. Lewis took angels seriously; he took the constant presence of the Holy Spirit seriously, as well. Telling a good story that would entertain its readers was his primary goal when writing *The Chronicles of Narnia,* but one of his motivations for writing the series was to create a modern mythological context for understanding the ways of God. This is ambitious, perhaps out of reach even for Lewis' genius, but it is why elements from Ancient Greek and Roman and Norse mythologies appear in *The Chronicles of Narnia* and why elements from folk tales from Europe and the Middle East appear in the novels. Lewis wanted his readers to see his telling of Aslan's relationship to the world He creates in *The Magician's Nephew* as all inclusive. It would be a mistake to call Lewis' views of mythologies "universalist," as if all were valid. He saw only Christianity as the one valid account of the world. He includes elements of other myths because he sees Christ as all-inclusive—that is, that Christ's life, crucifixion, resurrection, and continuing ministry are for every person everywhere, every era. His technique for showing this in *The Chronicles of Narnia* is to include traditions from several different cultures.

NORSE MYTHOLOGY

As with many of the world's mythologies, there are more than one version of the central events of Norse mythology, which did not necessarily bother the people who believed them; it is primarily modern peoples who are bothered by the seeming inconsistencies in the myths. These seeming inconsistencies were not at all seen as inconsistencies by ancient peoples; instead, variations in stories were often taken as examples of how hard it is to understand the supernatural, especially God. Thus, where the varying accounts of the creation of Adam and Eve in Genesis may seem to be evidence that one, the other, or both may be untrue to modern readers, to the Ancient Hebrews, as well as to Christians for much of the Christian era, the varying accounts are both true. That is, Eve was both made from Adam's rib and was made simultaneously from the same earth as Adam. The problem is not with the telling of the stories but with the human ability to understand them.

One of the most accepted Norse accounts of creation is Snorri Sturluson's version in the *Prose Edda*. He was a medieval Icelandic author whose literary works are exceptionally good. He based his accounts of Norse mythology on ancient poetry (called "eddaic poetry") and fragments of old accounts, many of which no longer exist. According to Sturluson, there was (and still is) a northern land called Niflheim, covered in ice and snow, and containing a spring from which seven rivers flow. To the south is Muspell, a frightening place of fire, and at the very southern end of Muspell is the fire giant Black Surt, who will mark the end of the world by attacking the gods and covering the world in flames.

These places reflect the harsh, pessimistic Ancient Norse view of the universe. In between them was Ginnungagap, an empty place into which the rivers of Niflheim flowed, creating an icy, salty, windy wasteland. Where the ice met the heat from Muspell, the melting water and salt formed the giant Ymir, an evil frost giant. There also formed a cow, whose milk Ymir drank. From one of his armpits grew a man and a woman, and from one of his legs grew a son. These were the ancestors of the frost giants whose evil threatens even the home of the gods. Meanwhile, the cow liked ice for its salt, and her licking slowly formed a man, who was named Buri. He had a son named Bor who married a frost giant named Bestla, and they had three children, first Odin, then Vili, and then Ve. During all these events, the world has not yet been created; there is a cold north, a hot south, and a void.

But the sons of Buri and Bestla murdered Ymir. His prodigious bleeding created a flood, drowning all the frost giants except two, who rode out the flood in a boat hacked out of a tree. Meanwhile, the sons of Buri and Bestla made the earth out of Ymir's body, using his bones to create mountains. The giant's blood formed lakes and the oceans that surround the world. This making of the world from Ymir's body is an idea shared by many mythologies. For instance, an ancient Chinese fragment of a myth (most Ancient Chinese myths exist only in fragments because an ancient Chinese emperor ordered all records prior to his time be destroyed, so that history might seem to begin with him) tells of a woman, maybe a witch, whose body was carved up into the world. In terms of *The Chronicles of Narnia,* one can see, here, the idea of evil giants living in frozen lands. That some of Narnia's giants are good would be in keeping with Lewis' idea that Aslan's (Christ's) redemption is for anyone who will accept it. Although in the Norse myths, the oceans that surround the earth are vast and perhaps uncrossable, Vikings (Norsemen) tried sailing as far as they could, with some landing in what is now called North America. (They called it "Vinland.") In *The Voyage of the "Dawn Treader,"* Lewis portrays a voyage that crosses a seemingly endless sea; the idea that Narnia's world is not a globe, but is somewhat flat (there seems to be an horizon), may derive from the Norse creation myth.

Odin, Vili, and Ve, the sons of Buri and Bestla, made the sky from Ymir's skull, and they made the sun, moon, and stars from the fires of Muspell. From Ymir's eyebrows, they formed Midgard. From the giant's brains, they made clouds. They gave northern lands to frost giants and rock giants, but the giants were so unruly and cruel that the sons of Buri and Bestla had to fortify the land around the giants, to hold them back from ravaging the earth.

The brothers found an ash tree and an elm tree on a beach of Midgard, and they made the trees into the first human beings, a man named Ask and a woman named Embla. This man and this woman lived in Midgard: Odin breathed life into them, Vili gave them intelligence and feelings, and Ve gave them sight and hearing. They were the ancestors of all human beings.

The idea of breathing life into someone is a common idea among mythologies and folk tales; Lewis put the idea to somewhat different use by having Aslan's breath revive and invigorate people (such as the statues in the White Witch's castle in *The Lion, the Witch and the Wardrobe*) and to convey the spiritual life of the Holy Spirit into people. The idea of there being two ancestors of humanity has a logic to it: one man, one woman, then children. In *The Magician's Nephew,* Aslan makes King Frank and Queen Helen the progenitors of a great people. The question about who their children married is common in such creations stories. The Ancient Egyptians had no trouble with the idea of incest, so they tell of brothers and sisters marrying. In other mythologies, including the Norse myths, the question is left open. In *Prince Caspian,* Lewis tells of how the Telmarines entered Narnia, hinting that migrations from earth to the world of Narnia would have supplied the necessary mates for King Frank and Queen Helen's children.

The sons of Buri and Bestla took the maggots that had been feasting on the flesh of Ymir and made them into dwarfs. Since they were maggots in the flesh of the giant, and the giant's flesh was made into the earth, the dwarfs live underground, with the earth that was once flesh. It is perhaps this part of the Norse creation myth that influenced Lewis to make his Dwarfs earthmen who love to dig into the ground. He rejects the maggot story by showing in *Prince Caspian* that Dwarfs and humans can intermarry and have children.

During the period after the creation of human beings, Odin became the Allfather, and he and his brothers were joined by gods and goddesses and other Aesir, the protectors of humanity.

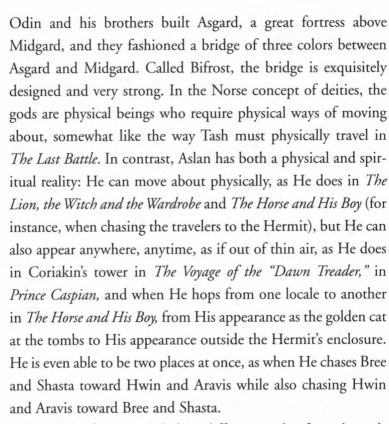

Odin and his brothers built Asgard, a great fortress above Midgard, and they fashioned a bridge of three colors between Asgard and Midgard. Called Bifrost, the bridge is exquisitely designed and very strong. In the Norse concept of deities, the gods are physical beings who require physical ways of moving about, somewhat like the way Tash must physically travel in *The Last Battle*. In contrast, Aslan has both a physical and spiritual reality: He can move about physically, as He does in *The Lion, the Witch and the Wardrobe* and *The Horse and His Boy* (for instance, when chasing the travelers to the Hermit), but He can also appear anywhere, anytime, as if out of thin air, as He does in Coriakin's tower in *The Voyage of the "Dawn Treader,"* in *Prince Caspian,* and when He hops from one locale to another in *The Horse and His Boy,* from His appearance as the golden cat at the tombs to His appearance outside the Hermit's enclosure. He is even able to be two places at once, as when He chases Bree and Shasta toward Hwin and Aravis while also chasing Hwin and Aravis toward Bree and Shasta.

The gods of Norse mythology differ somewhat from the gods of many other mythologies by being mortal, in the sense that they can die of old age. What keeps them youthful and alive for thousands of years are golden apples from a special orchard that they protect from intruders. The apples are magical and can be found only in the one orchard. This idea of immortality given by fruit is paralleled by the Tree of Life in *The Chronicles of Narnia.* By eating the fruit of the Tree of Life, a person can live forever, barring misadventure. When eaten without Aslan's permission, the fruit is a curse; Jadis eats the fruit and is doomed to an immortality of misery and self-loathing. When the fruit is eaten in Aslan's Country, it no longer delivers immortality, because Aslan has already granted immortality to all He welcomes into His country, but it expresses the sheer pleasure of being in Aslan's Country by being beautiful and richly tasty. In *The Magician's Nephew,* fruit from a tree that grew from the fruit from the Tree of Life is powerful enough to heal disease on earth, which is what it does when Digory feeds it to his mother, with Aslan's blessing. Both the golden apples of the Norse Gods and the fruit of the Tree of Life do not guarantee eternal life; those who eat them can be killed. In the Norse myths, the best-loved of all the gods, Baldur, is killed and his spirit goes to the underworld of the dead, and in *The Lion, the Witch and the Wardrobe,* Jadis the White Witch is slain by Aslan.

The end of earth depicted in Norse mythology is dramatic, stirring, and violent, and the final battle between good and evil they called "Ragnarok." The end of the world is preceded by degeneracy among mankind, including lechery and incest, as well as murdering one's own kin and the waging of wars for petty reasons. The land where humanity lives, Midgard, will then be gripped by an unending winter that sounds much like the winter created by the White Witch in Narnia, except that it lasts for a few years rather than a hundred.

The Father of Lies, Loki will have fathered three offspring by a giantess: Fenrir (or Fenris, as Lewis spells the name), Jormungand, and Hel. Fenrir was a wolf who continually grew, but was tied up by dwarven bonds so that he could not harm anyone. Jormungand was a gigantic snake who was thrown into the depths of the oceans that surrounded earth, and he grew so large that he encircled the world until his mouth could bite his tail. Hel was sent by Odin into the depths of the earth, where she was to care for the spirits of the dead.

During the great winter, a giant wolf named Skoll will eat the sun, and the moon will be destroyed, and blood will fall on the earth. Even the stars will be gone. These events will shake the earth and free Fenrir from his bonds. He will be joined by the evil giants and by Jormungand in his vengeful attack on Asgard. They will overwhelm the guards of Bifrost and swarm to Asgard's huge plain Vigrid. Although Bifrost is an incredibly strong bridge, the destructive forces loosed in Midgard will rock the world so violently that the bridge will collapse behind the army of evil.

Ragnarok will take place on Vigrid, with all of Asgard's champions charging forth to meet their enemies. The gods will be there, the Aesir will be there, and the spirit heroes chosen by the Valkyries for their courage in battle will protect Odin. The battle will be long and brutal, but the valiance of the forces of good will be to no avail. Odin will face gigantic Fenrir, whose mouth has grown so large that when open it spans the space between the ground and the sky. Beside Odin, the greatest warriors of Asgard will be overwhelmed, although they take a great toll on the enemy. Eventually, Fenrir seizes on a momentary advantage and eats Odin. Jormungand will have poisoned Asgard and Midgard with his venom, but Thor will kill him just before dying of the poison. Loki will be killed by the god Heimdall, who will then perish of his wounds. Amid the carnage and ruin, Vidar, son of Odin, will take hold of Fenrir's upper and lower jaws, and in a fury will tear the giant wolf to pieces.

The fire giant Black Surt, who existed before the world began, will send fire across Midgard. There will be no one to protect humanity, and he will wield a sword of flames as he slaughters humanity and smashes everyone he finds. Asgard, Midgard, the whole world, will burn; eventually the earth will sink into the ocean. Nearly every being, monsters, giants, dwarfs, gods, human beings, will die.

It is possible that Lewis borrowed two elements from the Norse view of a catastrophe that ends the world. One is the battle itself. Against great odds, King Tirian and the forces of good make a last valiant stand against evil in *The Last Battle*. The other element is the defeat of the forces of good. In the Ancient Norse view, all the feats of gods and mortals come to nothing. In a universe that cares nothing for or against life, all that lives is doomed to pass away (by drowning), as if it had never been. In *The Last Battle*, the terrible defeat of Tirian results only in a temporary victory for evil. When Tirian peers through crack in the stable door from Aslan's Country, he sees confused Calormenes who are not sure what they should do.

When Aslan calls forth Father Time to blow his horn, Lewis probably draws more on the Norse myth of Heimdall than on the Biblical account in Revelations. Heimdall was the watchman of the gods, and when the forces of evil invade Asgard, he blows the sacred horn Gjall, which is heard throughout the universe. Heimdall blows to summon the forces of good and in effect announces the end of the gods has come; Father Time blows to announce to the universe of Narnia that the end has come. The world of Narnia is as thoroughly scourged as that of Midgard, and the dramatic intensity of Lewis' description of the end reflects the tragic drama of the Norse myth.

Christianity took hundreds of years to find its way into

Norse mythology. The essentially pessimistic view of life of the Norse did not easily shift to a view of redemption, but around 1000 some writers created a new ending for the end of the world. It is a tacked-on version that follows the horrible destruction. According to it, there will be a few survivors of the scourging of the world. Odin's son Vidar will survive, along with several other children of the gods, and two human beings will survive. Eagles will survive and will soar above a new land that arises out of the ocean. This land will be bountiful and will provide food crops without anyone having to plant them. The two human beings will have many children, who will eventually repopulate the world. The gods will build great halls and will be just. All the world will be green with plants, beautiful, and at peace.

This ending of rebirth was probably influenced by Christianity and may mark the beginning of the end of faith in the old gods. The verdant landscape of the new world is reflected in Aslan's Country in *The Last Battle* where the land is rich in good things to eat.

ANCIENT GREEK AND ROMAN MYTHOLOGY

Like the Ancient Norse, the Ancient Greeks had a fairly pessimistic view of the supernatural world. Their gods tended to have the good and bad qualities that humans have, only magnified. For example, Zeus is a benevolent god who sometimes wanders the earth disguised as an old man, rewarding those who treat him (and old people) well, yet he also lusted after human women and would rape them, sometimes while taking the form of an animal. Worship could take the form of asking the gods to reflect their good qualities on the person praying while asking them to reflect their bad qualities on the worshipper's enemies.

It is the good fortune for readers of Greek myths that the Greeks loved to write. From almost the instant they learned to write (by adapting the Phoenician alphabet), Greeks were recording their mythologies. Eventually three views of the creation of the world and of human beings emerged. The first is mystical and involves beings that are very dissimilar to humans; the second involves the "five ages of man" and takes an historical approach to creation; and the third is analytical, a result of the development of Greek philosophy. This third approach rejected the myths of a pantheon of gods, but did allow for a supreme being. Aristotle, for one, thought he could prove through reason that there was a single god, although he would not much resemble the God of the Old and New Testaments. Lewis draws on Plato for many of his discussions of spiritual life and believed that thought itself was a supernatural act. He found in Plato's discussions of how the human mind works a model for explaining how a mind can be physical (the brain) yet spiritual.

As with the Ancient Norse myths, the Greek myths survive in different versions. The Greeks had only one text that was meant to remain unaltered, Homer's *Iliad,* which tells of the war against Troy and was thought by the Greeks to embody the essence of what Greeks were supposed to be. Otherwise, poets, playwrights, and storytellers reshaped myths to suit their tastes, the tastes of their audience, and the needs of the plots of the stories

they wished to tell. Throughout the many retellings of the Greek myths, the gods are cantankerous, vain, selfish, and powerful. The gods seemed like ill-tempered human beings. Some of the Greek creation myths relate to *The Chronicles of Narnia.*

– The First Gods –

There is more than one version of the Greek creation myth, with variations in the details. Just as the Norse had a void out of which arose the earth, the Greeks had *Chaos,* although Chaos is a living being, not a void. At first, Chaos was all that existed. Chaos was a thinking being, but its mind was nothing like the human mind and its behavior and reasoning could not be understood by human beings. Perhaps bored or lonely, or for no particular reason, Chaos created out of itself *Nox,* meaning Night. Chaos and Nox mated, resulting in *Erebus,* meaning Darkness. Erebus and Nox then mated, resulting in *Hemera,* meaning Day, and *Aether,* meaning Light. Thus out of Chaos had formed night and darkness, day and light.

The offspring of Hemera and Aether was *Eros,* the god of love. With the aid of Eros, Mother Earth (Gaia) and the Oceans were formed. Eros shot his arrows into Gaia, and from them came the air we breathe and plants and animals. Thus the creation of life on earth was an act of love. Out of Gaia arose the Heaven, personified as Uranus. At first, there was a perpetual springtime, the opposite of Narnia's long winter without Christmas, and there was happiness.

But after Uranus and Gaia mated, she gave birth to the Titans, who were monstrous, huge beings who overthrew

Uranus and ruled the earth. There was a prophesy—some accounts say was made by a witch, others say it was a curse by Uranus—that *Chronos,* the ruler of the Titans and god of Time, would be overthrown by his own children. Some accounts say that he mated with his sister Rhea, others that he mated with Gaia. In either case, the union brought forth the rebellious gods. Mindful of the prophesy against him, Chronos seized each child soon after birth and swallowed it whole, much to the misery and anger of their mother. Eventually he was fooled. In one version, Rhea gave him a stone covered in baby clothes, which Chronos swallowed whole without looking. Because Chronos thought that he had eaten the last child, Rhea was able to hide the child, Zeus, in deep caves. In another version, Gaia herself hid the child deep within herself. When Zeus grew up, he fought a ferocious battle with his father, and winning it, he seized Chronos and forced the Titan to vomit forth all of Zeus' brothers and sisters, who became the Greek gods and goddesses. After a war against the Titans and a few more gigantic, frightening monsters, the gods became supreme rulers of the earth and settled on top of the sacred mountain Olympus. Zeus assigned different gods to rule over different parts of the world. For instance, Hades ruled the underworld where spirits went after death and Poseidon ruled the world's oceans.

— The Creation of Man —

Some versions say Zeus, but others say Eros, gave an order that the animals of the world be endowed with qualities that would help them survive in the wild: birds could fly, antelope could run swiftly, fish were excellent swimmers. But when it came time to endow Man with special skills and instincts, there was little was left over for human beings who, far from ruling the animals, hid in caves and feared the dark. Prometheus, a son of the Titans but subservient to Zeus, observed the pitiful plight of humanity and wanted to help, but Zeus refused to allow humanity to have the one thing that would be necessary for their survival: fire. The ability to make fire was to be the property of the gods alone. Zeus threatened terrible punishments to anyone who gave away the secret of fire.

Even so, Prometheus' conscience was troubled by the misery human beings endured. Therefore, he sneaked a burning ember out of Olympus and secretly took it to human beings, showing them how to use it. This aspect of the creation story was exceptionally important to the Greeks because the fire Prometheus brought to humanity represented conscious thought and self-awareness: Prometheus taught them how to think. This gift made it possible for humans to overcome their physical weaknesses and rule over nature.

Unfortunate Prometheus paid an awful price for helping humanity. When Zeus saw spots of fires spreading across the world, he knew that someone had stolen fire. It took only a short time to discover that Prometheus was the culprit. Not at all contrite, Prometheus declared that he had done what was just. Zeus had Prometheus bound by chains to a rock high over a sheer cliff, and he bade a giant eagle to come everyday and tear out Prometheus' entrails and eat Prometheus' liver. Being immortal, Prometheus could not die, and he endured agonizing pain everyday, forever. Some late versions of the myth have

Hercules rescuing Prometheus, but most versions leave Prometheus bound to that rock, suffering forever so that human beings might live better lives.

— The Formation of Greek Religion —

If you find some of the Greek creation myth confusing, especially the stories about Chaos and Nox, don't worry. It is confusing. Greek Mythology was formed out of at least two already well-developed mythological traditions, one probably matriarchal (the female gods ruled) and the other patriarchal (the male gods ruled). The matriarchal religion was likely that of the Achaeans, the people who went to war against Troy. Their legacy can be seen in the importance of Athena, goddess of wisdom, Diana, goddess of hunting, and other prominent goddesses. The other people, now called the Ancient Greeks, were a pastoral group that migrated from the north into the Greek peninsula. Their culture eventually replaced the earlier one, and their gods, such as Zeus, became the dominant ones. Important female gods of the earlier culture often became sterile or were associated with male activities; for example, Athena, although beautiful, became too haughty and stern to accept the love of men, and her power to bear children was taken from her.

Of importance for *The Chronicles of Narnia* is another aspect of Athena. She was associated with a particular place, a region eventually dominated by the city of Athens. This is a relic of a very old tradition that predates both the matriarchal and patriarchal religions. It is the result of a system of beliefs that anthropologists call *animism*. In animism, the universe is filled with

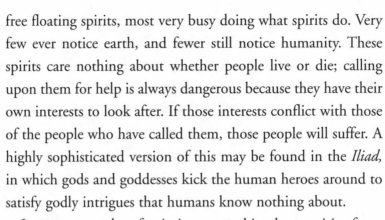

free floating spirits, most very busy doing what spirits do. Very few ever notice earth, and fewer still notice humanity. These spirits care nothing about whether people live or die; calling upon them for help is always dangerous because they have their own interests to look after. If those interests conflict with those of the people who have called them, those people will suffer. A highly sophisticated version of this may be found in the *Iliad,* in which gods and goddesses kick the human heroes around to satisfy godly intrigues that humans know nothing about.

In most examples of animism, everything has a spirit of one sort or another. Rocks, trees, animals—all have spirits. This is the reason behind the legendary buffalo dance of America's plains Indians (Native Americans). The dance is part of a ritual to thank the spirits of the buffalo that were slain in a hunt, to apologize to those spirits, and to help them move on to new buffalo bodies. Places also have spirits; in many early religions, lakes, rivers, mountains, and other places may have their own spirits. In the stories of King Arthur, these beliefs linger on in the form of the Lady of the Lake, a water spirit, and Sir Lancelot du Lac, another water spirit. At one time, each of these figures would have had its own special lake.

This aspect of animism fostered, often grudgingly, respect among religions. The gods and goddesses of mountains, lakes, and other places would be thought of as valid by migrating people, so for example, Athena, who was once a mountain goddess, would still be thought of as the goddess of her particular mountain by new arrivals in her territory. The legacy of this belief is found throughout the later religions of Europe and the Middle East. For example, the goddess Ishtar or Isis was shared by

Egyptians and Babylonians, who thought that each was a version of the other. The most spectacular result of the idea that place gods were equally valid to different religions is found in the Romans' wholesale adoption of Ancient Greek mythology. While keeping the names of their original gods, the Romans adapted the Greek gods. Jupiter was Zeus; Pluto was Hades; Poseidon was Neptune, and so on. This is why Ancient Greek mythology is often called Greek and Roman mythology or Greco-Roman mythology.

– Narnia and Greek Mythology –

By now, you may have begun to recognize the elements of Greek mythology that appear in *The Chronicles of Narnia*. It may seem odd to have parts of pagan mythology appear in novels in which Aslan (Christ) appears, but keep in mind that good storytelling came first when Lewis wrote *The Chronicles of Narnia,* and the symbolism was a secondary consideration. Further, Lewis began stories by first seeing a picture in his mind and then making up a tale about that picture. One of the earliest pictures that he thought of was of the faun Mr. Tumnus, a figure based on Greek mythology, in which fauns are forest spirits. Around Mr. Tumnus, Lewis formed the Lantern Waste, a woodland full of forest spirits.

Although the creation of Narnia's world has much more to do with Genesis than the Ancient Greek creation myth, borrowings abound in *The Chronicles of Narnia*. Dryads, hamadryads, naiads, the River God, nymphs, fauns, satyrs, silvans, are all beings taken from the early animistic form of Greek

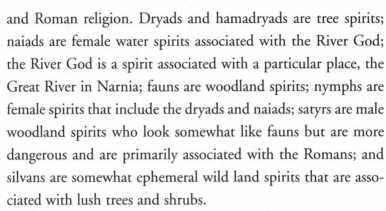

and Roman religion. Dryads and hamadryads are tree spirits; naiads are female water spirits associated with the River God; the River God is a spirit associated with a particular place, the Great River in Narnia; fauns are woodland spirits; nymphs are female spirits that include the dryads and naiads; satyrs are male woodland spirits who look somewhat like fauns but are more dangerous and are primarily associated with the Romans; and silvans are somewhat ephemeral wild land spirits that are associated with lush trees and shrubs.

Lewis has fun with these mythological beings, weaving them into an intricate carpet of spirits interacting with people. Most of his depictions remain true to the Ancient Greek creatures, except for their recognition of Aslan as their lord. Further, their inclusion in *The Chronicles of Narnia* helps to underscore the universality of the stories Lewis tells. These Greek figures are known worldwide, and form a part of the world's literature; they are bound to be recognized by many readers. In addition, they serve to illustrate the immense creative power of Aslan. The Lion sings a song of creation and the ground becomes astoundingly fertile. In *The Magician's Nephew,* animals arise out of the ground, trees grow to great heights in minutes, and even a piece of a street lamp grows into a new lamp that always glows. The Greek nature spirits arise out of Aslan's song, glorious examples of Aslan's spiritual strength, giving even trees spirits of their own. Throughout *The Chronicles of Narnia,* these nature spirits are reminders of the magic of Aslan's creation of the world, and of the magical mysteries that make the novels fun to read.

Centaurs and minotaurs are also from Greek mythology. The centaurs may be a legacy from the encounter of people who did not ride horses with some who did. They are nearly always associated with warfare and violence. On the other hand, Narnia's centaurs are learned creatures whose knowledge of science makes them good physicians and astronomers. Rather than being especially violent, they are especially wise. They also eat enormous amounts of food.

Minotaurs come from the myths about Theseus and the minotaur of Minos. Every year, Greeks were forced to send young people to Minos to be sacrificed to the minotaur who lived in a labyrinth beneath a palace. Theseus was a prince who slew the Minotaur and saved his people from having to send young people to their deaths. This all is very likely based on actual history. The Minos palace has been found and excavated by archeologists; at one time the Minoan empire ruled much of the Mediterranean Sea. Theseus may be based on a real-life person who led a war against the Minoan empire that freed the Greeks from paying tribute. Murals in the Minos palace show young men and women doing acrobatics on the backs of bulls. The bull may have been a symbol of Minoan power, and the myth about Theseus slaying the Minotaur, with the head of a bull and the body of a man, may be a symbolic account of a Greek war against the Minoan empire. Lewis remains true to the Greek myth by depicting minotaurs as allies of evil, of the White Witch.

Bacchus, Silenus, and the maenads are from Greek and Roman mythology. *Bacchus* is the Roman name for the Greek god *Dionysus*. Silenus was either Bacchus' father or teacher, depending on which version of the myths you read. *Maenads* is the Greek name for the woman followers of Dionysus; the Romans called them Bacchantes. In Greek mythology, Dionysus/Bacchus was the god of wine and merrymaking; he was also the protector of women. Thus, in Greek religious practices Dionysus/Bacchus had primarily female worshippers and priestesses, who would sometimes become very drunk during their religious celebrations. In Greek myths, the great musician Orpheus is torn apart by frenzied maenads. Even so, men could sometimes partake of religious celebrations of Dionysus/Bacchus, as represented by Silenus, who is often depicted as drunkenly riding a donkey.

In *Prince Caspian,* Bacchus and Silenus are followers of Aslan. Lewis thought that drinking wine was good for a person; after all, Jesus turned water into wine for people to drink. Further, Lewis liked to drink strong, "meaty," wine. Thus, in *Prince Caspian,* Bacchus is a good, faithful follower of Aslan, whose wine brings good health and happiness to those who drink it. His maenads may be very athletic dancers, but they are not drunkards in Lewis' portrayal of them. They represent unself-conscious, carefree joy in Aslan's presence, as is meant by their lack of clothing and cheerful attitudes. When a schoolgirl in Beruna joins them, she experiences the joy of being unfettered and able to be fully herself without having to hold back. She is not only freed from a nasty school, but she becomes free to enjoy Aslan's blessings without interference.

Bacchus has destructive power, but he only wields it at Aslan's command. He destroys the bridge that chains the River God. That Aslan would have him do this shows Aslan's continuing concern for the welfare of all beings, in this case the River God, and it shows Aslan's supremacy over all who might be gods: only the Emperor-over-sea is more powerful than Aslan. Further, the freeing of the River God represents a releasing of nature, which had been cruelly treated by the Telmarine humans who ruled Narnia. Bacchus becomes a liberator, not only for women such as the schoolgirl, but for the natural world.

— The Five Ages/Races of Man —

Two other significant Ancient Greek views of the universe, one embodied in the Five Ages/Races of Man, and the other a philosophical view of the supernatural, add to the richness of *The Chronicles of Narnia*.

When the Greeks first learned to read and to write, they recorded much of their religious belief. One very interesting document from that early time tells of the Five Ages of Man. Don't let it bother you that the Five Ages of Man contradicts the main creation myth that I earlier summarized. It did not bother the Greeks. They expected contradictions; their gods were very contradictory beings.

The first human beings to be created were Golden, and their age was the Golden Age. Chronos ruled earth at that time, and he did a good job of providing for them. The Golden people lived very long, had wonderful crops and large, meaty herds, and they were always happy. After death they became the spirits of places such as mountains and lakes. They remained benevolent and friendly to the peoples who followed them. After their passing came the Silver people, who were immature and quarrelsome. Because they were cruel and violent, they offended Zeus, who now ruled the earth, and he swept them away. Their spirits still wander the earth as demonic apparitions.

The Bronze people of the third age were very large and very

muscular. They were warlike and wore armor made from bronze and wielded weapons made from bronze. They were bitter, angry people. Even so, their feats of bravery were amazing. When they died, their spirits went to the underworld, probably to Tartarus, the worst part of the underworld.

At first, the fourth age was more promising. Sometimes called the Iron Age, its people were noble and honest. They were possessed of great courage and strength. Their society and customs were just and kind. But eventually, there were conflicts among their tribes. Oedipus and Achilles and other great men were caught up in long wars, especially the war against Troy which lasted for ten years. It is interesting to observe that the tellers of the Five Ages of Man recognized that a people different from them, someone they would displace, actually fought the Trojan War that was made central to their idea of "Greekness" (the behavior, values and ideals of the culture) in the *Iliad*.

The wars of the fourth age were catastrophic, but the iron-age people were essentially noble, although foolish. When they passed away, they were sent to a beautiful afterlife that had been earned by their courage. The fifth age, the era of the Ancient Greeks, was lamentable; people were mean spirited and selfish. They understood little about the richness of life, focused as they were on petty comforts. This was one way that the Greeks viewed themselves—as cowardly, disrespectful of the good, and selfish—when they finally began recording their history.

Of interest for reading *The Chronicles of Narnia*, is the assumption implicit in the concept of the Five Ages of Man that creation has a history. That is, human experience can be divided into historical eras that succeed one another in a clear chronological order. This is one of the significant aspects of the Old Testament, in which creation is shown to be part of the history of the world. This means that the people who created the Five Ages of Man shared with the writers of the Bible the notion that religious history can be world history; that religious events can be placed in particular eras, with significant religious events following one another in an identifiable order, with past influencing present.

This varies from many of the world's religions at the time, which saw little history in their gods, instead viewing religious events as part of something timeless, with little to do with what people did from one generation to the next. This idea that the past influenced the present logically led to the possibility that the present could influence the future. For the Ancient Greeks, this led to a freedom of outlook rare in the ancient world, because the Five Ages of Man implied that change could be made to happen, that people had some influence on their destiny, and that there was no religious rule that prohibited change.

This same sense of history is found in *The Chronicles of Narnia*. It is worth noting that in Narnia's short life of 2555 years, peoples arose and disappeared. In *The Silver Chair*, the ruined city of giants is testimony to a civilization that had flourished and then passed away, being replaced in Harfang by a dissolute culture. In *Prince Caspian*, change has come upon the land, with the Great River having carved a gorge, Cair Paravel being on an island, and Glasswater Creek appearing. In *The Lion, the Witch and the Wardrobe*, the kingdom of Frank and Helen had disappeared; in *Prince Caspian*, the kingdom of Peter, Lucy, Edmund, and Susan was almost forgotten history.

As in the Five Ages of Man, peoples followed peoples, some better, some worse. What does not change is Aslan's abiding interest in all the people of the world. From one novel to the next, He binds everything together.

— Greek Philosophy and Narnia —

At the same time that the Five Ages of Man was giving the Greeks a sense of history and the gods of Olympus form the core of their religion, some Greeks were developing a new field of study, philosophy. The history of Greek philosophy is complex but two aspects of it are important for the discussion of *The Chronicles of Narnia*. One is the trend toward atheism. Some philosophers decided that the Greek gods and goddesses were fantasies; they noted how some were obviously primitive deities for rivers and woodlands. As the Greeks began to amass scientific knowledge through research, proving that the earth was round, creating the science of medicine, mathematics, and philosophy, some scholars argued that science was the only explanation for the world. They rejected the possibility of the existence of any kind of supernatural world.

Among the Greek philosophers, Plato and his student Aristotle disagreed with the atheistic view. Lewis has Professor Kirke mention Plato ("it's all in Plato"), and Plato's view of how the human mind functioned was essential to Lewis' own highly sophisticated view. Plato argued that the mind existed apart from the body. He cited as evidence of this the ability to conceive of objects that one has not seen and the ability to carry a concept in one's memory. This allows a person to imagine a chair that he or she has never before seen and know by its shape that it is a chair. It was part of Plato's reasoning that a mind that was only physical (the brain) would not retain ideas that were not physical. In the case of chairs, a mind that was based only in physical bodies would have to relearn *chair* every time it saw a new chair. Abstract thought would be nearly impossible. It was Lewis' view that the mind was as Plato argued it was, separate from the body. Aristotle's contribution to philosophy surpassed Plato's in a number of ways. For instance, he developed the process of empirical reasoning, a fundamental aspect of what is now the scientific method. Rather than just thinking out answers to questions, he tested the reasoning against experience by conducting experiments. With empirical reasoning, he founded the science of botany by making careful observations of plants and testing his ideas against his observation of what plants actually did.

Aristotle was not only a scientist, but a mystic. He believed that the human mind was not only not physical but a sign of a world of existence apart from the physically observed world. With this as a start, he created in his *Metaphysics* a complicated rationale for the existence of God. Lewis, too, believed that the mind was evidence of the spiritual world. For him, the very act of thinking was supernatural. The mind was evidence of the soul and evidence of a world beyond the physical senses. Aristotle's view of God was not like that of Lewis or of other Christians. Aristotle lived hundreds of years before Jesus, and although he had ample opportunity to interact with Hebrews, there does not seem to be evidence that their view of God influenced his own thinking. To Aristotle, God was the creator and

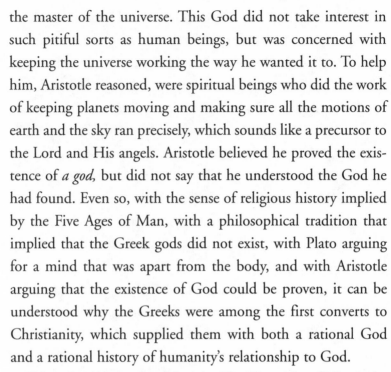

the master of the universe. This God did not take interest in such pitiful sorts as human beings, but was concerned with keeping the universe working the way he wanted it to. To help him, Aristotle reasoned, were spiritual beings who did the work of keeping planets moving and making sure all the motions of earth and the sky ran precisely, which sounds like a precursor to the Lord and His angels. Aristotle believed he proved the existence of *a god,* but did not say that he understood the God he had found. Even so, with the sense of religious history implied by the Five Ages of Man, with a philosophical tradition that implied that the Greek gods did not exist, with Plato arguing for a mind that was apart from the body, and with Aristotle arguing that the existence of God could be proven, it can be understood why the Greeks were among the first converts to Christianity, which supplied them with both a rational God and a rational history of humanity's relationship to God.

When Lewis mentions Plato in *The Chronicles of Narnia,* he is recalling Plato's logic that the mind exists apart from the body, implying that the mind, or soul, is part of a supernatural experience. In *The Chronicles of Narnia,* the very *act* of thinking connects each person to God, because thinking involves the soul and involves the supernatural world.

JOHN MILTON'S COSMOS, *PARADISE LOST* AND THE *CHRONICLES OF NARNIA*

John Milton's epic *Paradise Lost* (1658-1663) is an example of an author trying to remythologize the Christian faith. Whereas Lewis' first priority in *The Chronicles of Narnia* is to tell a good story, with his religious themes being subtexts to his accounts of high adventure, Milton's purpose is educational, to "justify the ways of God to men." It was his hope to explain some of the fundamental elements (what Lewis would call "true myth") of the creation and Fall of humanity. Further, he believed that he was inspired by God to write *Paradise Lost,* and he said that he had visions from God about what he was to write. Milton took his faith very seriously, and he took much solace from it. For instance, he believed that his going blind had a high purpose: that he could see God's will more clearly in his mind without the distraction of sight. Lewis did not have similar ideas about his *The Chronicles of Narnia.* Much of his early conception of the series was based on images that had come to his mind when he was a teenager, and he often said that he began his fiction first with a mental picture, and then he wrote a story about the picture. In *The Lion, the Witch and the Wardrobe,* he combined images of a faun loaded with packages and an isolated street lamp to create the striking scene Lucy first sees upon entering Narnia. But Lewis did not credit these images that came to him as visions from God; he took a humble view of himself as a workman, not a spokesman for the Lord.

The men's temperaments were even more different than their expectations for their works. Milton was a hard man who sometimes treated his daughters poorly, as if they were disappointments to him. One of his daughters suffered from what was probably a neurological disease, and he treated her as an affront, not even passing on to her some of his knowledge of Greek and Latin as he did to his other daughters. And even with the healthier daughters he did not necessarily tell them the meanings of

the Greek and Latin words of the texts he insisted that they read aloud to him. On the other hand, Lewis was exceptionally patient with sick people. When Minto's health fell into decline and she became querulous and unpleasant, he treated her with compassion and gave much of his time over to her care once she was bedridden. Where Milton seemed to hold woman's work in contempt, Lewis cheerfully washed dishes, cleaned floors and whatever other chores needed to be done. Among family and among company, Milton was a temperate man, somewhat reserved, but Lewis drank to excess, swore loudly and often, and loved to argue with guests about almost anything. Even so, he and Milton shared some expectations of their company: that none make light of the Bible or of God's works.

In their public lives, the two men also contrasted. Milton was a faithful public servant during Oliver Cromwell's dictatorship. (Cromwell led the parliamentary forces during the English Civil War that overthrew King Charles I. Cromwell became "lord protector" from 1653-1658 and established a tyrannical dictatorship.) Milton tended to reserve his political commentary to his writings, and even in those he was circumspect. Much different was Lewis, who relished public conflict and was ready to debate anytime. His dismay at the policies of Labor Party governments was plainly expressed. During his period of atheism, he would shout down those who disagreed with him; after his conversion to Christianity, he participated in many public debates in which he spoke of atheism with contempt. His writings about Christianity alienated academics at Oxford, which cost him promotions. Milton had the advantage of writing during an era in which faith was exalted and disagreements were primarily over religious doctrine rather than whether or not God existed. Even so, Milton must have felt the roots of atheism that would form part of the Age of Enlightenment, in which some philosophers, such as Voltaire, insisted that the many calamities that befall humanity prove that there is no God to prevent them, and others, called *deists,* such as Thomas Jefferson, believed in God but rejected the idea that the Bible is divinely inspired. Why else write an epic poem to "justify the ways of God to men" unless there were people who doubted both God and His word?

— Milton and Lewis' Use of Mythology —

As does Lewis in *The Chronicles of Narnia,* Milton incorporates Greek Mythology into his *Paradise Lost.* He frequently mentions Chaos and Chaos' mate, Night. It is out of Chaos that Hell and the earth are formed, with Chaos unhappy about them both. Uranus is also mentioned as being Heaven. These references to Classical Mythology are probably influenced by the time in which *Paradise Lost* was written: England was in the tail end of the Renaissance, a period of revival of the cultures of Greece and Rome, resulting in their profound influence on all of Europe. Milton's referring to Chaos and to God forming the earth out of Chaos would in his day seem fairly natural for him to do. Yet, the mixing of Chaos, Night, Uranus and other classical figures into the telling of the creation of the world and the Fall of Eve and Adam suggests that like Lewis, Milton was creating a new mythological view of God's work, perhaps in the same hope of reinvigorating the core ideas of Christianity for an audience that may no longer find the Biblical accounts energizing.

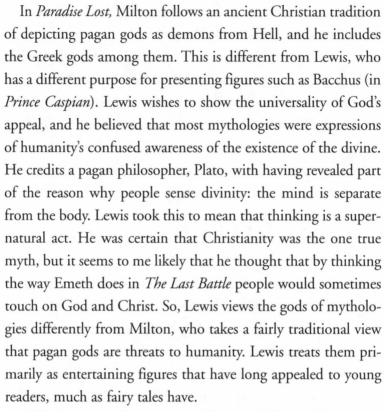

In *Paradise Lost,* Milton follows an ancient Christian tradition of depicting pagan gods as demons from Hell, and he includes the Greek gods among them. This is different from Lewis, who has a different purpose for presenting figures such as Bacchus (in *Prince Caspian*). Lewis wishes to show the universality of God's appeal, and he believed that most mythologies were expressions of humanity's confused awareness of the existence of the divine. He credits a pagan philosopher, Plato, with having revealed part of the reason why people sense divinity: the mind is separate from the body. Lewis took this to mean that thinking is a supernatural act. He was certain that Christianity was the one true myth, but it seems to me likely that he thought that by thinking the way Emeth does in *The Last Battle* people would sometimes touch on God and Christ. So, Lewis views the gods of mythologies differently from Milton, who takes a fairly traditional view that pagan gods are threats to humanity. Lewis treats them primarily as entertaining figures that have long appealed to young readers, much as fairy tales have.

Still, the two authors agree to the extent that Lewis suggests that pagan gods can be demons. His Tash, chief god of the Calormene's many gods, is a demon, and when he is banished to his proper world, it seems as though he was sent back to Hell, although Lewis does not outright say so. The demon-god Moloch of *Paradise Lost* is like Tash; Moloch, "horrid King, besmeared with blood/Of human sacrifice, and parents' tears; Though, for the noise of drums and timbrels loud,/Their children's cries unheard that passed through fire/To his grim idol." Like the worshippers of Tash, the worshippers of Moloch practiced human sacrifice, and as Milton says, they burned babies alive in their rituals. Milton's Moloch dwells in Hell with his master Satan, and in Milton's conception Hell even predates the creation of earth. Hell is a place apart from earth, which is why Satan must sneak out of Hell and creep his way to earth. Lewis may share this view of Hell as a place apart from earth. Although folk tradition places Hell inside earth, probably following the Ancient Norse and Ancient Greek and Roman view of spirits going to underground realms after death, in the world of Narnia there is Bism, an amazing, vibrantly alive place inhabited by the Earthmen who drink liquid emeralds and dwell among salamanders (lizardlike animals who live in fire). There is no Hell underground unless it is the Underworld ruled by the green witch, a place destroyed in *The Silver Chair*. Thus, when Tash is ordered to return to his own place in *The Last Battle*, it seems to be a place apart from Narnia, just as the Hell of *Paradise Lost* is apart from earth.

Calormen and *Paradise Lost* have something else in common, too. In his epic, Milton tells of the demon Belial, who reigns in "courts and palaces" and in "luxurious cities, where the noise/Of riot ascends above their loftiest towers,/And injury and outrage; and, when night/Darkens the streets, then wander forth the sons/Of Belial, flown with insolence and wine." This sounds like Tashbaan in *The Horse and His Boy*, a chaotic city that revels in its decadent luxury.

— Satan, Jadis, and the Garden of Eden —

Both Milton and Lewis depict the first evil beings in their worlds as outsiders. For Milton, the outsider is Satan, who has

lost a war against God and has been hurled into Hell. He sneaks to earth. For Lewis, the outsider is Jadis, who has murdered an entire world of people. Both of them try to corrupt humans: Satan tries to corrupt Adam and Eve, while Jadis tries to corrupt a Son of Adam, Digory Kirke in *The Magician's Nephew*. Milton's Satan and Lewis' Jadis enter the sacred garden in similar ways. Milton writes:

> So on he [Satan] fares, and to the border comes
> Of Eden, where delicious Paradise,
> Now nearer, crowns with her enclosure green,
> As with a rural mound, the champain head
> Of a steep wilderness whose hairy sides
> With thicket overgrown, grotesque and wild.

In *The Magician's Nephew*, the garden, called Paradise by Milton, is surrounded by a high wall; Milton refers to barrier as "The verdurous wall of Paradise." What Satan sees from the outside is similar to what Digory sees outside Aslan's walled garden; in *Paradise Lost* Satan sees:

> . . . and overhead up-grew
> Insuperable highth of loftiest shade,
> Cedar, and pine, and fir, and branching palm,
> A sylvan scene, and, as the ranks ascend
> Shade above shade, a woody theatre
> Of stateliest view.

Digory, Polly, and Fledge see:

All round the very top of the hill ran a high wall of green turf. Inside the wall trees were growing. Their branches hung out over the wall: their leaves showed not only green but also blue and silver when the wind stirred them.

Perhaps Lewis' imagery, here, was inspired by *Paradise Lost*. Both Milton and Lewis picture the wall as verdant, that is green and consisting of plants. Further, they both have their characters see trees above and beyond the wall.

Digory is able to enter Aslan's garden properly, through its gate, because he has been invited. Neither Satan nor Jadis have invitations:

> One gate only there was, and that looked east
> On the other side. Which when the Arch-Felon saw,
> Due entrance he disdained, and, in contempt,
> At one slight bound high overleaped all bound
> Of hill or highest wall . . .
>
> *Paradise Lost*

Digory and his companions "walked nearly all the way round it [the top of the hill] outside the green wall before they found the gates: high gates of gold, fast shut, facing due east." In *Paradise Lost*, the placement of the gate is partly symbolic, because it opens to the rising sun, representing the coming of the enlightenment that comes from Christ and God. In the case of *The Magician's Nephew*, the east is the direction from which Aslan came, and the gates open to the rising sun, representing the immense creative and life-giving power of Aslan and His Father.

Both Satan and Jadis go over the wall; the gates will not open for them. Then both try to persuade the humans to disobey God and eat the fruit of the Tree of Life, promising immortality. In *The Chronicles of Narnia,* this is a valueless promise because, as *The Last Battle* shows, faith in Aslan (Christ) assures immortality, anyway. In *Paradise Lost,* as in the Bible, Satan succeeds in persuading Eve to eat of the fruit of the tree. In Milton's version of the Fall (mankind's fall from Grace because of disobedience to God), Adam decides that he would rather perish with the woman he loves, Eve, than allow her to perish alone, which is why he eats the fruit of the Tree of Life. In *The Magician's Nephew,* Digory rejects Jadis' effort to tempt him to eat the fruit Aslan has plainly told him not to eat, just as God plainly tells Eve and Adam that they will die if they eat the forbidden fruit. By having Digory obey Aslan, Lewis shows that the world of Narnia is truly separate from earth and that his *The Chronicles of Narnia* are about a world other than earth. Further, Lewis implies that there was the possibility of Eve and Adam making another choice, of choosing to do as God told them to do, and that the history of earth might have been very different from what followed the Fall of the first man and the first woman.

In *Paradise Lost,* when Adam is told about how the Son of God shall redeem humanity, Adam says:

> "O goodness infinite, Goodness immense,
> That all this good of evil shall produce,
> And evil turn to good—more wonderful
> Than that which by creation first brought forth

> Light out of darkness! Full of doubts I stand,
> Whether I should repent me now of sin
> By me done and occasioned, or rejoice
> Much more that much more good thereof shall spring . . ."

Lewis disagreed with this view of the Fall. Milton suggests that the Fall was a blessing, that much good shall eventually come from the evil that has been unleashed on earth, because the Son of God's death and resurrection will be great triumph of salvation for humanity. Lewis believed that God had a wonderful plan for humanity if Adam and Eve obeyed Him. When they ate the forbidden fruit, God put aside that plan, and humanity will never know what it was. Thus, Lewis did not see good coming from evil; obeying God is the best action to take, on earth as well as in Narnia's world.

Paradise Lost and *The Chronicles of Narnia* share views about Christ's role in creating the world. They were both probably inspired in this notion by John 1:3: "All things were made by him [the Word, meaning Christ], and without him was not any thing made that was made." This passage means that the Word, Christ, was God's instrument in creating the universe. In *Paradise Lost*, God says to His Son, "And thou, my Word, begotten Son, by thee/This I perform; speak thou, and it be done!/My overshadowing Spirit and might with thee/Within appointed bounds be heaven and earth." In *Paradise Lost*, the Son of God need only speak to create earth; in *The Magician's Nephew*, Aslan, Son of the Emperor-over-sea, sings Narnia's world into being. The creative power given Them by Their Father is immense in both Milton's *Paradise Lost* and Lewis' *The Magician's Nephew*. Grass spreads across the land, and plants of all sorts spring from the ground. Even animals climb out of the ground, already full grown. As Milton put it, "The grassy clods now calved; now half appeared/The tawny Lion, pawing to get free/His hinder parts—then springs, as broke from bonds,/And rampant shakes his brinded mane" or "the swift Stag from underground/Bore up his branching head." This reads much like Aslan's song raising trees to full height and making animals spring from the ground: "And the humps [in the ground] moved and swelled till they burst, and from each hump there came out an animal . . . The stags were the queerest to watch, for of course the antlers came up a long time before the rest of them."

Both Milton and Lewis were probably inspired to visualize animals climbing out of the ground by Genesis 2:19: "So out of the ground the Lord God formed every beast of the field and every bird of the air, and brought them to the man to see what he would call them; and whatever the man called every living creature, that was its name." And God said, 'Let the earth bring forth the living creature after his kinde, cattell, and creeping thing, and beast of the earth after his kinde:' and it was so." They also may have been mindful of Genesis 1:24: "And God said, 'Let the earth bring forth living creatures according to their kinds: cattle and creeping things and beasts of the earth according to their kind.'" As fine as Milton's depiction of the creation of life by God, I think that in this instance, Lewis' imaginative rendering of the act of creation is superior to Milton's in both thematic depth and vivid description.

For the Last Judgment, Milton and Lewis have divergent views about Heavenly paradise. In *Paradise Lost,* Christ will sit with God in judgment, "When this world's dissolution shall be ripe,/With glory and power, to judge both quick and dead—/To judge the unfaithful dead, but to reward/His faithful, and receive them into bliss,/Whether Heaven or Earth; for then the Earth/Shall all be Paradise." Milton places the paradise that follows the Judgment on a remade earth, but Lewis places the best of earth in Aslan's Country (Heaven), in *The Last Battle,* asserting that the earth which humanity presently knows is merely a shadow of the heavenly earth.

IDEAS FOR REPORTS AND PROJECTS

1. How do the Norse myths reflect the culture of the Norsemen (Vikings)?

2. The final battle between good and evil in Asgard is huge, with all the warriors of each side participating. This gives the battle a truly apocalyptic feel as even the greatest warriors of each side fall amid great carnage. Why would Lewis choose not to follow this pattern and instead make the Last Battle a contest among three small forces?

3. Both the Norse and the Ancient Greeks had codes of honor. How are these codes reflected in their myths? How do these codes differ from Aslan's code?

4. How are women treated in Norse or Greek mythology? How does their treatment differ from the way they are treated in *The Chronicles of Narnia*?

5. In *The Lion, the Witch and the Wardrobe,* Peter, Lucy, and Susan are given magical items that aid them in their fight

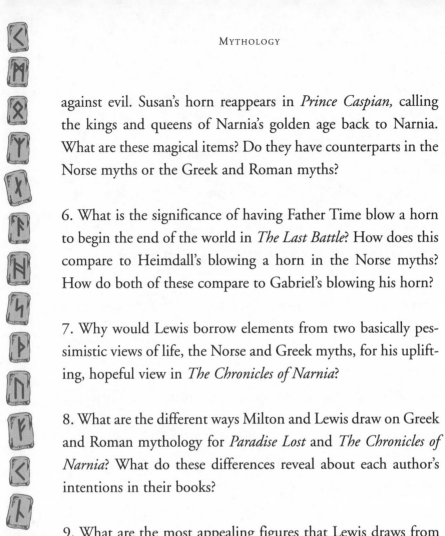

against evil. Susan's horn reappears in *Prince Caspian,* calling the kings and queens of Narnia's golden age back to Narnia. What are these magical items? Do they have counterparts in the Norse myths or the Greek and Roman myths?

6. What is the significance of having Father Time blow a horn to begin the end of the world in *The Last Battle*? How does this compare to Heimdall's blowing a horn in the Norse myths? How do both of these compare to Gabriel's blowing his horn?

7. Why would Lewis borrow elements from two basically pessimistic views of life, the Norse and Greek myths, for his uplifting, hopeful view in *The Chronicles of Narnia*?

8. What are the different ways Milton and Lewis draw on Greek and Roman mythology for *Paradise Lost* and *The Chronicles of Narnia*? What do these differences reveal about each author's intentions in their books?

9. What are the most appealing figures that Lewis draws from Greek and Roman mythology? How does Lewis make them appealing? Are they as appealing in their original Greek and Roman myths? What is Lewis' purposes in including them in *The Chronicles of Narnia*?

10. Why would Milton and Lewis have different views about where people would be after the end of the world? Which has the more Biblical support for his depiction of where the paradise of the next life is to be found?

CHAPTER 6

HISTORICAL BACKGROUND

Lewis was severely wounded in combat during World War I. His experiences were horrifying as he saw men killed in many different ways. For instance, he was wounded when a German shell blew to pieces his sergeant, who was standing beside him. As an officer, he was responsible for the lives of men, some of whom perished under his command.

The effects on him of his ordeals were profound. He changed from a shy young man who had spent his school years being bullied and pushed around by others to a more confident, commanding personality. The war also confirmed for him his atheism; like many others who have seen much suffering, he seems to have thought God would not allow such evil if He really existed.

World War I also gave impetus to the cultural movement called "Modernism," named by the Modernists who thought theirs was the last, penultimate movement in society and the arts. They believed this because they saw World War I as Western civilization's great watershed. All the old rules of life had led to an utter catastrophe, and therefore all those rules were wrong and had to be replaced by new rules that would reflect the world's new reality.

EXISTENTIALISM

One of spinoffs of the Modernist Movement was existentialism, a philosophy that says that only that which can be physically sensed exists. Further, it maintains that each individual person must come to terms with his or her personal isolation from other people and from the universe at large. In addition, existentialists regard the universe as being indifferent to human beings; there is no good or evil in it, merely the workings of a cosmos governed strictly by physical laws. This leads to relativistic thinking: That is, what is good or bad for people is determined by their personal experiences and the nature of the individual situations in which they find themselves. Some philosophers argued that emphasizing physical rather than spiritual meaning would make a person more logical and better able to cope with the unique qualities of each individual problem.

Although Lewis was never an existentialist philosopher, when he began teaching at Oxford University, he showed that he believed that a person could only be logical by sticking to physical facts. Spiritual beliefs in particular would, in his view, merely cloud the mind. By the time Lewis wrote *The Chronicles of Narnia,* he was utterly committed to Christianity, but elements of his old atheistic views show up in *The Lion, the Witch and the Wardrobe,* to be shown to be false. Thus, in the early chapters, Peter and Susan insist on relying on physical fact. For instance, they test the back of the wardrobe and find that it has a back; from this, they conclude that Lucy is lying. Yet, with such evidence in hand, they find themselves contradicted by Professor Kirke, a powerful logician who, like Lewis' beloved tutor William Kirkpatrick, taught reason with unrelenting logic. It seems that Lewis remembered Kirkpatrick's lessons in organizing his arguments logically, but until he became Christian, he had forgotten or chosen to ignore any spiritual elements his tutor may have tried to impart.

In *The Lion, the Witch and the Wardrobe,* Professor Kirke is sharp with Peter and Susan, taking into account elements of life that are beyond the physical. He suggests that they approach

their problem not from an existential point of view, but from their knowledge of their sister Lucy. Has she ever lied to them? No, she has always told the truth. Is she insane? No, both Peter and Susan have been with her enough to know that she is a rational person. Therefore, it is possible that she is telling the truth. What Kirke asks for is that Peter and Susan look beyond their limited physical world to see a larger picture of life in which experience and personality matter; experiencing life is more than assembling physical facts. Had Peter and Susan learned the lesson Kirke tries to impart, they might have discounted Edmund's insistence that he and Lucy had only played a game in which they pretended to go to Narnia. They would have factored into their reasoning Edmund's history as a bully and liar.

Until he was about thirty years old, Lewis argued for atheism with enthusiasm. His experiences during World War I seemed to confirm the idea that there is no good or evil and that the universe was utterly indifferent to what happened anywhere, anytime. The capricious death of his sergeant exhibited strong evidence that life and death are random. Much of *The Chronicles of Narnia* contradicts this view, instead reaching for an older view of the cosmos in which God is a transcendent being Who is so interested in human beings that He sacrificed His Son for their sins. In such a cosmos, *good* and *evil* have meaning: They are choices people can make, and they help determine each individual person's salvation. When Emeth meets Aslan, He calls the young man "beloved" and knows not only of his life but of his spiritual journey which has finally led to Aslan, the true Source of good.

Much of *The Horse and His Boy* is devoted to depicting how divine providence can work in lives. Shasta suffers much during his adventures, and his early childhood was one of miserable labor, but his experiences are not random events, for he is expected to learn from them. He must learn to respect people, especially women, and he must learn that his own life has meaning not just for himself, isolated from others, but for all those he meets and for many people he will never meet. Although Shasta's adventure is like a fairy tale, the point that experiences are opportunities for spiritual growth can be applied to anyone's life.

WORLD WAR I

World War I shows up in *The Chronicles of Narnia* in the way battles are depicted. The only time Lewis slips from realistic accounts of battle is in his depiction of Peter fighting the White Witch in the first battle of Beruna in *The Lion, the Witch and the Wardrobe*. Peter's sword is said to be flicking faster than the eye can see, suggesting a skill in swordsmanship that Peter has had no time to learn. But the sword is meant to represent the Holy Spirit, and it fights for Peter against evil as the Holy Spirit is supposed to fight for the souls of faithful Christians. Otherwise, the give-and-take of warfare is realistic in its hacking, stabbing, and tromping. Lewis had experienced men killing men first hand, and he harbored no romantic notions about glory in killing, even though the Talking Mice of *Prince Caspian* and *The Voyage of the "Dawn Treader"* seem to do so. Thus, when the traitors Glozelle and Sopespian lead a charge of Telmarine troops, High King Peter matter-of-factly lops off Sopespian's head. There is no romantic conflict, just death.

Experiences in World War I seem to have affected Lewis' mature spiritual beliefs in yet another way, frequently expressed in *The Chronicles of Narnia*. The bitter, angry young man who was severely wounded in war became a man who saw war as sometimes unavoidable because evil people will insist on harming others, forcing good people to resist. When he has Narnians come to the aid of Archenland in *The Horse and His Boy*, he is suggesting that good people should sometimes take violent action in the defense of others, somewhat as the British defended France against Germany in World War I, and as they were doing while he wrote *The Lion, the Witch and the Wardrobe* during World War II.

WORLD WAR II

In 1939, Germany and the Soviet Union made a pact with each other to conquer and divide Poland and the Baltic nations, and both armies invaded Poland, the Germans from the west and to Soviets from the east. After years of appeasement, in which millions of people's lives in Czechoslovakia, Alsace-Lorraine, and elsewhere were sold out to the Germans in order to maintain peace, France and Britain declared war on Germany. The badly organized French army was outmaneuvered by the Germans, and the British army was soundly defeated, fleeing to the coast and then being ferried back to Britain. The Germans then began bombing British airfields. Britain managed to launch air raids against Germany, even hitting Berlin, Hitler's military headquarters and the capital located deep in the heartland of a heavily defended part of Germany. Soon, the Germans began bombing London and other British cities. British civilians took it as a point of pride to remain in the cities, carrying on the business of a nation at war, and thousands of them were killed by German bombs. Many of these Londoners were parents who wanted their children kept out of harm's way, and thousands of children were sent to live in the country. During the war, Lewis took in many such children, giving them safe harbor.

Lewis regarded World War II as a contest between good and evil. It was plainly a war that good people had sought to avoid, but they had to choose between submitting to an evil enemy or standing up to that enemy and fighting it. In so doing, the British were not only defending themselves, something they had every moral right to do, but were helping those European peoples who could not fight. Most of the Narnian novels were written after World War II, when the full evil of the Nazi regime had been revealed. By the end of the 1940s, some of the evils of the Soviet regime (after Germany attacked the Soviet Union, the USSR became an ally of Britain) were also discovered, including forced labor camps, the murders of millions of civilians who had resisted collectivization, and the full apparatus of a police state.

In *The Lion, the Witch and the Wardrobe*, characteristics of the Nazi and Soviet regimes appear and would have been readily recognized by young readers at the time the novel was first published. The most obvious characteristic is the White Witch's secret police, led by the wolf Fenris Ulf. The secret police carry off Mr. Tumnus to the White Witch after his failure to report Lucy is discovered. The White Witch uses her secret police to terrorize Narnians; Mr. Beaver for one wants to flee his home the moment he realizes that the secret police may be on their way. Mr. Tumnus tells Lucy that not only are the secret police to be feared, but so are their many collaborators, of which, Mr. Tumnus sadly confesses, he is one. Even some Talking Trees are among the White Witch's spies.

Both World War I and World War II featured enormous battles involving tens of thousands of soldiers, but the battles in *The Chronicles of Narnia* generally involve hundreds of combatants, although the second battle of Beruna in *Prince Caspian* may have involved thousands. The smaller battles may reflect the smaller populations of the nations of Narnia's world, or they may simply be smaller because that makes them somewhat easier to depict. Bree's tales in *The Horse and His Boy* suggest that the Calormenes may have had larger battles with their neighbors than Narnia is used to seeing. The smaller battles also harken back to the earth's Middle Ages, when the notions of chivalry were born.

CHIVALRY

Although astronomy is a very highly developed science in Narnia, thanks to the centaurs, the society and technology of Narnia's world does not surpass those of early Renaissance Europe. It is worth noting that during the Middle Ages many knights were merely thugs who cared not a wit about the rights of others. In England, comedians have long been fond of pointing out that some members of English nobility are descended from cattle thieves. Even so, medieval society formed itself first around knights who became nobility and second around kings who ruled with the blessings of the Church.

Women of the noble class seem to have inspired the creation of a code of honor that became known as the "chivalric code." Among other elements, the code contained rules for the treatment of women. For instance, a true knight would protect a woman's honor, which included defending her from assault. In *The Lion, the Witch and the Wardrobe,* the chivalric code shows up when Lucy and Susan are given long-range weapons and are forbidden to engage in hand-to-hand combat; the idea of women being hacked in the middle of a battle is said to be too horrible to contemplate. This may be regarded as a sexist attitude, but Lewis is reflecting the attitude inherent in the chivalric code that women should not be exposed to mortal danger. His attitude toward women matured as he wrote the Narnian novels, with women becoming active in conflicts.

Although Susan and Lucy are primarily devoted to helping the wounded in *The Lion, the Witch and the Wardrobe,* in *Prince Caspian* Susan proves herself to be a crack shot with a bow and arrow by conking a couple of soldiers on their helmets, and in *The Horse and His Boy* Lucy is a deadly archer. In *The Last Battle,* Jill Pole is right in the thick of battle, even though the bow and arrow are her primary weapon, and she kills some of her enemies.

The chivalric code also shows up in the speech and relationships of people. Kings Peter and Edmund and Queens Lucy and Susan speak in a somewhat stilted, very sophisticated way at the end of *The Lion, the Witch and the Wardrobe,* and Lewis explains that kings and queens are supposed to speak that way. The chivalric code also implies duties to all those who practice the code. When in *The Magician's Nephew* Aslan tells King

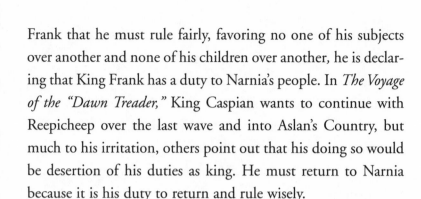

Frank that he must rule fairly, favoring no one of his subjects over another and none of his children over another, he is declaring that King Frank has a duty to Narnia's people. In *The Voyage of the "Dawn Treader,"* King Caspian wants to continue with Reepicheep over the last wave and into Aslan's Country, but much to his irritation, others point out that his doing so would be desertion of his duties as king. He must return to Narnia because it is his duty to return and rule wisely.

Thus the chivalric code governs how men and women should treat each other and defines the duties that powerful people have toward others. This does not mean that women are relegated to secondary status; in *The Chronicles of Narnia,* the chivalric code liberates women. In Narnia, where chivalry is taken seriously, women are free to do as they please. In Calormen, where scheming and warfare substitute for chivalry, women are property. Susan learns this to her dismay when she visits Tashbaan. Further, in Calormen, people's rights are determined by their social status. For example, in Tashbaan the rights of way on city streets are determined by social class, with the nobility able to push around everyone else and the slaves unable to do anything if anyone is in the way. In Narnia, the chivalric code specifies that all are to be treated with respect. Caspian and Peter show this in *Prince Caspian* in their behavior toward Dwarfs and Talking Animals. For instance, even though the Talking Bears tend to doze off and suck on their paws, Peter includes one among his Marshals of the Lists because bears have an hereditary right to that honor. Although he is High King and the greatest of Narnia's monarchs, he is as bound to respect the rules of conduct as anyone else.

ARMS AND ARMOR

Lewis devotes only one scene to an account of arms and armor, that of the Narnians' preparation for battle in *The Horse and His Boy*. Particularly frightful are the heavy boots the giants strap on for stomping on the enemy. In general, Lewis' characters use the weapons and armor of the early Middle Ages. Armor consists of chain mail, a helmet, and metal gloves, much like European and Byzantine knights wore during the Dark Ages. Calormen warriors wear helmets topped by points and wrapped in turbans. This is meant to give them a slightly Middle Eastern look, which is accentuated by their fondness for telling tales as if they were from *The Arabian Nights*. Knights and other nobility wear tunics over their armor, usually with symbols of their rank and allegiance. Shields, too, usually have such symbols on them: High King Peter's shield is silver with a bright red lion, representing Aslan, on it. When Prince Rilian picks up his shield after slaying the serpent in *The Silver Chair*, it resembles Peter's shield. During battles, women as well as men, wear armor.

Weapons are primarily swords, spears, and bows and arrows, although Narnian Talking Beasts often use their fangs or claws, and the giants use armored boots. Calormen warriors seem to prefer swords over other weapons, and Peter and other kings of Narnia favor swords, too. In Peter's case, the sword and shield have significance beyond their physical reality: They are gifts from Father Christmas in *The Lion, the Witch and the Wardrobe* and represent the Holy Spirit and Faith. In *The Silver Chair*, Prince Rilian's shield also represents faith. These are weapons and shields of Aslan's Father. A parallel may be found in the medieval tales of King Arthur; in the earliest tales, Arthur carries a shield that is white with a red cross on its outside and a painting of Jesus's mother Mary on the inside. Like the Crusaders, his shield represents his commitment to the Christian faith and Christian behavior.

MILITARY TACTICS

The military tactics are very basic and appropriate for the small size of the battling armies in *The Chronicles of Narnia*. Attacking from high ground offers an advantage for the White Witch's forces in *The Lion, the Witch and the Wardrobe,* as well as Lucy's archers in *The Horse and His Boy*. At first, the White Witch's higher ground seems to be a decisive advantage, but it is overcome when Edmund hacks her wand and through Peter's swordsmanship and determination. In the case of the battle at Anvard, the Narnian archers help to create chaos in the Calormene force by raining arrows down on them. The higher ground makes it easy for the archers to see their targets and to aim. All in all, seizing the high ground is classic military strategy used by many armies for thousands of years.

Otherwise, tactics are of the rush-and-bump-into-each-other variety. When Glozelle and Sopespian rally the Telmarine troops to attack the Old Narnians, they lead a pell-mell charge into the midst of their enemy. In *The Horse and His Boy,* King Edmund leads a charge into the right flank of the Calormenes, turning the battle into a swirl of battling horsemen. From Bree's accounts, it seems that the Calormenes, too, favor charging into an enemy and grappling in hand-to-hand combat. The only figures that try a more strategic approach to battle are Peter and the White Witch in *The Lion, the Witch and the Wardrobe*. Aslan praises Peter for thinking ahead and trying to plan for the inevitable battle against the White Witch. When Aslan and His companions return to the field of battle from the White Witch's castle, they see the White Witch's forces arrayed in line and working together to kill Peter's forces.

THE MEDIEVAL EUROPEAN CHURCH

Lewis borrows a little from the role of the Roman Catholic Church in medieval politics. After Charlemagne was crowned Holy Roman Emperor with the blessings of the Church in A.D. 800, kings and queens tried to have their authority confirmed by the Church, and over hundreds of years the doctrine of the divine right of kings evolved. This doctrine held that monarchs are ruled by God's choice, and therefore their decisions were sanctified by God. This resulted in terrible atrocities in which people were mass murdered because their views of Christ differed from what the monarchs thought to be correct doctrine. For instance, French kings mistakenly thought that the Roman Catholic Church would support them if they slaughtered the Huguenots, who were Protestants whose doctrines differed somewhat from the doctrines of Roman Catholicism.

In *The Chronicles of Narnia*, King Frank, High King Peter, King Edmund, Queen Lucy, Queen Susan, and King Caspian are all confirmed in their offices by Aslan Himself, somewhat as a bishop might have crowned a king or queen in the Middle Ages.

In this sense, these kings and queens rule by Aslan's authority. A crucial difference is in the concept of *duty*. During the Middle Ages, monarchs generally considered it the duty of all their subjects to be obedient, regardless of what Church authorities might say about caring for their subjects. In *The Magician's Nephew,* Aslan makes it plain to King Frank that his office is one of duty, of caring for the welfare of his subjects. In *Prince Caspian* and *The Horse and His Boy,* Miraz and the Tisroc are bad rulers in part because they fail to fulfill their duty to rule justly; they are selfish and rule for their own benefit. The idea that Aslan's blessing brings responsibility with it is made emphatic in *The Voyage of the "Dawn Treader"* when Caspian is reminded that he is bound by duty to return to Narnia, regardless of what he may prefer to do.

In *The Last Battle,* the potential danger of putting religion at the service of politics is shown. The hoax of the donkey pretending to be Aslan is created in order that Shift may become powerful and used by the Calormenes so that they may rule Narnia and plunder its resources. The claim that Aslan has given them political authority over Narnians is accepted by many Narnians; they fail to recognize that those who claim to rule by Aslan's command show no sense of duty. Like medieval tyrants, Shift and Rishda Tarkaan insist that Aslan's will is that people serve them. King Tirian contrasts with Shift and the Calormenes because he tries to do his duty to his people. His struggle is plainly to help liberate his people, not to make them his servants. In this, Lewis slips into a seemingly modern attitude, but one that may also be found in the tales of King Arthur. Those who have power deserve their high offices only so long as they do so for the benefit of those beneath them.

NORSE EXPLORATION

When he was a boy and first read a book about Norse mythology, Lewis' imagination was fired, and he never lost his passion for studying Norse lore and culture. In *The Voyage of the "Dawn Treader,"* Lewis borrows from ancient Norse sagas that tell of the westward exploration of the Vikings to Iceland, Greenland, and Vinland (North America). The *Dawn Treader* has some of the traits of a Viking longboat, with oars as well as sail, and an evocative shape of a dragon. Like the Vikings, when the crew of the *Dawn Treader* wished to look warlike, they hung their shields along the sides of their ship to catch the sunlight and to intimidate their enemies. The shields imply that every crewman is a warrior, ready to do battle. On the other hand, the *Dawn Treader* has traits of later English sailing ships, with multiple decks and square rigging.

The history of Viking explorations westward from Scandinavia, although motivated by greed, is one of courage, determination, and sorrow. Exploration was inherent in their culture, inherited from their Germanic ancestors who had pushed into Scandinavia and Northern Europe in the first century B.C. One reason they explored was to stay alive. As is the case with the Calormenes in *The Chronicles of Narnia*, kings were not secure in their positions. Sometimes kings would execute their brothers in order to eliminate significant rivals. Therefore, younger brothers would sometimes flee their homeland with their retainers in search of a safer place to live. In the epic poem *Beowulf,* Beowulf himself has left such a dangerous situation. In the case of Eric the Red, politics put his life in dan-

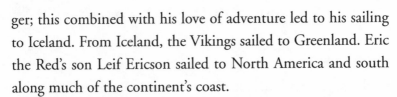

ger; this combined with his love of adventure led to his sailing to Iceland. From Iceland, the Vikings sailed to Greenland. Eric the Red's son Leif Ericson sailed to North America and south along much of the continent's coast.

The colonies of Iceland thrived, and descendants of the Norsemen who settled it in the Middle Ages are still there. The colonies on Greenland thrived for a time, but a change in climate made the colonies too cold for raising crops and their inhabitants failed to adapt to the change, even though the Inuits who migrated into southern Greenland about the same time as the Norse did well. The North American colonies were abandoned soon thereafter, perhaps because of conflict with Native American tribes but more likely because the colonists felt too isolated from other Vikings after the colonies in Greenland failed.

Out of this complex history, Lewis takes elements for *The Voyage of the "Dawn Treader."* Just as the Vikings did, the Narnians sail into an ocean full of unknowns with perhaps only vague rumors of lands beyond their known world. Caspian and his crew head southeast to the Lone Islands and then east to find what they can; the Vikings set out to the west, again hoping to find land. Navigating must have been challenging for the Norsemen, who sailed in stormy, unforgiving seas. For the crew of the *Dawn Treader,* navigating involves luck; sometimes they just barely see a new island to the southeast, and they follow a string of islands toward the edge of the world. For the Vikings, their explorations across thousands of miles of ocean may well have seemed as though they were headed to the world's end.

KINGS, QUEENS, AND SOCIETY

Lewis' depiction of royalty, nobility, and society in *The Chronicles of Narnia* has three sources: 1) European fairy tales and Medieval history; 2) Middle Eastern, primarily Arab, folklore; and 3) Ottoman Empire history. The influence of European fairy tales is evident throughout the novels. The reign of the Pevensies at Cair Paravel is like a fairy tale in its splendor and its adventures. The presence of magic is a quality typical of fairy tales, and the elevation of common people through magic and great deeds is typical of fairy tales.

EUROPEAN FAIRY TALES AND MEDIEVAL HISTORY

The primary attraction of the novels as stories may be their fairy-tale atmosphere in which anything can happen, and most importantly where good is rewarded and evil is punished. In justifying the violence that is typical of the fairy tale, Lewis argued that children in particular want to see good behavior rewarded and evil behavior punished definitively. Thus, the shoving of the witch into her own oven in "Hanzel and Gretel" is not only a poetic ending, but a satisfying one: The murderer of children dies the very way she has killed her victims. This element of fairy tales is evident in most of the novels of *The Chronicles of Narnia*.

For instance, in *The Lion, the Witch and the Wardrobe*, the White Witch, whose crimes are awful and beyond count, perishes at the very hands of those she sought to kill. It is interesting to

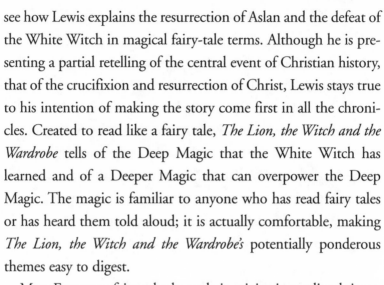

see how Lewis explains the resurrection of Aslan and the defeat of the White Witch in magical fairy-tale terms. Although he is presenting a partial retelling of the central event of Christian history, that of the crucifixion and resurrection of Christ, Lewis stays true to his intention of making the story come first in all the chronicles. Created to read like a fairy tale, *The Lion, the Witch and the Wardrobe* tells of the Deep Magic that the White Witch has learned and of a Deeper Magic that can overpower the Deep Magic. The magic is familiar to anyone who has read fairy tales or has heard them told aloud; it is actually comfortable, making *The Lion, the Witch and the Wardrobe's* potentially ponderous themes easy to digest.

Most European fairy tales have their origins in medieval times. There are later ones and some that may be earlier, but the vast majority reflect the era in which they were composed. They have kingdoms and kings and queens, and there are dukes and duchesses aplenty. Ordinary people had very little power and could often be abused by richer people or nobility without being able to resist. Thus, many fairy tales are stories about how ordinary people become powerful. Puss'n'boots is a talking cat whose cleverness enables him to obtain his master a fine home, at the expense of a nasty troll (someone who would victimize defenseless people). In *The Magician's Nephew,* a cab driver and his wife are made the first king and queen of Narnia, by no less than the creator of Narnia, Aslan Himself. In *The Lion, the Witch and the Wardrobe,* children hiding in the countryside from German bombs become the saviors of Narnia and its monarchs. For *The Horse and His Boy,* Lewis plays upon a common sort of wish fulfillment, the story of a child who really is not just poor and powerless, but is actually a prince.

Like fairy tales, *The Chronicles of Narnia* are vague about the details of "happily ever after" and the day-to-day aspects of being kings and queens. What details Lewis provides are a blend of medieval practices and Biblical precepts. Whereas some monarchs of the Middle Ages and the Renaissance claimed to rule by divine right, asserting that they were designated by God to do as they chose, Lewis has some of his characters actually be chosen by Aslan (Christ). In real life, the monarchs were a mixed bunch, with some actually trying to do good, while others used God's name as an excuse to commit great evil, much as Shift and the Calormenes do in *The Last Battle*. But King Frank and Queen Helen, Kings Peter and Edmund and Queens Lucy and Susan, and King Caspian are given their commissions by Aslan, and they actually rule as Aslan would wish them to.

The results for Narnia are happy ones. Under King Frank and Queen Helen, all Narnians are treated fairly and none are favored over others. Peter, Edmund, Lucy, and Susan reign over a golden age, the high point in Narnia's history in which the nation enjoys wonderful prosperity, and its enemies are defeated. *The Horse and His Boy* offers a glimpse of how the court of the Pevensies is constituted, with a faun, Mr. Tumnus, and a raven, Sallowpad, advising Queen Susan and the others while in Tashbaan. The golden-age court seems to be an inclusive one, with all sorts of Narnians a part of it.

A knight named Peridan is also part of the Narnian court. Apparently, the social hierarchy in the era of High King Peter includes nobility. In *The Lion, the Witch and the Wardrobe,* Peter was knighted by Aslan, so it seems reasonable that there would be other knights. In *The Horse and His Boy,* Peridan is an advisor to the kings and queens and, as a medieval knight would be, he is also a warrior. He carries a pennant in the battle at Anvard, and he is present when Rabadash is brought before King Lune. Peridan's presence in *The Horse and His Boy* suggests that Narnia's social structure includes nobility who act as lieutenants of the monarchs. Peridan's pointing out to King Lune that the monarch has a right to execute Rabadash hints that Peridan is aware of the legal rights and responsibilities that come with power, which would include his own power.

By the time of Caspian the Navigator (*Prince Caspian, The Voyage of the "Dawn Treader,"* and *The Silver Chair*) there are lords and ladies at the court. Lord Drinian is an important figure in *The Voyage of the "Dawn Treader,"* in which he captains the ship Caspian sails on to the end of the world. In *The Silver Chair,* he is a trusted courtier and close friend of Caspian. At first glance, Caspian's court seems very much like a medieval European one, replete with courtiers, inside advisors, servants, and pomp and circumstance, but a closer look reveals that Lewis slips in one of his own ideals. The idea that people should merit their positions is personified in the Dwarf Trumpkin, an ordinary Dwarf who has been elevated to the king's inner circle because of his courage and faithfulness. When Caspian sails from Narnia in *The Voyage of the "Dawn Treader"* and *The Silver Chair,* he designates Trumpkin as his regent—the person who serves in the king's stead. There is no hint of anyone thinking that Trumpkin, who lacks noble ancestry, should not have the position of ultimate authority in the king's absence.

Narnia is at its best when its inhabitants work together and respect one another's rights. It is at its unhappiest when they fight one another and deny each other's rights. Thus, during the Winter without Christmas, Narnians spy on one another, and even Talking Trees can be spies. It is a nation of fear. Later, in *Prince Caspian,* Old Narnians hide from a tyranny. They fear extermination by the Telmarine humans who have pushed them off of much of their land. All is not happy for the humans, for they fear ghosts and the Eastern Sea; they fear the great Lion who was said to have come from the east. Thus, Narnia is at its happiest when free from fear, when Narnians may venture outside safely whenever they want, and when they share Narnia with each other.

MIDDLE EASTERN SOURCES

In addition to European fairy tales and history, Lewis draws from Middle Eastern sources. As one might guess from reading *The Chronicles of Narnia,* Lewis loved stories and storytelling, and his admiration for Middle Eastern storytelling is apparent in *The Horse and His Boy* and *The Last Battle.* Among the best stories of mystery and enchantment are those from Middle Eastern folklore, many of which are familiar to Western readers from the various versions of the *Arabian Nights* that have been published over the last couple hundred years. In *The Horse and His Boy,* Bree mentions the high Calormene style of storytelling, a form at which he is good, and Aravis proves herself to be adept at it, as well, when she tells her own story to Bree and Shasta. It is one of several aspects of Calormen that may account for its being found in Aslan's Country after the end of the world. In addition to Aravis' story in *The Horse and His Boy,* the high Calormene style is displayed in Emeth's story in *The*

Last Battle, in which he describes Aslan in grand terms, at one point comparing the Lion's fierceness to a great volcano.

Calormene society reflects primarily Arab folk tales, with its fabulous gardens, ornate palaces, and grand personages recognizable from the *Arabian Nights.* Even the sculduggery of the Tisroc has its antecedents in the *Arabian Nights*: the premise of the *Arabian Nights* is that a woman tells a story every night to a king who intends to execute her, as he has others, and she postpones her execution because he wants to hear how her stories end. He is a ruthless man; the Tisroc is no worse.

The society of Calormen is much more rigidly structured than that of Narnia. As Lasaraleen, in *The Horse and His Boy* shows, notions of one's place in Calormen society can be very deeply impressed upon young people. She cannot understand why Aravis would not want to marry a wretchedly toadying old man because the man is rich and powerful, apparently the sort of man well-born young Calormene women are expected to aspire to marry. The streets of Tashbaan show a little of how social standing works in Calormen. There seems to be only one traffic rule: those of higher social station get to travel along a street before those of lower station do.

The only way of advancing outside of being well born is by distinguishing yourself in battle, although even in battle the men of higher station seem to receive preferential treatment. It was Bree's good fortune that he was put into the service of a high Calormene lord, who commanded respect and took a central place in combat. Apparently women are excluded from battle, as they are from most activities that would offer them opportunities to distinguish themselves. As Aravis' story shows, high-born women are expected to marry whomever they are told to marry. All Calormen women are treated primarily as property of men. Thus, *The Horse and His Boy* is not just a fairy tale about Shasta becoming a king, it is a fairy tale about Aravis being able to fully mature beyond the level of Lasaraleen, and to be free to live life on her own terms. This last is not so much a reflection of medieval Middle Eastern folklore as it is the times in which Lewis himself lived; many people were fleeing oppressive conditions in their Eastern European homelands to find greater freedom in Western democracies.

OTTOMAN EMPIRE

Some of the notions about how Calormen's government works may be drawn from the history of the Ottoman Empire, which ruled much of the Middle East and some of southern Europe for hundreds of years. Like Calormen, the Ottoman Empire grew by conquering its neighbors, and in the Middle Ages its leaders seemed preoccupied with warfare. By the late nineteenth and early twentieth centuries, the court of the Ottoman Empire had become notorious for its debauchery and treachery; murdering rival family members apparently happened often. The court of the Tisroc features a great deal of treachery, with concerns over gaining and holding power that even override concerns about family. It would seem that a government in which sons often murdered their fathers would be an unstable one, but *The Chronicles of Narnia* imply that the Calormene government was more stable than that of Narnia. From the era of High King Peter in *The Horse and His Boy* to the end of the world in *The Last Battle,* Calormen seems to have had the same sort of government and society without change.

IDEAS FOR REPORTS AND PROJECTS

1. Take note of the descriptions of the *Dawn Treader* in *The Voyage of the "Dawn Treader"* and make a drawing of the ship based on them. Look up Viking longboats in the library and make a sketch of one. Show how the *Dawn Treader* and the ancient Viking longboats are similar and how they are different. From what you have learned, could the *Dawn Treader* have been inspired by Viking ships?

2. Read about how the Norse colonized Iceland, and using what you have learned about the process, write a story about how people first colonized the Lone Islands.

3. Research the process for sending British city children to country homes in England during World War II? Who assigned the children to homes? How were the homes chosen? Why would Lewis' home have had many children stay at it at different times, rather than the same children all the time? How is this aspect of World War II reflected in *The Chronicles of Narnia?*

4. Lewis' personal experience of war involved huge armies battling over vast quantities of territory, often just to secure a small amount of actual ground. Why would he make the wars in *The Chronicles of Narnia* smaller affairs? What advantages are there to the storyteller?

5. What is the history of the chivalric code? Who first wrote it down and why? What were the purposes of the code? Why would Lewis include aspects of the code in his Narnia books?

6. What arms or armor does Lewis invent for *The Chronicles of Narnia*? What is their purpose? How do they affect the tones of the narratives?

7. In the first century B.C., in the era when Germanic peoples were migrating into northern Europe, Celtic and Germanic women were often warriors. Typically, the men were expected to go to the field of battle, and the women were expected to defend the wagons if they were nomads and their villages if they were settled. Often, children were armed and expected to back up the women. Women often distinguished themselves in battle, and among the Celtic peoples women were often field commanders, leading warriors into battle. By the coming of the Middle Ages this had changed. Why did it change? How does Lewis borrow from this history for his portrayal of women in battle?

8. In many medieval and early Renaissance tales of King Arthur, the rule of law is important. The Arthurian ideal is that even the king himself is constrained by law, and that by law the monarch and nobility must treat common people according to law. Even the queen may be punished for violating the law (having an extramarital affair with Lancelot). This was a very attractive principle to ordinary people. How is it reflected in *The Chronicles of Narnia*?

THE FOODS
OF NARNIA

INTRODUCTION

C. S. Lewis liked rich, meaty foods, and *The Chronicles of Narnia* reflect his preferences. When he describes wine, the best wines are hearty, almost like beef broth; wines fortify and satisfy his characters. What may be somewhat controversial is the drinking of alcoholic beverages by children in *The Chronicles of Narnia,* sometimes with Aslan's approval, and wine almost always has beneficial effects on youngsters in the novels. Lewis himself liked to drink, often to excess; he considered it a manly thing to do. He expected his college students to drink with him in taverns and to attend gatherings where Lewis would encourage students to drink a great deal; some of his students disliked the drinking parties. His Biblical authority for supporting his depictions of drinking wine is the story of Jesus turning water into fine wine at a feast and the sacrament of communion. Lewis imagines this wine to have healing properties, given it by Jesus, and in *The Chronicles of Narnia,* given to wine provided by Aslan. No feast in *The Chronicles of Narnia* is complete without wine or other alcoholic beverages.

Another Biblical reference is to Christ feeding the multitudes. When a large crowd had gathered to hear Christ speak, they were in need of food, but there was not enough fish and bread to go around. Jesus instructed his disciples to distribute the few fishes and loaves of bread to several thousand people; miraculously, the food never ran out and there always seemed to be enough bread and fish to give to the hungry people. Aslan performs a similar miracle in *The Lion, the Witch and the Wardrobe*: After the first battle at Beruna, the victors have high tea. "How

Aslan provided food for them all I don't know." What they ate is not described, but given the feast served at Aslan's Table in *The Voyage of the "Dawn Treader,"* it was probably very filling.

What amazing feasts there are in *The Chronicles of Narnia*: an abundance of food symbolizes prosperity and contentment. The feasts provided by Aslan Himself represent His generous nature and His creative power. Even without Aslan around, Narnians know how to prepare and serve food that will satisfy even the heartiest of appetites.

In *The Voyage of the "Dawn Treader,"* a feast is served every day at Aslan's Table on the island of Ramandu: "There were turkeys and geese and peacocks, there were boar's heads and sides of venison. There were pies shaped like ships under full sail or like dragons and elephants, there were ice puddings and bright lobsters and gleaming salmon, there were nuts and grapes, pineapples and peaches, pomegranates and melons and tomatoes." This passage probably reflects Lewis' own preferences—turkeys, geese, and peacocks, as well as fare from fairy tales: boars' heads and venison. Thematically, the feast represents satisfaction and reward after weeks of poor meals in *The Voyage of the "Dawn Treader,"* and symbolizes the spiritual bounty offered to the ungrateful Dwarfs in *The Last Battle*: "Aslan raised his head and shook his mane. Instantly a glorious feast appeared on the Dwarfs' knees: pies and tongues and pigeons and trifles and ices, and each Dwarf had a goblet of good wine in his right hand." Although food represents the spiritual bounty that Aslan offers, those to whom it is offered must make the effort to accept it. He can offer the feast, but He cannot force the ungrateful Dwarfs to partake of it.

Lewis tends to choose English cuisine when describing feasts, as he does for the voyagers at the Island of the Dufflepuds in *The Voyage of the "Dawn Treader"*: "mushroom soup and boiled chickens and hot boiled ham and gooseberries, red currants, curds, cream, milk, and mead." In a letter to a young fan of *The Chronicles of Narnia,* Lewis explains that fat for frying is scarce in England; therefore the English tend to boil their food. In *The Voyage of the "Dawn Treader,"* Lewis reports that this meal is exceedingly messy with hams, chickens, fruit, milk and mead. Everyone drinks the mead, but only Eustace regrets doing so. Later in the novel, the wizard Coriakin treats Lucy to a midday meal which is more like the food she is accustomed to eating on earth. The meal is a robust, English-style feast of a piping hot omlette, cold lamb, green peas, lemon-squash to drink, and for desert strawberry ice and a cup of chocolate.

The inhabitants at Cair Paravel know how to put on a feast (from *The Silver Chair*): "each course came in with trumpeters and kettledrums. There were soups that would make your mouth water to think of, and the lovely fishes called pavenders, and venison and peacock and pies, and ices and jellies and fruit and nuts, and all manner of wines and fruit drinks." This great feast comforts both Jill and Eustace, and provides a sense of security at a time when they are under considerable stress. Yet, the revelers at Cair Paravel are not the only Narnians who know how to prepare a wonderful meal. The Dwarfs feed Jill and Eustace "great mugs of frothy chocolate, and roast chestnuts, and baked apples with raisons stuck in where the cores had been, and then ices just to freshen you up after all the hot things."

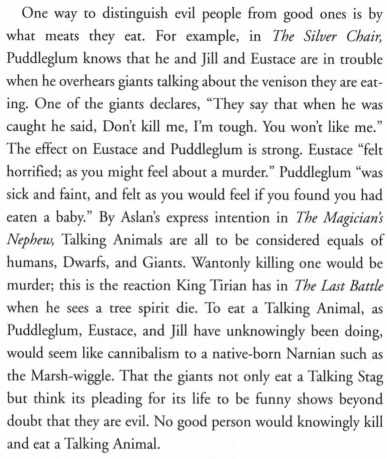

One way to distinguish evil people from good ones is by what meats they eat. For example, in *The Silver Chair,* Puddleglum knows that he and Jill and Eustace are in trouble when he overhears giants talking about the venison they are eating. One of the giants declares, "They say that when he was caught he said, Don't kill me, I'm tough. You won't like me." The effect on Eustace and Puddleglum is strong. Eustace "felt horrified; as you might feel about a murder." Puddleglum "was sick and faint, and felt as you would feel if you found you had eaten a baby." By Aslan's express intention in *The Magician's Nephew,* Talking Animals are all to be considered equals of humans, Dwarfs, and Giants. Wantonly killing one would be murder; this is the reaction King Tirian has in *The Last Battle* when he sees a tree spirit die. To eat a Talking Animal, as Puddleglum, Eustace, and Jill have unknowingly been doing, would seem like cannibalism to a native-born Narnian such as the Marsh-wiggle. That the giants not only eat a Talking Stag but think its pleading for its life to be funny shows beyond doubt that they are evil. No good person would knowingly kill and eat a Talking Animal.

Lewis' strong opinions about food included comments on vegetarianism, which he thought was bad for people and even an affront to God, Who had provided animals for people to eat. To him, vegetarianism was a rejection of the bounty God has given to humanity. While describing the Dwarfs' wholesome feast, he mentions that Jill had all sorts of sausages to choose from. He also disliked "health food," so his adventurers eat heartily like all worthy adventurers.

FOOD FOR FEASTS

Part of the great creative power of Aslan is His ability to serve incredible bountiful feasts, but in *Prince Caspian,* He has Bacchus, Silenus, and the Maenads perform a wild, "magic dance of plenty" that conjures up a feast of amazing propor-tions. There is roasted meat, wheat and oat cakes, honey, sugar, cream, at least seven kinds of fruit—"pyramids and cataracts of fruit"—and wines of almost all kinds. It seems every Talking Animal has something it would like to eat, and even the Talking Trees are given "rich brown loam" as an appetizer, followed by a light pink earth, then chalky soil, then desserts of gravel or sand. They even drink wine, which, Lewis reports, "made the Hollies very talkative." In *The Voyage of the "Dawn Treader,"* the as yet still invisible Dufflepuds serve Lucy and the others from the *Dawn Treader* their idea of a good feast, which consists of "mushroom soup and boiled chickens and hot boiled ham and gooseberries, red currants, curds, cream, milk, and mead," as well as very boring conversation consisting of agreeing with whatever the Chief Dufflepud says. This sounds like it would be a very agreeable meal to people who had been at sea as long as the crew of the *Dawn Treader* has been.

A candidate for all-time great feast has to be that served at Aslan's Table on Ramandu's Island. This is the last island before the End of the World to the east, and the table is laid out with a feast everyday at Aslan's order for any voyagers who should sail to the island from the lands such as Narnia far to the west. Lewis says, "There were turkeys and geese and peacocks, there were boar's heads and sides of venison, there were pies shaped

like ships under full sail or like dragons and elephants, there were ice puddings and bright lobsters and gleaming salmon, there were nuts and grapes, pineapples and peaches, pomegranates and melons and tomatoes." There are fruits and wine in abundance. At first, Caspian and his companions think that the food might be poisonous and responsible for the long sleep of the three lords they find at the table, but after Ramandu's daughter assures them that the food is safe to eat and after Reepicheep drinks some of the wine, the food proves to be a great feast. The idea underlying the feast is that those who dine at Aslan's Table—those who worship Aslan (Christ)—will have a great, endless spiritual bounty.

Boar's heads figured in medieval European feasts because their meat was considered especially tender and flavorful. Boar's heads at feasts reflect the medieval character of societies in the world of Narnia. They are served at Aslan's Table in *The Voyage of the "Dawn Treader."*

Chickens are served boiled by the Dufflepuds.

Cream seems to be great for any occasion in the known world of Narnia. It is mixed with fruits or used as a topping.

Curds are served by the Dufflepuds in *The Voyage of the "Dawn Treader,"* but what sort of curds is a mystery. They could be what Americans call "cottage cheese," solids taken from milk, but curds come in many flavors and are usually creamy, often served as desserts.

Geese are traditionally served at feasts in England. They are usually not as plump as turkeys, but they have a gamier, sharper flavor.

Gooseberries are greenish berries from a shrub. They are served by the Dufflepuds to Lucy and company in *The Voyage of the "Dawn Treader,"* and must be very welcome fruit for people who had been long at sea.

Grapes are cultivated in Narnia for making wine, but Bacchus and his crew conjure up some table grapes for feasting in *Prince Caspian.* Aslan's Table also features grapes in *The Voyage of the "Dawn Treader."*

Ham is served boiled by the Dufflepuds. Lewis explains in a letter to a young reader that a shortage of cooking fat in England results in many foods being boiled, but in Narnia fried fish, bacon, and eggs are common. On an island like that of the Dufflepuds, like England, oil and fat for frying must be rare.

Honey seems to have been favored for feasts on earth since time immemorial. In Narnia, honey is used to flavor many kinds of food.

Lobsters are eaten by the wealthy in Calormen and by voyagers who eat at Aslan's Table on Ramandu's Island in *The Voyage of the "Dawn Treader."* They are examples of the extraordinary bounty that is to be had at Aslan's Table.

Mead is honey wine, and although it was popular during the Middle Ages, it was reported to have an unpleasant taste. Perhaps today's mead is different because it tastes very good. The sailors of the *Dawn Treader* would love it.

Melons come in many varieties, but Lewis does not specify which appear at Aslan's Table in *The Voyage of the "Dawn Treader."* Perhaps they all do. Calormen has an abundance of melons.

Milk is served by the Dufflepuds in *The Voyage of the "Dawn Treader,"* which suggests that they have cows or goats someplace.

Mushroom soup is served on cold nights at sea in *The Voyage of the "Dawn Treader."*

Nectarines are so named because they are as sweet as nectar. On earth, they are a very ancient form of peach and may have been among the first cultivated crops. In Narnia, they are part of the feast celebrating the Old Narnians' victory in *Prince Caspian*.

Nuts are mentioned here and there throughout *The Chronicles of Narnia* as good to eat, and are served at Aslan's Table. In *The Horse and His Boy,* almonds in particular are mentioned.

Oat cakes are favored by Centaurs.

Peaches are among the fruits grown in Narnia. In the era of Caspian the Navigator, there must be many orchards in Narnia, because there are many fruits. Peaches are served at a feast at the end of *Prince Caspian*. They are served at Aslan's Table in *The Voyage of the "Dawn Treader,"* and would be welcomed eating for sailors who had been long at sea.

Peacocks may not come instantly to everyone's mind as food, but these large pheasants have been parts of Asian feasts for ages and may show up in Western feasts as "pheasant." They complete the trio of fowl served at Aslan's Table in *The Voyage of the "Dawn Treader"*: turkey, goose, and peacock.

Pears are cultivated in Narnia in *Prince Caspian* and are served at the feast celebrating the defeat of the army of the usurper Miraz.

Pies can be fruit or meat. I suspect that the pies at Aslan's Table on Ramandu's Island in *The Voyage of the "Dawn Treader"* are fruit filled, but given the hearty meats that are also served, some could be meat filled.

Pineapples originate in the tropical Americas but are now grown in most of the world's tropical areas. In the world of Narnia, they are most likely to be grown in Calormen and other southern countries. They are served at Aslan's Table on Ramandu's Island.

Plum pudding is a rich cakelike desert made from plums and other fruits, flour, sugar, flavorings such as vanilla, and it is usually soaked with rum or other liquor. The alcohol is usually burned off by lighting with a match. It is a traditional favorite for Christmas time in England. In *The Lion, the Witch and the*

Wardrobe, it is eaten as part of the celebration of the return of Christmas.

Pomegranates are fruits with a tough rind containing edible seeds. In Asian fairy tales, they make regular appearances at feasts, and in *Prince Caspian,* they are among the fruits culti- vated in Narnia. They are a delicacy found at Aslan's Table on Ramandu's Island in *The Voyage of the "Dawn Treader."* Pomegranates are also known as "passion fruit" because their juice suggests Christ's blood during His crucifixion.

Puddings can be served hot or cold and are often custards. At Aslan's Table, they are cold. Americans and the English can con- fuse each other over what is meant by "pudding," but in the case of Aslan's Table, it seems likely to be a sweet dessert.

Raspberries are served at the feast at the end of *Prince Caspian.*

Red currants grow in clusters on a shrub. They tend to be tart but are very good in cakes and breads. The Dufflepuds serve them in *The Voyage of the "Dawn Treader."*

Salmon was hard to find in English streams in Lewis' day, and had not been seen in the Thames since the early 1700s, but efforts to clean up England's streams resulted in a return of the Atlantic salmon in the 1970s, even to the Thames. For Lewis, salmon would be a treasured dish, served hot with herbs. Salmon are among the meatiest of fish and would be good eating at Aslan's Table in *The Voyage of the "Dawn Treader,"* served hot or cold.

Strawberries are among the sweets eaten in *Prince Caspian*.

Sugars appear in many dishes. In the feast after the second battle at Beruna in *Prince Caspian,* "many- coloured sugars" are served. Perhaps a little food dye has been added.

Tomatoes are originally from South America. They are a good source of vitamin C, something that would be important to voyagers who might suffer from scurvy. They are valued for their juicy, sharp-flavored pulp, and they are served at Aslan's Table on Ramandu's Island.

Turkeys are a North American game bird and a variety of North American domesticated bird. The second of these has been carried around the world and is kept and eaten in many different cultures. They would provide filling meat at Aslan's Table.

Venison is the meat of deer. It is valued in the northern countries, including Narnia itself, in the world of Narnia. Narnians take care not to kill Talking Deer, who look much like their counterparts among the nonintelligent game deer. To kill a Talking Deer for food is murder. Venison of the right sort is served at Aslan's Table on Ramandu's Island.

Wheat cakes are probably favored by Centaurs and Talking Horses.

Wines of nearly all kinds are served at Narnian feasts. In *Prince Caspian,* Bacchus goes all out to serve "dark thick ones like

syrups and mulberry juice, and clear red ones like red jellies liquefied, and yellow wines and green wines and yellowy-green and greenish-yellow" wines. In *The Voyage of the "Dawn Treader,"* Aslan's Table has many wines.

FOOD FOR BREAKFASTS

As Shasta learns in *The Horse and His Boy,* Caspian learns in *Prince Caspian,* and Jill learns in *The Silver Chair,* there is nothing better to prepare for a good adventure than a good breakfast.

Bacon, when it sizzles, has a smell that helps to awaken Narnians.

Beer is drunk by Centaurs for breakfast in *The Silver Chair,* but it is not recommended for everyone.

Coffee is the preferred breakfast drink of Dwarfs and Centaurs.

Cream is for pouring on porridge.

Eggs, usually fried, are standard fare for a Narnian breakfast. Orruns, a faun, and Jill prepare scrambled eggs near the end of *The Silver Chair.* These and toast must have been very welcome to Jill, as well as the bedridden Puddleglum.

Ham, served cold, is sometimes part of a Narnian breakfast.

Kidneys are part of breakfasts for Centaurs in *The Silver Chair.*

Marmalade, usually meaning orange marmalade, is often served with toast.

Milk is often served hot by Narnians at breakfast.

Mushrooms are mixed with eggs and bacon for breakfasts preferred by Dwarfs.

Omelettes are not breakfast food in Narnia, but they sound good as part of a Centaur's breakfast.

Pavenders are fish, eaten for breakfast by Centaurs, according to the faun Orruns in *The Silver Chair*.

Porridge is boiled oatmeal, favored by Centaurs in *The Silver Chair*, but eaten by almost everybody.

Toast is prepared by the faun Orruns and Jill for breakfast near the end of *The Silver Chair*. It is served with scrambled eggs and often with orange marmalade.

FOOD FOR TEATIME

In *The Voyage of the "Dawn Treader,"* the magician Coriakin tries to serve Lucy something like she would get at one o'clock in England: a hot omelette, cold lamb, green peas, strawberry ice, lemon squash, and hot chocolate.

Hot chocolate is served as a drink to finish a meal in *The Voyage of the "Dawn Treader."*

Lamb and green peas is lamb boiled with green peas, spices, and herbs. When served cold, it is usually accompanied by mint or some other jelly.

Lemon squash is a soft drink with a sweet, rich lemon flavor. It is fine anytime, but great on hot days.

Omelettes are eggs mixed and fried and folded over cheeses, vegetables, meats, fruits, or some combination of these. They tend to be meals all by themselves, but Lucy eats much more besides her omelette in *The Voyage of the "Dawn Treader."*

Strawberry ice seems to be a world favorite. It is crushed ice flavored with strawberry syrup or containing frozen sliced strawberries.

FOOD FOR HEARTY MEALS

In *The Lion, the Witch and the Wardrobe,* the Beavers have a well-stocked larder, including hams and strings of onions. They feed the Pevensie children beer drawn from a barrel, fried fish, boiled potatoes, creamy milk, "deep yellow butter," marmalade rolls, and tea. The Calormenes have their own version of hearty eating, which Shasta is served in *The Horse and His Boy* when people think he is Prince Corin. He is served "lobsters, and salad, and snipe stuffed with almonds and truffles, and a complicated dish made of chicken-livers and rice and raisins and nuts, and there were cool melons and gooseberry fools and mulberry fools, and every kind of nice thing that can be made with ice. There was also a little flagon of the sort of wine that is called 'white' though it is really yellow." Shasta had never eaten so well, but he seems to handle the rich food just fine.

The folks at Cair Paravel, in Caspian the Navigator's time, knew how to serve hearty meals. In *The Silver Chair,* they serve Jill and Eustace soups, pavenders, pies, venison, peacock, ices, jellies, fruit, nuts, wines and fruit drinks. This is regular eating in Cair Paravel, the seat of government of a prosperous nation. The giants of Harfang have their own versions of hearty meals, one of which is served to Puddleglum, Jill, and Eustace. It consists of cock-a-leekie soup, roast turkey, steamed pudding, roasted chestnuts, and an abundance of fruit, which would probably be imported from the south.

In *The Silver Chair,* Jill, Eustace, and Puddleglum are treated to a fine dinner after they climb out of Underworld and into Narnia. They are fed sausages—"And not wretched sausages half full of bread and Soya Bean," Lewis notes—hot chocolate, roasted potatoes, roasted chestnuts, baked apples with raisins, and ices.

Almonds are a nut that is popular just about everywhere. Germans love to make it into a sweet paste, Americans eat it as a snack, and it appears in many Chinese dishes. They should be plentiful in Calormen, which has a climate ideal for growing almond trees.

Apples are cored, stuffed with raisins, and baked for the dinner served to Jill, Eustace, Puddleglum, and Prince Rilian for their first dinner after leaving Underworld in *The Silver Chair.*

Beer is an almost universally savored drink in the world of Narnia. A dark, woody taste seems to be preferred.

Butter is good for pastries.

Chestnuts are encased in prickly husks and are grown on trees. They are served roasted by the Harfang giants in *The Silver Chair*. In America, they are common winter treats.

Chicken livers are valued by some and disliked by other eaters for their sharp, pungent flavor. They are often made into pastes for topping crackers, but in *The Horse and His Boy*, they form the foundation for a rice and raisin dish.

Hot chocolate had to be wonderful for Jill, Eustace, Puddleglum, and Prince Rilian after their time in Underworld in *The Silver Chair*. Lewis says the chocolate was "frothy."

Cock-a-leekie-soup consists of leeks, a vegetable that would grow in Harfang's climate, and chicken meat. After freezing for days, Jill and Eustace cannot be blamed for relishing it in *The Silver Chair*.

Fish may be served at any occasion, but fried fish are preferred for ordinary meals.

Fools are mixtures of sugar, heavy cream, and pureed fruit.

Fruit drinks, as varied as the kinds of wine, are served at Cair

Paravel to Jill and Eustace in *The Silver Chair*. This may be Lewis' lone concession to those who would prefer nonalcoholic beverages, although the lemon squash served Lucy by Coriakin in *The Voyage of the "Dawn Treader"* might be another.

Gooseberries are small, somewhat bitter fruits that grow on spiny shrubs. They are more popular in England than America, but they make very fine preserves and fools.

Hams are large, heavy cuts of pork. They are the sort of meat Narnians would smoke and hang in dry places. Cuts of ham may show up at breakfast.

Ice is very special in the world of Narnia, because the cultures of Narnia do not have an industrial age in which ice can be manufactured in freezers. Calormenes serve a wide variety of sweets made with ice. In *The Silver Chair*, Jill and Eustace are served ices (desserts of flavored ice or ice cream) at Cair Paravel at the outset of their adventure. They are also served ices for their first dinner after leaving Underworld near the end of the novel.

Jellies are served at Cair Paravel in *The Silver Chair*. These would probably be fruit preserves.

Lobsters are standard fair for well-to-do Calormenes. Whether they are broiled or boiled, Lewis does not say.

A **marmalade roll** is a cake with orange marmalade folded into its batter. A "gloriously sticky" marmalade roll is mentioned in

The Lion, the Witch and the Wardrobe, while Narnia is in the grip of its winter without Christmas, so the oranges probably came from Calormen.

Milk is a favorite for children in Narnia, although its source, from dairy cows or whatever, is mysterious.

Melons—actually Lewis mentions "cool melons" as food in Calormen. Not only is Calormen a fine land for growing fruits, but it is hot. Thus chilled melons would be a favorite Calormene dish.

Mulberries are the sweet fruits of trees called "red mulberry" and "white mulberry."

Nuts are served at Cair Paravel in *The Silver Chair*. Lewis does not specify which sorts of nuts, although he mentions almonds being served in Tashbaan in *The Horse and His Boy*.

Onions are not discussed much in *The Chronicles of Narnia*, but they are part of the Beavers' larder in *The Lion, the Witch and the Wardrobe*.

Pavenders are fish that live off the coast of Narnia. They are served at feasts and everyday meals. In *Prince Caspian*, fried pavenders are eaten by the Pevensie children and Trumpkin while they are on the island with the ruins of Cair Paravel. In *The Silver Chair*, they are part of the regular diet of Narnians.

Peacock is a large pheasant served at Cair Paravel in *The Silver Chair*.

Pies can be filled with meat or filled with fruit, and can be a main dish or a dessert. Lewis mentions them next to ices and jellies in *The Silver Chair*, so they are probably desserts in that instance.

Potatoes tend to be boiled in Narnia, but they form an important part of a filling meal. In *The Silver Chair*, Jill and her companions are served roasted potatoes as part of their first dinner after leaving Underworld. Narnians are fond of mixing herbs and other seasonings into the foods they roast, so these potatoes were probably very flavorful.

Raisins are dried grapes and have long been favorites for livening up dishes because of their sweet flavor and ability to keep fresh for long periods. Calormen is surely rich in raisins.

Salads are more Calormene fare than they are Narnian. Calormen seems to be richer in leafy vegetables than Narnia.

Sausages are especially favored by Dwarfs, but most people like them. Lewis himself seems to have been fond of them if they were properly made, without fillers. They are part of a hearty meal fed to Jill, Eustace, and Puddleglum after they return to Narnia in *The Silver Chair*.

Snipe is a European bird that is likely to be unfamiliar to Americans. It is smaller than turkeys and geese, but Calormenes

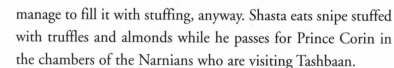

manage to fill it with stuffing, anyway. Shasta eats snipe stuffed with truffles and almonds while he passes for Prince Corin in the chambers of the Narnians who are visiting Tashbaan.

Soups are served at Cair Paravel in *The Silver Chair*. Perhaps these are mushroom and fish soups.

Steamed pudding is made with flour, milk, and usually fruit. It makes for a rich, filling dessert. It is served by the Harfang giants in *The Silver Chair*.

Tea is good anytime, but for a hearty meal, it accompanies dessert.

Truffles are edible fungi that grow underground. They tend to be very expensive but are esteemed by many eaters. They are part of a meal eaten by Shasta while he passes for Prince Corin, and they show that the meal Shasta eats was intended for someone wealthy.

The turkey of the Harfangs is roasted. Originally a North American bird, the domesticated turkey is now found through most of the world; in Narnia's world, it seems popular, too. It is even a part of the feast at Aslan's Table in *The Voyage of the "Dawn Treader."* In *The Silver Chair*, it is served to Jill, Eustace, and Puddleglum.

Venison is the meat of deer and the staple of the diets of northern peoples in *The Silver Chair*. To their horror, Puddleglum, Jill, and Eustace learn that the Harfang giants eat Talking Deer, which is considered murder in Narnia and by any follower of Aslan. It is okay to eat the meat of nonintelligent, ordinary, deer.

White wine is a fermented drink made from white grapes. Calormenes like to serve it with lobster.

Wines are served to Jill and Eustace at Cair Paravel at the start of their adventure in *The Silver Chair*. "All manner of wines," says Lewis. Wines are an important part of meals in Narnia, and an abundance of different kinds of wines represents a nation's prosperity.

FOOD FOR ADVENTURES

When Caspian must flee for his life from the usurper Miraz, his tutor Doctor Cornelius sees to it that he has cold chicken, venison, bread, an apple, and wine to take with him. Centaurs have their own views about what makes for good eating while traveling. When adventuring with Caspian in *Prince Caspian*, they bring "cakes of oaten meal, and apples, and herbs and wine and cheese."

Apples show up in different ways in *The Chronicles of Narnia*. The Apples of Life from the walled garden in the Western Mountains in *The Magician's Nephew* are magical and not like the ordinary apples of *Prince Caspian*, which Peter, Lucy, Edmund, and Susan eat when they are stranded on an island or the apple Doctor Cornelius packs for Caspian. The apples the Pevensie children eat are connections with their past, coming from an ancient orchard planted when they were the kings and queens of Narnia.

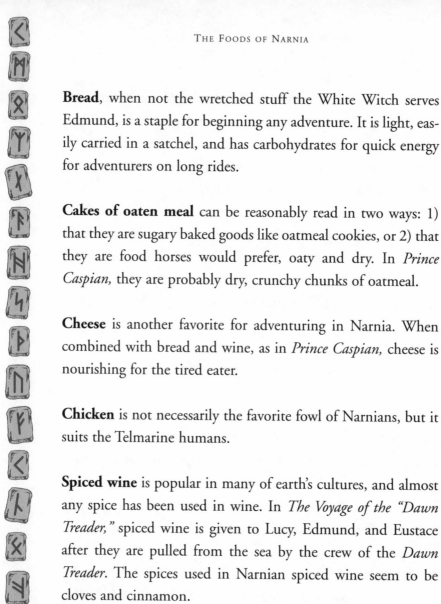

Bread, when not the wretched stuff the White Witch serves Edmund, is a staple for beginning any adventure. It is light, easily carried in a satchel, and has carbohydrates for quick energy for adventurers on long rides.

Cakes of oaten meal can be reasonably read in two ways: 1) that they are sugary baked goods like oatmeal cookies, or 2) that they are food horses would prefer, oaty and dry. In *Prince Caspian,* they are probably dry, crunchy chunks of oatmeal.

Cheese is another favorite for adventuring in Narnia. When combined with bread and wine, as in *Prince Caspian,* cheese is nourishing for the tired eater.

Chicken is not necessarily the favorite fowl of Narnians, but it suits the Telmarine humans.

Spiced wine is popular in many of earth's cultures, and almost any spice has been used in wine. In *The Voyage of the "Dawn Treader,"* spiced wine is given to Lucy, Edmund, and Eustace after they are pulled from the sea by the crew of the *Dawn Treader.* The spices used in Narnian spiced wine seem to be cloves and cinnamon.

Wine seems to be of value for any Narnian adventure. Narnian wine is especially good, because it is made strong and has rich, hearty flavor.

FOOD OF UNDERWORLD

At the Queen of Underworld's palace in *The Silver Chair,* Jill, Eustace, and Puddleglum are entertained by a dissolute man. He serves them pigeon pie, cold ham, salad, honey cakes, and something to drink, likely wine. He mentions that food is imported from other countries in Overworld. The Earthmen who populate Underworld are from the Really Deep Land, and their very busy commerce probably includes shipping food to the capital of Underworld. In their land, Bism, the Earthmen eat rubies and drink diamond juice.

Cold ham is, well, ham that is cold. Jill, Eustace, and Puddleglum are probably being served leftovers late at night.

Diamond juice is said by the Earthman Golg to be squeezed from living diamonds. The diamonds of Bism grow like fruit, unlike the "dead" diamonds known to Overworlders such as Prince Rilian, Eustace, Jill, and Puddleglum.

Honey cakes are probably pastries made of flour, honey, and butter.

Pigeon pie is a meat pie featuring boneless pigeon meat. It likely has onions and other vegetables in it.

Rubies are like berries in Bism, growing in bunches, and eaten by the Earthmen. The rubies that Overworlders know from their mines are considered "dead" by the Earthmen.

Salad is often served at dinners in Narnia. The salad likely consists of leafy vegetables.

FOOD OF PARADISE

Glimpses of the food of Paradise are offered in *The Magician's Nephew* and *The Voyage of the "Dawn Treader."* In *The Magician's Nephew*, the fruits of the walled garden are described as "apples," although they are more like the magical apples of Asgard of Norse mythology than ordinary apples. They are references to the fruits of the Garden of Eden, including the forbidden fruit. In *The Voyage of the "Dawn Treader,"* the Lamb offers roasted fish to the children. In *The Last Battle,* there is a fuller account of some foods to be found in Aslan's Country. In a grove of trees near the stable door, inside Aslan's Country, are golden, yellow, red, and purple fruits that defy description, being unlike any fruits known on earth. All earthly and Narnian fruits would taste foul in comparison to these fruits that have no pits. Aslan's food in His country is as bountiful as that found on His table on Ramandu's Island in *The Voyage of the "Dawn Treader."* For instance, he serves the ungrateful Dwarfs, who are huddled inside Aslan's Country just beyond the stable door, a feast of pies, tongues, pigeons, trifles, ices, and wine.

Apples of Life (also called "Apples of Youth") come from the Tree of Life and are found in the walled garden in the Western Mountains (*The Magician's Nephew*) and in Aslan's Country (*The Last Battle*). Those who eat one without permission "Shall find their heart's desire and find despair," according to a verse outside the garden. Jadis eats one without permission and receives immortality but loses her ability to enjoy living. When eaten with Aslan's permission, an apple can have great healing properties. Everyone in Aslan's Country is allowed to eat the fruit, which is delicious.

Fish are roasting over a fire beside the Lamb Who is Aslan at the end of *The Voyage of the "Dawn Treader."* The Lamb offers the fish to Lucy, Edmund, and Eustace for breakfast. You may remember that one of Christ's miracles was to feed the multitudes with a fish and five loaves of bread.

Ices are sweet desserts, usually made with crushed ice, although they may be ice cream or sherbets.

Pies are offered the ungrateful Dwarfs in *The Last Battle*.

Pigeons are usually roasted, and probably are roasted in *The Last Battle*, but they are in pies in *The Silver Chair*.

Tongues are probably beef tongues, considered a delicacy by many Europeans and Americans.

Wine is a special drink when Aslan serves it. It should be nourishing, but the ungrateful Dwarfs in Aslan's Country in *The Last Battle* think it is "dirty water."

FOOD OF EVIL

Edmund is seduced by Turkish Delights in *The Lion, the Witch and the Wardrobe,* but he receives only stale dry bread and water at the White Witch's castle, whereas the Beavers serve a sumptuous meal. The almost inedible bread and water symbolize the spiritual meanness of the witch, but the hearty meal served by the Beavers represents the spiritual richness that good creatures enjoy. In Harfang, in *The Silver Chair,* the giants serve the meat of Talking Animals, and for their autumn festival, special treats are human boys and girls. They also eat Marsh-Wiggles. All of these, the Talking Animals, humans, and Marsh-Wiggles are people, not animals, and eating them is akin to cannibalism.

Dry bread is served to the traitor Edmund at the White Witch's castle. He had hoped for Turkish Delights, but dry bread is all he is worth to the White Witch now that he is hers to command.

Mallard is the dish listed before Man in the cookbook Jill reads in the kitchen in Harfang.

Man is "valued as a delicacy" by the Harfang giants in *The Silver Chair.* Jill and Eustace are to be eaten by the king and queen of the Harfangs during their Autumn Festival. The green woman has sent them to die.

Marsh-Wiggles are not considered good eating by the Harfang giants in *The Silver Chair.* They are too stringy and "muddy" flavored, although there is a recipe for cooking them that reduces the unpleasant flavor. Puddleglum is probably in as much danger as the humans Jill and Eustace.

Sirloins in Chapter 7 of *The Silver Chair* probably refer to beef sirloins, but they exist only as figments of the imaginations of Jill and Eustace. The thought of the sirloins makes them even more quarrelsome than they already were, thus making their mindfulness of Aslan's signs even weaker.

Talking Stags are people in Narnia, so serving them for food is evil. Puddleglum and Eustace are horrified to learn that they have been dining on the meat of a Talking Stag in Harfang in *The Silver Chair*, with Puddleglum so certain that he has violated Aslan's laws that he seems ready to die. That the Harfang giants eat Talking Animals is an indication that they are evil.

Turkish Delights are jellied candies made from fruits and nuts. In real life, they have their origins in Turkey, perhaps among the ethnic Armenians. In *The Lion, the Witch and the Wardrobe*, they are temptations for Edmund, who cannot get enough of them from the White Witch. Edmund spoils for himself a very good meal at the Beavers' home because he thinks constantly about wanting more Turkish Delights.

Water tends to have magical properties in *The Chronicles of Narnia*, but in *The Lion, the Witch and the Wardrobe*, it is what Edmund receives to drink at the White Witch's castle. Compare this to the beer and tea his brother and sisters receive at the Beavers' home!

CHAPTER 8

THE GEOGRAPHY
OF THE WORLD
OF NARNIA

*See the endsheets for a map of the Known World
at the End of the Reign of Caspian the Navigator.*

THE GEOGRAPHY OF
THE WORLD OF NARNIA

The action in *The Chronicles of Narnia* takes place in only a fraction of the world. Beyond the Western Mountains are creatures and lands scarcely alluded to in *The Last Battle*. Only one land is given a name, Telmar, where the South Sea pirates from earth were transported, and from which the Telmarine kings of Narnia come. The southernmost nation given a name in *The Chronicles of Narnia* is Calormen, a vast kingdom created by conquering neighboring nations. The stories of Bree in *The Horse and His Boy* make it clear that there are many nations near Calormen, and Calormen is often at war with them. At the end of *The Horse and His Boy*, Rabadash distinguishes himself by using clever diplomacy to keep the peace with many potential enemy nations during his reign as Tisroc. In his notes and in the Narnian novels themselves, Lewis makes it clear that there are many places in Narnia's world yet to be seen, and many more stories of children and Aslan in Narnia than he actually tells. In *The Voyage of the "Dawn Treader,"* he even hints that he may someday tell the story of how the Lone Islands came to be part of greater Narnia (but he does not).

The world of Narnia is not shaped like the earth; although it seems to have a horizon, curving like the earth's, the world of Narnia has an edge along its eastern side. Beyond that edge is part of Aslan's Country, high atop cliffs that overlook land and

sea. To the west of Aslan's Country is the Last Wave, a body of water in the shape of a wave at its crest but which never breaks on the shore of Aslan's Country. In the southeastern sea is a low bit of land where Lucy, Edmund, and Eustace meet the Lamb that turns into the Lion Aslan.

To the south of this bit of land is a sea covered by white lilies. The water of this part of the sea is shallow enough for the children to walk through it. The water, here, and to the west is sweet; that is, it is like fresh water and can be drunk safely. This water not only quenches thirst, it gives its drinkers energy, and it helps their eyes see in the very bright sunlight of the End of the World, as the eastern edge is called. The sun is much larger in the east because people are closer to it. In fact, the sun of Narnia's world has birds living on it that fly to Ramandu's Island for a daily meal.

Everything in Narnia's cosmos seems much closer to the world than do the celestial bodies of earth. The stars are living beings with personalities of their own. Although they follow movements that centaurs can track and predict, the stars have lives of their own and can even commit transgressions as Coriakin has or retire as Ramandu has. They are close enough to Narnia's world to fall on it at the end of the world.

The world of Narnia has only one known continent, in the west, and between it and the End of the World is the Eastern Sea. To the north of Cair Paravel is the island nation of Galma, famous for building fine ships and providing excellent sailors. To the east of Galma is the island nation of Terebithia. In *The Voyage of the "Dawn Treader,"* the people of Terebithia have suffered a terrible plague and are known to be pirates. From there, to the east or southeast, are the Seven Isles, of which Muil and Brenn are the main islands, with the capital city of Redhaven on Brenn.

To the east or southeast of the Seven Isles are the Lone Islands. The westernmost is Felimath, an unpopulated island where King Caspian and others are kidnapped by slave traders in *The Voyage of the "Dawn Treader."* Just east of Felimath is the main island of Doorn. The capital city of the Lone Islands is Narrowhaven, which is on the western side of the island and which features are large bay and a very active seaport. Narrowhaven is a major trading center for the islands and the nations along the western edge of the sea. The city does not seem to be laid out in a distinct pattern, although a gate in its eastern wall opens directly on a road that leads to the governor's castle. In the northwest part of Narrowhaven is where slaves are traded until King Caspian puts an end to slavery. Most of the rest of Doorn is taken up by towns, villages, and farmlands. Avra, where Lord Bern lives, may have towns and villages, but it is given over mainly to agriculture.

To the southeast of the Lone Islands are Dragon Island, Burnt Island, Deathwater Island, Island of the Dufflepuds, the Darkness and Dark Island, and Ramandu's Island, which is the easternmost island in the sea. All of these islands are described in more detail in the chapter on *The Voyage of the "Dawn Treader."* Of particular interest are the sea people east of Ramandu's Island. The sea people have a well-developed civilization, with cities, roads, agriculture, and castles. They live in the shallow waters of the eastern sea because deeper levels are more dangerous; the sea serpent that attacks the *Dawn Treader*

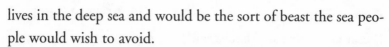

lives in the deep sea and would be the sort of beast the sea people would wish to avoid.

The continent that lines the western edge of the sea seems to be very large; its exact dimensions are not known because the lands west of the Western Mountains are scarcely mentioned. They could be vast and extend for thousands of miles. There might even be a sea beyond them. That they may be large can be inferred from *The Last Battle* when Aslan greets hordes of western creatures at the door to Aslan's Country at the end of the world. The Telmarine rulers of Narnia came to Narnia by way of Telmar, a western country, and the Calormenes may have fought wars against western nations.

The portion of the continent mentioned in *The Chronicles of Narnia* extends to the far north, where Jadis the White Witch lived for hundreds of years, but not to the far south. The southernmost place given a name by Lewis is Calavar, a province of Calormen where Aravis' father's palace is. South of the frozen north is the stronghold of Harfang, where sophisticated but evil giants live during *The Silver Chair*. Giants have lived in northern lands at least since the time of *The Lion, the Witch and the Wardrobe*. In *The Horse and His Boy*, High King Peter wages a war against them, and in King Tirian's time, before *The Last Battle*, Narnia seems to have fought against them.

The legacy of the giants may be an ancient one by the time of *The Silver Chair*. A short run south of the stronghold of Harfang is an ancient ruined giant city. Harfang pales in comparison to the architectural magnificence of the ruined city, which covers a large plateau. Far to the south is a magnificent, huge old stone bridge that may be crossed safely even though it is very old and has not been maintained. It suggests that the ancient giants were great builders.

Between this thinly populated region and eastern Narnia is Ettinsmoor (meaning "giants land"), home to dull-witted evil giants who off and on raid Narnia. These are presumably the giants that Tirian would have fought, but it is possible, even likely, that Peter fought the giants who were the great builders to the north. Perhaps his successful campaign marked the end of their civilization.

To the west of Ettinsmoor and the north of the Lantern Waste in Narnia are lands that have been the home of bandits by the time of *The Last Battle*. In *The Magician's Nephew*, the tree of protection would have been planted along the Great River just south of this area, marking the farthest south Jadis the White Witch could hope to go for the first several hundred years of the world's existence. Narnian kings are curiously unin- terested in conquest, choosing to live within Narnia's tradition- al borders, so the region several miles north of the Great Waterfall and Great River seems to have never had a govern- ment but to have always been wild.

The Western Mountains line the western edge of Narnia, Archenland, the Great Desert, and Calormen. In these moun- tains is the walled garden that Digory enters in *The Magician's Nephew*. It may have always been there during the existence of Narnia's world, but it marks the farthest west any character in *The Chronicles of Narnia* travels. In the northwestern corner of Narnia is the Great Waterfall, which is fed by a river from the mountains. The waterfall feeds the Cauldron Pool, from which flows the Great River. Just south of that area is the Lantern

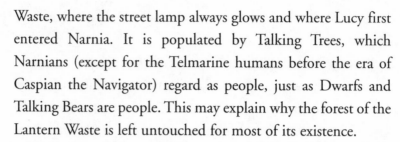

Waste, where the street lamp always glows and where Lucy first entered Narnia. It is populated by Talking Trees, which Narnians (except for the Telmarine humans before the era of Caspian the Navigator) regard as people, just as Dwarfs and Talking Bears are people. This may explain why the forest of the Lantern Waste is left untouched for most of its existence.

The Great River flows southeast, meeting the River Rush somewhat east of the center of Narnia; the two flow together and are called the Great River until the river reaches the sea. The River Rush flows northeast from the mountains of Archenland. Archenland occupies the mountain range that lines the southern border of Narnia from the sea to the Western Mountains. The nation was founded in Narnian year 180 by a son of Narnia's King Frank and Queen Helen, and is the world's second oldest country after Narnia, which was founded by Aslan at the beginning of the world.

South of Archenland is the Great Desert, across which Shasta, Aravis, Bree, and Hwin trek in *The Horse and His Boy*. It is dry, with only a little desert vegetation. It has at least one oasis to the northwest of Tashbaan, but in general it serves as a buffer between Archenland and Calormen. Tisrocs of Calormen have wanted to seize control of the northern nations, but have been discouraged by the desert. The one effort to conquer Archenland that Lewis tells about ends in failure in *The Horse and His Boy*. In *The Last Battle*, it takes traitors such as Shift the Ape and careful planning to enable Calormen finally to conquer Narnia. The cost to Narnia is horrible, because the Calormenes are cruel and kill wantonly.

Calormen extends only a little north into the desert, probably because there is nothing in the desert Calormenes value. There is a river that flows eastward from the Western Mountains to the sea. It is lined on both sides by beautiful homes and glorious gardens and must be quite a sight. At the western end of the river, beside the desert is the city of Tehishbaan, where Emeth of *The Last Battle* comes from. In the eastern river, a few miles from the sea is the capital city of Tashbaan, which covers a mountain-island in a wide spot in the river.

South of the river are cities, farmlands, wild lands, lakes, and hills. Bree and Shasta at first travel through a range of hills along the coast of Calormen in *The Horse and His Boy*. They and Aravis and Hwin then travel through rural areas that suggest that Calormen has a large agrarian economy. Where Aravis begins her journey, at her father's palace, there is a forest to the northwest with shrines to gods in it. Apparently, Calormen preserved large tracts of wild lands within its borders. As evil as he was, Rabadash made it clear that he wanted Narnia left intact, which makes mysterious the Calormene clearcutting of the forests of Narnia in *The Last Battle*. Perhaps something changed in the culture of Calormen between Rabadash's era and that of *The Last Battle,* so that Calormenes no longer valued the wild. To the south of Calormen are some of the nations against whom it periodically wages war.

SECTION III

ANALYSES OF THE
SEVEN NOVELS
OF NARNIA

CHAPTER 9

THE MAGICIAN'S NEPHEW

OVERVIEW

When he was asked in what order *The Chronicles of Narnia* should be read, Lewis always put *The Magician's Nephew* first. It explains the origin of Narnia, the origin of the White Witch, the origin of the Talking Animals and how they were set apart from "dumb" beasts, and how evil was brought into Narnia. Lewis notes, "It is a very important story because it shows how all the comings and goings between our own world and the land of Narnia first began." Of great interest is Digory Kirke's bringing Jadis, the White Witch, into the new world. Aslan is very unhappy about it, and He sets a task for Digory—that of bringing an apple from the Tree of Life back from a remote sacred garden.

THE GEOGRAPHY OF
THE MAGICIAN'S NEPHEW

The events in *The Magician's Nephew* take place in a block of a London residential neighborhood in 1900, in the Wood Between the Worlds, in Charn near the end of its existence, and in Narnia during its first days of existence. The novel begins in houses that are wall-to-wall with each other from one end of a block to another, with all sharing one long attic in common. In front of the houses is a sidewalk lined with street lamps. It is an arm from a street lamp in front of the Ketterleys' house that will give rise to the lamp of the Lantern Waste in Narnia. The street is busy with horse-drawn cabs, and police officers patrol on foot. The depiction of the street resembles neighborhoods in London such as Kensington even today.

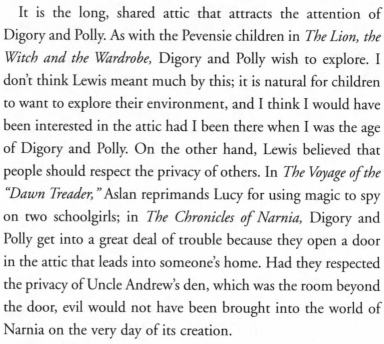

It is the long, shared attic that attracts the attention of Digory and Polly. As with the Pevensie children in *The Lion, the Witch and the Wardrobe,* Digory and Polly wish to explore. I don't think Lewis meant much by this; it is natural for children to want to explore their environment, and I think I would have been interested in the attic had I been there when I was the age of Digory and Polly. On the other hand, Lewis believed that people should respect the privacy of others. In *The Voyage of the "Dawn Treader,"* Aslan reprimands Lucy for using magic to spy on two schoolgirls; in *The Chronicles of Narnia,* Digory and Polly get into a great deal of trouble because they open a door in the attic that leads into someone's home. Had they respected the privacy of Uncle Andrew's den, which was the room beyond the door, evil would not have been brought into the world of Narnia on the very day of its creation.

The Wood Between the Worlds appears only in *The Magician's Nephew* in *The Chronicles of Narnia.* It is a quiet place where evil magic does not work well, and it has tall trees and many ponds. It is a way station between worlds; jump into a pond and you end up in a new world. In contrast, Aslan's Country leads to all worlds and is a far more spectacular place. Perhaps the Wood Between Worlds is a part of Aslan's Country, acting as a place where people can go to Shadow worlds such as earth and the world of Narnia that are outside of Aslan's Country.

Charn is a desolate place, with little life. The city is intimidating with its high doorways and vast rooms and courtyards; it was built for people much taller than most human beings. The only person still living in Charn is Queen Jadis, who is awakened by Digory's ringing the bell. She is proud and cruel, and seems to believe that she has the right to kill anyone she pleases; in fact, she said the Deplorable Word with all the proper rites and killed every being on Charn's world except herself, rather than surrender her queenship to her sister. Charn serves as a warning to earth, for Aslan points out that earth could die as Charn has died. *The Magician's Nephew* was written soon after World War II, and millions of people had been killed in combat and by the byproducts of war such as disease and famine. Furthermore, the Germans, Italians, Fascist French, and Japanese had deliberately slaughtered millions of civilians. More than twelve million people were exterminated in German death camps; more than twenty million Manchurians died as Japan tried to clear the land for Japanese settlement. Thus, Lewis is mindful of how destructive evil can be when he has Aslan point to Charn as an example of what could happen on earth.

The depiction of a dead, cold, lifeless land probably comes in part from Lewis' experiences during World War I. Lewis did not just see "no man's land," he was immersed no man's land. The battles of World War I had made vast tracts of land uninhabitable; nothing lived in these dead cold places except soldiers and the rats that lived in the trenches with the soldiers. Lewis likely saw the French cities that had been made desolate by the conflict. He had ample firsthand experience for describing Charn.

When Digory, Polly, and the rest first land on the world that will become Narnia's world, it is cold, empty, and dark. It must have air, because no one chokes and everyone, except Strawberry, seems able to talk. Lewis describes the creation of

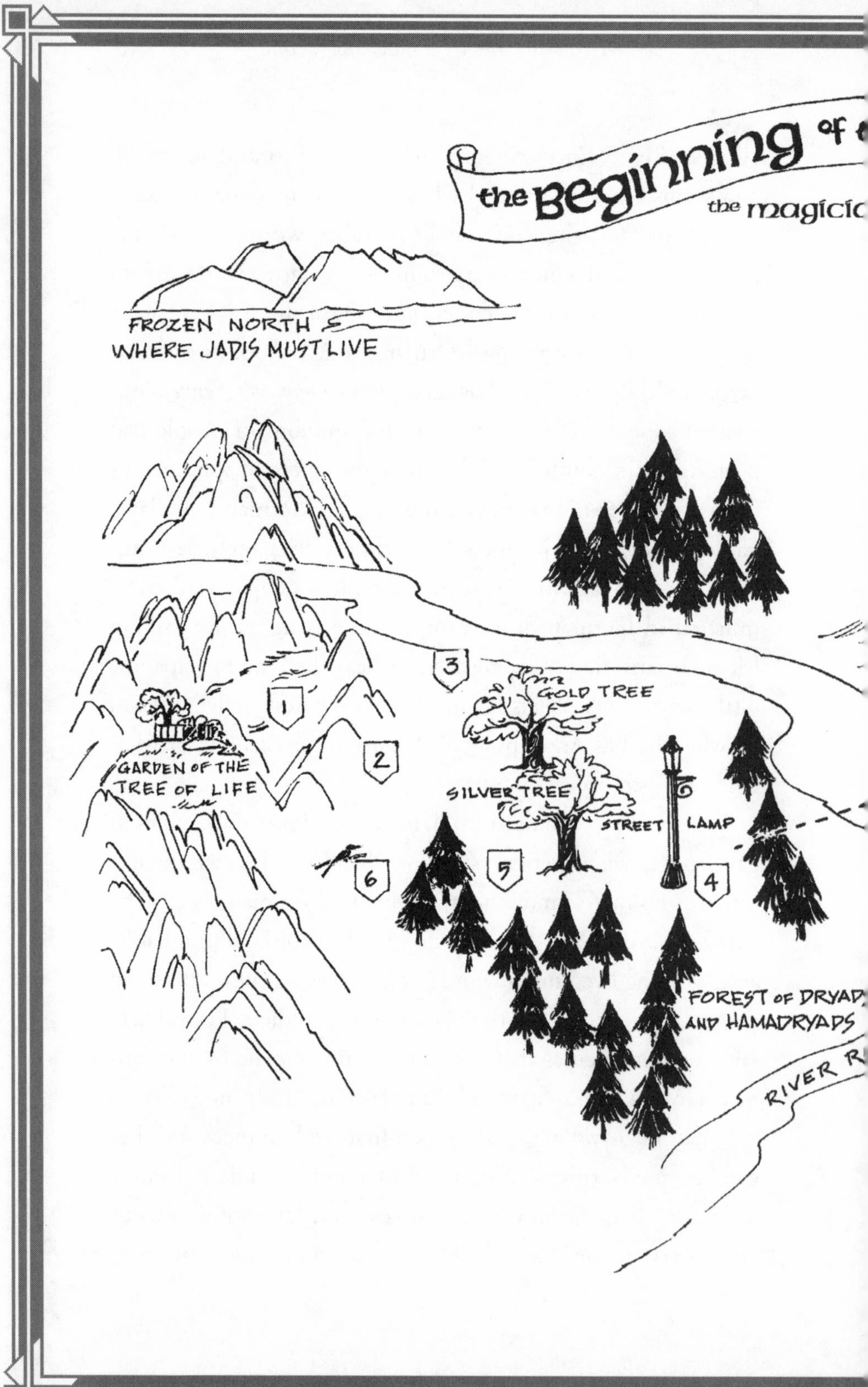

the Beginning of e

the magicia

FROZEN NORTH
WHERE JADIS MUST LIVE

GARDEN OF THE
TREE OF LIFE

1

2

3

GOLD TREE

SILVER TREE

STREET LAMP

5

6

4

FOREST OF DRYAD
AND HAMADRYADS

RIVER R

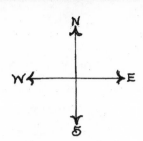

orld in narnia

hew

RIVER SHRIBBLE

ASLAN'S ROUTE ←

GREAT
RIVER

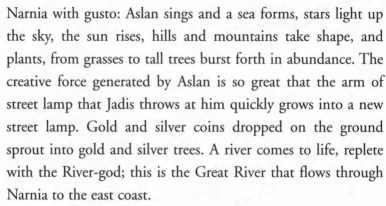

Narnia with gusto: Aslan sings and a sea forms, stars light up the sky, the sun rises, hills and mountains take shape, and plants, from grasses to tall trees burst forth in abundance. The creative force generated by Aslan is so great that the arm of street lamp that Jadis throws at him quickly grows into a new street lamp. Gold and silver coins dropped on the ground sprout into gold and silver trees. A river comes to life, replete with the River-god; this is the Great River that flows through Narnia to the east coast.

Digory has brought evil into the world, against Aslan's hope that the people of Narnia would have hundreds, perhaps thousands, of years of happiness before evil found its way in, so He is unhappy with the boy. Strawberry is turned into the winged horse Fledge and is given the gift of speech. At Aslan's command, he flies Digory and Polly westward into a tall mountain range, in search of a walled garden that has special trees with special fruit. The distance to the garden is about two days flying for Fledge, with time off for sleeping at night. The trio rest in a valley, there planting toffee and growing a toffee tree for food. There may be other such small valleys, but the mountain range is mostly steep sides and peaks.

The garden is entered only by Digory, who has permission to go through the gate in the wall. Climbing over the wall is forbidden, as is taking the fruit without permission, but Jadis does both, giving her eternal life along with eternal misery. Digory notices that the garden seems larger on the inside than on the outside, much as the stable in *The Last Battle* is. This may be a brief glimpse of Aslan's Country, which is enormous on the inside.

THEMES AND CHARACTERS

Aslan pointedly refers to Digory as "Son of Adam" and Polly Plumber as "Daughter of Eve," and he gives Digory a task that echoes Adam's fall in the Garden of Eden. Digory must retrieve an apple from a tree in a garden far to the west of Narnia. Once there, he must enter it properly, through the gates, and he must take one apple without eating any of the fruit of the tree. Where Adam transgressed against God's commandment, Digory does not; he picks the apple, and although sorely tempted by the promise of eternal life that eating the apple would give him, he brings the apple to Aslan. It is flung into a river bank and grows into a barrier that will keep Jadis trapped in the northern wilderness for hundreds of years. This aspect of *The Magician's Nephew* may be Lewis' speculation about how matters might go were Adam to be tempted a second time; it also illustrates the ability of the sinner (Digory) to find his way into God's (Aslan's) good graces through obedience and trustworthy behavior.

Jadis, revived by Digory, had killed all the people of her home planet rather than lose her position as Queen. She has great magical powers, although they curiously do not work when Digory brings her to earth. A megalomaniac, she intends to make herself queen of earth; Digory manages to snatch her from earth, only to bring her to Narnia. She instinctively loathes Aslan, but in an example of His Higher Magic, she is unable to harm Him. In fact, her terrifying magic is useless even against the Higher Magic of the tree planted to protect Narnia. For all her destructive power, she is no match for the creative

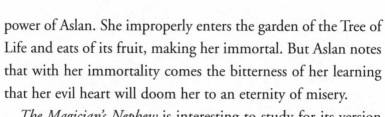

power of Aslan. She improperly enters the garden of the Tree of Life and eats of its fruit, making her immortal. But Aslan notes that with her immortality comes the bitterness of her learning that her evil heart will doom her to an eternity of misery.

The Magician's Nephew is interesting to study for its version of the creation story. Although Lewis was very suspicious of Darwinism (the theory of the evolution of species), he nonetheless studied and absorbed much that modern science has to offer. His imagination had no trouble encompassing the idea that the universe was not only composed of one galaxy of billions of stars—as was supposed until the discoveries of Edwin Hubble and others in the 1920s—but is composed of billions of galaxies with billions of stars each and possibly trillions of planets. He also was not *earth centric,* a phrase meaning a belief that the earth is the most important part of the universe. In Lewis' view, there could be a multitude of creation stories, with planets populated by their own unique peoples. This is the meaning of the Wood between the Worlds, which has many pools of water, each a conduit to a unique world.

Lewis says that in *The Magician's Nephew* he imagined how God might have created a world other than earth. The creation story for Narnia has some of the basic elements of the story found in Genesis. Note how the world that is to become Narnia appears when Digory, Polly, Uncle Andrew, and Jadis first land on it:

> And it [the world] was uncommonly like Nothing. There were no stars. It was so dark that they couldn't see one another at all and it made no difference whether you kept

your eyes shut or opened. Under their feet there was a cool, flat something which might have been earth, and was certainly not grass or wood. The air was cold and dry and there was no wind. (Chapter 8: "The Fight at the Lamp-Post")

This is not only a fine portrait of a nonliving world awaiting its Creator, but a fine conception of an earth that was lifeless until God made it alive. Note how Genesis 1:1-2 describes it:

In the beginning God created the Heaven, and the Earth. / And the earth was without form, and void, and darkness *was* upon the face of the deep: and the Spirit of God moved upon the face of the waters.

This sounds very like the state of affairs for the world-yet-to-be when Aslan begins His singing. Thus *The Magician's Nephew,* more than anything else, is a story of creation, and of the power creation has over destruction.

Yet, note that what God creates, He gives to the people he creates, and in so giving, gives them the power to destroy His worlds. This is the lesson of Charn; it was annihilated by Jadis and the Deplorable Word. Aslan notes that it is gone, as if it never existed. This, He says, could happen to earth and to Narnia, and it is a source of dramatic tension throughout *The Chronicles of Narnia,* for the series is about a frightful war between the forces of creation and destruction for the hearts of the people of Narnia's world, as well as those of the young people who come from earth to Narnia.

CHAPTER-BY-CHAPTER DEVELOPMENT OF THEMES AND CHARACTERS IN *THE MAGICIAN'S NEPHEW*

– Chapter 1: The Wrong Door –

As he does in *The Lion, the Witch and the Wardrobe,* Lewis gives us a mysterious building to explore. In *The Lion, the Witch and the Wardrobe,* it is great old country house; in *The Magician's Nephew,* it is a row of London town houses, all connected by a common attic stretching from one end of the city block to the other. When Digory and Polly begin their adventure, it appears that the strange attic will be the source of suspense and mystery, but Lewis takes a sharp turn. There is an abandoned house on the block that Digory and Polly hope to explore, but when they open the attic door, they come out of the attic one house too soon, into Digory's Uncle Andrew's house.

Digory begins *The Magician's Nephew* as a smart aleck. When Polly tries to apply some common sense to the mystery of the abandoned house by citing her father's view, Digory contemptuously says, "Pooh! Grown-ups are always thinking of uninteresting explanations." He is plainly a very immature young man, and one of the important aspects of the narrative of *The Magician's Nephew* is his growth into a responsible person.

"The Wrong Door" is constructed so as to lure readers into the plot of *The Magician's Nephew*. The principle characters Digory and Polly and their situations are quickly sketched, followed by the surprise of Uncle Andrew's secret room, and then the remarkably evil behavior of Uncle Andrew. The key aspect of Uncle Andrew's contribution to the themes of *The Magician's Nephew* is laid out in the next chapter. In this chapter, he persuades Polly to touch a yellow ring and she immediately vanishes. Polly's disappearance shows that Uncle Andrew is probably the "magician" of *The Magician's Nephew*. It also shows that Uncle Andrew is villainous, because he has enticed a little girl into doing something dangerous that she probably would not wish to do if she knew the consequences. Further, it makes a fine cliffhanger: Where has Polly gone? Is she in danger? At this place in the novel, only Lewis knows.

— Chapter 2: Digory and His Uncle —

Lewis believed that there were certain moral laws that were universal in all cultures. In *The Magician's Nephew*, he defines evil partly by how it defies such laws. Thus, in this chapter, Uncle Andrew declares that rules of moral conduct do not apply to him because he is a great thinker: "Men like me who possess hidden wisdom, are freed from common rules." This is one of the major themes in *The Magician's Nephew*, with the evil Jadis proclaiming herself to be above all moral codes because she is a queen.

Uncle Andrew is revealed to be a megalomaniac (a person who fantasizes about having wealth, power, or omnipotence) and the magician of the title, making Digory the nephew of the title. Digory displays a couple of his positive characteristics, loyalty to a friend and enough insight into other people to recognize that his Uncle Andrew is a wicked, cruel magician. He may be impulsive, but he is self-assured and clear headed while facing down his despicable uncle.

– Chapter 3: The Wood between the Worlds –

"It's not the sort of place where things happen. The trees go on growing, that's all," says Digory about the woods between the Worlds. In this chapter Lewis tells about the organization of the Narnian universe and in so doing reveals some of the care with which he constructs his narrative. Digory's characterization gains added depth when he suggests that Uncle Andrew talked of only one world but that dozens of other worlds might exist. Digory shows himself to have the intelligence and imagination to recognize some of the complexity represented by the Wood between the Worlds.

Digory compares the woods to the tunnel under the slates at home: from the tunnel you can enter any of the houses in the row. The tunnel and the Woods between the Worlds are similar to the attic that spans all the houses along the block? It too connects many places with one room, but when Digory and Polly opened a door in the attic, they emerged into a very bad place, where evil was afoot. Their stepping into a pool to travel to a world is much like their opening an attic door without knowing what was on the other side. In "The Wood between the Worlds," they again emerge in a bad place, Charn. This image of doorways or pools offering passage to other places is repeated in *The Magician's Nephew*. Of special interest is what happens when Digory knows where he is going when he reaches the western garden in Narnia; the results are very different when he has knowledge of what he is doing, rather than acting on impulse. Lewis said that "Digory was the sort of person who wants to know everything, and when he grew up he became the famous Professor Kirke who comes into other books." It is interesting to note that Lewis had already written *The Lion, the Witch and the Wardrobe* by the time he wrote *The Magician's Nephew,* so he is able to make remarks that help tie the series of Narnia novels together. Such remarks also help give Narnia a history, as if it were a real place.

— Chapter 4: The Bell and the Hammer —

Is fear good or bad? This is the nettlesome question raised in "The Bell and the Hammer." In his determination to show no fear Digory does something very foolish. It is not so much his ringing the bell that is foolish as his ignoring Polly's warning and then hurting her just to satisfy his impulse. Had he listened to his fear, he might have avoided doing great harm. This is a curious idea, that fear can be good, but it is typical of Lewis to express a curious idea in order to make a point. What Digory actually does when he hurts Polly is to ignore his heart; throughout *The Chronicles of Narnia* God speaks through the heart, and His voice is ignored only at great peril.

Digory impulsively ignores fear to enter a strange room, then to enter a strange pool, and then to ring a bell just because an inscription dares him to do it. When he thinks, he does better. He overcomes his fear to go to help Polly after a yellow ring whisks her away by considering his alternatives. Fear shows up in many characters when they do not understand their circumstances. Of special note is the fear Jadis and Uncle Andrew feel when they hear the singing of Aslan.

– Chapter 5: The Deplorable Word –

This is an important chapter not only for *The Magician's Nephew* but for the Narnian series as a whole. In *The Lion, the Witch and the Wardrobe,* Lewis creates one of literature's most frightful and awesome villains. Jadis' claiming of Edmund as her lawful prey is just plain terrifying. Since *The Magician's Nephew* is meant to be the novel that introduces the major aspects of *The Chronicles of Narnia,* the introduction of Jadis in "The Deplorable Word" needs to be carefully considered.

Given her awesome stature in *The Chronicles of Narnia,* Lewis' method of fleshing out Jadis' personality is an odd combination of utter evil and pathetic ridiculousness. She is over seven feet tall, carries herself proudly, and is a megalomaniac of grand proportions. She declares, "I, Jadis, the last Queen, but the Queen of the World." Her world is Charn, a dead and desolate place. The city that Digory and Polly explore is magnificent, built on a monumental scale. Once it teemed with people, but now it is dead. The horrible meaning of Jadis's statement is that she was about to be overthrown by her sister, and rather than lose the crown, she spoke "the Deplorable Word"—a word that if spoken a special way will kill everything on Charn: "It had long been known to the great kings of our race that there was a word which, if spoken with the proper ceremonies, would destroy all living things except the one who spoke it." By speaking it, Jadis made herself both the last queen and the Queen of the World, even though she is queen of the world because no one lives to challenge her rule.

She is a mass murderer on an enormous scale. She killed everyone just so she could call herself Queen. This makes her a truly evil enemy—someone who would defy Aslan rather than acknowledge His supremacy. On the other hand, Lewis under-

cuts her grand vision of herself, and in so doing invites us to observe her pathetic foolishness. He does this by paralleling her

with a truly pathetic megalomaniac, Uncle Andrew. She tells Digory and Polly that "what would be wrong for you or for any

of the common people is not wrong in a great Queen such as I." This attitude is exactly that of Uncle Andrew as we have seen

in the first two chapters. But where Uncle Andrew's insistence that no moral rules apply to him endangers the lives of a cou-

ple of innocent youngsters, Jadis shows how the rejection of universal moral laws carried to its ultimate logical end results in

horrors that defy full understanding. It is hard to imagine mur-

dering billions of people all at once!

At the time Lewis wrote *The Magician's Nephew,* some read-

ers thought that Jadis was his expression of Hitler, Mussolini, and Stalin, but in Jadis, Lewis attains a more universal expres-

sion of his ideas of what constitutes evil. It is easy, these many decades later, to see her action duplicated by dictators in

Cambodia by Pol Pot, in Uganda by Idi Amin, and by others who believe themselves to be above the moral laws of common

people. They are all hateful, and when compared to Aslan (Christ), they are every bit as ridiculous and foolish as Uncle

Andrew. With his presentation of Jadis in "The Deplorable Word," Lewis further develops his ideas of how evil may be

founded in utter selfishness, as well as his belief that moral conduct may be found in respect for the lives of others. Both these themes have by now become central to the purpose of *The Magician's Nephew*.

— Chapter 6: The Beginning of Uncle Andrew's Troubles —

Lewis notes, "In Charn, she [Jadis] took no notice of Polly (till the very end) because Digory was the one she wanted to make use of. Now that she had Uncle Andrew, she took no notice of Digory. I expect most witches are like that. They are not interested in things or people unless they can use them; they are terribly practical." Uncle Andrew finds himself in the company of his own kind, but where he is a dabbler in the occult, she is a mighty practitioner. Much of the humor in this chapter derives from Uncle Andrew's receiving a taste of his own medicine. Lewis further develops his theme of evil grounded in selfishness by noting how practical witches are; they use people and do not respect them.

The notion of witches and witchcraft in *The Chronicles of Narnia* is taken primarily from the multitude of folk tales from many cultures that Lewis had read, but he did, in fact, believe the occult was a fact, and he regarded it as utterly evil. He even ascribed the insanity of an acquaintance to that man's dabbling in the occult. Thus, what Uncle Andrew has been doing is very dangerous and results in the bringing of great evil—Jadis—to earth.

— Chapter 7: What Happened at the Front Door —

It is important to note that the Narnia novels are not all heavy thinking about morals and morality: all of the novels have abundant comedy. Thus, in this chapter not only the important work of showing how pathetic Jadis's monomania is, but entertaining comedy is presented. When Jadis's magic does not work in London, there is a hint of the humiliation to come, and Uncle Andrew's praise of her as a "dem fine woman" adds to the picture of her as someone who has seriously misjudged earth and its people. When Jadis appears, standing atop a hansom cab, seven feet tall and lashing a whip while her royal charger races along the street, she is at once a magnificent, amazing sight, and ridiculous. Her charger is Strawberry, a horse that spends its days pulling a cab along the streets of London. Her carriage is a wobbly, two-wheeled affair, and her airs of royalty are silly in a world that knows nothing about her. As for why her magic does not work, could it be that on earth Christ has already made His sacrifice, enabling people to draw on the Deeper Magic of God and making the powers of the occult weak, even trivial?

Digory's Aunt Letty hints that Digory's mother is dying. "I'm afraid it would need fruit from the land of youth to help her now," she says to Digory. "Nothing in *this* world will do much." These remarks offer the foundation for Digory's behavior in the last few chapters of *The Magician's Nephew*, and help explain the ending.

— Chapter 8: The Fight at the Lamp-Post —

There is no telling what damage Jadis might have done on earth had she stayed in London very long, but she would have needed more than her ego, height, and great physical strength to make herself ruler of the world. The crowd gathered at the lamp-post hails her as "Hempress of Colney 'Atch" (Colny Hatch was an insane asylum) and even as she bows in recognition of their acclaim they burst into laughter.

But she might have preferred the rough indignity of a crowd on a London street to what awaits her in the world she next visits. Weakened to the point of being crippled in the Wood between the Worlds, she manages to trick Digory into letting her grab hold of him when he, Polly, and Uncle Andrew leap into a pool. Where they end up is utterly desolate. There is nothing but darkness and the ground, to Jadis an empty world, nothing.

This marks the beginning of Narnia's creation story. Lewis said that he imagined God creating another world, and then imagined how that world's creation might progress—he did not think it would be identical to that of earth. For Narnia, it begins with a voice that turns out to be that of Aslan, a large golden lion, who by singing different songs creates the various elements of Narnia's world, from a sunrise to oceans to mountains to plants, especially trees, and to living creatures. Creating a whole world in minutes out of nothing must be a very challenging task, and Aslan explains that the newly created world is going through a brief period of ferocious fertility. Trees sprout up and are full grown in moments; the piece of the lamp-post, once on the ground, sprouts up into a full lamp-post. Coins dropped on the ground become golden and silver plants.

John writes (John 1:1-3), "In the beginning was the Word, & the Word was with God, and the Word was God./The same was in the beginning with God./All things were made by him, and without him was not any thing made that was made." In the present chapter, Lewis writes, "A voice had begun to sing." For Digory the noise "was, beyond comparison, the most beautiful noise he had ever heard." This voice makes the ground shake deep inside, and it gives rise to a young, magnificent sun. According to Lewis, "If you had seen and heard it, as Digory did, you would have felt quite certain that it was the stars themselves who were singing, and that it was the First Voice, the deep one, which had made them appear and made them sing." The Song of Aslan parallels the Word of Christ. Lewis' achievement, here, is extraordinary. He takes the idea of Christ as the Word that created the world and hears It as a Song, that the act of creation was magnificent music, and makes the event come alive with vivid descriptions. One can imagine such a Song making plants and animals spring out of the earth, as they do in the next chapter.

Lewis also touches on one of the important *mysteries* of the Christian faith: that God and the Word were separate and yet the same, as John says in his second verse. Aslan creates the world of Narnia at His Father's behest, which means that Aslan and the Emperor-over-sea are two separate beings, yet Aslan's song comes from the power of His Father, something that is emphasized throughout *The Chronicles of Narnia*. This makes Them One. Thus Aslan is a singer and an instrument of His

Father, yet He also personifies the act of creation, a power that comes from the Father. This power unifies Father and Son. In *The Horse and His Boy,* when Shasta hears three voices in the fog of Archenland's mountains, Lewis adds the Holy Spirit to the mix, because the Holy Spirit is a separate presence in each faithful person and also a manifestation of God.

In the Bible, evil comes early in earth's history, with the destruction of paradise. In *The Magician's Nephew,* evil is present at the moment of creation. This angers Aslan, because He sees another paradise about to be spoiled. He uses Digory, Polly, and Fledge to help salvage at least a few hundred years of happiness for Narnia, but He already knows of the sacrifice to come.

— Chapter 9: The Founding of Narnia —

Here is found the theme of creation. The singing of Aslan frightens Uncle Andrew, but it seems to terrify Jadis, who flings the arm of the lamp-post at Aslan, striking Him in the forehead. He shows no sign of having noticed the blow. "The Witch shrieked and ran: in a few moments she was out of sight among the trees." "A spirited gel, sir. It's a pity about her temper," says Uncle Andrew of Jadis, once again missing the point of what he observes. Evil despises and fears Aslan's power to create; it dwarfs evil's ability to destroy.

Lewis offers a wonderful account of the creation of living things. Animals burst out of humps in the ground, the "grassy land bubbling like water in a pot." The Lion says in "the deepest, wildest voice they had ever heard": "Narnia, Narnia, awake. Love. Think. Speak. Be walking trees. Be Talking Beasts. Be divine waters." His words make the world come alive, with all sorts of animals and plants appearing. The thinking beasts and trees immediately gravitate toward Aslan.

— Chapter 10: The First Joke and Other Matters —

The undercurrent of this chapter is the revelation that Aslan is not a one-dimensional serious Lord. At the command that ended the previous chapter, "Out of the trees wild people stepped forth, gods and goddesses of the wood; with them came Fauns and Satyrs and Dwarfs. Out of the river rose the river god with his Naiad daughters." To some of the animals, Aslan gives speech, and in an awkward moment the Jackdaw is heard to cry "No fear!"—making the other animals laugh. "Laugh and fear not, creatures. Now that you are no longer dumb and witless, you need not always be grave. For jokes as well as justice come in with speech," says Aslan. This is important for developing Lewis' view of Aslan; he sees Him as having a sense of humor, as taking pleasure in the happiness and fun of His people.

While Digory, Polly, and the cabby enjoy what they see and marvel at Aslan, Uncle Andrew is frightened. Where the others hear animals speaking and making jokes, Uncle Andrew hears only growling and grunting: "For what you see and hear depends a good deal on where you are standing: it also depends on what sort of person you are." In Lewis' view, the truth of God manifests itself for anyone who will make an effort to see it. He attributed his own years of atheism to an effort to deny the evidence of God's existence that was all around him. In *The*

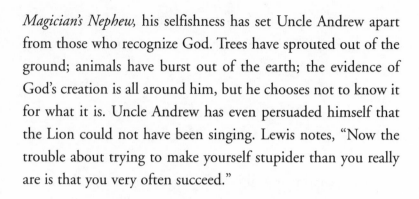

Magician's Nephew, his selfishness has set Uncle Andrew apart from those who recognize God. Trees have sprouted out of the ground; animals have burst out of the earth; the evidence of God's creation is all around him, but he chooses not to know it for what it is. Uncle Andrew has even persuaded himself that the Lion could not have been singing. Lewis notes, "Now the trouble about trying to make yourself stupider than you really are is that you very often succeed."

— Chapter 11: Digory and His Uncle Are Both in Trouble —

Aslan distinguishes between Digory and Polly and the people of Narnia by calling Digory "Son of Adam" and Polly "Daughter of Eve." Lewis will use these phrases to distinguish people of earthly ancestry from those of Narnian ancestry throughout *The Chronicles of Narnia*.

In this chapter Lewis draws the strongest parallels between Narnia's situation and that of earth. Aslan says, "Evil will come of that evil [Jadis], but it is a long way off, and I will see to it that the worst falls upon myself." Here, Aslan predicts his sacrifice in *The Lion, the Witch and the Wardrobe,* paralleling the notion that Jesus knew ahead of time that he was to be sacrificed for the sins of humanity. Further, Aslan declares, "And as Adam's race has done the harm, Adam's race shall help to heal it." This recalls I Corinthians 15:21, which says, "For since by man *came* death, by man *came* also the resurrection of the dead."

Aslan declares the Cabby Frank and his wife Helen the first King and Queen of Narnia, making them something akin to

Noah and Noah's wife. As is the case with the descendants of Noah, the descendants of Frank and Helen spread out of Narnia and throughout their world, to such places as "Archenland which lies yonder over the Southern Mountains." There seem to be plenty of humans for the descendants of Frank and Helen to marry without inbreeding.

— Chapter 12: Strawberry's Adventure —

Aslan proves Himself not only capable of fun and laughter, but of feeling grief, as well. When Digory pleads for help to save his mother's life, Lewis notes that great shining tears stood in the Lion's eyes. Aslan sends Digory and Polly on a mission to retrieve an apple from a tree in a walled garden in the Western Wild. This must be especially difficult on Digory, who must retrieve the apple to compensate for bringing evil to Narnia, even while not knowing whether Aslan will help his mother, who lives in another world.

Aslan performs many miracles in *The Magician's Nephew,* and one of the most spectacular is the one he performs on Strawberry, whom Aslan renames "Fledge": "'Be winged. Be the father of all flying horses,' roared Aslan in a voice that shook the ground. 'Your name is Fledge.'" This is another example of Aslan's great creative power. From the air, the trio of Fledge, Digory, and Polly see some of the immensity of Aslan's creation, with "jagged mountains appearing beyond the northern moors, and plains of what looked like sand far in the south."

– Chapter 13: An Unexpected Meeting –

In a letter to a young reader named Patricia, Lewis says, "Jadis plucking the apple is like Adam's sin, an act of disobedience, but it doesn't fill the same place in her life as his plucking did in his. She was *already* fallen (very much so) before she ate it." (C. S. Lewis, *Letters to Children*, 1985, pp. 92-93.)

Lewis had once thought he would become a great poet, which may be why he scatters verses through his fiction and nonfiction. In *The Magician's Nephew,* he places this one on the gate to the private garden:

> Come in by the gold gates or not at all,
> Take of my fruit for others or forbear.
> For those who steal or those who climb my wall
> Shall find their heart's desire and find despair.

The point of entering through the gates is that only those who are legitimately invited may enter the garden. This why the gates open easily for Digory, but Jadis must climb the wall. She is not welcome. The fruit may only be gifts; the theme of selfishness is implied, here. Taking the fruit for oneself results in a contradictory sort of disaster: having one's heart's desire while simultaneously finding despair. Jadis illustrates how this works by eating fruit that was not hers to take. She receives eternal life, but the evil in her heart makes that life a misery.

The garden seems to have a personality like Aslan's: quiet, with the pleasant sound of a fountain in the garden and lovely smells. "It was a happy place but very serious"; much like

Aslan, Who is happy and serious at the same time. Like the Serpent in the Garden of Eden, Jadis urges Digory to eat the fruit, and Digory is very tempted to do so: he longed to eat the fruit. But this is in the world of Narnia, not on earth, and Narnia veers away from earth's events when Digory resists temptation and retrieves the apple. Whereas he was an impulsive, unthinking youngster at the start of *The Magician's Nephew,* he has become more thoughtful, taking the time to use his mind to think through the meaning of the verses at the gate, as well as his promise to Aslan. With this thoughtfulness comes power: He is able to resist a terrible temptation and to stand up to Jadis, who had frightened him. He may not know it, but he has through trials and intelligence become a dangerous adversary.

— Chapter 14: The Planting of the Tree —

Digory had warned Uncle Andrew that he would be punished for his evil deeds, and Uncle Andrew gets what he deserves. That the Talking Animals mistake him for either a dumb animal or a plant is funny; it also suggests how much Uncle Andrew has debased himself. Even the innocent people of Narnia do not recognize him as a thinking being. As far as Uncle Andrew is concerned, he is being manhandled by a bunch of wild animals; he does not understand their speech. In their turn, they call him "Brandy," because he is constantly saying that word. He has worked so hard at making himself stupid that he does not even understand the beautiful, loud voice of Aslan, Who notes that "he has made himself unable to hear my voice." There is a world of wonders around Uncle Andrew, and he sees none of its miraculousness and beauty.

Aslan is forgiving, and once Digory has planted the silver apple, He tells Digory to take of the fruit of the tree to his mother. It is notable that while Jadis's evil magic fizzles on earth, Aslan's Deeper Magic seems to work everywhere. He needs no magic rings to bring Helen from earth to Narnia, and He plainly expects a magical apple from Narnia to work on earth. The point is that Aslan's power is universal, for all creation is His.

— Chapter 15: The End of This Story and the Beginning of All the Others —

Most of this chapter is devoted to setting up the rest of the novels in the Narnia series, but there is an allusion to the affairs of the people of earth:

> "When you were last here [the Wood between the Worlds]," said Aslan, "that hollow was a pool, and when you jumped into it you came to the world where a dying sun shone over the ruins of Charn. There is no pool now. That world is ended, as if it had never been. Let the race of Adam and Eve take warning."

Lewis avoids being preachy through almost all of *The Chronicles of Narnia*, but he may be forgiven for being a little bit preachy, here. He began *The Chronicles of Narnia* just as World War II broke out, and wrote much of *The Lion, the Witch and the Wardrobe* during the war. He also had served in World War I, during which he was not only gravely wounded but had seen men, friends of his, literally blown to pieces, including one who was standing right beside him. Given the terrible evils perpetrated during both wars, Lewis has Aslan point out that humanity needs to improve its behavior, to take warning from the fate of a world in which everyone but one died in its last war.

"The Apple of Life" Aslan gives to Digory offers a connection between *The Magician's Nephew* and *The Lion, the Witch and the Wardrobe*. Eating the apple cures Digory's mother—it is like a miracle, says her doctor, and that is what it is. It is also further proof that Aslan's power extends over earth as well as Narnia. Where Digory buries the apple core, a tree quickly grows. A storm blows the tree over, and Digory, now grown up, has it made into a wardrobe. He inherits the great big house in the country (the same as in *The Lion, the Witch and the Wardrobe*), and in it he puts the wardrobe. This wardrobe was made from a tree that had its origins in the Tree of Life, a part of the Deeper Magic that works everywhere in the universe, including earth. Thus it has magical powers that Lucy Pevensie discovers in *The Lion, the Witch and the Wardrobe*. This makes for an elegantly smooth transition from one novel to the next.

VOCABULARY FOR
THE MAGICIAN'S NEPHEW

CHAPTER 1: THE WRONG DOOR
do a sum: do an arithmetic problem
I'm game: I'm willing
We'd better bunk: an archaic phrase meaning run away or run

and hide
duffer: stupid person

Chapter 2: Digory and His Uncle
paid out in the end: to be punished for one's evil deeds

Chapter 3: The Wood between the World
pluck as in never had the pluck: courage or daring
gassing about it: talking excessively (a mildly insulting phrase)

Chapter 6: The Beginning of Uncle Andrew's Troubles
be decent: be honorable or unselfish
we'll call it Pax: we'll stop fighting
Pax: peace
eye-glass: monocle
dem: damn

Chapter 7: What Happened at the Front Door
sal volatile: smelling salts
hansom: a horse-drawn carriage with two wheels, a covered
    seat, and a seat above and behind, where the driver sits;
    commonly used as taxicabs in London before the advent of
    automobiles; Jadis must have been quite a sight standing
    seven-feet tall on top!
trams: streetcars
footpath: sidewalk

Chapter 8: The Fight at the Lamp-Post
spirits: alcoholic beverage

CHAPTER 9: THE FOUNDING OF NARNIA

Yeomanry: Uncle Andrew is probably referring to a cavalry unit in the Territorial Army

CHAPTER 11: DIGORY AND HIS UNCLE ARE BOTH IN TROUBLE

It's a fair treat: It's delightful

chap: man

use it hardly: be cruel to it

CHAPTER 12: STRAWBERRY'S ADVENTURE

curvetted: A horse is said to *curvet* when it leaps in the air with all four legs off the ground, with the forelegs returning to earth before the hind ones; *curvet* also means to prance; either way, Fledge is enjoying himself.

rum go: odd sight.

tuck in: eat heartily

CHAPTER 13: AN UNEXPECTED MEETING

herb called honesty: a European and Asian plant with fragrant, purple flowers and seed pods that are flat, white, and paperlike.

What's your game?: What's your scheme or plot? The phrase implies that someone is trying to dupe someone else into doing something stupid or wrong.

REFERENCES TO THE BIBLE IN
THE MAGICIAN'S NEPHEW

The passage from *The Magician's Nephew* is first quoted, followed by the relevant passage in the Bible. A transliteration of

the 1611 edition of the King James version of the Bible is used for the Biblical quotations. Comments then follow.

— Chapter 8: The Fight at the Lamp-Post —

1. "And really it was uncommonly like Nothing. There were no stars. It was so dark that they couldn't see one another at all and it made no difference whether you kept your eyes shut or opened. Under their feet there was a cool, flat something which might have been earth, and was certainly not grass or wood. The air was cold and dry and there was no wind."

> **Genesis 1:2:** "And the earth was without form, and void, and darkness *was* upon the face of the deep; and the Spirit of God moved upon the face of the waters."

Comments: Lewis is following the creation pattern outlined in Genesis. He is trying to convey what creation would be like to someone actually witnessing it.

2. "A voice had begun to sing. It was very far away and Digory found it hard to decide from what direction it was coming. Sometimes it seemed to come from all directions at once. Sometimes he almost thought it was coming out of the earth beneath them. Its lower notes were deep enough to be the voice of the earth herself. There were no words. There was hardly even a tune. But it was, beyond comparison, the most beautiful noise he had ever heard. It was so beautiful he could hardly bear it."

Genesis 1:2, conclusion: ". . . and the Spirit of God moved upon the face of the waters."

Comments: The song is Lewis' way of depicting God's Spirit moving across the world; it is a way of making the passage in Genesis concrete.

3. "One moment there had been nothing but darkness; next moment a thousand, thousand points of light leaped out—single stars, constellations, and planets, brighter and bigger than any in our world."

> **Genesis 1:14:** "And God said, 'Let there be lights in the firmament of the heaven, to divide the day from the night: and let them be for signs and for seasons, and for days and for years.'"

Comments: What Lewis describes seems well suited to the idea of creating a night sky that will provide signs and help identify seasons. These are the literal signs of the constellations that help ships navigate and which change throughout the year. The signs are also symbolic of God's power and will.

4. "If you had seen and heard it, as Digory did, you would have felt quite certain that it was the stars themselves who were singing, and that it was the First Voice, the deep one, which had made them appear and made them sing."

> **Job 38:7:** "When the morning star sang together, and all the sons of God shouted for joy."

Comments: Lewis here draws a parallel with a time of innocence, when the universe itself seemed to sing for joy.

— Chapter 9: The Founding of Narnia —

5. "Can you imagine a stretch of grassy land bubbling like water in a pot? For that is really the best description of what was happening. In all directions it was swelling into humps. They were of very different sizes, some bigger than mole-hills, some as big as wheelbarrows, two the size of cottages. And the humps moved and swelled till they burst, and the crumbled earth poured out of them, and from each hump there came out an animal."

> **Genesis 1:24:** "And God said, 'Let the earth bring forth living creatures according to their kinds: cattle and creeping things and beasts of the earth according to their kind,' and it was so." (See also Genesis 2:19, quoted in number 7, below.)

Comments: Lewis brings imagination and color to the idea of earth bringing forth animals. This is an example of his imagining how creation might look on another world.

— Chapter 11: Digory and His Uncle Are Both in Trouble —

6. "And as Adam's race has done the harm, Adam's race shall help to heal it."

I Corinthians 15:21: "For since by man *came* death, by man *came* also the resurrection of the dead."

Romans 5:19: "For as by one man's disobedience many were made sinners: so by the obedience of one, shall many be made righteous."

Comments: This is more than just a parallel with a Biblical passage; it is an example of Aslan and God's fairness and compassion. Those who have sinned are given the chance of redemption.

7. "You shall rule and name all these creatures, and do justice among them, and protect them from their enemies when enemies arise." (Aslan speaking to the Cabby.)

Genesis 2:19: "And out of the ground the LORD God formed every beast of the field, and every foul of the air, and brought *them* unto Adam, to see what he would call them: and whatsoever Adam called every living creature, that *was* the name thereof."

Comments: Even though the Cabby, a Son of Adam, is from earth, not Narnia, in Narnia as in Eden, man is charged with naming the animals, implying a supremacy over the animals.

— Chapter 12: Strawberry's Adventure —

8. "'My son, my son,' said Aslan. 'I know. Grief is great. Only you and I in this land know that yet.'"

> **II Samuel 18:33:** "And the king was much moved, and went up to the chamber over the gate, and wept; and as he went, he said, 'O my son Absalom, my son, my son Absalom. Would I have died instead of you.'"

Comments: Digory is surprised by Aslan's tears, but Lewis refers to a famous scriptural passage to clarify; the passage is about overwhelming grief. It also suggests the sacrifice Christ will make by dying for God's children, as well as Aslan's sacrifice for Edmund in *The Lion, the Witch and the Wardrobe*.

— Chapter 14: The Planting of the Tree —

9. "'Well done,' said Aslan in a voice that made the earth shake." (Aslan here praises Digory for bringing Him an apple from the Tree of Life.)

> **Matthew 25:21:** "His lord said unto him, Well done, thou good and faithful servant, thou hast been faithful over a few things, I will make thee ruler over many things: enter thou into the joy of thy lord."

Comments: The passage in Matthew refers to the servant who turned a few talents into many; given opportunity, he has made himself a better man. So, too, has Digory developed his own resources of intelligence, wisdom, courage, and fortitude.

DISCUSSION QUESTIONS AND PROJECTS FOR *THE MAGICIAN'S NEPHEW*

— Overview —

1. Lewis says that *The Magician's Nephew* is a very important story because it shows how the connections between our own world and the land of Narnia first began. Does the novel answer all your questions about why people from earth are found in the world of Narnia?

2. Although Lewis says that *The Magician's Nephew* is the first book to read in *The Chronicles of Narnia,* some readers believe that *The Lion, the Witch and the Wardrobe* should be read first because it was written first. Present your ideas for both arguments.

3. Why would Aslan be angry at Digory for bringing Jadis to Narnia? Was this Digory's fault?

4. What is the significance of Digory's faithfully bringing the silver apple to Aslan?

5. Lewis said that *The Chronicles of Narnia* was in part his speculation about how God might interact with a world other than earth. Discuss the parallels and differences in *The Magician's Nephew* between God creating the earth and Aslan creating Narnia.

6. In what ways does Digory mature during *The Magician's Nephew*? What qualities does he possess at the novel's end that he did not have at its start?

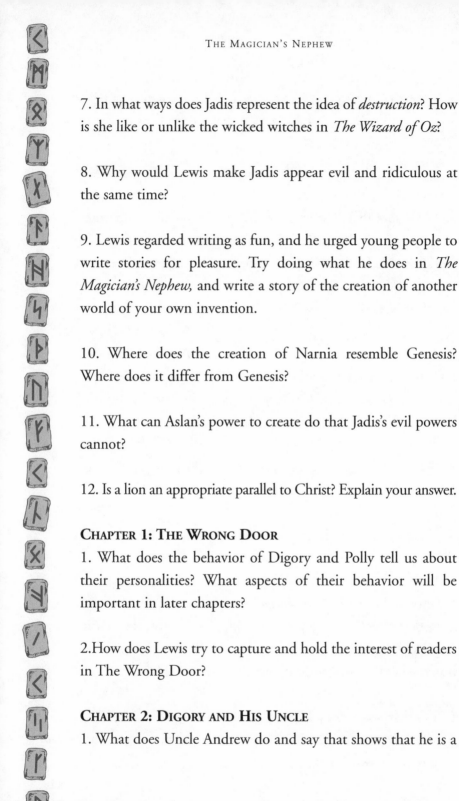

7. In what ways does Jadis represent the idea of *destruction*? How is she like or unlike the wicked witches in *The Wizard of Oz*?

8. Why would Lewis make Jadis appear evil and ridiculous at the same time?

9. Lewis regarded writing as fun, and he urged young people to write stories for pleasure. Try doing what he does in *The Magician's Nephew*, and write a story of the creation of another world of your own invention.

10. Where does the creation of Narnia resemble Genesis? Where does it differ from Genesis?

11. What can Aslan's power to create do that Jadis's evil powers cannot?

12. Is a lion an appropriate parallel to Christ? Explain your answer.

CHAPTER 1: THE WRONG DOOR
1. What does the behavior of Digory and Polly tell us about their personalities? What aspects of their behavior will be important in later chapters?

2.How does Lewis try to capture and hold the interest of readers in The Wrong Door?

CHAPTER 2: DIGORY AND HIS UNCLE
1. What does Uncle Andrew do and say that shows that he is a

bad man? How will his bad traits result in his being punished in the end?

2. What moral laws does Uncle Andrew violate in this chapter?

CHAPTER 3: THE WOOD BETWEEN THE WORLDS

1. Why do Digory and Polly enter the pool that takes them to Charn?

2. The Wood between the Worlds has many pools. Write a story in which someone uses the pools to visit other worlds. What would the worlds be like? Would they offer adventures like those in Charn and Narnia?

CHAPTER 4: THE BELL AND THE HAMMER

1. In Chapter 3, Lewis points out that Digory likes to acquire knowledge, and this characteristic may explain his wanting to ring the bell, but why would he hurt Polly in order to do so?

2. Does his ringing the bell make Digory responsible for Jadis?

CHAPTER 5: THE DEPLORABLE WORD

1. Why would Jadis be proud to be the queen of an unpopulated world?

2. Does Lewis trivialize mass murder in this chapter?

CHAPTER 6: THE BEGINNING OF UNCLE ANDREW'S TROUBLES

1. In what ways is Jadis terribly practical?

2. Why does Uncle Andrew admire Jadis?

CHAPTER 7: WHAT HAPPENED AT THE FRONT DOOR
1. What is comical about this chapter?

2. What does Jadis's behavior reveal about her?

CHAPTER 8: THE FIGHT AT THE LAMP-POST
1. What happens at the lamp-post that ties in with *The Lion, the Witch and the Wardrobe*?

2. Why is Jadis almost crippled in the Wood between the Worlds?

CHAPTER 9: THE FOUNDING OF NARNIA
1. Why would Lewis choose to have Aslan sing Narnia into being?

2. What is the order in which the new world is created?

3. Why does Aslan not do something about Jadis when she throws the piece of lamp-post at Him, hitting Him in the head?

CHAPTER 10: THE FIRST JOKE AND OTHER MATTERS
1. Why does Lewis make a point of laughter being part of Narnia's creation?

2. What are the important differences among the points of view of Digory, Polly, the Cabby, and Uncle Andrew?

3. What does Lewis mean by "Now the trouble about trying to make yourself stupider than you really are is that you very often succeed"?

CHAPTER 11: DIGORY AND HIS UNCLE ARE BOTH IN TROUBLE
1. What does Aslan mean by "And as Adam's race has done the harm, Adam's race shall help to heal it"?

2. Why does Aslan emphasize that Digory and Polly are outsiders by calling them Son of Adam and Daughter of Eve?

3. Why does Aslan declare the Cabby Frank and his wife Helen the first King and Queen of Narnia? Is this symbolic?

CHAPTER 12: STRAWBERRY'S ADVENTURE
1. Why are there tears in Aslan's eyes? What does this say about Him?

2. Why does Aslan rename Strawberry? Is there a meaning behind the name "Fledge"?

CHAPTER 13: AN UNEXPECTED MEETING
1. Why does Digory not eat the silver apple when Jadis tries to persuade him to do so? How does he resist eating the apple when its smell makes him very thirsty and hungry?

2. Would the Digory of Chapter 1 have eaten the apple? What changes have occurred in him that makes it easier for him to resist temptation?

CHAPTER 14: THE PLANTING OF THE TREE

1. Why do the Talking Animals of Narnia think Uncle Andrew is a dumb beast or a plant?

2. Why would Digory and his mother have been miserable if he had taken an apple from the Tree of Life without Aslan's permission?

CHAPTER 15: THE END OF THIS STORY AND THE BEGINNING OF ALL THE OTHERS

1. Are you satisfied with how *The Magician's Nephew* ends? Is there anything missing?

2. Why would Aslan want the rings disposed of?

3. Write a story about what would happen if some people accidentally dug up the rings. They might be construction workers or children playing a game.

CHAPTER 10

THE LION, THE WITCH
AND THE WARDROBE

OVERVIEW

This was the first published and is the most famous of the Narnian novels. Lewis began it in the late 1930s, having been inspired by Tolkien's work on *The Hobbit* and *The Lord of the Rings*. Initially, Lewis hoped primarily to write an entertaining book. As he worked on *The Lion, the Witch and the Wardrobe,* his research on the mythologies of cultures other than his own, as well as his studying of Christian theology, found their way into the narrative.

Lewis said that he became a Christian when he realized that Christianity was a "true myth." He believed that the world's mythologies and religions (which he often suggested were the same thing) were expressions of humanity's awareness that there is a spiritual aspect to life; they were, and are, ways to explain the supernatural. When Lewis was an atheist, he used this idea to attack all religions, including Christianity; he said that they were all nonsense—just inventions of imagination. When in 1929 he realized that God in fact existed, he slowly worked his way to the idea that one of the world's mythologies might be true. It would still be very much like other mythologies in its effort to explain God and the universe, but its distinction would be that it was truth. He eventually concluded that Christianity was the "true myth."

What he tries to do in *The Lion, the Witch and the Wardrobe* is make that "true myth" come to life in the narrative. His pulling together mythical beasts from different cultures, even his inclusion of Father Christmas, is an effort to show the inclusiveness of the Christian view; Aslan is the Lord of everybody and excludes nobody. Further, Lewis is trying to rephrase Christianity in terms a twentieth-century audience can understand; his creatures are rooted in our favorite bedtime stories, folklore, and popular culture. For example, although Father Christmas—or Santa Claus or Saint Nicholas—is not part of the New Testament, he is part of popular culture and is easily recognizable, but the significance of his giving to others is not only important to the events in *The Lion, the Witch and the Wardrobe* but an important aspect of the "true myth" of Christianity. Giving is mentioned many times in the New Testament as very important, and the custom of giving gifts at Christmas—as paralleled by the gifts of the Magi to the Christ child— is embodied through Father Christmas in the novel.

THE GEOGRAPHY OF *THE LION, THE WITCH AND THE WARDROBE*

Events in *The Lion, the Witch and the Wardrobe* take place in Professor Kirke's house and in Narnia. The house is in the country, where the children have been sent from London to escape the German bombing of the city. It is very large; Professor Kirke has at least four servants taking care of it. To the children's delight, the house has many rooms and good places for hiding and playing. Lucy thinks she has found a good hiding place in an upstairs room with a wardrobe in it. When she hides in the wardrobe, she tries to make her way to its back, probably to make it as hard to find her as possible, but there seems to be no back but instead a long array of soft coats, then scratchy tree branches, and then snow.

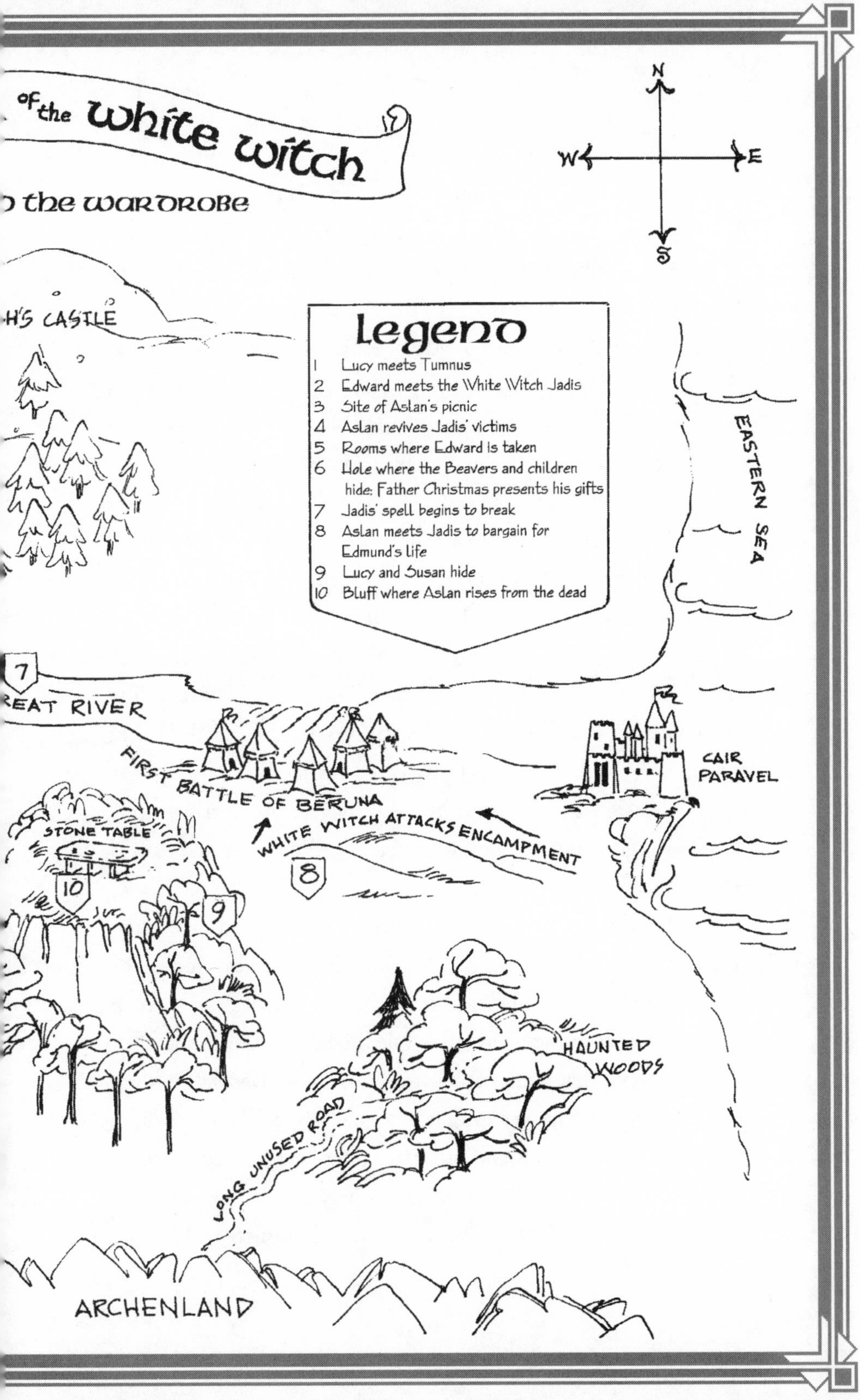

the **Wardrobe**

N
W ← → E
S

H'S CASTLE

Legend

1 Lucy meets Tumnus
2 Edward meets the White Witch Jadis
3 Site of Aslan's picnic
4 Aslan revives Jadis' victims
5 Rooms where Edward is taken
6 Hole where the Beavers and children hide: Father Christmas presents his gifts
7 Jadis' spell begins to break
8 Aslan meets Jadis to bargain for Edmund's life
9 Lucy and Susan hide
10 Bluff where Aslan rises from the dead

EASTERN SEA

7

REAT RIVER

FIRST BATTLE OF BERUNA

STONE TABLE

10

9

WHITE WITCH ATTACKS ENCAMPMENT

8

CAIR PARAVEL

HAUNTED WOODS

LONG UNUSED ROAD

ARCHENLAND

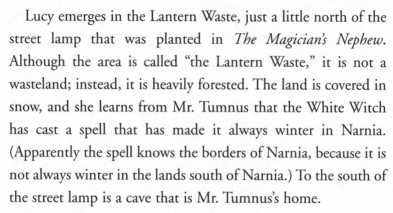

Lucy emerges in the Lantern Waste, just a little north of the street lamp that was planted in *The Magician's Nephew*. Although the area is called "the Lantern Waste," it is not a wasteland; instead, it is heavily forested. The land is covered in snow, and she learns from Mr. Tumnus that the White Witch has cast a spell that has made it always winter in Narnia. (Apparently the spell knows the borders of Narnia, because it is not always winter in the lands south of Narnia.) To the south of the street lamp is a cave that is Mr. Tumnus's home.

When Edmund enters Narnia for the first time, he becomes lost and wanders to the east where he encounters the White Witch. Although the ground is snowbound, she may be following an old road. When all four children enter Narnia, they are guided by a bird along a route through the Lantern Waste that avoids the road. To the southeast, on the Great River, is the Beaver Dam, where Mr. and Mrs. Beaver live, and Mr. Beaver escorts the children there. This seems to be an area with few trees, because when Edmund hikes upriver to the northwest, he slogs through snow in open country. The White Witch's small castle is near the river to the northwest.

The Beavers know the banks of the river well and take Lucy, Peter, and Susan downriver to a hole in which they can hide. The White Witch apparently passes by them without seeing them because she is atop the riverbank while the hole is next to the river. It is at this spot that Father Christmas stops and gives the children gifts. Downriver, they see evidence of the White Witch's passing: a celebration of squirrels and others that has been turned to stone.

It is somewhat hard to visualize where all the places mentioned near the end of the novel are in relation to each other, because Lewis does not offer much in the way of directions. But the area of Beruna is along the Great River, far downstream from the Beavers' home. It is on grassy, solid ground south of the river that Aslan's army makes camp. To the south is where Aslan and the White Witch meet to discuss the terms for sparing Edmund's life. It is considerably to the west, near the river, that Peter kills Fenris Ulf and is knighted by Aslan.

If one were to draw a triangle from the army camp to where Aslan meets the White Witch to the place where Peter kills Fenris Ulf and back to the camp, one could then draw a line from the camp southwest, bisecting the line between where Aslan and the witch meet and where Fenris Ulf dies, pointing at where the Stone Table is. This would be one triangle with a line through it, looking a little like an arrow pointing northeast.

THEMES AND CHARACTERS

Lewis wanted to be very clear that he was not rewriting Christianity, nor are his Narnian books theological treatises. To a youngster named Patricia, he writes:

> But I'm not exactly "representing" the real (Christian) story in symbols. I'm more saying "Suppose there were a world like Narnia and it needed rescuing and the Son of God (or the "Great Emperor Oversea") went to redeem *it*, as He came to redeem ours, what might it, in that world, all have been like?" (C. S. Lewis, *Letters to Children*, 1985, p. 92.)

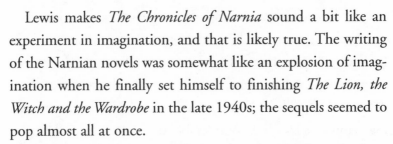

Lewis makes *The Chronicles of Narnia* sound a bit like an experiment in imagination, and that is likely true. The writing of the Narnian novels was somewhat like an explosion of imagination when he finally set himself to finishing *The Lion, the Witch and the Wardrobe* in the late 1940s; the sequels seemed to pop almost all at once.

Having set before himself the idea that God might have other worlds that would have their histories of their relationships with Him, Lewis plunged himself into the exploration of how events might go a little differently from what happened on earth. In *The Magician's Nephew,* we have already seen how evil entered Narnia's world but failed to persuade Digory, a Son of Adam, to violate the promise Adam and Eve had violated; the sin of eating the fruit of the tree of life without permission was not committed on Narnia. This does not prevent evil from existing in Narnia's world, but Digory's planting of the fruit, as commanded by Aslan, succeeds in giving Narnia hundreds of years free from evil—years earth did not have.

It is probably true that Lewis did not realize how his imagination, stirred by his work on *The Lion, the Witch and the Wardrobe,* would explode into a storm of creativity, which meant that he struggled somewhat to keep events and themes consistent throughout *The Chronicles of Narnia.* Still, basic themes are laid out in *The Lion, the Witch and the Wardrobe* that tend to remain important in the books that follow.

The Lion, the Witch and the Wardrobe establishes Narnia as a nation state among nation states; it is not the whole world, but only part of a world with other nations. In fact, in *The Horse and His Boy,* it will be established that Narnia is a fairly small nation compared with others. This is one reason why Narnia is subject to attack. If the White Queen does not try to conquer Narnia then the giants to the north or the Calormenes to the south will.

Another reason Narnia must sometimes defend itself is its close association with Aslan. In *The Magician's Nephew,* we learn that Narnia is where Aslan created the world's Talking Animals, and they tend to congregate in Narnia in large numbers—partly because people in other parts of the world are hostile toward them. Some are also hostile toward Aslan, the Lord of the wood. The Calormenes regard Aslan as an evil demon and fear Him; their occasional efforts to conquer Narnia stem not only from their greed but from their desire to suppress Aslan. In *The Lion, the Witch and the Wardrobe,* the White Witch hates Aslan, and forcing Narnia to submit to her will is her way of oppressing Aslan. Thus *The Lion, the Witch and the Wardrobe* is not just about four children defeating a vile witch, it is about a contest of wills between the White Witch and Aslan, between pure evil and divine goodness.

This contest is further developed in *The Horse and His Boy, Prince Caspian, The Silver Chair,* and *The Last Battle.* In these novels, someone defies Aslan and there is a contest between evil people and Aslan; the children in the novels become Aslan's representatives. Their victories over Narnia's enemies are also victories of the spirit. In *The Lion, the Witch and the Wardrobe,* Aslan saves the spirit of Edmund, a traitor who has given himself over to evil. The resistance of Eustace, Jill, Puddleglum, and Rilian against the green witch's effort to cloud their minds is another kind of victory for Aslan; Puddleglum declares that

even if Aslan's world were only a dream, it would be better than the witch's world.

Lying is also an important theme in *The Lion, the Witch and the Wardrobe*. It is introduced quickly when Peter, Susan, and Edmund believe that Lucy has made up her adventure in Narnia and is lying when she insists it actually happened. Note how Professor Kirke applies logic to the matter of lying and how his noting that Lucy does not lie confuses Peter and Susan. Also note how Edmund lies about visiting Narnia and meeting Lucy there; Edmund is a habitual liar whose viciousness is obvious to everyone, yet his denials are more readily believed by Peter and Susan than Lucy's avowals. Edmund's lies are comfortable ones; they reinforce prejudice; Lucy's truths are disturbing because they suggest a world and a life that is outside everyday experience.

There is more to this than first appears, because Narnia itself is in the grip of lies. The White Witch has made the telling of lies essential. She herself insists that she is a human being, a Daughter of Eve, and therefore fit to rule Narnia; yet, she is not at all human. Her ancestry as a daughter of a jinn and a giant is somewhat vague in *The Lion, the Witch and the Wardrobe,* but Lewis clarifies it in *The Magician's Nephew* by showing that she is from a world other than earth or Narnia. She rules with lies, seduces Edmund with lies, and defies Aslan with lies. In fact, she glories in lies. When she declares that after she kills Aslan she will then kill Edmund, even though she had agreed to exchanging Aslan's life for Edmund's, she is delighted in the lie. Aslan, on the other hand, puts an end to lies. Perhaps Lucy has such a profound understanding of Him partly because she tells the truth even when lying would save her embarrassment and misery. In any case, Peter and Susan's refusal to believe Lucy is very nearly disastrous; the White Queen counts on people believing convenient lies rather than difficult truths.

CHAPTER-BY-CHAPTER DEVELOPMENT OF THEMES AND CHARACTERS IN *THE LION, THE WITCH AND THE WARDROBE*

— Chapter 1: Lucy Looks into a Wardrobe —

Peter, Susan, Edmund and Lucy Pevensie have been sent to live in the country because of the air-raids. It is World War II, and Germany is bombing London day and night, killing thousands of people. While adults cling to their lives in the city, they send their children away to where they are less likely to be victims of bombs.

Their guardian in the country is Professor Kirke, an elderly, shaggy white-haired and bearded man. Although the children liked him almost at once, Lucy is a little afraid of him because of his odd looks, and Edmund stifles laughter because he thinks Professor Kirke looks funny. As is usually the case when it comes to judging people, Lucy's apprehension is a better measure of the man than is Edmund's laughter. It is likely that when he wrote his description of Professor Kirke in this chapter, Lewis had yet to begin *The Magician's Nephew*. It is interesting how he imagines the youthful Digory Kirke as impulsive, whereas the older version is cautiously logical and given to muttering about how poorly schools teach children.

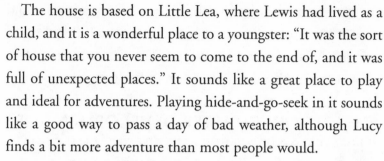

The house is based on Little Lea, where Lewis had lived as a child, and it is a wonderful place to a youngster: "It was the sort of house that you never seem to come to the end of, and it was full of unexpected places." It sounds like a great place to play and ideal for adventures. Playing hide-and-go-seek in it sounds like a good way to pass a day of bad weather, although Lucy finds a bit more adventure than most people would.

Lucy hides in the wardrobe, then walks to the back, eventually finding herself in someplace cold and wet. "Lucy felt a little frightened, but she felt very inquisitive and excited as well." These are important traits of Lucy; she is curious and quick to learn; she finds discovering something new exciting. These traits are part of what make her an attractive character and fun to read about.

She contrasts already not only with Edmund, who seems her opposite, but with Susan. Edmund does not often tell the truth, but he comes close when he accuses Susan of "Trying to talk like Mother." In other books, Susan is described as a "wet blanket." In the first chapter of her first adventure, we already see in her the trait that will eventually separate her from Aslan and Narnia—her persistent effort to be more grownup than she is or needs to be. This trait will eventually make her very difficult to have around during an adventure.

When Lucy explores the Lantern Waste a little, she sees a faun. (Lewis said that he had visualized the faun when he was a teenager and that his image helped inspire *The Lion, the Witch and the Wardrobe*.) This faun is Mr. Tumnus, a gentleman if there ever was one. Fauns are figures from Roman mythology (see page 144) and look much like Mr. Tumnus, only without the umbrella. Fauns are sometimes thought to be the same as satyrs, but although satyrs sometimes look like fauns, they are actually woodland gods and can have other forms. This helps explain why Lewis occasionally mentions that fauns and satyrs, as well as dryads and the like, inhabit Narnia; they are different creatures. It is worth noting that the inclusion of fauns and satyrs in *The Chronicles of Narnia* was probably part of what Tolkien objected to in the series. They are part of Lewis' multi-cultural borrowings and are inconsistent, supposedly, with the inclusions of beings from other, non-Roman mythologies. This said, their inclusion is consistent with Lewis' Biblical sources:

> The wild beasts of the desert shall also meet with the wild beasts of the island and the satyr shall cry to his fellow, the shriekchowl also shall rest there, and find for herself a place of rest. Isaiah 34:14

When we get to *The Last Battle*, we will find that unicorns too are consistent with Lewis' Biblical themes.

— Chapter 2: What Lucy Found There —

Although Lucy is excited by Narnia, for the people living there, life is miserable. Mr. Tumnus notes that it has been winter in Narnia for a long time; in fact the winter is so bleak that it is "always winter and never Christmas." In this chapter, Lewis uses Mr. Tumnus to foreshadow later events. Mr. Tumnus' book *Is Man a Myth?* is partly a joke; it is like having a book titled *Are Fauns a Myth?*—but it suggests more. It suggests that someone at one time knew about humans and that someone in Narnia is

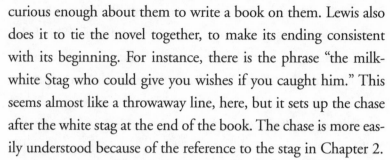

curious enough about them to write a book on them. Lewis also does it to tie the novel together, to make its ending consistent with its beginning. For instance, there is the phrase "the milk-white Stag who could give you wishes if you caught him." This seems almost like a throwaway line, here, but it sets up the chase after the white stag at the end of the book. The chase is more easily understood because of the reference to the stag in Chapter 2.

Mr. Tumnus is a strange fellow, and not just because he lives in a cave. He confesses that he works for the White Witch, which is a surefire way to get himself turned into stone, since he is supposed to turn Lucy in to the secret police and not tell her that she is in danger. He says that even some of the trees are on her side. Even though he thinks to harm her, Lucy forgives Mr. Tumnus. The theme of forgiveness is a powerful one in *The Chronicles of Narnia*. Remember Aslan's making a point of Polly's forgiving Digory in *The Magician's Nephew*? By forgiving Mr. Tumnus, Lucy displays one of the traits that Aslan values the most.

Mr. Tumnus notes that "until the four thrones at Cair Paravel are filled" the winter without Christmas will not end. If we are alert readers, we should note that there are four children and four thrones. It sounds as though the Pevensies may have a kingdom to claim. On the other hand, there is the problem with Edmund in Chapter 3; if he returns home or is an unworthy subject, that would leave only three children for four thrones.

— Chapter 3: Edmund and the Wardrobe —

Edmund is a beast, a cruel, spiteful youngster who delights in the pain of others. He especially likes causing the pain. When he walks into Narnia, he does not react as Lucy did. He does not like the place, has no spirit of adventure, and almost heads home before the White Witch comes by. He shouts for Lucy, who has gone her own way, and Edmund, with his usual condescension toward females, remarks, "Just like a girl," because he thinks she will not answer him and accept his apology. Such behavior is not at all in Lucy's character; later, she is eager to share the adventure in Narnia with Edmund, willing to give Edmund the benefit of the doubt. She forgives his nasty behavior, whereas Edmund is inventing reasons to feel insulted by his younger sister. The behavior he imputes to her is actually how he would behave. He spends much of the novel assuming that others would behave as miserably as he would.

Jadis, the White Witch, is a striking figure when she makes her appearance. She is very tall and wears white fur up to her throat, and on her head is a golden crown. In her right hand is a wand. Although its power has yet to be displayed, it is clearly a weapon. That the White Witch carries it in her hand even while riding in a carriage suggests that she feels threatened when she travels. Perhaps the most striking feature of this very striking figure is her face, which "was white—not merely pale, but white like snow or paper or icing sugar." She is beautiful, "but proud and cold and stern." This is the terrible enemy of Aslan; in her years in the north of Narnia's world she has learned the Deep Magic that has existed since time began.

— Chapter 4: Turkish Delight —

Turkish delights are in fact delightful. They are fruit candies, often dipped in powdered sugar. That Edmund should want some is understandable, but he is taking candy from a strange woman and, having a tendency toward cruelty already, he is easily captured by the magic in the candy. The witch might have had a more difficult time with Lucy, who probably would not let her greed for treats override her common sense, but Edmund is ruled by the worst in himself.

When Lucy declares to him, "And she [the White Witch] has made a magic so that it is always winter in Narnia—always winter, but it never gets to Christmas," Edmund's reaction is one of discomfort. He realizes that he has met the White Witch, but he also wants more Turkish Delight and will do what he must to get it.

— Chapter 5: Back on This Side of the Door —

When he returns to the house, by walking back through the wardrobe, Edmund has a clear choice: He can tell the truth, however uncomfortable that might be, and thereby be a good brother to Lucy, or he can lie, which would be comfortable for Peter and Susan to hear, and would cause Lucy much unhappiness: Edmund decides to let Lucy down. The lie is much easier to tell.

Peter is not stupid, a matter of concern for a future High King. He knows that Edmund is being cruel to Lucy: "I believe you did it simply out of spite," when it seems that Edmund has been encouraging Lucy in her supposed fantasy, only to let her down. "You've always liked being beastly to anyone smaller than yourself; we've seen that at school before now." Edmund is a bully, although his bullying will be attributed to experiences at school.

In this chapter, Lewis shows off a couple of the traits that made his tutor William Kirkpatrick his favorite teacher: compassion and ruthlessly applied logic. He notes that "a charge of lying against someone whom you have always found truthful is a very serious thing," when Peter and Susan come to him about Lucy's tales of Narnia. "'Logic!' said the Professor half to himself. 'Why don't they teach logic at these schools?'" This will become the Professor's catch phrase and eventually the cause of merriment in *The Last Battle*.

Professor Kirke logically deduces that Lucy is telling the truth. The children expect that he will uphold the adult view of life, which would probably insist that Narnia cannot exist. Instead, he surprises Peter and Susan by suggesting that they should believe Lucy until they have good reason otherwise; her story being farfetched is not a good reason. This seems unnerving to the brother and sister. When the professor remarks, "I should not be at all surprised to find that that other world had a separate time of its own; so that however long you stayed there it would never take up any of *our* time," he seems willing to believe Lucy. Thus, as Chapter 6 begins, we have a distressed Lucy, a lying Edmund, and confused Peter and Susan.

— Chapter 6: Into the Forest —

This is a transitional chapter. In it, the four children hide in the wardrobe in order to stay out of the way of a tour group that is being led through the house. Finding one's way into Narnia seems to be a matter of accident as much as design, with Peter and Susan wandering into it much as Lucy and Edmund had. It is odd that when they tried to pass through the wardrobe earlier, when Lucy first told them about Narnia, they could not do so; they found a solid wooden back to the wardrobe.

In this chapter, Edmund proves himself a liar to Peter and Susan. He mentions veering to the left to find the lamp-post, something he would not know about if he had not already been in Narnia. Instead of embarrassment, he feels anger, as if the others were mistreating him. The failure of evil folks to recognize their responsibility for their own behavior is a common theme in *The Chronicles of Narnia*.

— Chapter 7: A Day with the Beavers —

Having entered Narnia, the Pevensies can no longer find their way back to the wardrobe. People being lost occurs often in *The Chronicles of Narnia,* but the lost tend to find their way whenever the Lord of the wood is mentioned: Mr. Beaver says that Aslan is on the move and may have already arrived. The mere mention of Aslan's name has a remarkable effect:

> At the name of Aslan each one of the children felt something jump in his inside. Edmund felt a sensation of mysterious horror. Peter felt suddenly brave and adventurous. Susan felt as if some delicious smell or some delightful strain of music had just floated by her. And Lucy got the feeling you have when you wake up in the morning and realise that it is the beginning of the holidays or the beginning of summer.

Throughout *The Chronicles of Narnia*, saying Aslan's name aloud has a similar effect. It reflects the inner natures of those who hear it; you may remember how Jadis hated the sight of Aslan in *The Magician's Nephew*. In *The Lion, the Witch and the Wardrobe*, she hates even hearing the name of Aslan. Edmund feels horror, because he is a traitor, a liar, and a bully. The reactions of Peter, Susan, and Lucy are meant to show how people should feel when contemplating the divine; for good people, it represents the joy of the interaction between people and their God. This is part of what Lewis means when he uses the word *joy* and why he used it in the title of his autobiography *Surprised by Joy*. The discovery of God thrills the hearts of good people. It also brings with it exquisite freedom: "Lucy got the feeling you have when you wake up in the morning and realise that it is the beginning of the holidays." Lewis hated going to school, and as an adult, school holidays remained symbols of liberty. Communion with the Lord brings liberty with it; in *The Lion, the Witch and the Wardrobe*, this is made plain by the liberation of the Narnians because of Aslan's reappearance. In the later novels, this theme will reappear.

— Chapter 8: What Happened after Dinner —

Mr. Beaver fills the children in on some of the facts about the White Witch. She is fearsome and unforgiving; her castle's courtyard is littered with statues—people whom she turned to stone. This is probably what has happened to Mr. Tumnus. She pretends to be human but she is really the descendant of jinns (genies) and giants. The children are in danger because of a prophesy that when the Sons of Adam and Daughters of Eve occupy the four thrones at Cair Paravel, the witch's life will end.

On the other hand, Aslan is the King, the Lord of the wood.

Mr. Beaver seems somewhat surprised that the children do not know who Aslan is, declaring, "I tell you he is the King of the wood and the son of the great Emperor-Beyond-the-Sea. Don't you know who is the King of Beasts? Aslan is a lion—*the* Lion, the great Lion." The children are to meet Him at the Stone Table, which will figure prominently in later events in *The Lion, the Witch and the Wardrobe* and again in *Prince Caspian.*

While Mr. Beaver tells about the White Witch Jadis and about Aslan, Edmund slips away. Mr. Beaver says that Edmund is about to betray them because he is going to tell the White Witch about the other children. This is the sin for which Edmund must perish. It is not just a betrayal of good principles; it is a betrayal of life, because his brother and sisters are sure to be killed because of him. This betrayal is like that of Judas, who betrayed Jesus to those who intended to kill Him.

– Chapter 9: In the Witch's House –

Edmund does not have much in the way of excuses for taking the White Witch's side, because "deep down inside him he [Edmund] really knew that the White Witch was bad and cruel." He knows that he has chosen evil over good, but instead of reacting as a good person should, which is to reject evil, "he [Edmund] thought more and more how he hated Peter, just as if all this had been Peter's fault." The trek to the White Witch's castle is difficult and cold, but Edmund nurses his petty hatred and it helps him to find the determination to undergo hardships to help the White Witch.

Not even the sight of the stone statues stops him from aiding the witch; he hesitates only because he at first thinks one of the stone lions is alive. Once he realizes that the lion is stone, he uses a pencil to draw a moustache and glasses on it, and he jeers at it, saying. "Yah! Silly old Aslan! How do you like being a stone? You thought yourself mighty fine, didn't you?" This foreshadows Aslan's murder and shows how far into evil Edmund has taken himself. It also shows the depth of Aslan's mercy that he undergoes the humiliation that Edmund acts out in order to save Edmund's life. Edmund meets the grey Wolf, Fenris Ulf, the Chief of the Witch's Secret Police, and he learns how evil treats its followers, as he is bullied and spoken to contemptuously. Edmund is a traitor, and as the witch will point out, that makes him her lawful prey, a contemptible being worthy of death.

— Chapter 10: The Spell Begins to Break —

The frantic hustle and bustle of the Beavers as they prepare to flee their home is reminiscent of the Noah pageants in medieval mystery cycles. A mystery cycle was a series of short plays depicting events from the Bible and were performed for a whole day or perhaps two or three days as part of religious celebrations. It was customary for the Noah pageant to be comical, with the wife of Noah being very difficult about leaving when the great flood begins. In *The Lion, the Witch and the Wardrobe*, Mrs. Beaver calmly goes about selecting supplies even while the others are eager to rush out the door and get away before the White Witch arrives. As in the medieval pageants, everybody gets away in time.

That Narnia's long winter is ending is made clear by the appearance of Father Christmas. It may seem that Father

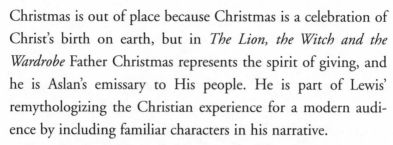

Christmas is out of place because Christmas is a celebration of Christ's birth on earth, but in *The Lion, the Witch and the Wardrobe* Father Christmas represents the spirit of giving, and he is Aslan's emissary to His people. He is part of Lewis' remythologizing the Christian experience for a modern audience by including familiar characters in his narrative.

Lucy, Susan, and Peter feel happy as well as solemn when they see Father Christmas, a complexity of emotion that appears often in *The Chronicles of Narnia*. It is a part of the sublime experience of meeting the truly good and sacred. Father Christmas gives each of the three Pevensie children gifts that they may use in their fight against evil. Of particular importance is Susan's horn; it will later call the Pevensies back to Narnia to aid Caspian in *Prince Caspian*.

Peter's gifts are particularly interesting because they suggest a passage from Ephesians: "Above all, taking the shield of Faith wherewith you shall be able to quench all the fiery darts of the wicked. And take the helmet of salvation, and the sword of the Spirit, which is the word of God." Ephesians 6:16-17. When Peter battles the White Witch, the source of evil in Narnia, he battles her on two levels: 1) the obviously physical level of life-or-death combat and 2) the spiritual level in which his gifts of Faith (the shield) and the Holy Spirit (the sword) both protect him from evil and enable him to fight evil. Father Christmas emphasizes that the shield and sword are tools not toys.

— Chapter 11: Aslan Is Nearer —

She may pretend to be human, but the White Witch Jadis plainly is not; she contemptuously calls Edmund "the human creature." He is little more than an animal to her. Perhaps it is the White Witch's mistreatment of him that begins to turn Edmund's heart: "And Edmund for the first time in this story felt sorry for someone besides himself. It seemed so pitiful to think of those little stone figures sitting there all the silent days and all the dark nights, year after year, till the moss grew on them and at last even their faces crumbled away." Thinking of the welfare of others seems to be an important quality that Aslan values; He expects good people to help others. Edmund may be on his way to admitting to himself the truth about the White Witch. If he does this, he may wish to know the truth about her and Aslan, and he may begin seeking Aslan because to seek the truth is to seek Him.

Remember how Jadis reacted to Aslan's name in *The Magician's Nephew*? Her reaction is hateful too, here in *The Lion, the Witch and the Wardrobe*: she will instantly kill both Dwarf and Edmund if they mention Aslan's name again. If Edmund's reaction to Aslan was horror, what feelings might the name of Aslan create in someone dedicated to evil, especially to inflicting misery on Narnia primarily because Narnia is Aslan's creation? It might cause pain.

— Chapter 12: Peter's First Battle —

In the Bible, Jesus declares the disciple Peter to be His rock, the foundation of His ministry. In *The Lion, the Witch and the Wardrobe*, Peter Pevensie seems to fill a similar role. He is to become High King of Narnia, and it is plain that he is expected to serve Aslan as the foundation of good. He fights the wolves (the secret police) and kills Fenrus, the chief of the secret police. Aslan then knights Peter, as a prophet of the Old Testament might have anointed a king, and dubs Peter "Sir Peter Fenris-Bane."

This chapter also gives a close view of the Stone Table: "It was a great grim slab of grey stone supported on four upright stones. It looked very old; and it was cut all over with strange lines and figures that might be the letters of an unknown language." This passage points out two important aspects of the Stone Table. One is that it is ancient, probably dating back to the creation of the world and thus associated with ritual. The other is that it has ancient, indecipherable writing on it, probably relating to the Deep Magic that will kill Aslan. This may also be an allusion to the tablets bearing the inscriptions for The Ten Commandments, and foreshadows the stone that was used to seal Christ's crypt after His crucifixion. At this point in *The Chronicles of Narnia*, the Stone Table seems to be more of a landmark than the mysterious, uncanny relic it will be in *Prince Caspian*.

— Chapter 13: Deep Magic from the Dawn of Time —

This chapter offers some notable contrasts. For instance, Aslan is a beautiful golden color; He is so beautiful that it can be difficult to look at Him without being overwhelmed. The White Witch is "dead-white"; it is as if her face has no life in it. She is the death of the spirit, an ending without remorse. That she should have trouble looking Aslan in the eyes is to be expected, because she is death and He is life, and His life is more powerful than her death, even if she does not yet realize it.

The contrast between death and life shows in their behavior.

One of the most dramatic passages in *The Chronicles of Narnia* is the White Witch's declaration: "You [Aslan] know that every traitor belongs to me as my lawful prey and that for every treachery I have a right to a kill." The White Witch is focused on killing, and for her part in negotiations with Aslan she tries to win a death. On the other hand, Aslan strives to preserve life. Although it is not mentioned in *The Lion, the Witch and the Wardrobe,* in *The Voyage of the "Dawn Treader"* Aslan will point out that He follows His own rules, which in this case means that evil belongs to evil. To save Edmund, who is well on his way to converting to Aslan's side and remains silent as the Lion dickers for his life, Aslan must fulfill the Deep Magic that was established when He first created the world. (As a note to remember later on, the idea of "lawful prey" is repeated at the end of *The Last Battle,* when Tash takes Rishda Tarkaan.) Where the White Witch wants to *take* a life, Aslan *gives* life by surrendering His Own for that of Edmund.

Although the White Witch threatens her Dwarf servant, Aslan is much kindlier toward Dwarfs. When we see, here, Aslan calling a Dwarf "Son of Earth," He does not intend to suggest Dwarfs are somehow less than other beings. This characterization of Dwarfs is repeated in other Narnian novels and in *The Silver Chair,* it is explained that Dwarfs love to dig; for them it is fun. Thus "Son of Earth" is a reflection of their passion for digging into the earth.

— Chapter 14: The Triumph of the Witch —

It is hard to read this chapter without weeping at least a little. Lewis has done a magnificent job of developing his charac-

ters, following his own rule in writing fiction: to show rather than explain. His characters have revealed themselves in their conduct throughout the novel. We have seen how Lucy remains truthful even under hardship, how Peter tends to take charge, how Susan is gentle, and how Edmund is cruel and selfish. In this chapter, we see the depth of Aslan's character, deepest of all the figures in *The Chronicles of Narnia*. This depth of characterization makes what happens to them seem like it could be happening to real people.

Edmund may seem utterly unworthy of sympathy, but Aslan champions him. Lewis explained that Edmund was like Judas, but that he repented of his evil, whereas Judas did not. Edmund's repentance, however unlikely it seemed, began with his feeling sympathy for the creatures Jadis has turned to stone. By this chapter he actually seems to be trusting Aslan. This is crucial to his salvation.

For such an unworthy person, Aslan trades His own life. He will later remark that many people die, that it is very common (in *The Last Battle*), but He dies to save the life and spirit of someone else. The manner of his death, which is prolonged and demeaning adds depth of feeling to the tragedy of this chapter. Aslan is shorn of His mane; He is taunted; He is brutalized. He is strapped to the Stone Table (as Christ is nailed to the cross). The White Witch has her moment of sublime triumph; she gloats:

> And now, who has won? Fool, did you think that by all
> this you would save the human traitor? Now I will kill you
> instead of him as our pact was and so the Deep Magic will

be appeased. But when you are dead what will prevent me from killing him as well? And who will take him out of my hand *then*? Understand that you have given me Narnia forever, you have lost your own life and you have not saved his. In that knowledge, despair and die.

But Aslan is wise, and the witch does not realize that her declaration that "you have given me Narnia forever" is ironic, that is it is the opposite of what actually happens. In medieval and Renaissance times, *despair* was often considered to be the ultimate sin, because to despair was to deny the possibility of salvation. Here, to despair and die means that the White Witch believes she is sending Aslan into permanent darkness, with no hope of salvation. In that case, she will be free to do as she wishes: She will kill the Pevensies and their Talking Animal companions. Her angry, hate-filled speech to Aslan is the height of her power, and her most glorious moment. Being powerful but not wise, she does not realize that her speech could mark the beginning of Aslan's triumph.

— Chapter 15: Deeper Magic from before the Dawn of Time —

Lucy and Susan have hidden nearby while Aslan is tormented and killed. When they emerge from cover to look at the Stone Table, they find the body of Aslan laid out on the Table. Field mice gnaw through the ropes that bind Aslan; for this service they will be made into Talking Mice. Their descendants will be among Aslan's most faithful followers.

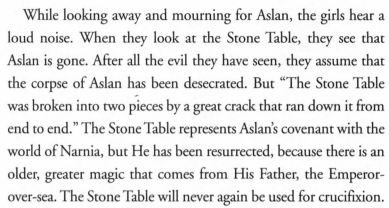

While looking away and mourning for Aslan, the girls hear a loud noise. When they look at the Stone Table, they see that Aslan is gone. After all the evil they have seen, they assume that the corpse of Aslan has been desecrated. But "The Stone Table was broken into two pieces by a great crack that ran down it from end to end." The Stone Table represents Aslan's covenant with the world of Narnia, but He has been resurrected, because there is an older, greater magic that comes from His Father, the Emperor-over-sea. The Stone Table will never again be used for crucifixion.

Out of the cracking of the old covenant is a new one. Lucy and Susan are thrilled to discover Aslan once again alive. Even His mane has regrown, so that He is no longer naked before His enemies. (Christ was crucified wearing only a loin cloth, but when he reappeared to his disciples after his resurrection, he was fully dressed.) Aslan explains that "though the Witch knew the Deep Magic, there is a magic deeper still which she did not know." Although the White Witch's knowledge goes back to the beginning of time (for Narnia's universe), there is a deeper magic that comes before the beginning of time. This is the Deeper Magic of the Emperor-over-sea, Aslan's Father. The White Witch is bound by time; she cannot, like Aslan, transcend time. Had she been able to look to before the beginning of time, "She would have known that when a willing victim who had committed no treachery was killed in a traitor's stead, the Table would crack and Death itself would start working backwards." Aslan has drawn on the Deeper Magic of His Father; this is an irresistible force of life; it is like the power that creates Narnia in *The Magician's Nephew*. The Stone Table represents the Deep Magic; the cracking of the table represents the breaking of the Deep Magic, and of death in particular.

Death "working backwards" means that Death now begins life; in other words, a truer life follows death. This is somewhat consistent with the Christian concept of two covenants, one preceding Christ's resurrection and one following Christ's resurrection. The apostle Paul explains that faith and doing good replace old laws of animal sacrifice, of dietary restrictions, of religious worship. In the New Testament and in *The Lion, the Witch and the Wardrobe,* the new covenant involves the defeat of death.

Important to note is how Aslan reacts to His resurrection. It is with joy; He plays like a frisky kitten with the girls. His Life is a celebration of life, and He is no solemn Deity. "The three of them rolled over together in a happy laughing heap of fur and arms and legs." Aslan is very large, much larger than an ordinary lion, but He plays with Lucy and Susan without their ever being in danger. This is the joyous, happy Lion that will be found in Aslan's Country in *The Last Battle.*

— Chapter 16: What Happened about the Statues —

Although giants are often villains in *The Chronicles of Narnia,* Lewis makes the point that some may be good such as "Giant Rumblebuffin." Salvation is open all those who choose good over evil; as Aslan breathes on each statue, He is bringing His salvation, life, to the victims of the White Witch. Although there is a terrible battle yet to be fought, Aslan brings His joy to Narnia before rushing to the battle. This pattern will be repeated in *Prince Caspian,* where Aslan works happy miracles before moving on to the crucial battle. Plainly, Aslan is a Lord of happiness before He is a Lord of wrath.

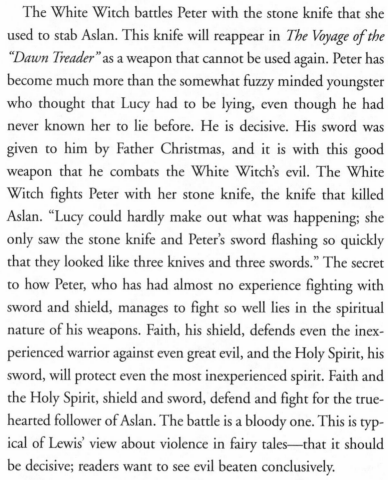

The White Witch battles Peter with the stone knife that she used to stab Aslan. This knife will reappear in *The Voyage of the "Dawn Treader"* as a weapon that cannot be used again. Peter has become much more than the somewhat fuzzy minded youngster who thought that Lucy had to be lying, even though he had never known her to lie before. He is decisive. His sword was given to him by Father Christmas, and it is with this good weapon that he combats the White Witch's evil. The White Witch fights Peter with her stone knife, the knife that killed Aslan. "Lucy could hardly make out what was happening; she only saw the stone knife and Peter's sword flashing so quickly that they looked like three knives and three swords." The secret to how Peter, who has had almost no experience fighting with sword and shield, manages to fight so well lies in the spiritual nature of his weapons. Faith, his shield, defends even the inexperienced warrior against even great evil, and the Holy Spirit, his sword, will protect even the most inexperienced spirit. Faith and the Holy Spirit, shield and sword, defend and fight for the true-hearted follower of Aslan. The battle is a bloody one. This is typical of Lewis' view about violence in fairy tales—that it should be decisive; readers want to see evil beaten conclusively.

Aslan leaps on the White Witch, who is both amazed and terrified. The Lion is no weakling; when action is called for, He is a terrible foe. Aslan is both loving and tough: He is a mighty soldier in battle.

In this chapter, Aslan talks about Deep Magic and Deeper Magic. This passage may have been inspired by I Corinthians 2:6-7, which draws a contrast between the wisdom of the world and the "hidden" wisdom of God. The wisdom of the world and the "Princes of this worlde" come to nothing when compared to God's hidden wisdom, which may only be known through God. The White Witch may be taken to be one of the "Princes" of the world; as great as her knowledge is, it comes to nothing compared to the wisdom of the Emperor-over-sea (God), which is the power Aslan draws on. His resurrection "means . . . that though the Witch knew the Deep Magic, there is a magic deeper still which she did not know."

— Chapter 17: The Hunting of the White Stag —

At last the Witch was dead. Lucy takes her vial of healing potion and uses it to heal Edmund's wounds, and she wishes to linger with Edmund to see the effect, rather than rushing to help heal other wounded, but Aslan says severely, "Must *more* people die for Edmund?" He is stern as well as playful and dangerous. Here, Lewis refers to "that horrid school which was where he [Edmund] had begun to go wrong," which seems to be a reference to Lewis' schools—the "concentration camps" that he loathed all his life. In *The Chronicles of Narnia,* schooling is primarily done by tutors, perhaps reflecting Lewis' happiest times with William Kirkpatrick and his dons at Oxford, where teacher and student working one-on-one was expected.

"Once a king or queen in Narnia, always a king or queen," announces Aslan when He crowns the Pevensies. This is important, because throughout the rest of *The Chronicles of Narnia,* Peter, Susan, Edmund, and Lucy are treated as Narnia's monarchs even by the kings who are reigning in their stead. In the case of Peter, he is always the High King, to whom all other rulers must submit.

The children grow up and rule Narnia for many years as "King Peter the Magnificent," "Queen Susan the Gentle," "King Edmund the Just," and "Queen Lucy the Valiant." In *The Horse and His Boy,* we shall see a little of why they are called these names. In *The Lion, the Witch and the Wardrobe,* they eventually stumble into the wardrobe and back into the Professor's house while chasing the white stag, with little earth-time having passed. This dissatisfied me when I was a youngster reading the novel for the first time (and the second through fifth times); I identified with the children and knew that I would want to remain a king of Narnia for all my life. Yet, having the Pevensies return to earth is a necessary plot device, without which the later novels would not be possible. It is the time element that is crucial: time passes at different speeds on earth and in Narnia, enabling the Pevensies and other children to return to Narnia hundreds of years, even thousands of years, after their earlier adventures. As dissatisfied as I may have been with the Pevensies' returning to England, I would not give up *Prince Caspian* and *The Voyage of the "Dawn Treader"* in order to have a different ending to *The Lion, the Witch and the Wardrobe.* I definitely would not wish to lose the gallant Reepicheep and the valiant Caspian.

Did you notice the Professor's remark "Once a King in Narnia, always a King in Narnia?" It parallels what Aslan said when the children were crowned. Does it mean that the Professor knows more about what is happening than he lets on?

VOCABULARY FOR *THE LION, THE WITCH AND THE WARDROBE*

CHAPTER 1: LUCY LOOKS INTO A WARDROBE
wireless: radio
blue-bottle: a fly with a metallic-blue body
muffler: a scarf worn around the neck for warmth

CHAPTER 3: EDMUND AND THE WARDROBE
you goose: you silly person
Make it Pax.: make peace; forgive.
sledge: (sled) a vehicle with runners instead of wheels and pulled by horses or other animals across snow and ice
instead of a rug: instead of animal skin or thick fabric shaped like a blanket

CHAPTER 4: TURKISH DELIGHT
Turkish Delight: jellied fruit candies, probably invented in Turkey

CHAPTER 5: BACK ON THIS SIDE OF THE DOOR
snigger: a particularly repellant and stupid snicker
jeering: taunting
beastly: cruel
beasts: cruel people
to see over it: to tour the house
taking a party over the house: showing a group of people around the house
sharp's the word: be alert
trippers: tourists

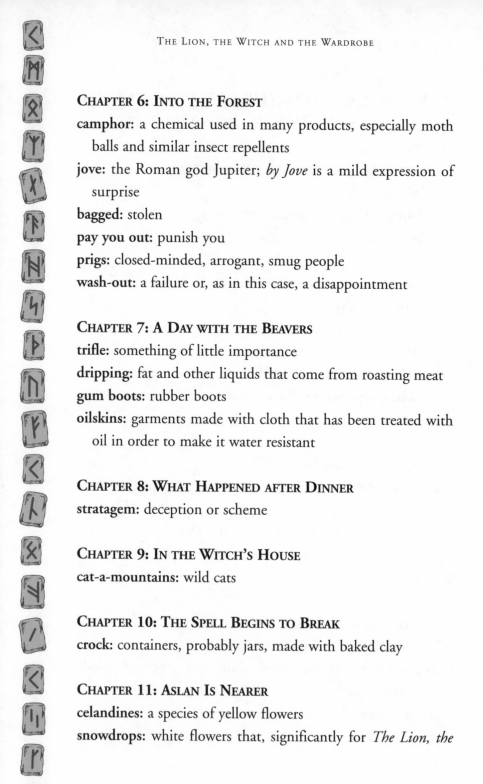

CHAPTER 6: INTO THE FOREST

camphor: a chemical used in many products, especially moth balls and similar insect repellents

jove: the Roman god Jupiter; *by Jove* is a mild expression of surprise

bagged: stolen

pay you out: punish you

prigs: closed-minded, arrogant, smug people

wash-out: a failure or, as in this case, a disappointment

CHAPTER 7: A DAY WITH THE BEAVERS

trifle: something of little importance

dripping: fat and other liquids that come from roasting meat

gum boots: rubber boots

oilskins: garments made with cloth that has been treated with oil in order to make it water resistant

CHAPTER 8: WHAT HAPPENED AFTER DINNER

stratagem: deception or scheme

CHAPTER 9: IN THE WITCH'S HOUSE

cat-a-mountains: wild cats

CHAPTER 10: THE SPELL BEGINS TO BREAK

crock: containers, probably jars, made with baked clay

CHAPTER 11: ASLAN IS NEARER

celandines: a species of yellow flowers

snowdrops: white flowers that, significantly for *The Lion, the*

Witch and the Wardrobe, bloom in the spring; they are signs of Aslan's return to Narnia

crocuses: several species of flowers with slender leaves and petals of a variety of colors that bloom in early spring

larches: trees with needles

birches: trees with whitish bark

laburnums: several species of bushes and trees with yellow flowers

beech: a tree with smooth bark and edible nuts

CHAPTER 12: PETER'S FIRST BATTLE

kingfisher: several species of birds with prominent crests

bluebells: plants with bell-shaped, blue flowers

thrush: song bird

elms: a tall, heavily branched shade tree

currant: a prickly plant whose berries are made into jelly

hawthorn bushes: a shrub with thorns and white or pink flowers

rampant: a stylized depiction of an animal (in this case a lion) showing the animal in profile, standing on one hind leg with the other raised and both forelegs raised

CHAPTER 13: DEEP MAGIC FROM THE DAWN OF TIME

Boggles: an evil goblin

Cruels: probably a being who likes to cause suffering

Hags: witches

Spectres: ghosts

chap: man or, in this case, a male Talking Animal

CHAPTER 14: THE TRIUMPH OF THE WITCH

Incubuses: evil spirits that rape women

Wraiths: apparitions or ghosts

Efreets: demons from Arabic myths

Sprites: pixies or elves; also an archaic definition for ghost

Orknies: perhaps a reference to monsters from Roman mythology, the orcs, who also appear in *Beowulf* and *The Lord of the Rings*

Wooses: frightful spirits

Ettins: an ancient word meaning evil giants; they are probably from Ettinsmoor, a land of giants, as Puddleglum says in *The Silver Chair.*

Chapter 15: Deeper Magic from
before the Dawn of Time

briar: a bush whose woody roots are made into tobacco pipes; rarer, a thorny bush; given Lewis' fondness for tobacco pipes, he probably means that kind of briar

goose bushes: probably gooseberries, spiny plants with edible fruit

heathery mountains: mountains with low-lying shrubs called heather, with pale purple flowers

Chapter 16: What Happened about the Statues

blowed: an expression of surprise

out of condition: out of shape; not physically fit

saccharine tablet: an artificial sweetener

gibbered: unintelligible babbling

Chapter 17: The Hunting of the White Stag

high tea: a substantial late-afternoon meal that would include a hot dish, bread and butter, and a dessert, as well as tea.

REFERENCES TO THE BIBLE IN *THE LION, THE WITCH AND THE WARDROBE*

The passage from *The Lion, the Witch and the Wardrobe* is first quoted, followed by the relevant passage in the Bible. A transliteration of the 1611 edition of the King James version of the Bible is used for the Biblical quotations. Comments then follow.

— Chapter 3: Edmund and the Wardrobe —

1. "The others [Peter, Susan, and Edmund] who thought she [Lucy] was telling a lie, and a silly lie too, made her very unhappy."

> **Mark 16:11:** "And they, when they had heard that he was alive, and had been seen of her, believed not."

> **Luke 24:11:** "And their words seemed to them as idle tales, and they believed them not."

Comments: Lucy will become the closest to Aslan of all the characters in *The Chronicles of Narnia*. In this passage, she is placed in a role similar to that of Mary, the mother of Jesus, and Mary Magdalene, who are at first not believed by disciples of Jesus when they say that they have seen Him alive after His internment.

— Chapter 8: What Happened after Dinner —

2. "At the sound of his roar"

Hosea 11:10: "They shall walk after the Lord: He shall roar like a lion: when He shall roar, then the children shall tremble from the West."

Comments: The passage in Hosea is possibly one of the passages that inspired Lewis to have Aslan take the form of a lion. In *The Chronicles of Narnia,* Aslan is very formidable, and He makes even good people tremble. The reference to the "West" may have been one reason why Narnia and the other major nations are set in the western part of the world.

3. "sorrows will be no more"

Isaiah 65:19: "And I will rejoice in Jerusalem, and joy in my people, and the voice of weeping shall be no more heard in her, nor the voice of crying."

Comments: Narnia is somewhat like Isaiah's Jerusalem, having been held in thrall by dark power, and the promise in *The Lion, the Witch and the Wardrobe* is the same: The coming of the Lord will put an end to the misery of the land and its people.

4. "When Adam's flesh and Adam's bone"

Genesis 2:23: "And Adam said, This is now bone of my bones, and flesh of my flesh: she shall be called woman, because she was taken out of man."

Comments: As the passage from Genesis suggests, "Adam's flesh and Adam's bone" refers to both men and women and therefore means both the boys and girls Pevensies.

— Chapter 10: The Spell Begins to Break —

5. "With these words he [Father Christmas] handed to Peter a shield and a sword. The shield was the colour of silver and across it there ramped a red lion, as bright as a ripe strawberry at the moment when you pick it. The hilt of the sword was of gold and it had a sheath and a sword belt and everything it needed, and it was just the right size and weight for Peter to use."

> Ephesians 6:16-17: "Above all, taking the shield of Faith, with which you shall be able to quench all the fiery darts of the wicked. / And take the helmet of salvation, and the sword of the Spirit, which is the word of God."

Comments: This passage in *The Lion, the Witch and the Wardrobe* works on three levels. The surface level is Peter accepting weapons that "are tools, not toys" that he will use in battle. On another level, his new weapons symbolize his becoming a man, ready to do a man's job in the war against evil. At another level, as the quotation from Ephesians suggests, Peter is taking on the spiritual defence of God, the shield, and the weapon of God, the Holy Spirit. The "word of God" is truth, and it defies evil's lies. Further, "the word" may represent Christ; in this sense Peter becomes a soldier of Aslan (Christ) both spiritually and literally. Peter will display his qualities of Faith and Spirit not only in *The*

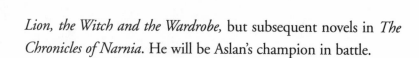

Lion, the Witch and the Wardrobe, but subsequent novels in *The Chronicles of Narnia.* He will be Aslan's champion in battle.

— Chapter 13: Deep Magic from the Dawn of Time —

6. "'Here is your brother,' he [Aslan] said, 'and—there is no need to talk to him about what is past.'"

> **Isaiah 65:16:** "That he who blesses himself in the earth, shall bless himself in the God of truth; and he that sweareth in the earth, shall swear by the God of truth; because the former troubles are forgotten, and because they are hidden from mine eyes."

Comments: Here, Aslan grants Edmund the all-encompassing forgiveness of God. Edmund having repented his betrayal of his sisters and brother, and having joined the side of Truth, Edmund's past will not be held against him—in fact, Aslan will treat it as forgotten. This represents one of the central tenets of what Lewis regarded as "mere Christianity," a universal truth on which all Christians may agree: that even the worst sin can be forgiven by God through true repentance of the sinner. In a letter to a young reader, Lewis asserts that God would have forgiven even Judas, the betrayer of Christ, had he truly repented.

7. "But Edmund had got past thinking about himself after all he'd been through and after the talk he'd had that morning. He just went on looking at Aslan. It didn't seem to matter what the Witch said."

Hebrews 12:1-2: "Wherefore, seeing we also are compassed about so great a cloud of witnesses, let us lay aside every weight, and the sin which does so easily beset us, and let us run with patience to the race that is set before us, / Looking to Jesus the Author and Finisher of *our* faith, Who for the joy that was set before Him, endured the cross, despising the shame, and is set down at the right hand of the throne of God."

Comments: Edmund's behavior from this moment on is a reflection of the commandment in Hebrews. He looks to Aslan (Christ) "as the Authour and finisher" of his faith, and he sets aside his allegiance to the White Witch.

— Chapter 14: The Triumph of the Witch —

8. "I [Aslan] should be glad of company to-night."

9. "I am sad and lonely. Lay your hands on my mane so that I can feel you are there and let us walk like that."

Matthew 26:37-38: "And He [Jesus] took with Him Peter, and the two sons of Zebedee, and began to be sorrowful, and very heavy. / Then said He to them, 'My soul is exceeding sorrowful, even unto death: stay here, and watch with me.'"

Comments: These passages stand out on two levels, both important. On one level, Aslan and Jesus are sad and want the companionship of those who love Them. Each knows what is coming but does not say what it is, putting Their remarks on a simple level of friendship. There is a grandeur in Their not using the dramatic plea of "I'm going to die tomorrow!"— instead taking comfort on the human level of, "I am sad." On another level, both the passage from *The Lion, the Witch and the Wardrobe* and Matthew show a link in the chain of witnesses— that is the crucial events are witnessed by honest people. Their testimony, or witnessing, will help to explain what Aslan and Christ have done through their sacrifices and defeat of death.

10. "'Stop!' said the Witch. 'Let him first be shaved.'
"Another roar of mean laughter went up from her followers as an ogre with a pair of shears came forward and squatted down by Aslan's head.'"

> **Matthew 27:28:** "And they stripped him [Jesus], and put on him a scarlet robe."

Comments: The baring of the skin represents the humiliation endured at the hands of cruel people. Both Aslan and Jesus are made naked before Their enemies, so that They appear helpless.

11. "'Why, he's only a great cat after all!' cried one.
"'Is *that* what we were afraid of?' said another.
"And they surged round Aslan jeering at him, saying things like 'Puss, Puss! Poor Pussy,' and 'How many mice have you caught to-day, Cat?' and 'Would you like a saucer of milk, Pussums?'"

Matthew 27:29-30: "And then they had braided a crown of thorns, they put it on His head, and a reed in His right hand: and they bowed before Him, and mocked Him, saying, 'Hail king of the Jews.' / And they spit on Him, and took the reed, and struck him on the head."

Comments: The power of Aslan and Christ are mocked. Their tormentors fail to recognize that Their power transcends Their fleshly bodies.

12. "In that knowledge despair and die."

Matthew 27:46: "And about the ninth hour, Jesus cried with a loud voice, saying *'Eli, Eli, Lamasabachthani,'* that is to say, 'My God, my God, why have thou forsaken me?'"

Mark 15:34: "And at the ninth hour, Jesus cried with a loud voice, saying, 'Eloi, Eloi, lamasabachthani?' which is, being interpreted, 'My God, my God, why have You forsaken me?'"

Matthew 27:50: "Jesus, when He had cried again with a loud voice, yielded up His ghost."

Mark 15:37: "And Jesus cried with a loud voice, and gave up His ghost.

Comments: In the Witch's terse sentence and Matthew and Mark's accounts, despair and death are united. In each Case, Aslan and Jesus are supposed to be doomed and out of reach of help. Later, despair and death are separated; death need not be

an ending. Through Christ, no one need despair in death. Lewis takes this notion literally, and in *The Last Battle,* those who die are shown to continue to live to have new adventures. Thus in Their dying, Aslan and Christ subvert despair.

— Chapter 15: Deeper Magic from before the Dawn of Time —

13. "At that moment they heard from behind them [Lucy and Susan] a loud noise—a great cracking, deafening noise as if a giant had broken a giant's plate."

14. "The Stone Table was broken into two pieces by a great crack that ran down it from end to end; and there was no Aslan."

> **Matthew 27:51-53:** "And behold, the veil of the Temple was torn in two, from the top to the bottom, and the earth did quake, and the rocks rent. / And the graves were opened, and many bodies of Saints which slept, arose, / And came out of the graves after His resurrection, and went into the holy city, and appeared to many."

> **Mark 15:38:** "And the veil of the Temple was torn in two, from the top to the bottom."

> **Luke 23:45:** "And the Sun was darkened, and the veil of the temple was torn in the middle."

Comments: Here, the Stone Table is meant to represent the temple, and both are meant to represent the old spiritual laws (the Deep Magic of *The Chronicles of Narnia*), which are often called "the First Covenant." These laws are split open to reveal a deeper law that transcends and overpowers the old ones. Called the Deeper Magic in *The Chronicles of Narnia,* this deeper law reveals God's abiding love and His power over death. Under the old law, death is an ending, and this is where the White Witch makes her fatal mistake; she believes it really is an ending. Aslan and Christ reveal that death is actually a beginning.

15. "'You're not—not a—?' asked Susan in a shaky voice. She couldn't bring herself to say the word *ghost.*"

Luke 24:37: "But they were terrified, and frightened, and supposed that they had seen a spirit."

Comments: Susan and Lucy at first react much as some of Christ's followers did when "Jesus himself stood in the midst of them" (Luke 24:36).

16. "The warmth of his breath and a rich sort of smell that seemed to hang about his hair came all over her."

John 20:22: "And when He said this, He breathed on them, and said to them, 'Receive you the Holy Ghost.'"

Comments: Aslan often breathes on people in *The Chronicles of Narnia,* and they feel secure, refreshed, and strong. The verse from John suggests that Aslan is passing to them the spiritual strength to be derived from the Holy Spirit.

17. "'Do I look it?' he [Aslan] said."

> **Luke 24:39:** "'Behold my hands and my feet, that it is I myself: handle me, and see, for a spirit has not flesh and bones, as you see I have.'"

> **John 20:20:** "And when He had so said, He showed them His hands and His side. Then were the disciples glad, when they saw the Lord."

Comments: Aslan does as Christ did; He invites witnesses to see for themselves the truth of His resurrection and defeat of death.

18. "'It means,' said Aslan, 'that though the Witch knew the Deep Magic, there is a magic deeper still which she did not know. Her knowledge goes back only to the dawn of Time. But if she could have looked a little further back, into the stillness and the darkness before Time dawned, she would have read there a different incantation.'"

> **I Corinthians 2:6-7:** "How is it that we speak wisdom among those that are perfect: yet not the wisdom of this world, nor of the Princes of this world, that come to nothing: / But we speak the wisdom of God in a mystery, *even* the hidden *wisdom* which God ordained before the world, to our glory."

Comments: The matter of Deep Magic often confuses even scholars, who blend Deep Magic with Deeper Magic as if they were the same. They are not. Deep Magic is very deep, indeed, because it goes back to the creation of Narnia and the beginning of Time; yet, even the evil witch can learn about it without the aid of God. God's magic is deeper still, and beyond her reach. As the passage from I Corinthians explains, only through God (the Emperor-beyond-the-Sea) may the wisdom from "before the world" (Deeper Magic) be known. Thus, even though the Deep Magic is well known to Him, Aslan (Christ) has access to a form of magic that is miraculous, and only through Him can it be known.

— Chapter 17: The Hunting of the White Stag —

19. "How Aslan provided food for them all I don't know; but somehow or other they found themselves all sitting down on the grass to a fine high tea at about eight o'clock."

> **John 6:10-11:** "And Jesus said, 'Make the men sit down.' Now there was much grass in the place. So the men sat down, in number about five thousand. / And Jesus took the loaves, and when He had given thanks, He distributed to the disciples, and the disciples to them that were seated, and likewise of the fishes, as much as they would."

Comments: Although he says, "I don't know," Lewis implies that Aslan performs a miracle similar to that when Jesus took five loaves of bread and two fishes and made them enough to feed thousands of people sitting on the grass.

20. "... Aslan solemnly crowned them and led them onto the four thrones amid deafening shouts of, "Long Live King Peter! Long Live Queen Susan! Long Live King Edmund! Long Live Queen Lucy!"

> **Isaiah 32:1:** "Behold, a King shall reign in righteousness, and princes shall rule in judgment."

Comments: Peter is the High King, and he rules righteously. Susan, Edmund, and Lucy show mercy, fairness, and courage.

21. "He [Aslan] doesn't like being tied down—and of course he has other countries to attend to."

> **John 10:16:** "And other sheep I have, which are not of the this fold: them also I must bring, and they shall hear my voice; and there shall be one fold, *and* one shepherd."

Comments: In *The Chronicles of Narnia,* Lewis takes the idea in John 10:16 and expands upon it, suggesting that there may be many other worlds besides earth that need Christ's ministry.

DISCUSSION QUESTIONS AND PROJECTS FOR *THE LION, THE WITCH AND THE WARDROBE*

— Overview —

1. Some literary critics say that *The Lion, the Witch and the Wardrobe* should be read before all the other Narnian books,

Checkout Receipt
Harris County Public Library
Renew your items online:
http://catalog.hcpl.net

Title: Chronicles Of Narnia. The
Voyage Of The Dawn ...
Call Number: YBLU-RAY CHRON
Item ID: 01087956
Date Due: 3/5/2024

Title: The Chronicles Of Narnia.
Prince Caspian [Blu...
Call Number: YBLU-RAY CHRON
Item ID: 01126624
Date Due: 3/5/2024

Title: The Chronicles Of Narnia. The
Lion, The Witch...
Call Number: C
Item ID: 34028084611038
Date Due: 3/5/2024

Title: Finding God In The Land Of
Narnia
Call Number: 823.912 Bru
Item ID: 34028057333255
Date Due: 3/5/2024

Title: Exploring C.S. Lewis' The
Chronicles Of Narni...
Call Number: 823.912 Bee
Item ID: 34028054050423
Date Due: 3/5/2024

Title: Chronicles Of Narnia, The
Voyage Of The Dawn ...
Call Number: YBLU-RAY CHRON
Item ID: 01087958
Date Due: 3/6/2024

Title: The Chronicles Of Narnia.
Prince Caspian [blu...
Call Number: YBLU-RAY CHRON
Item ID: 01126624
Date Due: 3/6/2024

Title: The Chronicles Of Narnia, The
Lion, The Witch...
Call Number: C
Item ID: 34028084611038
Date Due: 3/6/2024

Title: Finding God In The Land Of
Narnia
Call Number: 823.912 Bru
Item ID: 34028067333266
Date Due: 3/6/2024

Title: Exploring C.S. Lewis' The
Chronicles Of Narni...
Call Number: 823.912 Hee
Item ID: 34028040680423
Date Due: 3/6/2024

even though Lewis said that *The Magician's Nephew* should be read first. What are the reasons that *The Lion, the Witch and the Wardrobe* should be read first? Are they better than the reasons for reading *The Magician's Nephew* first?

2. Why does Aslan redeem Edmund?

3. Why would Lewis tell a story of a Lion giving up His life for Edmund as a way of retelling the crucifixion and resurrection of Christ?

4. Why cannot the children return to Narnia through the wardrobe at the end of *The Lion, the Witch and the Wardrobe*? Why couldn't they just stumble through again, sometime? (This is a deceptive question because Lewis has both thematic and structural considerations for *The Chronicles of Narnia* at work, here.)

5. In the course of the narrative of *The Lion, the Witch and the Wardrobe,* Lewis mentions many places in Narnia. Draw a map showing where these places are (do not forget the entrance from the wardrobe!) and then trace the paths of the different children from one place to the next.

6. If Aslan is too beautiful to look at, what makes it possible for people to see Him?

7. Lucy is the point-of-view character for most of *The Lion, the Witch and the Wardrobe,* which makes her characterization par-

ticularly important. How does Lewis round her out, making her seem real? Does she grow in any important ways?

8. How does Lewis show that the White Witch and Aslan are opposites?

9. Why is there violence in *The Lion, the Witch and the Wardrobe*? What purpose does it serve?

10. What is the difference between Deep Magic and Deeper Magic?

11. How is Aslan playful, dangerous, loving, and stern?

12. What was life like for children sent from London to live away from their parents in the country during World War II?

13. Why does evil expect evil from others, as in Edmund's case?

14. Why would Lewis make Jadis absolutely white?

CHAPTER-BY-CHAPTER DISCUSSION QUESTIONS

CHAPTER 1: LUCY LOOKS INTO A WARDROBE
1. How is it that the Pevensies have fun even though they are away from home and their city is being bombed?

2. Is Professor Kirke what you would expect Digory Kirke (from *The Magician's Nephew*) to be like when he grew up?

3. Does the Professor's house seem like a good place for children?

4. How interesting a figure is Mr. Tumnus when you first see him?

CHAPTER 2: WHAT LUCY FOUND THERE
1. Why would Lucy find Narnia exciting while Mr. Tumnus would describe it as miserable?

2. What does "Always winter and never Christmas" tell about Narnia?
3. What does Lewis write in this chapter to make us want to continue reading?

CHAPTER 3: EDMUND AND THE WARDROBE
1. Does Edmund seem to have any redeeming qualities in this chapter?

2. When you first see the White Witch, what does she seem like? Does she appear evil at first?

CHAPTER 4: "TURKISH DELIGHT"
1. What are Turkish delights? How are they made? Where were they invented?

2. Why does Edmund not accept Lucy's view that the White Witch is evil?

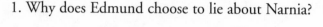

CHAPTER 5: BACK ON THIS SIDE OF THE DOOR

1. Why does Edmund choose to lie about Narnia?

2. Why does the Professor's logic about Lucy's telling the truth seem to be lost on Peter and Susan?

3. What makes the Professor's behavior surprising?

CHAPTER 6: INTO THE FOREST

1. Why does the wardrobe have a solid wooden back when Peter and the other children tested it earlier but in this chapter is open to Narnia?

2. How do the other children respond to proof that Edmund had been lying?

CHAPTER 7: A DAY WITH THE BEAVERS

1. What do the reactions of the Pevensies to the mention of Aslan's name tell about their personalities? Do they later behave in harmony with what we learn from their reactions here?

2. What do the Beavers do that makes them seem like good people? (Note how the food they offer differs from that which the White Witch offers Edmund, both in the woods and later at her castle.)

CHAPTER 8: WHAT HAPPENED AFTER DINNER

1. Why does the White Witch pretend to be human?

2. What does Mr. Beaver mean when he says that Aslan is "the Lord of the whole wood"?

3. Why does Lewis mention the Stone Table in this chapter?

CHAPTER 9: IN THE WITCH'S HOUSE

1. If Edmund knows "deep down inside him" that "the White Witch was bad and cruel," why does he go to her, overcoming much difficulty, in order to betray his brother and sisters? How evil does this make him?

2. Why does the White Witch treat Edmund badly once he tells her about his brother and sisters being at the Beavers' home? Why not give him all the Turkish delights he wants?

CHAPTER 10: THE SPELL BEGINS TO BREAK

1. What makes Mrs. Beaver calm while everyone around her is frantic?

2. Does Father Christmas seem out of place in this chapter?

3. What do the gifts to Lucy, Susan, and Peter suggest about the personality of each? How well rounded are their characterizations by now?

CHAPTER 11: ASLAN IS NEARER

1. Why does the White Witch call Edmund "the human creature"? What does this tell us about her?

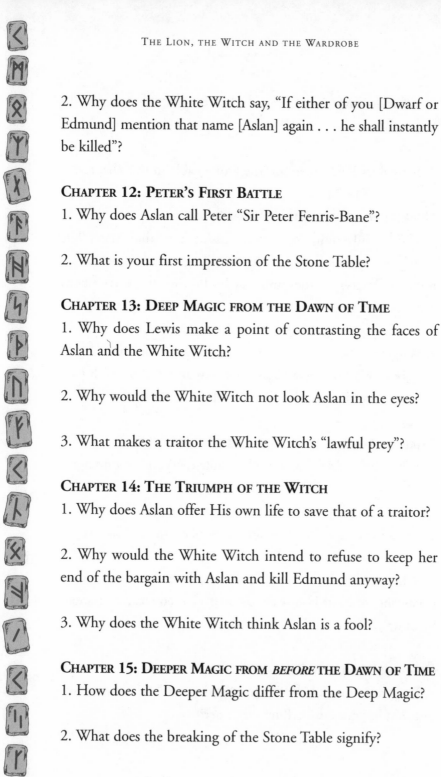

2. Why does the White Witch say, "If either of you [Dwarf or Edmund] mention that name [Aslan] again . . . he shall instantly be killed"?

Chapter 12: Peter's First Battle

1. Why does Aslan call Peter "Sir Peter Fenris-Bane"?

2. What is your first impression of the Stone Table?

Chapter 13: Deep Magic from the Dawn of Time

1. Why does Lewis make a point of contrasting the faces of Aslan and the White Witch?

2. Why would the White Witch not look Aslan in the eyes?

3. What makes a traitor the White Witch's "lawful prey"?

Chapter 14: The Triumph of the Witch

1. Why does Aslan offer His own life to save that of a traitor?

2. Why would the White Witch intend to refuse to keep her end of the bargain with Aslan and kill Edmund anyway?

3. Why does the White Witch think Aslan is a fool?

Chapter 15: Deeper Magic from *before* the Dawn of Time

1. How does the Deeper Magic differ from the Deep Magic?

2. What does the breaking of the Stone Table signify?

3. What does Aslan mean by "Death itself would start working backwards"?

4. Why does Aslan frisk with Lucy and Susan?

Chapter 16: What Happened about the Statues
1. What has made Peter into a skilled and valiant warrior?

2. Is the violence in this chapter appropriate for the subject?

3. What does this chapter tell us about Aslan?

Chapter 17: The Hunting of the White Stag
1. Just how dead is the White Witch? There are hints in *Prince Caspian* and *The Silver Chair* that she may be revived.

2. What does Aslan mean when he says, "Must *more* people die for Edmund"?

3. Why does Lewis have the Pevensies return to the wardrobe after they have become great kings and queens? Would losing them be good for Narnia?

CHAPTER 11

THE HORSE
AND HIS BOY

OVERVIEW

In *The Horse and His Boy*, Lewis offers a somewhat more traditional tale of adventure than those in *The Lion, the Witch and the Wardrobe* and *The Magician's Nephew*. In it a boy who was like a slave makes a journey through exotic lands to his true home. His companions are two Talking Horses, Bree and Hwin, and a Calormene girl Aravis, who is running away from an arranged marriage to an old man she does not like. As is common in folk tales, Aravis is haughty and treats the boy, Shasta, as inferior because he is poor and she was rich; on the other hand, also typical of folk tales, Shasta dismisses her because she is a girl. Through their adventures, each will learn to value the other and to set aside their false assumptions of superiority that are based only on the prejudices attached to their birth.

THE GEOGRAPHY OF
THE HORSE AND HIS BOY

The Horse and His Boy offers the only good look at Calormen in *The Chronicles of Narnia*. It is a big nation, probably larger than any other in Narnia's world. Its northern border runs along the desert that separates Calormen from Archenland. Deep in the south is the Calormene province of Calavar, which is ruled by Aravis' father Kidrash Tarkaan. Aravis and Hwin flee to the northeast in order to avoid cities and towns directly to the north.

Probably not as far south as Kidrash Tarkaan's palace and at the seashore is the small home in which Shasta and Arsheesh live. Shasta had washed up in a boat, along with a dead sailor,

the WORLD of Shasta, Late
Queen and the talkir
the ho

DETAIL
OF THE
BATTLE
OF
ANVARD

10

9

7 4

TO NARNIA

1

5

3

6

8

TO DESERT

2

DESE

Legend

1 Rabadash's warriors hammer Anvard's main gate
2 Lucy leads archers against Calormene warriors
3 Where Calormene warriors are assembled
4 Edward leads cavalry, followed by Narnian Dwarfs and Giants
5 Battle site where Shasta falls
6 Route where some Calormenes flee
7 King Lune charges Calormenes at the gate killing some and forcing others to flee
8 Forest where defeated Calormenes flee
9 Rabadash is captured on a wall
10 Rabadash refuses to redeem himself before Aslan and is transformed into a donkey

TEHISH BAAN

CALORMEN

ARAVIS' HOME

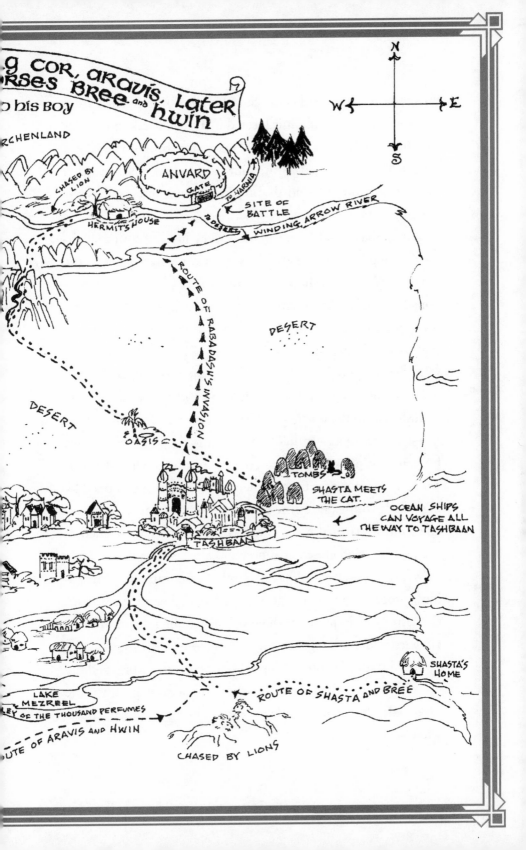

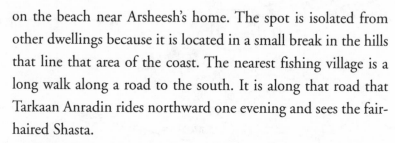

on the beach near Arsheesh's home. The spot is isolated from other dwellings because it is located in a small break in the hills that line that area of the coast. The nearest fishing village is a long walk along a road to the south. It is along that road that Tarkaan Anradin rides northward one evening and sees the fair-haired Shasta.

When Shasta and Bree run away, they head north to north-west, trying to avoid roads and stay in the wilder parts of the range of hills, but a lion chases them toward the west, where lions had chased Aravis and Hwin toward the east. From there the quartet heads in a northerly direction, veering this way and that to avoid busy roads, as well as towns and cities. The cities seem heavily populated but the countryside sparsely so.

Eventually they climb atop a low hill and see the capital city of Tashbaan to the northeast. Tashbaan is on a mountain-island in a wide area of a river that flows east into the sea. It has a large, busy area of piers and quays along its southern edge; it is evidently a major center for commerce. The city is surrounded by high walls with gates to the north and south (maybe northeast and southwest) that lead to bridges. These gates are opened in the morning and closed at sunset and are well guarded.

Within its walls, Tashbaan is a confusing mixture of build-ings, progressively more spectacular the higher they are, with the Tisroc's main palace at the top. The winding streets are very crowded and hard to get through. The main traffic rule is based on social station; people of higher station get to go before those of stations lower than theirs. So, the Tisroc gets to go anywhere unimpeded, but poor people have to wait on the sides of streets while rich people pass by.

Across from the northern bridge, at the edge of the desert, are the twelve tombs of ancient kings. They seem to be very old, and they are shaped like gigantic beehives rising out of the desert; their doors are black. It is among the tombs that Shasta, Bree, Aravis, and Hwin agree to meet if they are separated in Tashbaan, which they are. While he waits, afraid of the tombs, Shasta meets Aslan in the form of a great golden cat that gives him comfort.

Shasta is foolish enough to think about crossing the desert without his friends, which would be a mistake. The desert is large, dry, and unforgiving. Without the others, Shasta might never have found the oasis to the northwest. The oasis is small and cannot satisfy the thirst of a large group, but two horses and two children are satisfied. Aravis knows that Rabadash intends to lead a military force north to attack Archenland, so she and the others cannot linger long at the oasis because Rabadash might find them there. Rabadash's two hundred horsemen are probably too many to be able to slake their thirst at the oasis, but Rabadash made it clear that he would be sure they were well equipped, so they probably carry enough water to get them across the desert safely.

The horses and children veer to the northwest as they cross the desert, whereas Rabadash remains to the east of them. They find a small gorge in which a river flows and a fruit tree may be found. The place is very comfortable and refreshing and sounds a bit like the walled garden in *The Magician's Nephew*. The gorge leads north; when the group emerges from it they are in west central Archenland, a mountain kingdom that stretches along the mountain range that forms the southern border of

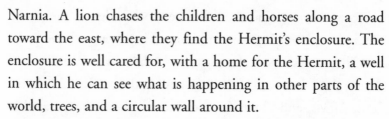

Narnia. A lion chases the children and horses along a road toward the east, where they find the Hermit's enclosure. The enclosure is well cared for, with a home for the Hermit, a well in which he can see what is happening in other parts of the world, trees, and a circular wall around it.

While the others may rest in the Hermit's home, Shasta must run eastward toward Anvard to warn of Rabadash's invasion. He runs along a path among stones and trees and eventually finds King Lune and a hunting party in an open area. From there lead roads to the east that have many twists and turns; one turn leads north to Anvard, another leads farther east then north along a narrow, treacherous mountain trail. It is on this trail that Shasta meets Aslan. The trail also leads into Narnia, where Shasta warns Talking Animals of Rabadash's plans, and a stag rushes off to Cair Paravel with the warning.

The road from Cair Paravel to Anvard is large and seems to be well used. On it, a small army of Narnians led by King Edmund marches south into Archenland and prepares to surprise Rabadash with an attack from the south and east. Anvard is a great walled city, with a courtyard within its main gate; it is in this courtyard that Aslan will give Rabadash a chance to repent and King Lune will show Shasta to others and declare Shasta to be Prince Cor. The gate is very strong, and Rabadash's men bang on it with a tree trunk to try to break it down. Just outside the main gate at least three roads meet: one from Narnia to the north, another to the west along which King Lune and his party would have raced to get back to Anvard before Rabadash reached it, and one to the southeast to the desert, on which Rabadash would have ridden, and on which some of his followers flee during the battle.

There is forest to the north of Anvard and north of the clearing in front of the main gate. There is a rise to the east of the clearing that is forested, as well. On this rise the Narnian archers take their places, looking down on the Calormenes. The rest of the Narnian army is hidden by the northern forest and a turn in the road. The battle begins with Narnian archers shooting at the Calormenes, followed by a charge into the ranks of the Calormenes by Narnian horsemen and foot soldiers. Then, King Lune leads an attack out of Anvard's gate, and the Calormenes have only one way to run, back down the road on which they came. A few do this. After a furious fight, the others are killed or captured, and Rabadash is trapped along Anvard's wall, north of the main gate.

THEMES AND CHARACTERS

The central characters of *The Horse and His Boy* are Shasta, supposedly the son of a poor Calormene fisherman, Bree, a warhorse of a Tarkaan, Aravis, daughter of a Tarkaan, and Hwin, a mare of Aravis' father's stable. Coincidences seem to abound as these four characters, far apart in home as well as social status, come together. They will find that a Lion has had much to do with their adventures, and the coincidences are not so coincidental after all.

The fundamental themes of *The Horse and His Boy* are friendship, love, trust, and faithfulness. The narrative is not only about four companions fleeing slavery for a promised land of liberty, but about how they grow together and learn to respect and

understand each other. This may sound too sweet to tolerate, but in their working out are attacks by lions, large, ancient burial grounds, palaces, a war, and plenty of suspense. Shasta, Aravis, Bree, and Hwin have several harrowing adventures and learn more than they may have wished about themselves.

CHAPTER-BY-CHAPTER DEVELOPMENT OF THEMES AND CHARACTERS IN *THE HORSE AND HIS BOY*

— Chapter 1: How Shasta Set Out on His Travels —

The Horse and His Boy begins, "This is the story of an adventure that happened in Narnia and Calormen and the lands between, in the Golden Age when Peter was High King in Narnia and his brother and his two sisters were King and Queens under him." This novel provides the only good look at the reign of the Pevensies, but it does not begin at Cair Paravel in Narnia, but along the seacoast in a remote area of Calormen.

Arsheesh, a "poor fisherman" and Shasta, a boy, eke out a meager living. Shasta has many chores to perform, and he is sometimes beaten for his trouble. (This is a violation of universal moral law, as Lewis sees it, in which the abuse of children is forbidden.) Shasta's life is a hard one, but he may be someone special.

Tarkaan Anradin, riding on his great warhorse, sees Shasta and knows that he cannot be Arsheesh's son. He says to Arsheesh, "This boy is manifestly no son of yours, for your cheek is as dark as mine but the boy is fair and white like the accursed but beautiful barbarians who inhabit the remote north." A *tarkaan* is a high nobleman in Calormen's feudal society, which means that a tarkaan's word carries much weight. He means to buy Shasta as a slave from Arsheesh. In Calormen, slavery is a widespread practice.

Slavery is a very hard matter for the slave, and when he over-hears Tarkaan Anradin's plans for him, Shasta wants no part of them. This is where the story takes a strange turn, at least for Shasta. The tarkaan's horse talks to him. The are no Talking Animals in the south of Narnia's world; they seem to be primarily in the north and on the eastern islands.

The horse is named "Breehy-hinny-brinny-hoohy-hah," which is a respectable name for a horse but is too hard for Shasta to pronounce. Therefore, Shasta dubs the horse "Bree," which may lose something in translation but still captures the flavor of the horse's full name. Bree is an experienced warhorse, a veteran of the Tarkaan Anradin's many battles; he has survived by his intelligence and common sense. Kidnapped from the north when he was young, Bree has never before let on that he could talk, but in Shasta's situation, he sees an opportunity to free himself, for he regards himself as little other than a slave of the tarkaan.

A boy journeying alone would be subject to capture and slavery; a horse wandering alone would be subject to capture and, to Bree's mind, slavery. But a horse and a boy together would look like a servant boy caring for his master's horse and might not attract attention. It does not take much to convince Shasta that running away is a good idea, so he and Bree head off toward the north, toward the capital city of Calormen, where the Tisroc, ruler of Calormen dwells.

— Chapter 2: A Wayside Adventure —

In this chapter, the major plot elements of *The Horse and His Boy* come together. First, Shasta learns to ride and to ride well, because "No one can teach riding so well as a horse," and Bree teaches him (and Bree wants nothing to do with spurs). As Shasta and Bree flee northward, some lions frighten Bree. These lions send him off toward a pair of riders, who turn out to be a mare and a girl. Remember these lions because they turn out to be important, later.

Perhaps Shasta may be forgiven his exclamation, "Why it's only a girl!" when he first meets Aravis. It may be attributed to an upbringing in which he met few people, and it may reflect Arsheesh's prejudices. Boys may make this exclamation or others like it too often; in *The Chronicles of Narnia* Lewis offers many examples of tough, courageous, capable women, and this particular girl, Aravis is among them.

Shasta has his embarrassing prejudice that experiences with Aravis will help him to put aside, and Aravis has hers. She regards the boy dressed in rags and obviously not of her noble social class as lacking in the courage and social graces that only one born of noble blood (to her way of thinking) can have. Perhaps she may be forgiven for her unenlightened view of Shasta, because she seems to have been raised by selfish, cruel people who cared nothing for enlightened thought. She is a *tarkheena*, a female of the level of nobility of the tarkaan.

Both Shasta and Aravis have prejudiced views of the horses. They have been raised in a land without Talking Animals and do not realize that the Talking Animals are deserving of respect.

At one point, Bree rebukes them by noting that "you might just as well say I stole *him*." From this comes the title *The Horse and His Boy* rather than *The Boy and His Horse*. After all, Bree is the older and wiser of the two. Hwin does not express herself as passionately as does Bree, but she is plainly smart and as deserving of respect as Bree.

Bree says to Aravis, "We're free Narnians, Hwin and I, and I suppose, if you're running away to Narnia, you want to be one too. In that case Hwin isn't *your* horse any longer. One might just as well say you're *her* human." Aside from reinforcing Bree's view of the relationship between the horses and the humans, this passage presents an idea that is repeated through most of *The Horse and His Boy*: the association of Narnia with freedom.

— Chapter 3: At the Gates of Tashbaan —

Aravis Tarkheena was not a slave, yet she could be bartered in marriage. The husband chosen for her was the husband she must accept. Aravis plans to plunge a dagger into her heart when a mare speaks up: "O my mistress, do not by any means destroy yourself, for if you live you may yet have good fortune but all the dead are dead alike," says Hwin. Hwin tells her of Narnia, a land of freedom. She says she has a great wish to be in that country of Narnia, and she seems to have sense enough to put more trust into a Talking Horse horse than in "Zardeenah, Lady of the Night and of Maidens," from whom little help is to be had. Thus, in Aravis' escape, although it was better planned than the escape of Shasta and Bree, it is the horse who actually comes up with the idea of escaping together.

Unfortunate Shasta listens to the tale of Aravis' escape and then to Aravis and Bree chatting about people and places he knows nothing about. Shasta will feel more and more excluded as he mixes with royalty, follows the orders of a hermit, and hides among the Tombs of the Ancient Kings. Tombs are where he and the others are to wait until all four are gathered again, after their perilous journey through Tashbaan.

— Chapter 4: Shasta Falls in with the Narnians —

In this chapter, old friends King Edmund, Queen Susan, and Mr. Tumnus from *The Lion, the Witch and the Wardrobe* reappear. They are not the focus of the plot, but it is fun to see them interact. Susan seems a little too easily taken in by Prince Rabadash, but she carries herself like a queen. Edmund has become a man, and he conducts himself with courage and good judgment. Mr. Tumnus is grayer than he was, but he is now a trusted advisor of the two kings and two queens of Narnia. By this time Peter and Susan and Edmund and Lucy had been Kings and Queens of Narnia for several years.

Lewis has some fun toying with expectations in this chapter. Shasta has been mistaken for Corin, a wayward prince of Archenland who has sneaked away from his lodgings in Tashbaan. This looks as though it may be a retread of the very old and tired theme of Mark Twain's *The Prince and the Pauper,* in which a prince and a commoner exchange places. Later, when Corin shows up, it is easy to wonder whether the boys have some closer connection beyond their resemblance; Lewis has been foreshadowing such a possibility ever since Tarkaan

Anradin pointed out that Shasta looked like a northerner.

Prince Rabadash is mentioned in this chapter, and he will become an important figure as the plot unfolds. He has shown himself to be dashing and valiant while visiting Cair Paravel; he has been impressive enough for Queen Susan to journey to Tashbaan with the thought of marrying him. Yet, Susan has seen how even women of the nobility are treated in Calormen—as property to be used as men wish. Edmund says that Rabadash is a proud, bloody, luxurious, cruel and self-pleasing tyrant, which led Susan to reply that "in the name of Aslan" they should leave Tashbaan. That phrase, "in the name of Aslan" will become more meaningful for Shasta as he continues his adventures.

— Chapter 5: Prince Corin —

While the king and queen and their advisors confer on how to escape on the "*Splendour Hyaline,*" Shasta listens and tries to be inconspicuous. He was raised by a cruel, selfish man, and he had therefore developed the habit of never telling adults anything if he could manage it, because "he thought they would always spoil or stop whatever you were trying to do." This is an attitude shared by many young people, and it helps to make Shasta more fully human—someone we can understand. Further, it explains why he does not say that he is not Corin. He has been severely abused by adults and expects the worst from them. Therefore, he can foresee nothing but trouble resulting from revealing who he really is. He has yet to learn that some adults are trustworthy.

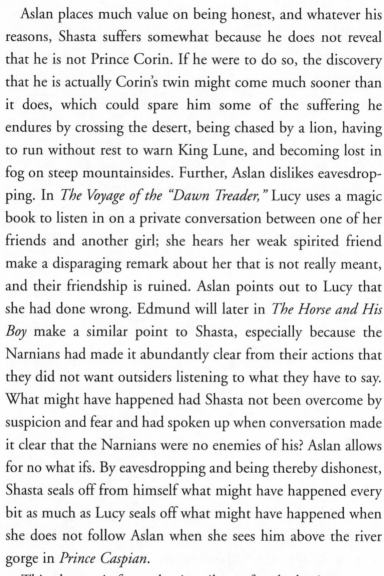

Aslan places much value on being honest, and whatever his reasons, Shasta suffers somewhat because he does not reveal that he is not Prince Corin. If he were to do so, the discovery that he is actually Corin's twin might come much sooner than it does, which could spare him some of the suffering he endures by crossing the desert, being chased by a lion, having to run without rest to warn King Lune, and becoming lost in fog on steep mountainsides. Further, Aslan dislikes eavesdropping. In *The Voyage of the "Dawn Treader,"* Lucy uses a magic book to listen in on a private conversation between one of her friends and another girl; she hears her weak spirited friend make a disparaging remark about her that is not really meant, and their friendship is ruined. Aslan points out to Lucy that she had done wrong. Edmund will later in *The Horse and His Boy* make a similar point to Shasta, especially because the Narnians had made it abundantly clear from their actions that they did not want outsiders listening to what they have to say. What might have happened had Shasta not been overcome by suspicion and fear and had spoken up when conversation made it clear that the Narnians were no enemies of his? Aslan allows for no what ifs. By eavesdropping and being thereby dishonest, Shasta seals off from himself what might have happened every bit as much as Lucy seals off what might have happened when she does not follow Aslan when she sees him above the river gorge in *Prince Caspian.*

This chapter is focused primarily on foreshadowing events, thereby creating suspense. The more suspenseful foreshadowing comes from the conversation among the Narnians in their chambers. For instance, Mr. Tumnus tells of a conversation with the Grand Vizier of Calormen in which he is asked how much he likes Calormen. Disliking everything about Calormen, Mr. Tumnus evasively said that he yearned for the cooler climate of Narnia, to which the Grand Vizier (the very same man who is supposed to marry Aravis) replied that the faun was welcome to return to Narnia *"always provided you leave us in exchange a bride for our prince."* Such threatening talk is common to the schemers of the Tisroc's court, especially for the Grand Vizier who is notorious for his underhanded methods. Plainly, the Tisroc plans to keep the Narnians captive in his capital city until Queen Susan weds the odious Prince Rabadash. This foreshadows conflict, and out of the conflict will arise the exciting action of the rest of the novel.

Lewis further uses this chapter to fill in some details that will become important later, as well as foreshadowing the romantic conclusion of *The Horse and His Boy.* He reveals that King Lune of Archenland is Corin's father. Archenland is a nation almost as old as Narnia, founded in the Narnian year 180 by a son of King Frank, Narnia's first king at the beginning of the world. It is south of Narnia, in the mountains on Narnia's border. This is why Rabadash will need to pass through it on his way to Cair Paravel. When Aravis learns in Chapter 8 that Rabadash plans to cross the desert to invade Narnia, we readers realize that he must pass through Archenland first, probably only after a struggle. In addition, the mistaking of Shasta for Prince Corin should already have us wondering about the boys. One has lived as a slave, working long hours out of doors, and he has made a long and dangerous trek through Calormen to Tashbaan; one would think he would be as tanned as he could

be and would bear the marks and bruises of a hard life of physical labor. Yet, his features are nonetheless so close to those of Prince Corin that he is thought to be Corin after Corin has gotten into a few scrapes in Tashbaan. When Corin and Shasta meet, the two boys suddenly knew that they were friends. This odd happenstance is foreshadowing for events that follow, because Lewis is too good a writer to mention this for no reason. Blood calls to blood, hinting at the relationship King Lune will eventually reveal.

— Chapter 6: Shasta Among the Tombs —

Tombs of the ancient kings are wonderfully mysterious and unusual. Each looks like a giant beehive, rounded at the top. It is easy to picture all sorts of frightful beings inhabiting the black structures, and as the sun sets, their shadows could hide ghouls or other menaces. It is no wonder that Shasta worries about whether he will be abandoned by his companions and whether he should get away from the tombs and head out across the desert on his own.

"She [Aravis] was proud and could be hard enough but she was as true as steel and would never have deserted a companion, whether she liked him or not," but Shasta cannot help but worry that while he was trapped in a palace, his companions had left without him. With the way Aravis has treated him with contempt, he thinks that abandoning him would be just the sort of thing that Aravis would do. But she will surprise him, just as he will surprise her when she is attacked by a lion in Archenland.

He thinks about setting off across the desert toward Narnia: "It was a crazy idea and if he had read as many books as you have about journeys over deserts he would never have dreamed of it. But Shasta had read no books at all." This idea of reading the proper books is repeated in *The Chronicles of Narnia*; Lewis thought that books could prepare their readers for life. In *The Voyage of the "Dawn Treader,"* he mentions some of the sort of readings that fail to teach people to think. In the present case, Lewis means that if Shasta had read adventure books, then he would know that crossing a desert by oneself, without supplies, would end in his death. Deserts are unforgiving, dangerous environments.

Pay close attention to the Cat in this chapter. The Cat brings comfort to Shasta among the suitably ominous tombs. Further, it leads Shasta to the desert side of the tombs and stares northward, across the desert to the far mountains. It also allows Shasta to sleep against it, giving him comfort in a setting that frightens the boy.

— Chapter 7: Aravis in Tashbaan —

Aravis has the good fortune to encounter a friend of hers, Lasaraleen, who does not understand why Aravis would pass up a chance to marry an important member of the Tisroc's court. Somewhat giddy, her gay, carefree personality is a marked contrast to Aravis' serious, brooding nature. Even so, she is willing to help her friend on her adventure. Lasaraleen might seem like a silly girl with a shallow mind, but pay attention to what she actually does. One thing she does not do is betray Aravis to any-

one. She knows how to help Aravis, and she manages to endure some very dangerous moments without giving herself and Aravis away. She is very frightened, it is true, but she is a true friend to Aravis. Perhaps she is one reason why Tashbaan appears in Aslan's Country in *The Last Battle*.

— Chapter 8: In the House of the Tisroc —

This chapter is a good example of Lewis' storytelling skills. In Chapter 4, through Shasta, Lewis shows what the plans of the Narnians are. In the present chapter, Lewis reveals through Aravis the plans of the Calormenes. This has three beneficial effects on the novel: 1) we readers are kept informed about everything that is going on; 2) when Aravis, Shasta, Bree, and Hwin reunite, they will be able to know what both sides are doing and therefore be able to work out a rational course of action; 3) it builds suspense, because the two plans may result in much danger for Aravis, Shasta, Bree, and Hwin.

As in Chapter 4, Lewis creates suspense in this chapter by creating the possibility of discovery. Although there is a great deal of exposition (people explaining what the situation is) in both chapters, Lewis holds the reader's attention with suspense. In Shasta's case, there is the possibility of his being discovered to be someone other than Corin, who could show up at any moment. In Aravis's case, the couch does not fully hide her and Lasaraleen. All the men in the room have to do is look in their direction to discover them; both Aravis and Lasaraleen know that if they are discovered they will be put to death. Thus, the conversation of the men, explaining what

they mean to do, has throughout it the possibility of the girls' discovery and murder.

The Tisroc, his son Rabadash, and the vizier are shown to be corrupt and without honor. For them, life as all about power. Normal family feelings are absent, replaced by political moves and countermoves. The Tisroc approves of Rabadash's invasion of Archenland partly on the chance that his son will be killed, thus removing a threat to the Tisroc's own life. Heroic princes have been known to kill their fathers and become Tisrocs themselves.

This chapter shows the bitter animosity the Calormenes have toward Narnia. For instance, the Tisroc says, "It is commonly reported that the High King of Narnia (whom may the gods utterly reject) is supported by a demon of hideous aspect and irresistible maleficence who appears in the shape of a Lion." In *The Magician's Nephew* and *The Lion, the Witch and the Wardrobe,* evil is recognizable for its animosity toward Aslan. Jadis loathed the sight of Aslan in *The Magician's Nephew* and threatened to kill Edmund and her Dwarf in *The Lion, the Witch and the Wardrobe* if either one said the name *Aslan* in her presence.

Lewis also shows the cultural bias against women that may be responsible for Shasta's own first response to Aravis: "For it is well known that women are as changeable as weathercocks." When they came to visit Tashbaan, Queen Susan and King Edmund discovered a society in which women are treated as inferiors to men. It would be a bad place for Susan or for Aravis to live. Occasionally, a disparaging comment about women in general appears in *The Chronicles of Narnia*; such comments reveal the wrongheadedness of the speakers, be they otherwise heroes or villains. In Shasta's case, the boy learns to appreciate women for what they do. In Rabadash's case, not all of his life is revealed, so there is a possibility of his learning to hold women in high regard, but given the depth of his villainy, it seems unlikely.

— Chapter 9: Across the Desert —

Literary critics have attacked poor Lasaraleen as being afraid and cowardly, but she serves as a good friend. She is not the only one who is afraid: Lewis points out that Aravis is herself trembling, probably from fear. Aravis threatens to run out into a corridor and scream, calling attention to Lasaraleen and her, and very likely getting them killed on the spot. "Oh you *are* unkind," says Lasaraleen. "And I in such a state!" This makes her sound weak, although not every person is going to have Aravis's unusual physical courage. But remember what Lasaraleen has already done: She has thought of a way her friend Aravis can leave Tashbaan unnoticed, she has entered a forbidden area of a shadowy old palace, and she has managed to keep quiet all the while listening to three men talk about killing people. So far, she has done well. In *The Last Battle*, Aslan tells Emeth that the young warrior's actions have spoken for him, earning His blessing; Lasaraleen's actions similarly speak for her. In the present chapter, Lasaraleen eventually pulls herself together, and at the imminent risk of her life, she takes Aravis to the small boat *and* embraces Aravis affectionately! That is more courage, forgiveness, and friendship than Aravis had any right to expect from Lasaraleen. People like Lasaraleen may be among the reasons Tashbaan makes it into Aslan's Country at the end of the world.

Bree is hard on himself later on, when he behaves like an ordinary horse and runs from a lion, but the value of his years of experience as a military horse is put to good use in crossing the desert. "Trot and walk," he tells the others, meaning they should cross the desert by trotting for awhile and then walking for awhile to conserve energy while still moving onward. He tells Aravis and Shasta that they should dismount during the periods of walking and walk, too, but Shasta responds to Bree by leaping on his back when the sand burns the boy's bare feet and remarking, "Can't be helped." His knowledge of how to march across a hostile landscape is invaluable for the group; his endurance, built up by years of carrying his master to battles against Calormene neighbors, enables him to bear the burden of Shasta; and his leadership shows his companions how to survive their dangerous crossing of the desert.

Further, he teaches Shasta valuable lessons by example. Lewis notes, "But one of the worst results of being a slave and being forced to do things is that when there is no-one to force you any more you find you have almost lost the power of forcing yourself." While his companions forge on, Shasta has trouble pushing himself. Aravis is too proud to show her feelings, which must be worn to exhaustion, and Bree is focused on completing his mission, but Shasta seems to lose the life in his spirit. Even though "mile after mile, there was nothing but level sand," Bree pushes on, and Shasta learns from him how to push on as well. Part of what he learns in this chapter is to motivate himself. The hardships of the desert prepare him for the challenges he will face in Archenland, especially his long run to King Lune.

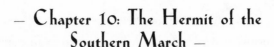

— Chapter 10: The Hermit of the Southern March —

Aravis admits that Shasta is the best one of them all, which is a big admission for her, and it is a strong sign of her personal growth. It also suggests that Shasta has broken free of the restraints on his spirit that were made during his years of servitude. What has he done? He has turned to face a lion that claws at Aravis while Bree runs away and Aravis and Hwin flee. This action requires him to think for himself and to take action motivated by his best nature, rather than what people tell him to do. Eventually, he discovers that his heroic actions were motivated by Aslan, that in fact Aslan has been motivating him, helping him, and teaching him throughout his adventures.

Whereas Shasta discovers in himself courage that he thought he lacked, having fled lions in Calormen and spent a night afraid at the Tombs outside Tashbaan, Aravis and Bree receive lessons of their own. For Aravis, proud and courageous, the lesson is physically painful: She is clawed on her back by the lion that chases her and her companions to the Hermit's home. Her first lesson is one in humility. Shasta, the seemingly weak-spirited slave boy, far beneath her in social class, not only faced the lion to save her but actually *ran back* to the lion to put himself between it and Hwin and her. It is not something she would even have thought of doing. To her credit, she realizes this almost as soon as she reaches the Hermit. Her second lesson is made clear only later, when she meets Aslan. She could be killed by the claws of the lion, but the cuts on her back are not deep enough to kill. Way back at the start of her adventures, she took advantage of a servant girl who was to watch over her. The girl was whipped for letting Aravis go; Aslan, who is actually the lion chasing the travelers in this chapter, claws Aravis as a lesson not to abuse others for her own selfish ends. This lesson is very important, because it will help Aravis be a good leader and Queen.

Bree is particularly hard on himself, and in spite of his excellent leadership during much of *The Horse and His Boy,* he probably should be. He has made much of his having been a great, proud warhorse, and he has bragged often about his exploits in battle, but who was it that beat everyone to the Hermit's home, fleeing in panic? Bree. This is a shocking, dispiriting lesson to learn about himself, and Bree believes that slavery is all he is fit for. Who turned and charged the lion, like a good warrior? The slave boy Shasta who had to be carried without walking across the desert. Having bragged about his battlefield exploits, his humiliation is great. The point Lewis makes, here, is that there is a difference between beating on those who are weaker, as the nonintelligent ordinary horses were that Bree confronted in battles in which the Calormenes were the stronger side. He has not known defeat; he has not known competition with equals. At the end of *The Horse and His Boy,* his true test will come when he must swallow his pride and live among Narnian Talking Horses as an equal.

The Hermit is a strange character who welcomes the four into his compound and then sends Shasta off to warn King Lune of the invasion of the Calormenes. This is very hard on Shasta, who has already accomplished plenty for one day. But he has learned to persevere, to find in himself the desire to push himself. It is a lesson athletes must learn, and he has learned to run the extra miles it takes to be a winner. The horses are too tired to carry him, so he must run. Lewis says that Shasta had not yet learned that one good deed usually leads to another and harder one. Unfortunately, Lewis had does not develop this idea further because it is an important part of his commentary on unselfishness. Shasta has plainly learned to be so unselfish as to offer his own life to protect the lives of others, and Bree has learned how selfish he himself can be. Perhaps Lewis here means to foreshadow the actions Shasta will take during the rest of the novel, with each conflict calling for more effort and courage from Shasta until he faces the great test of his patience, book learning and getting an education.

— Chapter 11: The Unwelcome Fellow Traveller —

Shasta's first impression of King Lune is a good one: He is "the jolliest, fat, apple-cheeked, twinkling-eyed King you could imagine." One of the wonderful aspects of very good writing is how it surprises by side-stepping an easy cliché and offers something better. In this case, the cliché would be for the jolly king to ridicule Shasta as only a little boy; instead, King Lune acts like a truly good king behaves. Any possibility of a threat to his people should be taken seriously, even from a tired, sweaty boy dressed in rags. King Lune says that the truth is in Shasta's face, showing that he is a good judge of character.

Soon, Lewis will reveal why King Lune "stared hard at Shasta again with that curious expression, almost a hungry expression, in his steady grey eyes." King Lune must be wondering about the significance of Shasta's looking like Prince Corin.

Meanwhile, Rabadash's cruelty is illustrated by his instruction to his warriors:

> Kill me every barbarian male within its walls, down to the child that was born yesterday, and everything else is yours to divide as you please—the women, the gold, the jewels, the weapons, and the wine.

Beyond the depth of his depravity, this passage indicates Rabadash's lust for power; the wealth matters less to him than conquering and controlling the kingdom.

Shasta is soon separated from King Lune and Lune's followers; he ends up lost in a mist, with something pacing him. To his inquiries, Shasta is told by a Voice:

> I was the lion who gave the Horses the new strength of fear for the last mile so that you should reach King Lune in time. And I was the lion you do not remember who pushed the boat in which you lay, a child near death, so that it came to shore where a man sat, wakeful at midnight, to receive you.

Shasta knows nothing of the truth about Aslan; he has been raised in Calormen, where Aslan is feared and hated. It must be a shock when Shasta turns to see a giant Lion, taller than the horse, pacing alongside him. The horse does not seem to mind. The light emanates from the Lion; shining is one of Aslan's qualities because He is the Bringer of light. "No-one ever saw anything more terrible or beautiful," Lewis declares.

Aslan as a source of light has Biblical sources; Christ is the Light of the world.

After one glance at Aslan's face, Shasta slipped out of the saddle and fell at His feet. As often happens when a true-hearted person meets Aslan, Shasta drops before Him. The warrior Emeth from Calormen will do the same in *The Last Battle*. It is a spontaneous acknowledgment of Aslan's supreme goodness, as well as a reaction to His overwhelming beauty. It is not an expression of cowardly fear, but instead of the fear one might reasonably have in meeting the greatest desire of one's heart.

A somewhat puzzling passage is that of the three voices. Without explanation, Shasta's question "Who are you?" is answered "Myself" in three voices, one deep, another loud and gay, and another that is like a whisper, but powerful. This is the only passage in *The Chronicles of Narnia* in which Lewis personifies the concept of the Trinity in one mysterious figure, the Father (the Emperor-over-sea), the Son (Aslan), and the Holy Spirit (Aslan's breath). Lewis did not claim to understand the concept of the Trinity, agreeing with a multitude of theologians that the concept is too large for human minds. Shasta's reaction of fear and joy is a response to being in the presence of God.

— Chapter 12: Shasta in Narnia —

In a series of novels in which children take charge of their lives and perform heroic deeds, it is somewhat jarring to hear King Edmund say that a boy in battle is a danger only to his own side. Prince Corin gives cause for concern when he injures the Dwarf Thornbut in a silly fight. On the other hand, Shasta has confronted a Lion that attacked Aravis (not knowing yet Who the Lion was), run to warn King Lune, and traversed dangerous mountain trails to Narnia. By now, he should be more respected, but as in the rest of the novel, he is underestimated.

It is interesting to see King Edmund at work at the end of this chapter. At the end of *The Lion, the Witch and the Wardrobe*, we learn that he will be called "King Edmund the Just," and he seems in *The Horse and His Boy* to be prone to making wise-sounding pronouncements. It turns out that in addition to being just, he is a good leader and a fine military commander; he is a true King of Narnia even if Peter is the High King. Later, when Rabadash is judged, Edmund will reveal that he is a compassionate man, ever mindful of his own treason in *The Lion, the Witch and the Wardrobe*.

– Chapter 13: The Fight at Anvard –

Where is Queen Susan, whose interest in Rabadash was an important factor in inspiring Rabadash's invasion of Archenland, to be followed by Narnia? Queen Susan is more like an ordinary adult, Corin tells Shasta when he asks where she is. She has no taste for battle and has remained behind at Cair Paravel rather than accompany Edmund and Lucy to fight. This does not mean that she lacks important skills; in *Prince Caspian*, she reveals great skill at using the bow and arrow when she shoots two soldiers on their helmets, knocking them down without killing them. But she is not a valiant fighter like Lucy. Even so, it seems irresponsible of her not to contribute in some way to the defense of Archenland and Narnia. This is one of Lewis' hints

about what is to come in *The Last Battle:* that Susan will not be
among the friends of Narnia at the end of the world.

The battle is a perilous one, with much give and take. The
map on page 334 shows some of the details about who stood
where and who did what. Lewis provides an interesting look at
how a Narnian military force would be arrayed. There is
strength in having many different kinds of talking beings to call
upon, with big cats like panthers and leopards on the left flank
and giants on the right flank. The giants seem especially formidable with their heavy armored boots meant for stomping on
enemies. The giants of Narnia tend not to be very bright, but
their courage is great, and they have a long heritage of honorable
service to their nation. The variety of fighting skills that Narnian
Talking Animals represent would seem to put the Calormenes at
a disadvantage, but the Calormene warriors are in constant
training, always preparing for another war, whereas the Narnians
are mostly volunteers who have lives apart from warfare. The
Narnians manage to surprise their enemy, with Lucy the
Valiant's archers raining arrows into the midst of the Calormenes
and King Edmund's cavalry and foot soldiers charging into the
flank of the Calormenes, but the Calormenes are much like
European knights of the 1100s, who were very strong and quick
and each able to fight alone or in formation. Many of the
Calormenes are on their horses in an instant and the battle
becomes heated. King Edmund has expressed a horror of having
children fight in battle, and events soon show why. Prince Corin
and Shasta charge into the melee and are stricken.

Back at the Hermit's home Aravis, Bree, and Hwin are very
worried about Shasta and the outcome of the battle. The Hermit

looks into a pool to see what might be happening at Anvard. Looking into water to see events far away or to look forward in time has an ancient history, probably dating back to before there were written languages. In medieval Europe, looking into pools of water, or even bowls of water, was a common practice for seers. However, the Hermit can only see the present, and when he looks into the pool, he sees Shasta fall. You may remember how Peter fought the White Witch to a stalemate in *The Lion, the Witch and the Wardrobe,* but he had a sword (the Holy Spirit) and a shield (faith), given him by Father Christmas, and he and his sword and shield are to the far north, where he is battling the evil giants in Ettinsmoor. Although Prince Corin is very strong and both he and Shasta are valiant, they are up against grown men who have trained all their lives to fight wars and who are perfectly willing to kill children, as Rabadash has asked them to do. Lost beneath the hooves of frantically moving horses, amid the weapons of a merciless enemy, Shasta is in deep trouble. Eventually, the Hermit announces that the Calormenes have been defeated. But what of Shasta?

While his friends at the Hermit's home worry about him, Shasta has new worries. He and Corin have both survived, but King Lune seems angry with them both for disobeying King Edmund's orders to stay out of the fray. Yet, King Lune seems proud of them both, too. The king pulls the boys together, and asks, "Has any man any doubts?" There is cheering, but Shasta does not understand why. Perhaps you and I have figured it out. If we remember the mistaken identity in the quarters of the Narnians in Tashbaan, we should have the clues we need for solving the mystery.

— Chapter 14: How Bree Became a Wiser Horse —

Hwin is eager to get moving, to finish her journey to Narnia, but Bree thinks they should wait a few days. Bree is not the only one reluctant to go to Narnia; Aravis herself wonders what she would do there. She also wonders why Bree often swears by the Lion, knowing how Bree fears lions. Bree says that Aslan is not actually a lion, but he has trouble explaining this to Hwin. It just must not be his day, for the truth of Aslan's nature is soon upon him.

Behind Bree, Hwin and Aravis "saw an enormous lion leap up from outside and balance itself on the top of the green wall; only it was a brighter yellow and it was bigger and more beautiful and more alarming than any lion they had ever seen." Perhaps, by now, you have noticed that Aslan loves to make dramatic entrances. His appearance next to Shasta on the mountain trails was mysterious and ominous; for Bree, Hwin, and Aravis He makes a surprising, breath-taking appearance.

Aslan helps Bree make the mental adjustment from being a great Calormene warhorse to just another Narnian Talking Horse in a community of Talking Horses. In Calormene, being a thinking horse, he was the master of ordinary horses in battle; they were not his equals in intelligence and lacked the ability to understand what was happening. Bree could understand what the Calormenes were saying and therefore what was expected of him. This made him proud; remember, he bragged through the long journey to Archenland about his deeds in battle. His pride was doing him no good.

The appearance of Shasta, now called "Prince Cor of

Archenland," is not entirely unexpected. Earlier King Lune placed Prince Corin and Shasta side-by-side and asked his court whether anyone had any doubts as to their relation. In true fairy-tale fashion, the lost boy who was washed up on a beach turns out to be the first-born twin son of King Lune; he stands to inherit Archenland.

— Chapter 15: Rabadash the Ridiculous —

Rabadash does seem like a fool as he rants and raves at his captors, but it is worth remembering that he is still a blood-thirsty murderer who treats women as commodities and relishes killing people, even newborns. With this in mind, Edmund's remark that "I have known one that did [mend]" is significant. Aslan turns Rabadash into a donkey and sends him back to Tashbaan in disgrace, but this gives Rabadash a chance to redeem himself. This helps explain Aslan's mercy, because Aslan gives second chances. Rabadash becomes a peacemaker because he dares not venture more than ten miles from Tashbaan; if he does, he will become a donkey permanently. And he does not want any of his generals becoming famous in battle and threatening his rule as Tisroc. Thus, Calormen has a period of peace as a gift from Aslan.

As happens in fairy tales, the young hero and the young heroine, Cor (Shasta) and Aravis marry. Their son is to be Ram the Great. Cor and Aravis seem to have a great marriage, one worthy of song and a book of its own. It is a sign of the richness of Lewis' Narnian world that there are many other tales that could become their own novels in the Narnia series.

VOCABULARY FOR
THE HORSE AND HIS BOY

Chapter 1: How Shasta Set Out on His Travels

heathery: covered with low-lying plants

thymy downs: aromatic low-lying herbs

plashing glens: lightly splashed or spattered glens; Lewis probably means this as a metaphor for the scattered light and shadow of the glen floors

Chapter 2: A Wayside Adventure

bother: forget

rum: strange, odd

trot: between a walk and a run

canter: a pace between a trot and a gallop

gallop: faster than a canter, slower than a run, this is a natural fast pace for a horse

Chapter 3: At the Gates of Tashbaan

lineage: a line of ancestry dating back to a specific ancestor

second watch of the night: a second period of being on guard; Aravis here refers to a period during which the first guards of the night for her father's palace have been replaced

ghouls: evil spirits who rob graves and eat corpses

Chapter 4: Shasta Falls in with the Narnians

terrace: flat areas cut out of the side of the mountain

pillared colonnades: columns set at regular intervals

minarets: slender towers with balconies

pinnacles: a small spire on a roof or wall

brazen gates: bright brass gates

sweetmeat: candy

pillared arcades: arches supported by pillars

tunics: loose garments that hang from the tops of the shoulders and end at the knees

scimitar: a curved sword with a sharp edge on its outer (convex) side; although it can be thrust forward, it is primarily a slashing weapon

hangdog: guilty

avouch: take responsibility

cypress trees: evergreen trees with small needles, usually found in warm climates

hastilude: a tournament with spears that resembles wartime combat

Chapter 5: Prince Corin

chafed: annoyed

Queen's grace: Queen's favors

Hyaline: like glass

snipe: a long-billed wading bird

gooseberry fools: a puree of gooseberries, cream, and sugar

mulberry fools: a puree of mulberries, cream, and sugar

stoup: a drinking vessel of almost any size, but probably a tankard, in this case

Chapter 6: Shasta Among the Tombs

queue: line

jackal: a member of one of three species of wild dog found in Africa and Asia

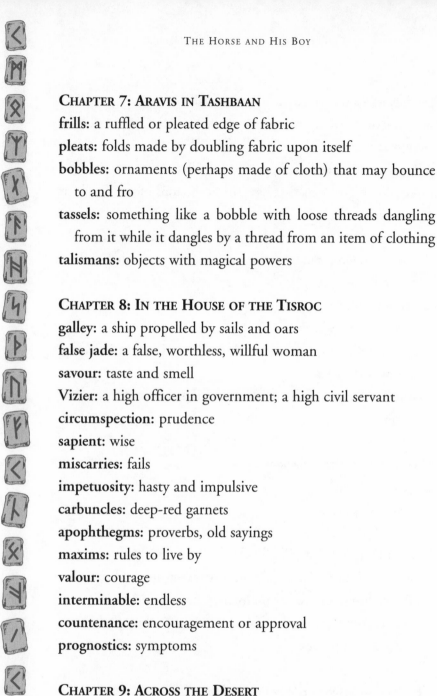

CHAPTER 7: ARAVIS IN TASHBAAN

frills: a ruffled or pleated edge of fabric

pleats: folds made by doubling fabric upon itself

bobbles: ornaments (perhaps made of cloth) that may bounce to and fro

tassels: something like a bobble with loose threads dangling from it while it dangles by a thread from an item of clothing

talismans: objects with magical powers

CHAPTER 8: IN THE HOUSE OF THE TISROC

galley: a ship propelled by sails and oars

false jade: a false, worthless, willful woman

savour: taste and smell

Vizier: a high officer in government; a high civil servant

circumspection: prudence

sapient: wise

miscarries: fails

impetuosity: hasty and impulsive

carbuncles: deep-red garnets

apophthegms: proverbs, old sayings

maxims: rules to live by

valour: courage

interminable: endless

countenance: encouragement or approval

prognostics: symptoms

CHAPTER 9: ACROSS THE DESERT

faugh: an expression of disgust

scullion: a lowly kitchen worker

punt: a small, square-ended, flat-bottomed boat that is propelled by a pole

quailed: cringed

victualled: supplied with food

prim: to look or act overly proper

CHAPTER 10: THE HERMIT OF THE SOUTHERN MARCH

fetlock: the part of a horse's leg behind and above the hoof

rowan: a deciduous tree native to Europe

heather: a low-lying plant

porridge: boiled oatmeal

CHAPTER 12: SHASTA IN NARNIA

morsel: a bit of food

haversacks: a large, sturdy bag with a single strap that is slung
over one's shoulder; it is used for carrying supplies

heart's-scald: an irritating pest

I'd as lief: I'd as soon

cordial: a thick liquid, usually for drinking in social situations

extremities: grave dangers

CHAPTER 13: THE FIGHT AT ANVARD

goosecap: foolish

horrid: unpleasant

sloped their huge clubs over their shoulders: the giants hold
one end of their clubs in their hand and lean the club back
to rest on their shoulders, somewhat like a modern soldier
may rest or slope a rifle while marching

girths: belts

portcullis: an armored grille that drops down to block the gateway to a fortress

funk: to flee in cowardly fright

a rod to your breech: a rod whipping your buttocks

CHAPTER 14: HOW BREE BECAME A WISER HORSE

rot: nonsense

an absolute brick: a very good man

bezzling: embezzling

CHAPTER 15: RABADASH THE RIDICULOUS

swap off: perhaps to slice off

noisome: disgusting and foul

gentilesse: good breeding

chafed: annoyed

pajock: fool

phantasm: an image of something that is not actually there

gape: open

estres: ethers

REFERENCES TO THE BIBLE IN *THE HORSE AND HIS BOY*

The passage from *The Horse and His Boy* is first quoted, followed by the relevant passage in the Bible. A transliteration of the 1611 edition of the King James version of the Bible is used for the Biblical quotations. Comments then follow.

— Chapter 14: How Bree Became a Wiser Horse —

1. "Touch me [Aslan]. Smell me. Here are my paws, here is my tail, these are my whiskers."

> **Luke 24:39:** "'Behold my hands and my feet, that it is I myself: handle me, and see, for a spirit does not have flesh and bones, as you see I have.'"

> **John 20:27:** "Then He said He [Jesus] to Thomas, 'Reach here your finger, and behold by hands, and reach here your hand, and thrust it into my side, and do not be faithless, but a believer.'"

Comments: As Christ does for his disciples, especially Thomas, Aslan does for Bree. He invites the horse to touch Him and learn for himself that He is not a phantasm or a metaphor but is a real, substantial lion. This is a fundamental principle of the Christian faith, that Christ is a physical being, that His resurrection was of the body as well as the spirit, proving a complete defeat of death. In the case of Aslan, Who appears in the world of Narnia for thousands of years, and Who was murdered by the White Witch in *The Lion, the Witch and the Wardrobe*, His physical reality offers proof of His victory over death.

DISCUSSION QUESTIONS AND PROJECTS FOR *THE HORSE AND HIS BOY*

— Overview —

1. How common is the bartering of women as brides, the way Aravis is bartered, in the world today?

2. Are King Edmund, Queens Lucy and Susan what you expected them to be?

3. Why does Aslan not just slay Rabadash?

4. Why would Rabadash's father and later Rabadash himself fear men who distinguished themselves in battle?

5. The Tombs of the Ancient Kings are imposing and mysterious. Write a story about how they came to be. You may wish to look at the "A Short History of Narnia" chapter of this book for ideas.

6. Write a story about King Cor and Queen Aravis. What adventure would be appropriate for them?

7. Write a story that shows why the son of King Cor and Queen Aravis would be called "Ram the Great."

8. During the events in *The Horse and His Boy*, High King Peter is leading a war against the northern giants. Read about the dif-

ferent kinds of northern giants in *The Silver Chair,* and then write a story about Peter's campaign. Which giants does he fight? Why does Narnia fight them? How do Narnians defeat people who are much larger than they are?

9. Why does Aslan allow Calormene to exist?

10. Women are spoken of as property several times in *The Horse and His Boy.* What do these occasions reveal about the characters of the speakers? How does this Calormene practice figure in the motivations of characters in *The Horse and His Boy?*

11. Why does Aslan only reveal Himself to Shasta and his companions near the end of the novel when he has been with them throughout their journey?

12. Why did Shasta not recognize Who the cat in the tombs was?

13. Draw, paint, or sculpt a representation of one of the palaces in Tashbaan. There are clues about what they look like throughout the chapters that take place in Tashbaan.

14. The city of Tashbaan is a splendid sight. Draw or paint a picture of it as it might have looked to Shasta, Aravis, Bree, and Hwin as they approached it. Lewis describes some of what it looked like, which should help you get started.

CHAPTER-BY-CHAPTER
DISCUSSION QUESTIONS

CHAPTER 1: HOW SHASTA SET OUT ON HIS TRAVELS

1. *The Horse and His Boy* begins, "This is the story of an adventure that happened in Narnia and Calormen and the lands between, in the Golden Age when Peter was High King in Narnia and his brother and his two sisters were King and Queens under him." Why is it important for Lewis to tell us this right at the beginning of his novel?

2. Why is it important for us to know that Shasta was beaten by Arsheesh?

3. Why would an accomplished warhorse like Bree wish to run-away from where he is admired and famous for his deeds in combat?

CHAPTER 2: A WAYSIDE ADVENTURE

1. Why does Bree suggest that it could be he who stole Shasta and that it could be Hwin who owned Aravis, instead of the other way around?

2. What do the lions do?

3. Is Shasta sexist? Is Aravis elitist? Is Bree conceited?

Chapter 3: At the Gates of Tashbaan

1. Lewis shifts the tone of the narrative when Aravis tells of her adventures in the formal Calomene style. How effective is his change of tone and diction (word choices)?

2. Why is it significant that Hwin comes up with the idea of how she and Aravis will escape together?

Chapter 4: Shasta Falls in with the Narnians

1. Have Edward and Susan become pompous? Why do they talk the way they do? (Take a look at the last chapter of *The Lion, the Witch and the Wardrobe*.)

2. Have you guessed by the end of this chapter what the resemblance between Shasta and Corin is about?

3. What does Sallowpad mean by "see the bear in his own den before you judge of his conditions"?

Chapter 5: Prince Corin

1. Lewis says, "The two boys (Corin and Shasta) were looking into each other's faces and suddenly found that they were friends." Why would this happen?

2. Are Shasta's reasons for not revealing himself good? Should he have taken Corin's welfare into consideration? After all, until the end of the chapter Corin is still missing.

3. Is the plan for Queen Susan's escape a good one?

CHAPTER 6: SHASTA AMONG THE TOMBS

1. Why does Shasta not realize that Aravis would not abandon him, that she is "as true as steel"?

2. Why does the cat stare across the desert at the far mountains?

3. How would having read books have helped Shasta's thinking in this chapter?

CHAPTER 7: ARAVIS IN TASHBAAN

1. Why does Lasaraleen think that the arranged marriage for Aravis is a good one? Why would Aravis disagree?

2. What motivates Lasaraleen to help Aravis?

CHAPTER 8: IN THE HOUSE OF THE TISROC

1. What does Aravis learn while in the house of the Tisroc?

2. How does Lewis create suspense in this chapter?

3. Why would the Tisroc consent to have his son die?

CHAPTER 9: ACROSS THE DESERT

1. How does each of the companions respond to the challenges of crossing the desert? What do their responses tell about their personalities?

2. Do any of the characters grow or mature in this chapter? How does it happen?

Chapter 10: The Hermit of the Southern March

1. Why would Bree say, "Slavery is all I'm fit for"?

2. Why does Shasta refuse to rest rather than do as the hermit says he should?

Chapter 11: The Unwelcome Fellow Traveller

1. Why does Shasta "after one glance at the Lion's face" slip out of the saddle and fall at His feet?

2. What is to be learned about the personality of King Lune during Shasta's first meeting with him?

3. How do you view the significance of Shasta's adventures after Aslan tells him that he had been with Shasta in various forms since Shasta ran away from Arsheesh?

Chapter 12: Shasta in Narnia

1. What is your impression of King Edmund in this chapter? Do you see in him the boy from *The Lion, the Witch and the Wardrobe*?

2. Why are Shasta and Corin supposed to remain out of the battle to come? Are the reasons for this good?

Chapter 13: The Fight at Anvard

1. Should Aravis, Bree, and Hwin be happy to learn of the defeat of the Calormenes at Anvard?

2. Why does Shasta disobey orders and fight? Is he right to do so?

3. Is Aslan protecting him, even now?

CHAPTER 14: HOW BREE BECAME A WISER HORSE

1. Hwin suggests that Bree does not wish to leave for Narnia right away because he is vain about his badly cut tail. Are there other reasons for his reluctance?

2. Why would Bree think Aslan was not really a lion?

3. What does Aslan give Aravis, Hwin, and Bree?

CHAPTER 15: RABADASH THE RIDICULOUS

1. Rabadash has caused many deaths, so why is he not executed?

2. Should Rabadash have a second chance?

3. Edmund had been a traitor. Is what he did in *The Lion, the Witch and the Wardrobe* worse than what Rabadash has done?

4. How satisfied are you with the ending?

Chapter 12

PRINCE CASPIAN

OVERVIEW

This novel is the beginning of a trilogy within *The Chronicles of Narnia,* consisting of *Prince Caspian, The Voyage of the "Dawn Treader,"* and *The Silver Chair.* In it, Lewis tells a little about the history of Narnia after the disappearance of Kings Peter and Edmund and Queens Lucy and Susan. Some pirates from the earth's South Seas stumbled on a deserted island that had a portal to Telmar in Narnia's world. Once established there, the pirates' descendants invaded Narnia and started a new line of monarchs, of whom Caspian is the direct descendant. The Telmarines were suspicious and afraid of the Talking Animals and other wondrous beings in Narnia and suppressed them. By Caspian X's era, the many nonhumans of Narnia are in hiding from the humans who rule the land; for many of the Telmarines, the fabulous animals and beings of Narnia are merely folk tales. Even so, they fear the eastern forests where they believe evil spirits live, and they fear the seacoast because it is from across the eastern sea that Aslan is said to come to visit Narnia. Aslan is much feared.

This hardly makes a good case for Caspian being the legitimate King of Narnia; he is the descendant of pirate kings who have persecuted Narnians. On the other hand, Lewis mentions no direct descendants of King Frank (from *The Magician's Nephew*), first King of Narnia, and he mentions no direct descendants of Peter, Susan, Edmund, or Lucy. Susan seriously contemplated marriage in *The Horse and His Boy,* and she or the others *could* have married and had children. Lewis is silent on this point.

Caspian's best claim to kingship is that he wants the Talking Animals and other Narnians to again live in Narnia as equals with humans. It is his sincere desire to win the freedom of the suppressed Narnians; that is his chief claim to their loyalty. That loyalty is hard to keep, as *Prince Caspian* reveals, and Caspian must show by deed as well as word that he means to rule well.

THE GEOGRAPHY OF *PRINCE CASPIAN*

The action of *Prince Caspian* takes place primarily in the southeastern region of Narnia, south from the Great River to the northern edge of the mountains of Archenland, east to Cair Paravel, now a ruin on an island at the mouth of the Great River, from a road that runs from Miraz's castle to Archenland. It is in this large area that many Old Narnians have managed to survive, because the Telmarine humans that rule Narnia are superstitious and believe that much of the woods, especially near the coast, are haunted. Even some Old Narnians such as Trumpkin think the rumors of ghosts may be true.

The landscape of this region has changed significantly from the era of *The Lion, the Witch and the Wardrobe*. The forest now covers nearly everything, right to the sea shore, as well as the new islands at the mouth of the Great River. The children at first do not recognize where they are because of the dense forest and because they are on an island. In *The Lion, the Witch and the Wardrobe*, Cair Paravel was beside the Great River, but as the children discover, it is now on one of several islands of the delta of the river. Further, the lower (eastern) part of the Great River now flows through a deep gorge; upon seeing this, the

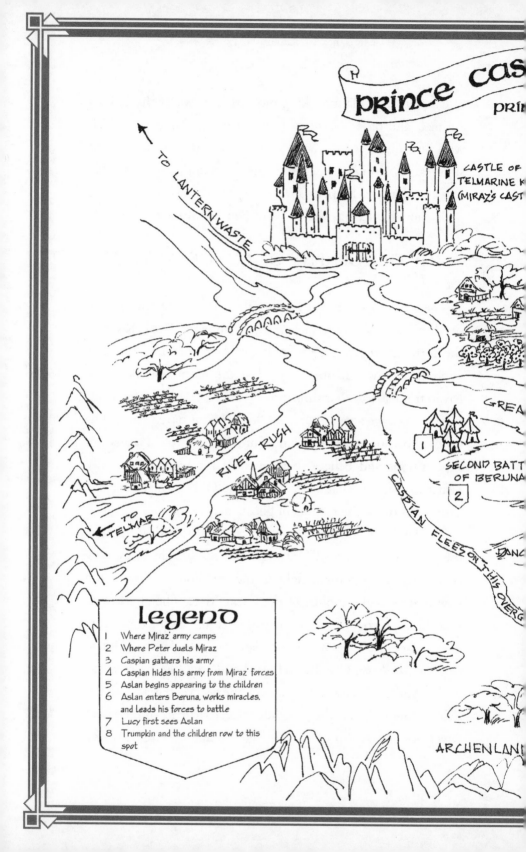

prince cas

prín

CASTLE OF
TELMARINE K
(MIRAZ'S CAST

TO LANTERN WASTE

TO TELMAR

RIVER RUSH

GREA

SECOND BATT
OF BERUNA

CASPIAN FLEEZ ON THIS OVER

DAN

ARCHENLAN

legend

1 Where Miraz' army camps
2 Where Peter duels Miraz
3 Caspian gathers his army
4 Caspian hides his army from Miraz' forces
5 Aslan begins appearing to the children
6 Aslan enters Beruna, works miracles, and leads his forces to battle
7 Lucy first sees Aslan
8 Trumpkin and the children row to this spot

children realize that it has indeed been a very long time since they were Narnia's kings and queens.

Well upriver is the small town of Beruna, on the north side of the river, across from where Peter and the White Witch battled in *The Lion, the Witch and the Wardrobe*. The Telmarine humans have settled along the Great River and the River Rush to the west, north, and south, and they have cultivated much of the land west of Beruna, and they have driven the Old Narnians into hiding. So long has it been since the presence of the Old Narnians has been felt that most humans believe Talking Beasts to be myths.

Miraz's castle is to the north. When Caspian flees, he takes an easternly route on a road that runs north-south through the "haunted" forest to Archenland; the road is so little used that it becomes overgrown as Caspian nears Archenland's mountains, and a tree branch knocks him from his horse. It is possible that the branch is part of a Talking Tree, and that the tree knocked him down on purpose. For most Telmarine humans, this would be proof enough that the forest is haunted, but Caspian is knocked unconscious, and when he awakes he has proof that Old Narnians are not myths when he sees a Talking Badger and two Dwarfs.

When the children and Trumpkin vote three-to-two to climb down the north side of the gorge, which is upriver from the mouth of The Great River, rather than follow in the direction of where Lucy saw Aslan, they make their trek much more difficult than it needed to be. The sides of the gorge are almost sheer, and finding a route through the rocky edges and along the rocky banks of the river is taxing. It turns out that by walking west along the north edge of the gorge, the children and Trumpkin would have had a much easier journey and would have found a ford upstream; there is even a bridge at Beruna. They might even have been able to join Aslan's march through the town.

Whereas the Stone Table was once in the open, a large mound has now been constructed over the table. The mound has many passageways and is large enough to hold the army of Old Narnians. Outside of the mound is mostly forest, although beyond some trees to the west is open ground, where the Telmarine army makes camp. There is no indication that the bluff at which Aslan roared after being resurrected in *The Lion, the Witch and the Wardrobe* is still there. Many of the trees are Talking Trees, and they manage to terrify the Telmarine humans during the second battle of Beruna by marching behind the Old Narnians.

THEMES AND CHARACTERS

According to Lewis, he began *Prince Caspian* after *The Lion, the Witch and the Wardrobe,* and it more than other subsequent Narnian novels continues the themes begun in *The Lion, the Witch and the Wardrobe.* There is betrayal, this time in the forms of King Miraz, who murdered his brother Caspian IX, and his lieutenants Lords Glozelle and Sopespian betray him.

The choosing of sides between good and evil is repeated in *Prince Caspian.* Caspian makes himself the focus of the rallying of the Old Narnians to defy King Miraz, but the Old Narnians are themselves divided about who should fight on their side.

Caspian specifically rejects the recruiting of a hag and ogre, both enemies of Aslan, but one of his chief lieutenants, the Black Dwarf (so called for his hair color) Nikabrik, recruits a witch to cast a spell to recall the White Witch. He notes that Dwarfs did all right under her rule. When Aslan appears at the battle, the Red Dwarfs (red haired) are astonished, but some of the Black Dwarfs edge away, foreshadowing future conflict and events in *The Last Battle*.

CHAPTER-BY-CHAPTER DEVELOPMENT OF THEMES AND CHARACTERS IN *PRINCE CASPIAN*

– Chapter 1: The Island –

The events in *The Lion, the Witch and the Wardrobe* "had all happened a year ago" at the outset of *Prince Caspian*. Peter, Susan, Edmund, and Lucy Pevensie are snatched away from earth; Susan sensibly tells the others to hold hands (she is not always a wet blanket) and "The four children, holding hands and panting, found themselves standing in a woody place." In *The Lion, the Witch and the Wardrobe*, Lewis used the opening chapters to establish time, place, and main characters. In *Prince Caspian*, he takes advantage of having done all that to thrust his characters directly into the story. Add to the presence of the children a mysterious island and more than a little magic, and the story is well under way.

Take note of their beginning the novel at a railway station. It is an apt place for beginning a journey, even if it is not the one they expected to make. Further, it foreshadows events in *The Last Battle*. The railway station is something like the ponds in *The Magician's Nephew*, which are passageways to various worlds. In *Prince Caspian* and *The Last Battle*, the train station is a passageway between earth and the world of Narnia and even between earth and Aslan's Country.

— Chapter 2: The Ancient Treasure House —

Susan is a stick-in-the-mud when she and the other youngsters find mysterious ruins and an old wooden door because she is afraid of an open door. It is dark and night is falling, and she is afraid of what might come out of the hole. This sounds like the Susan who would choose to stay behind at Cair Paravel rather than fight the Calormenes at Anvard in *The Horse and His Boy*. One of the undercurrents of *Prince Caspian* will be her lack of the spirit of adventure. Lucy rebuffs Susan, but a few minutes later Peter reminds her that she is a queen in Narnia and that they cannot behave like children.

Peter sets the tone for this chapter, although Lucy's excitement at having an adventure helps set the tone for later chapters. When the children realize that they are in their old treasure chamber from when they ruled Cair Paravel, Peter takes charge. He says that they must take the gifts that Father Christmas had given them in *The Lion, the Witch and the Wardrobe*. Later, the others observed that Peter had a different tone in his voice, and they all felt that he was really Peter the High King, again. Peter's taking serious his role as High King is important for the success of their adventure, and his step-

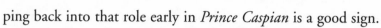

ping back into that role early in *Prince Caspian* is a good sign.

A bad sign is the decay of Cair Paravel. The seat of the past kings and queens of Narnia has plainly been abandoned for a long time. This is a mystery to be solved. Another bad sign is the treasure room. While it is good that the Gifts and other important items are where the youngsters can find them, the room's being untouched suggests a collapse of the government of Narnia soon after the children left it. Had they had successors, the treasure in the room would have been moved about and even used. The Gifts would have been revered and taken when the kings or queens moved from Cair Paravel. The room suggests that the Golden Age of Narnia soon ended after the Pevensies returned to earth.

—Chapter 3: The Dwarf —

The Dwarf of this chapter is Trumpkin, who will become one of the greatest Narnians, advisor to kings and a trusted regent (someone who rules a kingdom in the absence of the king or queen). He has been sent to see whether the Kings Peter and Edmund and Queens Lucy and Susan have shown up where Cair Paravel used to be. That he does not know that he has found them is logical: As the children themselves realize in this chapter, they have returned as earth children, not the grownup monarchs they were when they left Narnia at the end of *The Lion, the Witch and the Wardrobe*.

At first, the Dwarf is in need of rescuing, for Telmarine soldiers have captured him and he has been carried off to the delta of the Great River to be drowned. This occasions a demonstration that the children's old Narnian skills may still be with them, even though they look like their earthly selves. Showing quick wits and initiative, Susan exhibits great skill in archery by knocking down one of the two soldiers without killing him, by hitting him on his helmet in one quick shot. Both soldiers splash into the water and flee. This action would suggest that Susan is ready and able to participate in a new adventure. Even her prideful remark that she was not aiming to kill, for fear someone would think she would miss her target at so close a range, suggests that she has pride enough to take a leader's role as she and her companions face new dangers. Lewis even points out that she is an excellent swimmer back on earth, suggesting that she is in excellent physical condition, and she seems to have no trouble swimming in her clothes to the Dwarf's boat and then, with Peter, pulling it in to shore. This makes her later behavior puzzling. By the time the group is at the edge of the river gorge, she seems to be a tiresome whiner. Does this mean that Lewis disapproves of her wish not to kill people? Or that her quick actions save the life of a Dwarf? Probably not. What may be happening, here, is that Lewis is experiencing some indecision about the direction he wants to take Susan's characterization. A master of well-rounded characters, Lewis is giving Susan fullness by showing that she has good qualities, but these particular qualities conflict with her later grating griping. If she is the well-experienced swimmer Lewis says she is, she should have more stamina and more endurance than her companions; she should be trudging over difficult terrain while the others struggle to keep up. Perhaps it is during the writing of this novel, which he began after *The Lion, the Witch and the*

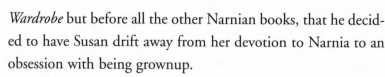

Wardrobe but before all the other Narnian books, that he decided to have Susan drift away from her devotion to Narnia to an obsession with being grownup.

This chapter is a lead in to the story of "Caspian the Tenth, King of Narnia," and leader of the Old Narnians. Once rescued, Trumpkin helps the children catch rainbow hued fish—pavenders, clearly good food for adventures—so he makes his value evident. It is much better to have eaten some fish baked in the ashes of a fire before an adventure than just apples, although Narnian apples are fine eating. The children are uncertain of why they are in Narnia, and we readers probably are, as well, so it is good to have the Dwarf tell them about why he was supposed to be drowned. He is in service to Caspian the Tenth and will tell them (thereby telling you and me) about the state of affairs in their old kingdom. Trumpkin becomes a literary triumph, a character seemingly present in the narrative only to tell about the adventures of other characters but who himself becomes not only a major actor in events but a full, well-rounded figure.

— Chapter 4: The Dwarf Tells of Prince Caspian —

Rather than have Trumpkin tell the history of Caspian, Lewis does it—to save time, he explains. This chapter introduces the basic Telmarine characters: Caspian, Miraz, and Doctor Cornelius. Miraz is introduced as "Miraz the King of Narnia," but Lewis will later call him "usurper Miraz." He is the uncle of Caspian and the murderer of Caspian's father King Caspian IX. This makes Prince Caspian, King Caspian X, the rightful ruler of the Telmarines. Miraz had assumed power, first as Regent—someone who runs the country until the rightful king is old enough to reign himself—but later he called himself the king. Miraz shows himself to be either ignorant or a liar when he tells Caspian that there is no such person as Aslan. He wants people to believe that Old Narnia is merely a bunch of old fairy tales without any truth in them. It turns out that he knows that the Old Narnians, the Talking Animals and woodland spirits, actually do exist.

When Caspian's nurse is sent away for telling him stories about Old Narnia, she is replaced by a tutor, Doctor Cornelius, whom Caspian thought that he would hate but who turned out to be the sort of person it is almost impossible not to like. Lewis loved his own tutor William Kirkpatrick, and it seems that he has given Caspian a tutor just as good. For one thing, Doctor Cornelius is diligent in giving Caspian good books to read, even though they are forbidden, and he provides Caspian with a great store of practical knowledge of how to live.

Lewis provides a fine description of Doctor Cornelius (you may wish to look it up), whose face "looked very wise, very ugly, and very kind." He is small and fat, with a grave voice and merry eyes, which make telling whether he means to be funny or serious difficult. Doctor Caspian provides the only incidence in *The Lion, the Witch and the Wardrobe* in which racism is an issue: When Caspian asks, he explains that he is part human and part Dwarf. This is a dangerous admission, since in the Telmarine court Dwarfs officially do not exist. The racism appears when it turns out that some Dwarfs find people of mixed ancestry such as Doctor Cornelius to be disgusting and

those Dwarfs discriminate against those who are like Doctor Cornelius. The Dwarfs' reaction to those like Doctor Cornelius is one way telling whether they lean toward evil.

Doctor Cornelius tells Caspian about the origins of the Telmarines, who are from "the Land of Telmar, far beyond the Western Mountains." The news that the Talmarines are descendants of pirates who stumbled by accident from earth into Telmar upsets Caspian some, because he would prefer nobler ancestors. More importantly, Doctor Cornelius tells Caspian about Aslan.

— Chapter 5: Caspian's Adventure in the Mountains —

After some years, Miraz' wife, Queen Prunaprisma gives birth to a son who will claim to be the rightful heir to Caspian's throne. During the previous years, Caspian has learned much about astronomy and other sciences. He also learned about Miraz's treachery. Miraz has killed or otherwise disposed of all who might favor Caspian as king, and Doctor Cornelius tells Caspian that Miraz persuaded the seven noble lords to sail away and look for new lands beyond the Eastern Ocean. As he intended, they never returned.

This is significant because the fate of these seven lords weighs heavily on Caspian's mind and will become the inspiration for his adventures in *The Voyage of the "Dawn Treader."* Doctor Cornelius is emphatic when he declares to Caspian that Miraz murdered his father.

With the birth of his son, Miraz will want to murder

Caspian, who is now his son's rival for the throne. Doctor Cornelius spirits Caspian away, urging him to take shelter with King Nain of Archenland. It seems that even after centuries since the events in *The Horse and His Boy* Archenland still holds together and is still a friend to justice.

Caspian remembers that he is "a Telmarine, one of the race who cut down trees wherever they could and were at war with all wild things; and though he himself might be unlike other Telmarines, the trees could not be expected to know this." As he races through the forest, branches whip at him, eventually felling him from his horse. Then he is discovered by a Talking Badger and two Dwarfs. The badger confirms what Doctor Cornelius has said about there being Talking Animals, but Caspian learns that it will be difficult to win over the Old Narnians to his cause. The badger Trufflehunter is kind to him, but the Dwarf Nikabrik is not sure that Caspian should not be put to death.

— Chapter 6: The People That Lived in Hiding —

"Now began the happiest times that Caspian had ever known." This is a curious way to open a chapter about the difficulties of rallying Old Narnians against Miraz, but it may reveal an important aspect of young Caspian's character: He is a man of action and relishes accomplishing something. This aspect of his character is part of his motivation for sailing across the sea to the east in *The Voyage of the "Dawn Treader"* and his seeking out Aslan in the Lone Islands, even though he is by then very old, in *The Silver Chair*.

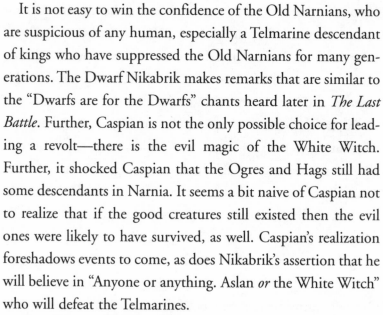

It is not easy to win the confidence of the Old Narnians, who are suspicious of any human, especially a Telmarine descendant of kings who have suppressed the Old Narnians for many generations. The Dwarf Nikabrik makes remarks that are similar to the "Dwarfs are for the Dwarfs" chants heard later in *The Last Battle*. Further, Caspian is not the only possible choice for leading a revolt—there is the evil magic of the White Witch. Further, it shocked Caspian that the Ogres and Hags still had some descendants in Narnia. It seems a bit naive of Caspian not to realize that if the good creatures still existed then the evil ones were likely to have survived, as well. Caspian's realization foreshadows events to come, as does Nikabrik's assertion that he will believe in "Anyone or anything. Aslan *or* the White Witch" who will defeat the Telmarines.

Reepicheep, the High Mouse, and his twelve companion mice are gallant and determined fighters, and Reepicheep himself will turn out to be one of the best friends Caspian could have. He will reappear in *The Voyage of the "Dawn Treader,"* in which he is said to be two-foot tall (rather than about one-foot tall, as said, here), and his gallantry, seen in battle in *Prince Caspian*, becomes the standard for courage for his companions, who will look to him to see how a gallant person should behave. Although the Old Narnians are gathering to prepare for war, this is a mostly humorous chapter. For instance, Reepicheep and his mice are delightfully valiant and speak in courtly terms. The courageous bears are fun as they bumble clumsily about and absentmindedly suck on their paws (considered an embarrassing habit by other Narnians). No sooner do fauns show up than Caspian and others are caught up in a joyful woodland dance.

– Chapter 7: Old Narnia in Danger –

In this chapter, Caspian and the Old Narnians take refuge in a large artificial hill that has many passageways. Here, Lewis brings the narrative of *Prince Caspian* back to the most momentous location in *The Lion, the Witch and the Wardrobe*, the Stone Table. In the center of the hill is "a stone table, split right down the centre, and covered with what had once been writing of some kind." For those of us who have just read *The Lion, the Witch and the Wardrobe*, the Stone Table is familiar, but for Caspian and his followers it is an ancient artifact that links them to an age when Old Narnians did not have to spend their days in hiding, and it is evidence that Aslan really did die and then return to life. The writing on the table would be mysterious ancient symbols of the Deep Magic, as evocative of an ancient past as ancient Egyptian hieroglyphs might be to modern readers. The table adds gravity to the events in this chapter because the Stone Table is where Aslan was slain and where he was resurrected. This split in the table represents the breaking of the Deep Magic and the coming of the Emperor-over-sea's Deeper Magic. There, at the most sacred spot in Narnia, the Old Narnians choose to make their stand.

– Chapter 8: How They Left the Island –

The children's looks are deceiving when they are in Narnia. Trumpkin tells the children that the Narnians have been imagining them as great warriors, and that the children look like something else—that is, children, not grownup fearsome warriors. To prove their worthiness, Edmund and Peter talk the Dwarf into a fencing match against Edmund, using real broad swords and Edmund wins by disarming Trumpkin. Then Susan challenges Trumpkin to an archery contest—Dwarf warriors are excellent archers—and beats him. The displays of warlike skills convince Trumpkin that "great warriors" may be exactly who have been summoned by Caspian's blowing on Susan's horn. He may even dare hope that some good may come from the summoning of the Pevensies. This chapter makes it clear that the children are still the kings and queens of Narnia's Golden Age, whatever they may look like, which helps build anticipation for battles to come. When Peter eventually takes on Miraz in single combat, there is reason to hope that he may be victorious. Lewis notes that the air of Narnia tends to make returning children recall their old skills and even toughens them. Edmund is already beginning to seem bigger, stronger, and quicker than he was on earth.

This is the chapter in which the children begin calling Trumpkin "D.L.F."—short for "Dear Little Friend," which he does not like. Trumpkin's characterization becomes a more rounded when he decides to let "D.L.F." pass, even though he does not like it. He has higher priorities and plainly likes the Pevensies as much as they like him. It also shows that he has the sense of a good diplomat. Further, he becomes endearing by his fortitude and his comic exclamations such as "Giants and junipers!" He is fond of alliteration (making consonant sounds that are alike, as in the *juh* sound in *g- iants* and *j-unipers)*. The combination of good sense, courage, and comedy are making him a deep figure, and by novel's end will have been shown to be someone who can be trusted with an entire kingdom while its monarch is absent, as he will be in *The Voyage of the "Dawn Treader"* and *The Silver Chair.*

Lewis was not consistent in his descriptions of directions and landmarks in his books, which is why maps of Narnia often disagree with one another. In this chapter, the children and the Dwarf are headed every which way. The best explanation for their movements out to sea one moment, south another, north another, and eventually toward the mainland is that they have several islands to get around before finding a suitable landfall. It is understandable if you have a hard time visualizing what they are actually doing.

— Chapter 9: What Lucy Saw —

Edmund again accuses Susan of being a wet blanket. In this case, she is not the only wet blanket, for Peter's behavior may be worse. Edmund's smart aleck remarks have already irritated Lucy when he told Peter and the Dwarf that girls can't carry a map in their heads. "That's because our heads have something inside them," Lucy retorts.

Edmund is a very much better person than he was at the start of *The Lion, the Witch and the Wardrobe,* but he still has room for growth. He should show more respect for Susan and Lucy, who have earned it. For all Susan's complaining, she endures the same difficulties as the boys and does not ever give up.

When Lucy sees Aslan, apparently leading her party up a hillside along the gorge, whereas the travelers are about to go down into a gorge, she is eager to follow Him. When going up or down is put to a vote, Edmund votes with Lucy for going up,

because he has finally learned that Lucy does not lie about what she sees. One would think Peter and Susan would have learned that lesson thoroughly after their bungling at the beginning of *The Lion, the Witch and the Wardrobe,* but they and Trumpkin vote for going down. When the children see Aslan later on, Lucy and Edmund will be the first to greet Him. The broader lesson to be learned is that following Aslan is not a matter of majority rule. He is to be followed regardless of what others think, as Lucy will come to realize.

— Chapter 10: The Return of the Lion —

Aslan is quite a sight when He reveals Himself to Lucy: "For *He* was there: the huge Lion, shining white in the moonlight, with his huge black shadow underneath him." His size amazes Lucy: "But every year you grow, you will find me bigger," Aslan tells her. Lucy is saddened to learn that she erred when she did not follow Aslan at the gorge. It seems as though the trek to the Stone Table would have been easier going Aslan's way up, instead of down into the gorge, but when Lucy asks Aslan what would have happened had she gone His way, Aslan says that she can never know.

This parallels Lewis' view on events in Genesis. In Lewis' view, God had a wonderful plan for the lives of Adam, Eve, and their descendants if they had obeyed Him and not eaten the forbidden fruit. Even though God has another wonderful plan for humanity, it is different from the original one and the nature of the original one will never be revealed. This idea that Aslan will not reveal what would have happened had His sign been followed will be repeated in *The Silver Chair.*

"And I thought you'd come roaring in and frighten all the enemies away—like last time," Lucy says to Aslan. He tells her that things never happen the same way twice and that she must tell her companions that she has seen Him while they slept, even at the risk of not being believed again. She has very good reason to worry that she will not be believed, although somewhere along the line her brothers and sister should get it into their heads that she would not lie about Aslan (in fact she never lies). Lucy buries her face in Aslan's mane, ashamed that she had not done what He wanted when she was at the edge of the gorge, but the touch of the mane strengthens her, causing her to sit up, erect. Aslan tells her that she is now a lioness.

— Chapter 11: The Lion Roars —

The Narnian air, which has a strengthening effect on the children who visit from earth, is having a notably good effect on Peter and Edmund, who look more like men than boys. Their old Narnian selves are returning. If we look closely, we can see that Lucy is again Queen Lucy the Valiant; she has not only the benefit of the Narnian air, but the benefit of Aslan's mane, which has invigorated her and given her confidence. When her companions do not see Aslan, she asserts herself as she had not done before, this time insisting that she will leave to follow Aslan on the instant. Even though none of the others sees Aslan, Peter decides all should follow Lucy. In this, she is like a Biblical prophet, because she sees Aslan and hears Aslan and knows what is to be done, while others follow her because they trust in her relationship with Aslan. One of her strengths

is being able to open herself to Aslan when others cannot or choose not to do so.

Having Aslan invisible to all but Lucy, at first, is very odd. As Peter points out, he and Edmund and Susan had always been able to see Him before. Eventually, Susan confesses that in spite of her ill-natured complaining that Lucy was only dreaming about Aslan, she felt deep inside her that Lucy was seeing the golden Lion. She was just too ill-tempered to accept His being there. This may explain not only Aslan's initial invisibility to all but Lucy but the order in which each member of the party first sees Him. Except for Lucy, the others were too irritable and unhappy to allow themselves to see Aslan. Edmund is determined to back Lucy up, not only in order to make up for his cruelty toward her in *The Lion, the Witch and the Wardrobe* but because he is certain that Lucy tells the truth, as well as the quite reasonable grounds that she has always been right about seeing Aslan before. He receives a "Well done" from Aslan, the Lion's highest praise, for his support of Aslan.

Peter and Susan are becoming too grownup, with too many grownup reasons for not believing in Aslan. Christ asks for a childlike faith, and Peter and Susan are not as willing as they had been to give that faith. Peter sees Aslan after Edmund does, and confesses his error to Aslan, who says, "My dear son," to him, a blessing. Peter has for a second time disbelieved Lucy even though he knows that Lucy tells only the truth. (During the last day before the crucifixion, the Disciple Peter denies Jesus three times.) Throughout *The Chronicles of Narnia*, Aslan wants people to seek the truth, not to shy away from it. Susan, who is determined to be grownup and who has been speaking to Lucy as if she were a grownup and Lucy a child, calling Lucy "naughty," even, and Trumpkin, who has been referring to Aslan as a fairy tale, both see Aslan next. Aslan breathes on Susan to give her strength, but her faith is plainly weak. Aslan tosses Trumpkin about with His mouth, gently catching the Dwarf in His paws, perhaps to demonstrate to Trumpkin that He is solid and real. They make friends.

Aslan's roar is remarkable. It is heard everywhere in Narnia and some distance beyond, even in the mountain strongholds of giants in the far north. Apparently His roar varies in meaning for different people. The Telmarine soldiers are bothered by it; other Telmarines are frightened. The northern giants are concerned. But from all over the place, from every direction, flowing over and through the land, come tree spirits, Bacchus and maenads and many others, all looking forward to a "Romp." This chapter ends with Lucy and Susan overwhelmed by a joyful celebration of being alive and of Aslan's works. This is another time in *Prince Caspian* that Lewis has balanced serious themes with comedy. Peter, Edmund, and Trumpkin have been sent off to the Great Mound over the Stone Table, where they will encounter great evil, and a battle in which lives will be lost seems imminent. Yet Aslan begins a joyous revel. How the joy is to be put to serious uses is to be shown in Chapter 14: "How All Were Very Busy."

— Chapter 12: Sorcery and Sudden Vengeance —

In this chapter Caspian, now Caspian X to the Old Narnians, has tough choices to make. The most important one comes from the Dwarf Nikabrik, who proposes to use evil magic to recall the

White Witch. He says that she is practical, a word we should we suspicious of. It is a word that evildoers are very fond of, and it is a word used to describe Jadis in *The Magician's Nephew*. Nikabrik insists that Jadis was a friend of the Dwarfs and that they are not afraid of her. This cynical, cruel attitude in which the welfare of others is cast aside for selfish interest is echoed by the ungrateful Dwarfs in *The Last Battle*.

Even though Nikabrik's words foreshadow events in *The Last Battle,* in this chapter they present Caspian with choices. The Dwarfs are very good fighters, and to go against Nikabrik could cost Caspian the help of the Black Dwarfs (black-haired Dwarfs). On the other hand, even at the outset of his adventure, his instinct was to reject the services of hags and ogres. He truly believes in Aslan and in the ideals he has learned from his nurse and Doctor Cornelius.

Doctor Cornelius reasonably points out that the Witch is dead. All the stories agree on that. The Hag, in a shrill, whining voice replies that the witch is not necessarily dead. "You can always get them back," she says of witches. The idea that the White Witch could return will be echoed in *The Silver Chair*; in fact, the woman in the green kirtle could be an incarnation of the White Witch. What the hag proposes, here, is recalling the original source of evil in Narnia's world back to the world. She may be lying about this; if she wanted the White Witch to return, why has she waited until this moment to try to bring her back? To his credit, Caspian knows exactly what to do, and Peter and Edmund learn—they are listening behind the door—which side of good and evil Caspian belongs to. It is fortunate that they are there to help Caspian.

— Chapter 13: The High King in Command —

Edmund cuts an intimidating figure, "For Aslan had breathed on him at that meeting and a kind of greatness hung about him." If, as Glozelle notes, the boy is King Edmund of old, then he would be very dangerous. More dangerous still is High King Peter, who challenges Miraz to single combat. Miraz seems to have mistaken himself for a real king, and not a usurper, for he reacts badly to the suggestion that he might be a coward or that his honor might be suspect if he does not fight Peter. Perhaps he has forgotten that he is king by treachery and that his example may be followed by others. Conspirators Glozelle and Sopespian see in Peter's challenge an opportunity to dispose of Miraz and seize power for themselves. Thus, a betrayer is himself betrayed.

— Chapter 14: How All Were Very Busy —

The betrayers in *Prince Caspian* meet unhappy ends. Miraz is stabbed in the back by one of his own lieutenants, Glozelle. Meanwhile, Sopespian no sooner begins to rally his men to battle than Peter lops off his head. Plainly, it is a very bad idea to go against Aslan's chosen High King! No sooner does the battle start than the wood attacks. This echoes a scene from Shakespeare's *Macbeth,* when a forest seems to march on Macbeth's castle; Macbeth is himself a murderer and usurper. "The wood! The Wood! The end of the world!" cry the Telmarine soldiers.

Meanwhile, Aslan makes Himself known in the nearby town or Beruna, where He and His people march through, making miracles. At a school, a man is beating a boy, a violation of universal moral law, as Lewis sees it. An end is put to it. School is out for any child who wishes to be with Aslan. Aslan works miracles, curing a dying woman (who turns out to be Caspian's nurse) and turning water into the best wine possible. At Aslan's order, the bridge across the river is broken by Bacchus, freeing the river-god. As Aslan walks, people dance, sing, laugh, and run about Him: the righteous join Him, the loving join Him, and the oppressed are freed.

There is more to this moving passage than Aslan and His people having a good time; it is the symbolic representation of His liberating the Telmarines of Narnia. He brings them joy and freedom. When He goes to the scene of battle, He has shown what He meant when He told Lucy that nothing happens the same way twice. In *The Lion, the Witch and the Wardrobe,* he conquered with wrath, but in *Prince Caspian* He conquers with joy.

— Chapter 15: "Aslan Makes a Door in the Air" —

"But a tail is the honour and glory of a Mouse," Reepicheep tells Aslan. The High Mouse had been badly injured; Lucy tries to use the Gift of the healing cordial to revive him but his tail, which had been chopped off, did not regrow. Aslan recalls how the mice chewed the ropes that bound him to the Stone Table and how He rewarded them by giving them the power of speech. When Reepicheep's fellow mice unsheathe their swords to cut off their own tails, so that they will not dishonor their leader by having tails when he does not, Aslan gives Reepicheep a new tail. Loyalty is one of the virtues Aslan rewards.

The battle has settled Narnia's future, assured Caspian's reign as king, and freed the Talking Beasts, the Dwarfs, Dryads and Fauns, and other creatures. In *The Voyage of the "Dawn Treader"* and *The Silver Chair*, Caspian rules justly and is much loved.

The explanation that he is the descendant of pirates leaves Caspian wishing that he came from a more honorable lineage (in this, he sounds a little like Reepicheek). Aslan tells him that he is descended from Lord Adam and Lady Eve, and that is "both honour enough to erect the head of the poorest beggar, and shame enough to bow the shoulders of the greatest emperor in earth."

The point, here, is that all people who are descendants of Adam and Eve are descendants of sinners; that Caspian's remote anscestors were pirates seems trivial in comparison to this larger truth. In any case, the tradition of having a descendant of Adam and Eve as ruler of Narnia seems to be important to the Narnians, perhaps because of the Golden Age when Peter, Susan, Edmund, and Lucy ruled, or perhaps because Aslan's first King of Narnia was a Son of Adam.

Aslan gives the Telmarines the choice of going to earth to live or remaining in Narnia. While many choose to leave, many others stay, thus making Narnia a land where humans and all Aslan's other creatures live as equals.

With the good news comes some bad: Peter announces that he and Susan will never return to Narnia. This must be particularly hard on the High King, who will no more be among his people. Although Aslan says that He is to be found on earth as well as on Narnia's world, this must be small comfort, because Peter will always be part of Narnia from his soul, as is shown in *The Last Battle*.

VOCABULARY FOR *PRINCE CASPIAN*

CHAPTER 1: THE ISLAND

junction: a place where different railroad routes meet or join

dimply pool: a pool with dimplelike ripples

rhododendrons: an evergreen shrub with clusters of flowers

Jove: a variant name for Jupiter, the chief god in Roman mythology

wallflowers: a plant whose European variety has orange, yellow, and brown flowers and a strong fragrance.

CHAPTER 2: THE ANCIENT TREASURE HOUSE

nettles: a plant with hair that secrets a stinging fluid on its leaves

fir-cones: pine cones

mer-people: mermaids and mermen

tapestries: thick fabric with colorful woven designs; it is typically hung on walls or used to cover furniture

all rot: all nonsense

CHAPTER 3: THE DWARF

can't swim for nuts: can't swim at all

gist: essence; a summary of something much longer

Wars of the Roses: an English civil war from 1455 to 1485

CHAPTER 5: CASPIAN'S ADVENTURE IN THE MOUNTAINS

theorbo: a stringed instrument, a lute, with two sets of strings and an *S*-shaped neck

cosmography: the study of the forces that govern the universe

rhetoric: the study of style, structure, and cadence in literature and public speaking

heraldry: a study of symbols used to decorate armor, such as High King Peter's red lion on his shield

versification: to write rhythmic cadences such as song lyrics and poems

physic: the study of medicine

alchemy: primitive chemistry and physics

pother: fuss

antechamber: a small room through which a person passes in order to go into a larger room; Caspian's antechamber seems unusually large

venison: meat from deer

flask: a small bottle with a neck and a cap; usually made of glass

satchel: a bag with at least one shoulder strap

usurper: some who seizes a position illegally, as Miraz has done by claiming the position of king

fervent: emotional and passionate

wild heaths: an area of wild lands covered by heather or similar low-lying shrubs

morsel: a small amount of food

CHAPTER 6: THE PEOPLE THAT LIVED IN HIDING

wolds: plains, heaths, or moors of rolling ground with few or no trees

subterranean: underground

ogre: a man-eating monster, usually of great size and strength

hag: a witch

foxgloves: a plant with long, purple flowers; nowadays, its leaves are a source of the medication digitalis

hedgerows: a row of bushes that form a hedge

martial: warlike

CHAPTER 7: OLD NARNIA IN DANGER

Signior: term of respect meaning *sir* or *mister*.

CHAPTER 8: HOW THEY LEFT THE ISLAND

seneschal: the chief household official of the king, in charge of the servants and household needs

more of a sucks for him: more of an embarrassment for him

cricket bat: a flattened club with a round handle used to play the sport of cricket; it is swung at a pitched ball

hauberk: a tunic of chain mail; it hangs from the shoulders down to the knees

junipers: shrubs and trees that produce berrylike, poisonous fruit

jibe: also spelled *gibe*; a taunt

CHAPTER 9: WHAT LUCY SAW

bracken: a tough fern with long fronds

bivouac: a military term for a temporary camp

wizened: withered and dry

you're a brick: you're a good person

chap: man

CHAPTER 10: THE RETURN OF THE LION

battledores: the paddles used to play an early form of badminton; Narnia's Dwarfs love such meaningless phrases as bottles and battledores

slanging: a now obsolete variation on the word *slang* meaning to speak badly of others, to run them down

CHAPTER 11: THE LION ROARS

bilge: nonsensical speech or foolish talk

cobbles: a rounded stone

rum: poor, as in poor light

blown: out of breath

rowans: deciduous trees native to Europe

Tig: tag

CHAPTER 13: THE HIGH KING IN COMMAND

abhominable: detestable

monomachy: combat between two people to determine the outcome of a battle between two armies, rather than fight the full battle; it is usually intended to save lives and to show the courage of the two people

jackanapes: foolish, misbehaving child

effrontery: insulting impudence

dotard: a senile person

dastard: coward

CHAPTER 15: ASLAN MAKES A DOOR IN THE AIR

cataracts: a large waterfall; in this case, it is used as a metaphor meaning the arrangement of the fruit resembled a large, cascading waterfall

mazers: a large bowl or cup for drinking, made of metal or wood

not canny: not natural

REFERENCES TO THE BIBLE IN
PRINCE CASPIAN

The passage from *Prince Caspian* is first quoted, followed by the relevant passage in the Bible. A transliteration of the 1611 edition of the King James version of the Bible is used for the Biblical quotations. Comments then follow.

— **Chapter 12: "Sorcery and Sudden Vengeance"** —

1. "The help will come. It may be even now at the door."

> **Mark 13:29:** "So you in like manner, when you shall see these things come to pass, know that it is near, even at the doors."

Comments: Lewis makes Mark's verse literal, because in *Prince Caspian,* help in the form of the Pevensies and a Dwarf is actually just behind a door.

— **Chapter 14: "How All Were Very Busy"** —

2. "But what was in it [the pitcher] now was not water but the richest wine"

> **John 2:7-9:** "Jesus said to them, 'Fill the water pots with water.' And they filled them up to the brim. / And He said to them, "Draw out now, and bear to the governor of the feast." And they bore it. / When the ruler of the feast had

tasted the water that was made into wine, and knew not where it was from (but the servants who drew the water knew), the governor of the feast called the bridegroom, / And said to him, 'Every man at the beginning sets forth good wine, and when men have well drunk, then serve that which is worse: but you have kept the good wine until now.'"

Comments: Aslan repeats the miracle of transforming water into excellent wine. It is a sign of His divinity and His life-giving power. It may also be the basis for Lewis giving wine special restorative powers in *The Chronicles of Narnia*.

DISCUSSION QUESTIONS AND PROJECTS FOR *PRINCE CASPIAN*

— Overview —

1. Why isn't Caspian called King Caspian at the start of the novel?

2. Take a look at the railway events in *The Last Battle* and compare them to the role the railway station plays in *Prince Caspian*. How are they similar? How are they different? What purpose in *The Chronicles of Narnia* is served by repeating the depiction of a railway station?

3. Why would Aslan (or Lewis) choose to keep children from returning to Narnia after they reach a certain age?

4. Why was Cair Paravel abandoned with its treasure room intact?

5. Peter challenges Miraz to combat, with the winner determining who wins the battle. What are the historical origins of this practice?

6. Miraz bears some similarities to Shakespeare's King Macbeth, also a usurper who murdered a king. What other parallels between the two figures can you find?

7. Why would Lewis choose to have Peter and Susan's adventures in Narnia end with *Prince Caspian*?

8. Why does Aslan first appear to Lucy before He appears to anyone else?

9. What do the goings on in the town of Beruna say about Aslan's intentions for Narnia?

10. In what ways does Susan sometimes prove helpful?

11. What does Lewis add to his portraits of Peter, Susan, Edmund, and Lucy that are not found in *The Lion, the Witch and the Wardrobe*?

12. It what ways does Lucy become a lioness?

CHAPTER 1: THE ISLAND

1. Why would Peter, Susan, Edmund, and Lucy return to Narnia as children rather than as the adults they were when the left Narnia in *The Lion, the Witch and the Wardrobe*?

2. What problems must the youngsters solve when they arrive on the island? How well do they solve them?

CHAPTER 2: THE ANCIENT TREASURE HOUSE

1. Why would Cair Paravel now be on an island when it was not in *The Lion, the Witch and the Wardrobe?*

2. What do the events in this chapter tell about each of the children? What do we expect of them?

3. Why are the Gifts important? What are they?

CHAPTER 3: THE DWARF

1. Why does Susan not kill the soldiers even though she could?

2. Why would Lewis choose to wait until Chapter 3 to mention Caspian?

CHAPTER 4: THE DWARF TELLS OF PRINCE CASPIAN

1. Why not have Trumpkin tell about Caspian in his own words? After all, in *The Horse and His Boy* Aravis tells her story her way.

2. Why does Doctor Cornelius take the risk to tell Caspian about forbidden topics?

CHAPTER 5: CASPIAN'S ADVENTURE IN THE MOUNTAINS

1. Why would Trufflehunter or any Old Narnian treat any Telmarine such as Caspian with kindness?

2. Does the forest actually attack Caspian or does it just seem that way?

CHAPTER 6: THE PEOPLE THAT LIVED IN HIDING
1. "Now began the happiest times that Caspian had ever known" is an odd phrase to begin a chapter about rallying people to fight a war. Why is this the happiest time Caspian has so far known?

2. Why do the Old Narnians think that war may be their best option for solving their problems with Miraz?

CHAPTER 7: OLD NARNIA IN DANGER
1. What are the reasons for the Old Narnians and Caspian making their stand at the Stone Table?

2. What leadership skills does Caspian reveal in this chapter?

CHAPTER 8: HOW THEY LEFT THE ISLAND
1. Are the Pevensies just showing off, or is there a purpose behind their displays of warrior skills?

2. How does Trumpkin respond to his "lesson"? What does this show about his character?

CHAPTER 9: "WHAT LUCY SAW"
1. Why does Edmund make disparaging remarks about girls?
2. Why does Edmund vote on Lucy's side? Why are Peter and Susan not persuaded by his reasons?

3. Why does Lucy not follow Aslan on her own? Should she follow Him regardless of what the others do, even if it means defying the High King Peter?

Chapter 10: The Return of the Lion

1. "But every year you grow, you will find me bigger," Aslan tells Lucy. Why would He get bigger as she grows?

2. Why would all Narnia be renewed by Lucy's obedience of Aslan?

3. Why would Aslan not reveal Himself to the others the way He reveals Himself to Lucy?

Chapter 11: The Lion Roars

1. Lewis says that "Everyone except Susan and the Dwarf could see Him [Aslan] now." Why would Susan, in particular, but Trumpkin, too, not be able to see Aslan by now if the others can? What is the significance of the order in which the Pevensies and Trumpkin see Aslan?

2. Why do Peter and Edmund look more like men than boys in this chapter?

3. What does the chapter title "The Lion Roars" signify?

Chapter 12: Sorcery and Sudden Vengeance

1. Why does entering the Mound seem like entering a prison to the boys?

2. Why would Nikabrik wish to recall the White Witch whose long winter hand been a misery for Narnians?

3. Is or is not the White Witch truly dead? Could she be recalled to Narnia?

CHAPTER 13: THE HIGH KING IN COMMAND
1. What does Aslan given Edmund by breathing on him?

2. Should Miraz have realized that he might be betrayed?

3. Is Peter wise in making a challenge of mortal combat?

CHAPTER 14: HOW ALL WERE VERY BUSY
1. Why would Lewis include a figure from Roman mythology, such as Bacchus, among Aslan's companions?

2. Why does Aslan not rush straight to battle rather than visiting the town of Beruna?

CHAPTER 15: ASLAN MAKES A DOOR IN THE AIR
1. What does Aslan mean when he says that coming of "the Lord Adam and the Lady Eve" is "both honour enough to erect the head of the poorest beggar, and shame enough to bow the shoulders of the greatest emperor in earth."

2. Why is Reepicheep able speak to Aslan so forthrightly when many others are tongue-tied in His presence?

CHAPTER 13

THE VOYAGE
OF THE
"DAWN TREADER"

OVERVIEW

Caspian X has sworn to spend a year and a day trying to find out what happened to the seven lords sent by Miraz to the east, across the sea, and on his ship *Dawn Treader*, Caspian and a crew of volunteers set out to visit the Lone Islands and to journey beyond until all the lords are found. Meanwhile, Edmund and Lucy have been sentenced to a sort of hell-on-earth. While their parents are overseas, they must stay with Eustace Scrubb's family of snobs. Eustace himself is poisonous; he looks forward to tormenting Edmund and Lucy. He has no friends and does not seem to care about it.

Eustace and his family are examples of some of what Lewis finds wrong in modern life and in modern education. The Scrubbs are "very up-to-date and advanced people": They are vegetarians, teetotallers, and nonsmokers who wear "a special kind of underclothes," and Eustace is allowed to call his parents by their first names rather than Mother and Father or Mom and Dad. Their house seems an uncomfortable place with very little furniture. It does not feel lived in. Eustace is allowed to read books only about facts and figures: no fiction of any kind. Much of *The Voyage of the "Dawn Treader"* is about how unprepared he is to deal with situations new to him and how incapable he is of thinking out problems that involve people. Thus he tries to fit his companions into his limited knowledge of facts and figures, irritating everybody and accomplishing nothing good. Much of *The Voyage of the "Dawn Treader"* is devoted to Eustace growing into a full human being; encouraged by his mother, he has been living a dehumanized life in which his only pleasure has been causing others misery; the snobbery of his mother in particular has encouraged him to view all other people as his inferiors, especially ones who talk about amazing places such as Narnia. Elsewhere, Aslan tells Lucy that she and her brothers and sister have been brought to Narnia so that they may know Him better when they are on earth; this is also the case for Eustace, who will be physically transformed into the monster he has always been and who will learn the value of other people as his equals and even superiors, and he will learn of the power of Aslan to cleanse away sin and give him a second chance at life.

Beyond this, in *The Voyage of the "Dawn Treader,"* Lewis tells a tale of high adventure and or repentance and redemption. Aslan has use of Lucy and Edmund, even of the annoying Scrubb, and the three children are drawn into a painting of a ship and from there into the water near the *Dawn Treader*. High adventure is what *The Voyage of the "Dawn Treader"* is about, and it is one of Lewis most imaginative achievements.

THE GEOGRAPHY OF *THE VOYAGE OF THE "DAWN TREADER"*

In *The Voyage of the "Dawn Treader,"* Caspian and a crew of volunteers have set out to discover what happened to the Seven Noble Lords that the usurper Miraz had sent on an expedition to the far east, in the hope that they would never return. When Lucy, Edmund, and Eustace appear in the water, the *Dawn Treader* is nearing the Lone Islands.

The Lone Islands are a cluster to the east of Narnia, and the king of Narnia is their emperor. Only three of the islands are

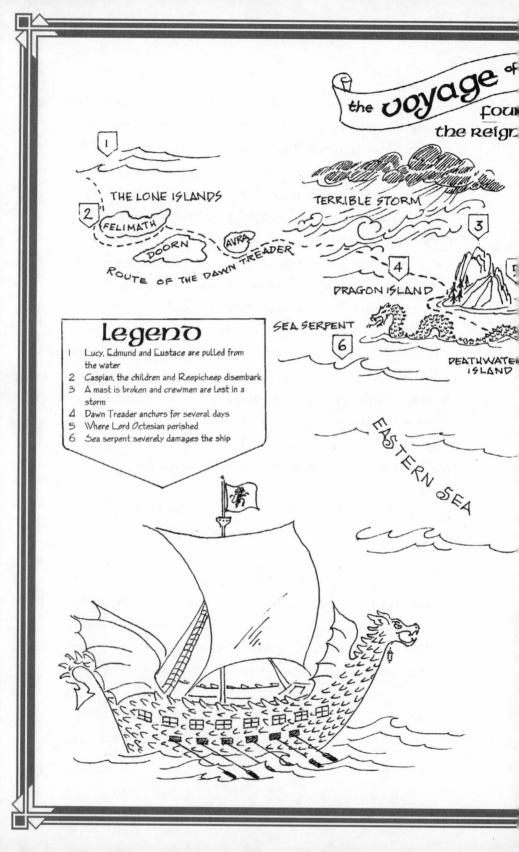

the **voyage** of

fou~~r~~

the reign

THE LONE ISLANDS

1

2 FELIMATH

DOORN   AVRA

ROUTE OF THE DAWN TREADER

TERRIBLE STORM

3

4

DRAGON ISLAND

SEA SERPENT

6

DEATHWATER ISLAND

EASTERN SEA

Legend

1 Lucy, Edmund and Eustace are pulled from the water
2 Caspian, the children and Reepicheep disembark
3 A mast is broken and crewmen are lost in a storm
4 Dawn Treader anchors for several days
5 Where Lord Octesian perished
6 Sea serpent severely damages the ship

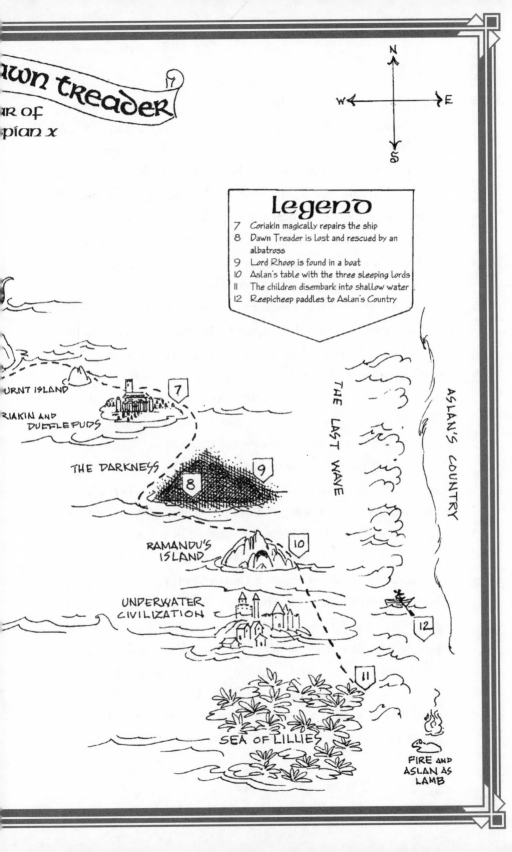

awn treader
ur of
pian x

N
W ← → E
S

Legend
7   Coriakin magically repairs the ship
8   Dawn Treader is lost and rescued by an albatross
9   Lord Rhoop is found in a boat
10 Aslan's table with the three sleeping lords
11 The children disembark into shallow water
12 Reepicheep paddles to Aslan's Country

URNT ISLAND

RIAKIN AND DUEFLEPUDS

THE DARKNESS

7

8

9

THE LAST WAVE

ASLAN'S COUNTRY

RAMANDU'S ISLAND

10

UNDERWATER CIVILIZATION

12

11

SEA OF LILLIES

FIRE AND ASLAN AS LAMB

named in *The Voyage of the "Dawn Treader"*: Felimath, Doorn, and Avra. Felimath is "like a lone green hill in the sea," and as the *Dawn Treader* approaches it, Lucy can also see Doorn, the main island. The grassy hills of Felimath make it an attractive place for a walk, but slavers kidnap Caspian and his companions among some trees near the island's eastern shore.

Along the west coast of Doorn is a large bay and many piers and quays, and beyond them is the city Narrowhaven, a busy center of commerce for voyagers from many nations. In its northwest area are the warehouses where slaves are kept, as well as the square in which they are sold. Caspian puts an end to the slave trade in Narrowhaven. The city's eastern edge is walled, with a gate in it. From the gate, it is a short walk east up a hill to the governor's castle. The castle seems fairly ordinary: When one enters its gate, one steps into a courtyard; beyond the courtyard is a building that is probably the keep.

Much of Doorn seems to be devoted to farming, and Avra, where Lord Bern lives, is also primarily farm lands. Bern's holdings are called Bernstead, and are just a short boat ride from Doorn. Bernstead is a large estate, worked by freemen. It seems to be a very pleasant place, but Caspian cannot linger there.

The *Dawn Treader* encounters a nasty storm to the east of the Lone Islands; a mast is lost, but the winds blow the ship to the southeast, where it encounters Dragon Island. There is a bay, probably in the northwest part of the island, where the ship can safely anchor. The bay is lined by a beach, and beyond the beach, east and south, is a forest. Rivers from the northeast and southwest flow into the bay. Snowcapped mountains rise high out of the forest to the east and south east.

It is up onto a southeastern mountain that Eustace climbs. When he tries to come down, he walks northeast to a valley between mountains. The valley has a lake at its western end, and has grass and trees. In a cave south of the lake lives a dragon. This elderly, pitiful creature takes one last drink from the lake and dies. It is in the dragon's cave, while sleeping on the dragon's piles of loot that Eustace is transformed into a dragon, the personification of the greedy, selfish person he is.

With a new mast made from a tree in the forest on Dragon Island, and with Eustace back to looking human, the *Dawn Treader* sails east to Burnt Island, which is low-lying, covered in grass, and populated by small animals such as rabbits. After Burnt Island, sailing becomes more difficult. There are windless calms to endure, and before reaching the next island, the ship is attacked by a huge sea serpent that tears off the dragon wings at the ship's aft.

The next island, Deathwater Island, seems unremarkable, but while exploring a western hillside, the clothing of one of the lost lords is found. Down slope, to the north, is a pool with a statue of a diving man in it. Edmund discovers that the pool's water changes things to gold (why the whole island isn't gold is not explained). The pool has an evil enchantment that quickly has Edmund and Caspian bickering over who the pool should belong to. Fortunately, Lucy keeps her head and points out that the pool must be affecting their minds. The statue is that of one of the lost lords. The explorers give the island the name Deathwater, because the magic pool kills people.

To the southeast, the voyagers discover an island populated by invisible beings, the Island of the Dufflepuds. Although the

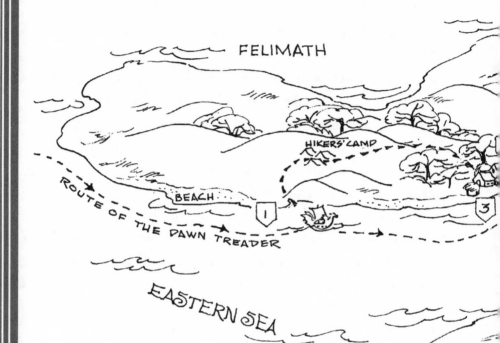

FELIMATH

HIKERS' CAMP

ROUTE OF THE DAWN TREADER

BEACH

1

3

EASTERN SEA

BEACH

Legend

1 Dawn Treader anchors; the children, Caspian and Reepicheep go for a walk
2 The children, Caspian and Reepicheep are captured by slave traders
3 Lord Bern buys Caspian; the others are taken to slave quarters
4 Bern greets his family
5 Caspian disembarks and is greeted by cheering crowds
6 Caspian, soldiers and crowd march to the governor's castle
7 Governor's castle; Caspian removes Gumpas from office and declares Lord Bern ruler
8 Square where slaves are sold and Caspian ends slave trade

Dufflepuds are threatening, their silly talk makes them seem somewhat ineffectual. The island is laid out in a square pattern, with straight roads lined with trees leading from the shores to the center of the island. At the center is the large home of the wizard who rules the island, and of whom the invisible people are afraid. There, Lucy climbs a tower and finds the spell for visibility, casting it and making all the invisible people visible, including the wizard Coriakin and Aslan, Who says He was made visible because He follows His own laws. Coriakin not only entertains the voyagers, he uses his magic to fix the aft of the *Dawn Treader*.

Still sailing southeast, the *Dawn Treader* encounters its most fearsome danger, the Darkness. Within the Darkness is Dark Island, where dreams come true. Not daydreams, but real dreams. Once the voyagers are in the Darkness, they can see nothing beyond the ship, but there is a mournful voice calling for help. It is Lord Rhoop, one of the lost lords. He has been trapped on Dark Island for many years and has been driven near to insanity by his stay. The Darkness is very confusing, and it seems to envelop the *Dawn Treader* no matter where it goes. A plea to Aslan brings a white albatross that leads the ship to safety. In the very first edition of *The Voyage of the "Dawn Treader,"* Lewis had the Darkness and the Dark Island disappear after the voyagers escape, but he changed the story thereafter so that both the island and Darkness remain. He thought that his first version made fun of children's nightmares, and he wanted to make clear that night terrors are serious and cannot be wished away.

Southeast of Dark Island is Ramandu's Island, named for the

retired star who lives on it. At the time the *Dawn Treader* visits the island, Ramandu has a beautiful, dignified daughter. She will eventually marry Caspian and be the mother of Prince Rilian. The island seems fairly flat from where the *Dawn Treader* anchors and the island's center, probably from the northern shore southward. Beyond the island's center, south and southwest are mountains, in which Ramandu and his daughter live. At the island's center is a great promenade of pillars, and among those pillars is Aslan's Table. Ramandu and his daughter set the table with a great feast every day, provided by Aslan, and every day, birds that live on the sun come to feed on the feast. The feast is not there just for the birds; Aslan has set the table for anyone who managed to sail that far east. At the table are three of the Seven Noble Lords, who were put to sleep when one of them grabbed the Stone Knife the White Witch had used to kill Aslan in *The Lion, the Witch and the Wardrobe*. Their enchantment can only be broken by sailing farther east.

East of Ramandu's Island live the sea people, who have created a great civilization in the shallow water of the far eastern sea. Lucy sees many roads, magnificent buildings, and many sea people, some working, some playing. The water in this region is sweet and can be safely drunk. Those who drink it find their eyesight much improved, and they can bear the brightness of the sun, which is much larger and brighter in the far east than in Narnia.

Eventually, the *Dawn Treader* reaches a sea covered by white lilies. To the east is the Last Wave, a wave of water at its crest, but never crashing down into the eastern shore, which the voyagers think is Aslan's Country (in *The Silver Chair*, Lewis con-

dragon island

DRAGON ISLAND

legend

1   Dawn Treader anchors in a deep bay:
    rowboat is beached
2   Camp is made here; a tree is felled for
    a new mast
3   Pool where old dragon dies
4   Dragon's cave where Eustace turns into a
    Dragon
5   Eustace the dragon positions himself
    between the boat and camp

DEATHWATER ISLAND and ISLAND of the DUFFLPUDS

ROUTE OF THE DAWN TREADER

BEACH

BEACH

ROUTE OF THE DAWN TREADER

1

2

3

4

5

DEATHWATER ISLAND

8

7

6

ISLAND OF THE DUFFLEPUDS AND CORIAKIN

firms that it is indeed Aslan's Country). The water is shallow enough to walk in, so when Reepicheep rows his little boat over the Last Wave, Lucy, Edmund, and Eustace walk south to a shore with a fire on it and a Lamb beside the fire. As they walk to the fire, they find themselves losing some of the physical strength they had gained during their voyage.

THEMES AND CHARACTERS

Lucy, Edmund, Caspian X, and Reepicheep return from previous Narnian adventures. Lucy loves adventure and has a great time, although almost being sold as a slave must have put a damper on her high spirits for a little while. She continues to grow and deepen, becoming an even richer, fuller figure than she was before. Edmund is not only a capable adventurer himself, but he serves as a reminder that people even worse than Eustace have been redeemed by Aslan. Caspian X is a worthy leader who has quickly brought peace to Narnia; it is only three years of Narnian time since he claimed his throne. Reepicheep offers comic relief with his eagerness to stand up to any danger and any challenge, and his whacking Eustace a few times with the side of his sword is a welcome comeuppance for a youngster who is making himself intolerable. Still, Reepicheep is more than just comic relief. His courage and honor are standards to which others aspire; when in doubt, others look to Reepicheep to show which course of action is the honest, honorable one. A delightfully daring and outspoken figure in *Prince Caspian*, he becomes a well-rounded character in *The Voyage of the "Dawn Treader."*

The themes of faithfulness and liberty wind their ways throughout *The Voyage of the "Dawn Treader."* Caspian's search for the lost lords is a matter of his keeping faith with an oath he made to Aslan in *Prince Caspian.* Although all crew members display a degree of faithfulness, the theme reaches its fullest form in the reformation of Eustace, who learns not only the value of friendship but of faithfulness in friendship. The theme of liberty is most obvious in the passages about the practice of slavery in the Lone Islands, which Caspian recognizes as evil and puts an end to as soon as possible, but the theme works its way through the relations of government to the governed in the Lone Islands, into the plight of the Dufflepuds, and subtly through the free association of Caspian's crew with their king. A people who have liberty are, the narrative implies, free to make good choices.

THE ODYSSEY AND THE VOYAGE OF THE "DAWN TREADER"

Near the end of *The Voyage of the "Dawn Treader,"* Ulysses is mentioned by Edmund, who agrees that if Caspian tries to leave the ship to go to Aslan's Country at the End of the World then Caspian should be tied to the ship's mast to prevent it, the way Ulysses was tied to the mast of his ship so that he could not leave the ship and perish against rocks by trying to reach the sirens, who lure sailors to their death with their beautiful songs. This makes Caspian angry, but more to the point, it is Lewis's one allusion in *The Voyage of the "Dawn Treader"* to one of the greatest seafaring tales ever composed: *The Odyssey,* an epic

poem by the Ancient Greek poet Homer. The poem is named for its main character, Odysseus, a Greek military leader who had fought in the Trojan War. The god of the sea Poseidon was the patron god of Troy, and he was very angry when the Greek invaders sacked and burned the city. Thus, he sends storms to toss Greeks ships about, and he sends Odysseus' ship far off course when he attempts to return home. The Romans' name for Odysseus was Ulysses, and that is the name not only Lewis but many English writers have used when writing about him.

King Caspian's adventures turn out much differently than those of Ulysses, who between the war and sailing from one strange island to another was absent from his home for twenty years. Caspian completes his mission in about a year. On the other hand, his sailing is preceded by the great second battle at Beruna in *Prince Caspian,* in which the long misguided persecution of the Old Narnians is put to an end, an event as far-reaching for Narnia as Troy's defeat was for the ancient Middle East. But whereas Ulysses wishes just to return home after his war, Caspian is motivated by a desire to find and rescue the seven lords who had been exiled by the usurper Miraz. When Ulysses finally reaches home, he finds his palace crowded with men trying to force Ulysses's wife Penelope to marry them, and in great anger, he kills all of them, even the man who was actually trying to protect Penelope rather than marry her. Caspian is a much more merciful sort. At the beginning of *The Voyage of the "Dawn Treader,"* he is kidnapped by slave traders and only by good fortune (or by Aslan) is he saved. Like Ulysses cleaning out his palace, Caspian cleans out the castle of the governor of the Lone Islands, but he chooses to avoid bloodshed. In *The*

Odyssey and *The Voyage of the "Dawn Treader,"* a palace is cleaned out of evil men, but Ulysses does it by brute force whereas Caspian does it through cleverness. Ulysses would almost certainly have killed the slavers, whereas Caspian spares their lives.

The Voyage of the "Dawn Treader" shares with *The Odyssey* a wandering structure in which the main characters sail from island to island, each of which presents an obstacle they must overcome before being allowed to continue toward their far off goal. Their ships are subject to the whims of the weather, with storms blowing each toward islands. But where Ulysses meets the witch Circe, Caspian and his companions meet a benevolent magician, Coriakin. Circe has the power to change people into animals and changes Ulysses' crew into pigs, something duplicated in *Prince Caspian* when the piggish schoolboys of the small town of Beruna apparently transform into fat pigs. Like Circe, Coriakin has the power to transform the shapes of others. Before the *Dawn Treader* reaches the island of Coriakin, he has transformed the Duffers from two-legged dwarfs into one-legged, one-footed dwarfs, who eventually adopt for themselves the name *Dufflepuds*. But where Circe is selfish and cruel, Coriakin turns out to be friendly and kindly. He has been appointed ruler of the Dufflepuds by Aslan Himself, and Coriakin is trying to help the Dufflepuds live wisely, something the Dufflepuds are not good at doing.

Ulysses sails to a realm reminiscent of the Dark Island in *The Voyage of the "Dawn Treader."* This is the realm of the shades, the ghostly figures of dead people. It is a nightmarish place, reached only after much struggle. Like the Dark Island, it is a place sensible people would wish to avoid, and escaping from it is like escaping from the Darkness into light. From the shadowy realm, Ulysses sails to the realm of the sun-god Helios, which finds its parallel in the sailing of the *Dawn Treader* toward an increasingly large and bright sun. Like the crew of the *Dawn Treader,* who fear that prevailing winds will prevent them from sailing westward toward home, the crew of Ulysses' ship fears that they will not be able to return from Helios' lands. But Aslan provides for Caspian and his companions, for the sea becomes fresh with liquid light, that when drunk makes it possible to bear the light from the sun, three times larger than in Narnia. In Ulysses' adventure, the possessions of Helios must not be touched. Some of Ulysses' crew eats of Helios' herds and are killed for doing so.

Thus the gods of *The Odyssey* and much different from Aslan in *The Voyage of the "Dawn Treader."* Although both take personal interest in the doings of the main characters, the Greek and Roman gods are unforgiving. When Helios complains to Zeus about Ulysses' crew, Zeus shatters their ship with a thunderbolt, but Aslan is forgiving. For instance, Ramandu, a retired star, says that the magician Coriakin is actually a star who committed a transgression serious enough to have him removed from the firmament of Narnia's world. His punishment, such as it is, is to rule the Dufflepuds benignly and to help them become wise. Aslan visits Coriakin and gives him encouragement. Ulysses spends much of his adventure dodging the various gods who are angry with him, and he must deal with fickle gods who may approve of him one moment and then disapprove the next. Aslan is constant in His love, and seeing Him is always welcome, although He can be as intimidating a presence as any Greek god: When Lucy decides to cast a spell making herself the most beautiful girl in the world, Aslan's face appears and is enough to cause Lucy to turn the page of the magician's book. When the curse of Deathwater Island is working itself by making Edmund and Caspian insane, a glance of Aslan's gigantic form walking on a hillside is enough to snap everyone back to their senses.

Another important difference between *The Odyssey* and *The Voyage of the "Dawn Treader"* is that the *Dawn Treader's* crew loses one member during the voyage, whereas Ulysses loses just about everyone. When the *Dawn Treader* is attacked by a sea serpent, Reepicheep figures out a way for the ship to escape, although only after much damage. When Ulysses sails past Scylla, a multi-headed serpentlike monster, several of his crew are eaten by the creature. Monsters seem invariably dangerous in *The Odyssey,* but not so in *The Voyage of the "Dawn Treader."* On Dragon Island lives an old dragon that dies almost as soon as Eustace sees it. Eustace himself is transformed into a dragon, the physical representation of his selfishness, greed, and cruelty, but he becomes nicer because he realizes that he really is a monster. As a dragon, he is friendly, helping find food and a tree suitable for replacing a broken mast.

Ulysses himself is a hard, sometimes cruel man. He is a soldier noted for his skills for killing people. In contrast, Caspian is stern but is concerned about the welfare of others. Like Ulysses, he has proven himself in battle, but when dealing with his crew he seems much more understanding of their needs and motivations than Ulysses is of his crew's. For instance, when his crew is reluctant to sail from Ramandu's Island to the End of the World, Caspian shrewdly declares that only the best may accompany him on the rest of his voyage; his crew does not wish to be found wanting, and some members compete to be included on the final part of the voyage. But when in the lands of Helios, Ulysses just tells his men not to take anything, especially the animals. His crew is hungry; they kill and eat some animals and doom follows. A skilled leader such as Ulysses should better understand how to motivate his men, but Ulysses seems accustomed to being obeyed without hesitation or explanation. In these instances, Caspian has the advantage of having a giving and loving Aslan on his side, whereas Ulysses must contend with selfish, remote gods: Aslan's Table is covered with a wonderful feast every evening, free for the eating, whereas Helios' lands are rich in good foods to eat but visitors are not allowed to touch any of it. On the other hand, the bountiful food makes crew members of the *Dawn Treader* reluctant to leave, whereas the unwelcome sign at Helios' place encourages a quick exit.

In the end, the combination of a benign God, psychologically shrewd leadership, and courage enable Caspian to accomplish far more than Ulysses does. Although Ulysses courage is great, he is brutal and prone to kill when there may be alternatives to killing. Thus, Caspian ends slavery in the Lone Islands, helps Eustace become a human being instead of a monster, keeps all but one of his crew alive, and sails to the end of the world and lives to tell about it. A well-rounded character, he has his weak points, including being stubborn as he is when he wishes to join Reepicheep in sailing to Aslan's Country, although he is motivated as much by a sense of honor, that he should not leave any challenge unattempted, as he is by a desire for adventure. Ulysses takes years to get home and manages to get a multitude of people killed; he may have had a great adventure, but he did not accomplish much.

CHAPTER-BY-CHAPTER DEVELOPMENT OF THEMES AND CHARACTERS IN THE VOYAGE OF THE "DAWN TREADER"

— Chapter 1: The Picture in the Bedroom —

Eustace Clarence Scrubb is self-important and willfully cruel. "I can't tell you how his friends spoke to him, for he had none," remarks Lewis. Edmund calls him "that record stinker, Eustace." Living with him would be nearly unbearable, and he could quickly become intolerable for readers too if his mother had not had bad taste in art (and in many other matters). She has hung a painting she does not like out of her sight in one of the children's rooms. It is a dramatic painting of a ship sailing the sea; it is very beautiful to Edmund and Lucy, and is nothing to Eustace. During *The Voyage of the "Dawn Treader,"* Eustace will begin to learn to appreciate beauty, but his education has been one without beauty, one that rejects beauty for facts. Lucy and Edmund are particularly drawn to the painting because the ship in it looks very much like ships from Narnia when they were a king and a queen there. As they look at it yearningly, the ship rocks, the waves shift, and water splashes on them, as well as Eustace. This may be an example of Aslan call-

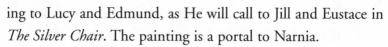

ing to Lucy and Edmund, as He will call to Jill and Eustace in *The Silver Chair.* The painting is a portal to Narnia.

In *Prince Caspian,* it is revealed that earth has more than one portal to Narnia. The Telmarines had entered Telmar in Narnia's world through a portal on a South Sea island. Edmund and Lucy have already walked through another portal, the wardrobe in *The Lion, the Witch and the Wardrobe.* They have also been summoned by Caspian blowing on Queen Susan's horn—just whisked away from a railway station. Therefore, they are not overcome by surprise when they find themselves splashing about in a sea; they have felt Aslan's summoning magic before. Understandably, Eustace is put out by finding himself in water; also understandably, the others are not happy that he entered the painting with them.

In this chapter, Caspian and Reepicheep, the Chief Mouse, are introduced, as well as Lord Drinian, the ship's captain. Lord Drinian is an interesting figure in two ways. In one, he is a stouthearted leader of good sense and courage; a very good person to have around. In another way, he serves to reflect Caspian's character. Lord Drinian is a bold man of strong will. That he would willingly follow Caspian and faithfully serve Caspian implies that Caspian is an exceptional leader who can capture and hold the faith of strong men. The theme of faithfulness begins with him in this chapter.

— Chapter 2: On Board the "Dawn Treader" —

It has been three years since Caspian and Edmund last saw each other. Once again the passage of time is at variance with that on earth, although it seems not nearly to have passed as quickly on Narnia as it did when Edmund, Lucy, Peter, and Susan spend one year on earth between *The Lion, the Witch and the Wardrobe* and *Prince Caspian* while hundreds of years passed on Narnia. The lack of consistency in the passage of time is one of Aslan's mysteries, perhaps explained a little in *The Last Battle* by the suggestion that time as experienced on earth or on Narnia's world has no meaning in Aslan's Country, the place Reepicheep hopes to reach during Caspian's expedition to find the seven lost lords: Revilian, Bern, Argoz, Mavramorn, Octesian, Restimar, and Rhoop.

In spite of the seriousness of the quest, this chapter plays primarily for comedy. When praising Trumpkin, who has been left in Narnia to serve as regent in Caspian's absence, Lord Drinian says he is "loyal as a badger," then "and valiant as—as a Mouse," having noticed Reepicheep's gazing at him. This is funny, but it serves a purpose, because it foreshadows events in which Reepicheep proves that Talking Mice set the standard for valiance. He may be small, but his deeds are large. Other comedy in this chapter arises from Eustace, who is whiny and blubbering much of the time. At home, he relished the prospect of tormenting Lucy and Edmund; on the *Dawn Treader,* the small Reepicheep seems a fine target for abuse, so Eustace sneaks behind the Mouse, grabs it be the tail and swings it, but Reepicheep is an accomplished warrior and quickly draws his sword, twists and jabs Eustace's hand. Once out of Eustace's grip, he paddles the boy with the flat of his sword. It is a serious matter at the end of the chapter, but a humorous one too, when Eustace "realised that everyone took the idea of a duel quite seriously" and were discussing how to properly arm Eustace to face Reepicheep in single combat. Perhaps the first sensible action of his life is when Eustace apologizes to the Mouse. He has new rules to live by, for honor is valued by King Caspian and his companions, and cruelty is punished rather than ignored. At the end of *The Silver Chair,* cruelty is again punished by beatings with the flats of swords. In Lewis' view, as well as Aslan's world, for right to prevail, evil must be punished.

— Chapter 3: The Lone Islands —

Matters look grim and adventuring seems much less fun when the children, Caspian, and Reepicheep are kidnapped by slavers to be sold in the slave market of Narrowhaven. This could mark the end of the quest to find the seven lost lords and turn into a wholly different kind of adventure. In this case, the kidnapping serves as an excuse to examine aspects of good and bad government. Caspian is somewhat too easily saved by being purchased by none other than Lord Bern, one of the missing seven. He had recognized in Caspian's face something of the old King Caspian's face, the face of Caspian's father. Caspian X is very displeased with what he has found in the Lone Islands and means to set matters right.

The Lone Islands have been part of the holdings of Narnia's crown ever since the Narnian year 302, when Narnia's King Gale had vanquished a dragon that plagued the islands. The grateful islanders declared the king their emperor. Yet it has been many years since a Narnian king has visited the islands and renewed his claim to them; 150 years have passed since the

Lone Islands last paid their tribute to Narnia. You may recall from *Prince Caspian* that the Telmarine kings who had ruled Narnia for generations feared the sea and would not go near it, so it is not surprising that the Lone Islands have lost contact with Narnia's kings. But Bern proves to be a noble person, eager to help Caspian and to rid the islands of slavery and their bad government, run by a timid, officious, greedy governor.

— Chapter 4: What Caspian Did There —

"Have you no idea of progress, of developments?" Gumpas says to Caspian. This reflects Lewis' attitude toward the cult of progress. At the time he wrote *The Voyage of the "Dawn Treader,"* the cult of progress had existed for over a hundred years, and it is strong, even today. The cult of progress is the belief that any change, particularly economic or technological, is automatically good. Lewis strongly disagreed with this view; to him, progress could be good or bad and it must justify itself. When it blighted or belittled people's lives, it was bad. He thought it particularly bad in religious belief, because he thought modern people had lost touch with the everyday presence of God by putting Him in a past tense. The notion that God existed beyond all things, a medieval notion that beyond the planets and beyond the stars was God, was something Lewis wanted people to return to, but he saw modern society becoming too focused on what good may be immediately realized from the present. To Lewis, God was reached by a lifetime of faith and action, not a few days or even a few years. In the case of the Lone Islands, the government has given itself wholly over

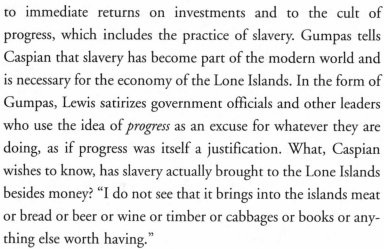

to immediate returns on investments and to the cult of progress, which includes the practice of slavery. Gumpas tells Caspian that slavery has become part of the modern world and is necessary for the economy of the Lone Islands. In the form of Gumpas, Lewis satirizes government officials and other leaders who use the idea of *progress* as an excuse for whatever they are doing, as if progress was itself a justification. What, Caspian wishes to know, has slavery actually brought to the Lone Islands besides money? "I do not see that it brings into the islands meat or bread or beer or wine or timber or cabbages or books or anything else worth having."

Governor Gumpas is eager to show graphs and statistics that illustrate what the trade in human lives brings, but he is unable to show anything that is actually of no use to anyone. This stinging portrait of a man given entirely over to cruelty and exploitation is likely to find a responsive chord in anyone who has had to deal with an officious, small-minded bureaucrat. Gumpas is little more than a bully, reaping wealth out of the misery of others. Lewis's particular disdain for "statistics" may stem from the raw reduction of human beings to abstractions by national socialist and communist dictatorships that served as an excuse for the murders of tens of millions of farmers in Ukraine and tens of millions of Jews, gypsies, other religious minorities, homosexuals, and other people whose deaths were engineered by the Nazis. A good government is one like that of King Caspian, that is concerned with actual people and their everyday needs rather than remote abstractions embodied in statistics and graphs and other busywork that separates the government from the realities of the lives of the governed.

From *Prince Caspian,* Caspian's courage and daring are already known, but in this chapter Lewis shows more of his intelligence: He not only puts Gumpas and other government bureaucrats' nonsense about slavery being good to the contemptible place it belongs, but he shows how to accomplish his ends without violence, by using his authority and knowledge of his opponents to win a good and just end without deaths. His potential enemies find themselves trapped in their own bureaucratic confusions.

— Chapter 5: The Storm and What Came of It —

Lucy remains Queen Lucy the Valiant, as good a companion on an adventure as one could wish: "Lucy thought she was the most fortunate girl in the world, as she woke each morning to see the reflections of the sunlit water dancing on the ceiling of her cabin and looked round on all the nice new things she had got in the Lone Islands—sea-boots and buskins and cloaks and jerkins and scarves" (all good to have on a sea journey in which one is expected to take action and not just be a passenger).

The passages in this chapter that explain Reepicheep's chess skills are a masterpiece of revealing character through action rather than exposition. Reepicheep is determined: he moves big chess pieces around with difficulty, but he plays many games with Lucy anyway. He is smart and sometimes wins games against Lucy. He is given to passion: he sometimes forgets himself and puts pieces in harms's way with the idea that they would fight against overwhelming odds, just as he would. He is good spirited: he may lose, sometimes by forgetting that he is

just playing a game, but he continues to play against Lucy without rancor.

The storm costs the crew one life, the only life lost on what is a perilous adventure into hostile waters. *The Voyage of the "Dawn Treader"* has a great deal of action, and Lewis puts the storm to use as motivation for action in the next chapter. When Eustace hears of all the work to be done after they have landed on an island, he chooses to make a difficult climb into the woods, away from work, convinced, as usual, that the others are scheming to make him miserable by making him work. Even so, Lewis notes that there has been some growth in Eustace, for when the climbing gets tough, Eustace sticks with it. The old Eustace would have given up the climb scarcely after it had started.

— Chapter 6: The Adventure of Eustace —

Eustace sees a dragon, but because he has not read the right books, he does not know what it is. To Lewis, reading fiction, especially adventures, fairy tales, and myths, is good for a person. They help one to become a good thinker. Lewis adds that the wrong books "had a lot to say about exports and imports and governments and drains, but they were weak on dragons." This remark ties Eustace's impoverished education with Gumpas' bad government, because both are about mindless data without consideration for consequences for people. Just as Gumpas was separated from the people he governed by pointless paperwork, so Eustace has been separated from companionship and affection. His home life has been the embodiment of the obsession with "progress" without thought to what *progress* ought to be. A more immediate problem is that Eustace has had such a pathetic intellectual life that he has no idea what a dragon is, not even after he is turned into one. His parents almost certainly would never have allowed him to read *The Chronicles of Narnia*.

The dragon is a sad sight, having "a long lead-colored snout, dull red eyes, no feathers or fur, a long lithe body that trailed on the ground, legs whose elbows went up higher than its back like a spider's, cruel claws, bat's wings that made a rasping noise on the stones, yards of tail." Lewis notes that even Eustace saw that it was an old dragon. It dies miserably, with only a self-centered, uncomprehending boy as a witness. The dragons of Narnia are greedy creatures, craving treasure above all else; the dragon's death is that of someone who cared nothing for anyone but itself. Yet, its cave is full of treasure, and Eustace is delighted with it.

He takes a nap and feels very awkward upon awakening. When he crawls to the pool, he sees the face of a dragon, which is really his own reflection. Lewis explains, "Sleeping on a dragon's hoard with greedy, dragonish thoughts in his heart, he had become a dragon himself." That might or might not happen on earth, but in Narnia's world, such transformations are known to happen. Having aspired to being rich and having become a pain to others, Eustace become the embodiment of pointless greed and affliction; he now looks like what he has aspired to be.

Yet the physical transformation is not as important as the transformation in Eustace's heart. As he flies back to the *Dawn Treader*, he realizes that he wanted to have friends with whom

he could talk and laugh and share things. He realizes that "he
was a monster cut off from the whole human race." In human
form, he already was a monster cut off from the human race.
Awaking as a dragon with a hoard of wealth, he finally realizes
that the hoard is without value if he is to be cut off from companionship, the way the pitiful old dragon was.

When Eustace lands on the beach, he is cause for concern.
Reepicheep is ready to have single combat with him, thinking
that Eustace is a dangerous dragon, but Caspian forbids it. Lucy
says that maybe the dragon will go away. Edmund says that he
hopes not: "If there's a wasp in the room I like to be able to see
it." This sounds very much like King Edmund in *The Horse and
His Boy*, often given to solemn pronouncements that may or
may not be wise. This reaction is not much different from the
attitude the crew already had toward Eustace, and now his
many sins, from self-pity to lying to stealing have become sym-
bolized by his heavy, thick dragon's skin, which sets him apart
from others.

— Chapter 7: How the Adventure Ended —

Caspian notes that the ring that painfully pinches Eustace's
foreleg is the Lord Octesian's arm-ring. The ring that bears
Octesian's insignia draws on the ring-giver custom of the Dark
Ages, as in the epic *Beowulf*, which also features a greedy dragon and a dragon's hoard of treasure. Such rings were a sign of
wealth and were often given by good kings to their followers.
The arm-ring suggests that Octesian died on the island, perhaps
killed by the dragon Eustace saw.

In a turn around that is masterfully handled by Lewis, Eustace, having become physically what his spirit had been like, begins to be liked by others: "It was, however, clear to everyone that Eustace's character had been rather improved by becoming a dragon." Thus the nasty boy, who wounded people for the fun of it, who now as a dragon could inflict as much pain as he wants, discovers that being liked and, still more the pleasure of liking other people, kept him from despair. He also learns that he is happiest doing others favors, such as flying them on his back high above the island.

At the end of this chapter, Eustace undergoes a miraculous transformation. When he sees a huge lion coming slowly towards him, he notes that although there was no moon, moon-light illuminated the lion. One the signs of Aslan is that He gives off His own light. In fact, He is so bright that He can be hard to look at, but His breath gives people the strength to look at Him.

What follows is a symbolic undressing of Eustace's sins. As he bathes and sheds layers of his dragon form, he symbolically washes away the layers of his spirit that he had created by his cruelty and selfishness. Removing these layers will make it easier for him to make friends, something he has recently learned to desire, and it will make him more open to Aslan's influence. Further, the bathing and the emergence of Eustace as a human boy exemplify Aslan's power to forgive and to wash away sin. It is a manifestation of the symbolism of baptism, the washing away of sin and representing a commitment to God. But the cleansing of his spirit is only a beginning towards Eustace's redemption. He will continue to make a pest of himself; even Edmund after all his years of living in the way of Aslan, still has bad moments.

– Chapter 8: Two Narrow Escapes –

When the sea serpent appears, Eustace shows that his character has strengthened; he valiantly attacks that beast, doing little good but being valiant. In so doing, he ruins the sword Caspian has given him. It seems particularly important that the two smallest crew members are the ones who most distinguish themselves in the battle against the sea serpent. One is Eustace, from whom nothing is expected but who shows his determination to be better than he has been, and the other is the Chief Mouse Reepicheep. He has shown much valor in battle, so his courage is unquestioned, but he demonstrates that his valor is matched by his composure and clear thinking. Edmund has shown the futility of hacking at the sea serpent's armored skin, and arrows have bounced off the creature, and the sea serpent is tightening its coil around the *Dawn Treader*. Apparently flummoxed, the crew watches Reepicheep charge to the sea serpent and push with all his might—the idea is to push the coil over the back of the ship before it tightens all the way. This is smart thinking and leadership, for once they see what Reepicheep means, everyone rushes to do as he is doing.

Having outwitted the sea serpent, the sailors find another island. It has a particularly insidious danger that some nearly fall prey to. They find remnants of armor on a hillside, then a pool with a golden statue in it. Only by good thinking do they figure out what has happened. "That water turns things into gold," says Edmund. This would seem like a great find—like having Midas' touch without the liability of not being able to touch anything without it turning into gold. Yet the golden statue of a man diving is a warning, seemingly an obvious one, because the clues are all there: the helmet and armor without any bones that should indicate that he shed his clothes voluntarily and dove into the pool.

But the place is cursed, for greed overwhelms Caspian and Edmund, who argue pointlessly about who should own the pool. When they see a huge Lion on the distant hillside, bathed in bright sunlight even though there was no sun, the people for once pay attention to Aslan's sign and leave the pool alone, promising to tell no one about it. The theme of *greed* again manifests itself. It has been shown in the form of a government ruining lives in the pursuit of money in the Lone Island, it has been personified by Eustace who actually becomes a creature that is supposed to be devoted only to the gathering of wealth, and here, two otherwise good people lose control over themselves at the thought of unlimited gold. In each case there are monsters. Gumpas and his government are monsters who rule over the Lone Islands just as if they were a dragon stealing its wealth; Eustace was a monster, a being devoted to inflicting pain on others, until he took the form of a monster; and the behavior of both Caspian and Edmund is here monstrous. The desire for gold has turned them into thoughtless creatures, with no more motivation or sense than a dragon. In each case, *greed* is pitted against *humanity*, with people suffering when greed becomes more important.

In this chapter is a cautionary tale of how even the best of people can lose their minds when they forget to be humane: The statue is a dead man. Think of him before one thinks of the gold and a humane perspective can be achieved. The statue is a man who has become the personification of what gold, when only gold is

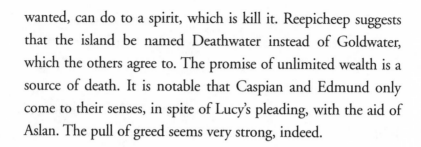

wanted, can do to a spirit, which is kill it. Reepicheep suggests that the island be named Deathwater instead of Goldwater, which the others agree to. The promise of unlimited wealth is a source of death. It is notable that Caspian and Edmund only come to their senses, in spite of Lucy's pleading, with the aid of Aslan. The pull of greed seems very strong, indeed.

— Chapter 9: The Island of the Voices —

This chapter begins the story of the Dufflepuds, mixing mystery, suspense, and comedy. Caspian and his party land at an island that appears to be inhabited, but without any people. Eventually, in addition to the thumps, they hear voices plotting mischief, and the landing party prepares for the worst. Invisible enemies seem to be between them and their landing boat. This chapter shows Lewis' penchant for juxtaposing opposites to create tension. The invisible people seem very dangerous, yet a chorus of voices always praising the main speaker is comical. Certainly the spear that flies into a tree trunk is ominous, but what of the thumping of the ground wherever the invisible people go? Such loud thumping warned Lucy of their coming, so invisible though they are, they would have trouble sneaking up on anyone. Their demand that Lucy read a spell from the book of a menacing magician who "uglified" them can be very ominous, or it could be ridiculous. After all, they confess that it was the leader's daughter who read the invisibility spell from the magician's book, so maybe they are just being silly. Lucy says to Caspian, "Don't you get the idea that these people are not very brave?" But there is that matter of a well-thrown spear.

— Chapter 10: The Magician's Book —

The invisible people are not entirely bad sorts. After Lucy agrees to climb up into the magician's lair and read the magician's book, out of which only little girls and the magician can cast a spell (or so they claim), they take her and the others to the magician's manor and serve a good meal. It is curious to watch serving platters leap high into the air and bounce a few feet before hitting the floor, and the food tends to get all over the place as it spills.

Lucy the Valiant is as good as her word, even though the winding stairs and the hallway into which she emerges are uncomfortably mysterious, with strange symbols on the doors, odd woodworking, and mysterious objects. When reading the magic book, she has four significant experiences: 1) She spies on two girls, one a friend of hers who says bad thing about Lucy; 2) she reads a spell that would make her the most beautiful woman in the world, and kings would fight terrible wars over her; 3) she reads a fabulous story that is so wonderful she feels as though she is living it, but she cannot remember what it was after she finishes it; 4) she finds and works the spell of visibility. This last brings a great surprise: in the doorway stood Aslan himself. Had He been there, invisible? Lucy is surprised that by casting the spell of visibility, she could make Aslan visible, as if she could make Him do anything. He says, "Do you think I wouldn't obey my own rules?" This is an important point that later is revived in Aslan's Country in *The Last Battle* when Aslan says that He will show what He *cannot* do as well as what He can when He offers the ungrateful Dwarfs a hearty meal. He follows His Own rules and He follows His Father's rules.

When Lucy thinks of actually casting the spell to make her supremely beautiful, she sees a picture where there had been no picture before. In it she found "the great face of a lion, of the Lion, Aslan himself, staring into hers. It was painted such a bright gold that it seemed to be coming towards her out of the page; and indeed she never was quite sure afterwards that it hadn't really moved a little. At any rate she knew the expression on his face quite well. He was growling and you could see most of his teeth." Lucy knows what this means and she turns the page.

Aslan points out that she was spying on her school friend, and that spying by magic is still spying. In fact, He says, Lucy's friend loves her but she is weak and said what she thought was wanted. But Lucy cannot forget what was said. Lucy thinks she has spoiled their friendship, and she asks Aslan what would have happened had she not spied on her friend. He tells her that as He explained to her once before, no one is ever told what *would have happened?* This refers back to Chapter 10 of *Prince Caspian,* when Aslan reveals Himself to Lucy in the woods. It seems to be important to Lewis that this point be made: that God will not tell us what He had planned for us had we made the choices He would have preferred.

About the wonderful story that Lucy cannot remember? Lewis provides a cryptic passage, a tantalizing mystery. The clues are "It was about a cup and a sword and a tree and a green hill." This is not much to go on. Perhaps the cup is Jesus's cup at the last supper, the sword the one that cut off a man's ear when Jesus was seized, and the tree and green hill representative of the night He spent with His disciples in a garden before His crucifixion. That would parallel the story about Christ's sacrifice for the people of earth. It is a story that bears many retellings and Aslan promises to tell it again and again.

— Chapter 11: The Dufflepuds Made Happy —

Among those who become visible when Lucy casts the spell is Coriakin. As an old man dressed in a red robe, Coriakin the magician is not particularly imposing. "His white hair was crowned with a chaplet of oak leaves, his beard fell to his girdle, and he supported himself with a curiously carved staff." Later, it will be revealed that Coriakin is a fallen star who has committed some unspecified offense, but in this chapter he seems like a pleasant old man. He says of Aslan, "it's not as if he were a *tame* lion," meaning Aslan's behavior is unrestrained.

The other previously invisible beings are Monopods, so called because they each have but one large foot (*mono*: one; *pod*: foot); they are also called Duffers, probably because they are somewhat deficient in intelligence. Although the Duffers believe themselves to be very ugly because they have only the one foot, they look like ordinary Dwarfs except for not having two legs. The visitors to their island help the Duffers forget how ugly they are supposed to be by showing them ways to enjoy using their big feet, and instead of being a frightening bunch, they turn out to be playful. They mingle the words *monopod* and *duffer* until they settle on a new name for themselves, calling themselves the "Dufflepuds." Once the sailors show them how to make small oars and how to use the oars, the Dufflepuds merrily paddle around the *Dawn Treader,* their big feet acting like small boats. The Dufflepuds are probably based on descrip-

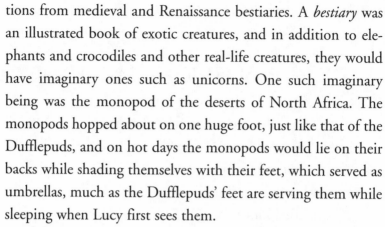

tions from medieval and Renaissance bestiaries. A *bestiary* was an illustrated book of exotic creatures, and in addition to elephants and crocodiles and other real-life creatures, they would have imaginary ones such as unicorns. One such imaginary being was the monopod of the deserts of North Africa. The monopods hopped about on one huge foot, just like that of the Dufflepuds, and on hot days the monopods would lie on their backs while shading themselves with their feet, which served as umbrellas, much as the Dufflepuds' feet are serving them while sleeping when Lucy first sees them.

Whatever Coriakin's offense may have been, he seems like a good person. He has used his magic to help the Dufflepuds learn how to fend for themselves, and it seems that the Dufflepuds would starve without Coriakin's guidance on how to grow crops and keep domesticated animals. He conscientiously conjures up a meal as close to an English tea as he can manage for Lucy, and later he feeds everybody very well, treating them to a fine feast. He magically repairs the stern of the *Dawn Treader* to its original condition, and he stores provisions for the ship to continue its journey eastward. He tells the voyagers that "the lords Revilian, Argoz, Mavramorn and Rhoop" made it to the island of the Dufflepuds.

For the next chapter, remember the happy Dufflepuds and how they seemed menacing when invisible but turned out to be just very silly. And remember how Coriakin turned out to be a nice person, even if the Dufflepuds sometimes tried his patience. In Chapter 12, the voyagers encounter another kind of invisibility—one that only faith can defy.

— Chapter 12: The Dark Island —

The voyagers have seen something interesting in the distance. "About nine that morning, very suddenly, it was so close that they could see that it was not land at all, nor even, in an ordinary sense, a mist. It was a Darkness." Perhaps wisely, the crew wishes to avoid the Darkness, but Reepicheep speaks up, saying, "But I hope it will never be told in Narnia that a company of noble and royal persons in the flower of their age turned tail because they were afraid of the dark." Reepicheep will turn out to be right (he is a smart as well as honorable mouse) and the crew will be somewhat in the wrong.

When the *Dawn Treader* enters the Darkness, the region around the ship becomes eerie and Lucy feels very cold. Then, suddenly, from somewhere they could not determine, came a cry of some inhuman voice or from someone who had lost his humanity. When they find the source of the voice, he is a terrible sight; a man nearly insane and unsure whether the *Dawn Treader* is real. The man has swum out from the Dark Island. He says that this is the island where dreams come true, which causes some happy excitement among the crew, who think of what they wish would come true: meeting lost friends, reliving a love affair, or having a second chance to right a mistake. They have some reason to think this, because they have managed to turn frightful adventures into happy ones. After all, the invisible Dufflepuds turned out to be a ridiculous lot, and their magician Coriakin was friendly with Aslan. Besides, people commonly speak of wishing their dreams would come true as something to be desired.

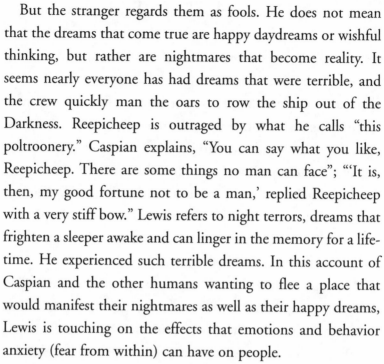

But the stranger regards them as fools. He does not mean that the dreams that come true are happy daydreams or wishful thinking, but rather are nightmares that become reality. It seems nearly everyone has had dreams that were terrible, and the crew quickly man the oars to row the ship out of the Darkness. Reepicheep is outraged by what he calls "this poltroonery." Caspian explains, "You can say what you like, Reepicheep. There are some things no man can face"; "'It is, then, my good fortune not to be a man,' replied Reepicheep with a very stiff bow." Lewis refers to night terrors, dreams that frighten a sleeper awake and can linger in the memory for a lifetime. He experienced such terrible dreams. In this account of Caspian and the other humans wanting to flee a place that would manifest their nightmares as well as their happy dreams, Lewis is touching on the effects that emotions and behavior anxiety (fear from within) can have on people.

You may remember how worked up Caspian and Edmund became over the water that turned things into gold; their baser selves were speaking without the inhibitions that good sense can provide. Dark Island offers the prospect where no inhibitions can govern the worst someone can think of; the effect of this on the crew is manifested in their panic. Already the island has begun to work on them; like Caspian and Edmund on Deathwater Island, their normally intelligent, courageous behavior degenerates into pointless fear. That the crew members each hear different noises and see different menaces approaching the ship or climbing over the ship shows that the menace is not exterior but interior, with each man creating his own awful terror. In *Prince Caspian,* Reepicheep showed much presence of mind, even calmness, after his tail was chopped off; when the *Dawn Treader* was attacked by a sea serpent he had the presence of mind to see how they could escape the sea serpent. Thus it is not entirely surprising that when menaced by his own worst nightmares Reepicheek's reaction is to confront them. This incident at Dark Island so sets Reepicheek apart from all the others that he alone will be welcomed into Aslan's Country at the novel's end; he has achieved a level of self-control and courage that all the others have yet to attain. When Lucy, Edmund, and Eustace want to know whether they can go into Aslan's Country, too, Aslan says not yet because they still have more to learn about themselves.

After considerable rowing, it becomes evident that the *Dawn Treader* is making little, perhaps no, progress out of the Darkness. Lucy prays, "Aslan, Aslan, if ever you loved us at all, send us help now." A spot of white appears. "At first it looked like a cross," perhaps suggesting God's spirit coming to the ship. The white cross turns out to be an albatross. Traditionally, albatrosses bring good luck; in this case, it shows the way out of the Darkness. Perhaps the only salvation from the worst of dreams is Aslan. Eustace found himself living a nightmare while he was a dragon; it took Aslan to free him from the burden of sins that had made him a dragon. Life itself can be like a nightmare. If the white cross means that the albatross is the Holy Spirit, then it represents Aslan's ability to guide people out of darkness and into light. In the case of Dark Island, Lucy's prayer and the coming of the albatross suggest one way to battle the terrors of the mind: Call to Aslan. Aslan's breath (the Holy Spirit) represents a connection to Aslan and His Father. Lewis believed that

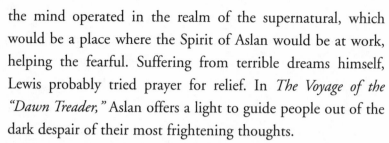

the mind operated in the realm of the supernatural, which would be a place where the Spirit of Aslan would be at work, helping the fearful. Suffering from terrible dreams himself, Lewis probably tried prayer for relief. In *The Voyage of the "Dawn Treader,"* Aslan offers a light to guide people out of the dark despair of their most frightening thoughts.

The stranger turns out to be the lord whose name Caspian has trouble remembering, Lord Rhoop. At last, the expedition has recovered a lost lord. Had Reepicheep not demanded courage of his shipmates, Rhoop may have been lost for all his life amide his most horrifying imaginings, all uncontrolled by his conscious mind.

There are major differences between the first British edition and the first American edition of this chapter. In the British edition, it seems as though the Darkness could be wished away, but in the American edition the fearsome Darkness and the Dark Island are treated more seriously. In the first British edition, Caspian asks the freshly rescued Lord Rhoop what boon he would like:

> "Never to bring me back there," he said. He pointed astern. They all looked. But they saw only bright blue sea and bright blue sky. The Dark Island and the darkness had disappeared forever.
>
> "Why!" cried Lord Rhoop. "You have destroyed it!"
>
> "I don't think it was us [meaning it was Aslan]," said Lucy.

It is apparent in this passage that Lewis wanted to point out another aspect of Aslan's power by suggesting through Lucy that

He destroyed the Dark Island. But Lewis knew by personal experience that prayer does not banish nightmares forever. Night terrors are persistent and very troubling. Suffering from night terrors himself and regarding them as very serious, Lewis did not wish to imply that they could be wished away or were mere childishness. The sources for his night terrors could have been the death of his mother, the brutality of his schools, and eventually his utterly horrifying experiences at the front during World War I. He rewrote some of Chapter 12 to more accurately reflect the ideas he wanted to say about the experience in the Darkness. Thus Lord Rhoop has a different reply for Caspian and the new passage is:

> "Never to ask me, nor to let any other ask me, what I have seen during my years on the Dark Island."
>
> "An easy boon, my Lord," answered Caspian, and added with a shudder, "*Ask* you: I should think not. I would give all my treasure *not* to hear it."

In this revision, Lewis allows the Dark Island to stand as a lasting threat to peace of mind, and it is more psychologically realistic than the passage he chose to discard. Further, it treats with respect the nightmares many young readers (perhaps all) experience, whereas the earlier one suggests that good thoughts could banish them. As I write this, there is a rumor that I have not confirmed that the parent publisher of *The Chronicles of Narnia* intends to return to the first British edition version of Chapter 12, discarding the revised version. This would be directly contrary to Lewis' own wishes, made manifest in his concern that the chapter more precisely conveys his ideas. The first American edition represents his final version of the chapter, which in the world of literary scholarship means that it is to be preferred for both research and criticism over earlier versions.

— Chapter 13: The Three Sleepers —

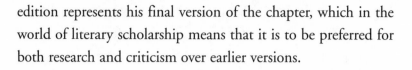

The voyagers visit another strange island and discover something odd: "What they now saw was a wide oblong space flagged with smooth stones and surrounded by grey pillars but unroofed. And from end to end of it ran a long table laid with a rich crimson cloth that came down nearly to the pavement. The crimson color is symbolic of Aslan and perhaps of Aslan's blood. It suggests that Aslan's Table is an altar and that dining at Aslan's Table is a sacrament in which the wine represent Aslan's blood and the food represents Aslan's flesh. At either side of it were many chairs of stone richly carved and with silken cushions upon the seats." Seated at this table, apparently asleep are three men whose exceedingly long hair hung over the backs of their chairs so that they were wholly concealed. The hair almost buries them, suggesting that they have been asleep in their places for many years. They are the Lords Revilian, Argoz, and Mavramorn.

A mysterious girl eventually calls the table "Aslan's table." She is remarkably poised; the way she carries herself engenders respect in those who see her. She explains that the three men quarrelled about whether to remain on the island, return to Narnia, or continue sailing eastward. One of them grabbed the Knife of Stone and instantly they fell asleep. Lucy recognizes it as the one the White Witch used to kill Aslan at the Stone Table. The girl confirms that it is the same knife. She says that it is kept with "honour" at the table until the world ends. It is odd that a knife used to slay Aslan would be honored, but it is the only knife to have done so, and from the blood it shed came Aslan's victory over death, a victory in which all Narnians may share. Still, it was not up to battling Peter and Peter's sword in *The Lion, the Witch and the Wardrobe,* so it is unlikely to be at the table because of its having special power. Indeed, having it at a place where people are supposed to feast is strange. Some people could be put off by it. On the other hand, if the crimson carpet represents Aslan's blood, and the wine and food Aslan's blood and flesh, then having the stone knife of Aslan's Table makes sense, because the carpet would represent the flow of blood from the Stone Table in *The Lion, the Witch and the Wardrobe,* and Aslan's Table would be the altar. From both the Stone Table and Aslan's Table comes life, but the Stone Table represented the Deep Magic that Aslan broke, thereby breaking the old covenant, whereas Aslan's Table in this chapter represents an affirmation of life, the Deeper Magic of the Emperor-over-sea. Thus there is more to the girl's statement that Aslan has provided the food to comfort those for those voyagers who come so far east. The feast also represents the spiritual feast Aslan has waiting for those who make their long spiritual journeys toward enlightenment.

— Chapter 14: The Beginning of the End of the World —

The voyagers are excited by the sunrise because the sun is larger than it had been before and they knew they had come to the beginning of the end of the world. Their host Ramandu is

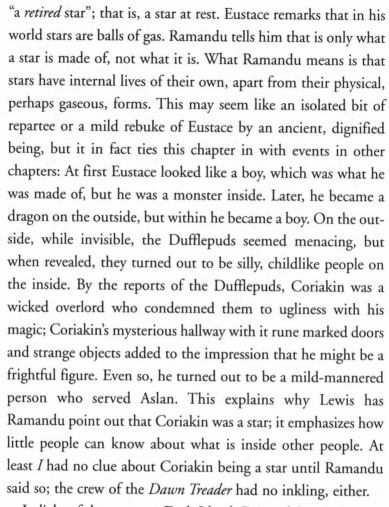

"a *retired* star"; that is, a star at rest. Eustace remarks that in his world stars are balls of gas. Ramandu tells him that is only what a star is made of, not what it is. What Ramandu means is that stars have internal lives of their own, apart from their physical, perhaps gaseous, forms. This may seem like an isolated bit of repartee or a mild rebuke of Eustace by an ancient, dignified being, but it in fact ties this chapter in with events in other chapters: At first Eustace looked like a boy, which was what he was made of, but he was a monster inside. Later, he became a dragon on the outside, but within he became a boy. On the outside, while invisible, the Dufflepuds seemed menacing, but when revealed, they turned out to be silly, childlike people on the inside. By the reports of the Dufflepuds, Coriakin was a wicked overlord who condemned them to ugliness with his magic; Coriakin's mysterious hallway with it rune marked doors and strange objects added to the impression that he might be a frightful figure. Even so, he turned out to be a mild-mannered person who served Aslan. This explains why Lewis has Ramandu point out that Coriakin was a star; it emphasizes how little people can know about what is inside other people. At least *I* had no clue about Coriakin being a star until Ramandu said so; the crew of the *Dawn Treader* had no inkling, either.

In light of the events at Dark Island, Ramandu's pointing out that there is a difference between what someone is made of and what he or she actually is has another ramification that Lewis may hope provides material for thought. At the Dark Island, the menace did not so much come from outside but from within. Each shipmate had his or her own nightmares; as they heard or saw frightening beings swimming to, climbing onto, swarming over, or flying over the ship, they were revealing inner aspects of themselves that they normally would repress. They were being reminded that they, like stars, were more than what they were made of. What Ramandu reveals is that Lewis has been working throughout *The Voyage of the "Dawn Treader"* on his view of the inner person, of the mind and therefore the soul being something apart from the body. Ramandu and Coriakin personify this idea because they were once stars shining in the firmament but have now taken the form of human beings. Yet, they are still stars. Whether the form is gas or flesh and bone, they are still their essential, inner selves. This idea will be expanded in the last chapter of *The Voyage of the "Dawn Treader,"* in which Aslan is both Lamb and Lion. Whatever His form, He like the people He creates remains the same person regardless. This idea will occur again in *The Last Battle,* in which the Pevensies, Digory, Polly, Eustace, Jill, and King Tirian all appear as young adults, although their ages are hard to define. This amazes Tirian, who had only minutes before seen Eustace and Jill as children, but you and I will have read *The Voyage of the "Dawn Treader,"* already, and realize that whatever their outward forms, these are same people we have shared adventures with throughout *The Chronicles of Narnia.* It also implies that *The Chronicles of Narnia* is in part a spiritual pilgrimage. Ramandu is pointing out a spiritual truth that the main characters are learning through direct experience, and it is a truth that will put them in closer touch with the realities of Aslan's Country.

Ramandu tells the voyagers that to break the enchantment of the three sleeping lords, they must sail to the end of the world, and one of them must not return; further, the *Dawn Treader* can only have a willing crew if the disenchantment is to work. This puts Caspian and the others who wish to sail onward in a bind, because most of the crew does not wish to sail farther eastward. One sailor points out that Ramandu's Island, with a feast served every evening for everybody would be a fine place to wait until the winds shift so that they can sail westward to Narnia. Caspian has already displayed his superior diplomatic abilities at the Lone Islands, in which he effected a change of government without bloodshed, but his handling of his crew shows that Narnia is indeed in good hands while he reigns. As men think of reasons not to continue their voyage, he announces that they have the matter backwards. Not everyone is to be allowed to sail farther east with him; that is a privilege to be earned, not one that everyone is to have. Reepicheep helps out by announcing his desire to continue (this is no surprize since we already know of his desire to find the End of the World and possibly Aslan's Country). One sailor immediately declares his desire to continue because he does not wish to be outdone by a Mouse. The talk shifts from not wanting to continue to who is to be allowed to continue.

— Chapter 15: The Wonders of the Last Sea —

Lucy sees underwater roads and magnificent cities populated by people. Lord Drinian warns her to tell no one because sailors have been known to jump overboard and drown in pursuit of sea maidens. This echoes a medieval seafaring tradition that mermaids would lure men off of their ships. This tradition may have its origins in Greek myths about the Sirens, who were supernatural maidens who would lure sailors to their deaths by singing to them. Homer included them in *The Odyssey*, and it is to the Sirens and *The Odyssey* that Edmund alludes in the next chapter when it is proposed that Caspian be tied up as Ulysses (Odysseus) was when his ship sailed past the rocky home of the Sirens. Drinian does not reckon with Reepicheep, who sees a sea man threatening the ship and takes it to be a challenge to battle—in he goes to duel with the challenger. In so doing, he makes a valuable discovery: the water is sweet, not salty. Most seawater is undrinkable because of its saltiness, but as the *Dawn Treader* approaches the End of the World, the water becomes drinkable—a sign that the ship may be approaching Aslan's Country. It is to Lord Drinian's relief that Reepicheep shouts about the quality of the water, not the sea people or their cities. This water would seem to fulfill part of the prophesy about Reepicheep sailing to Aslan's Country: "Where the waves grow sweet,/ Doubt not, Reepicheep,/ There is the utter East."

Such water would be a good home for an underwater civilization, and it seems a sign that the end of the world is nearer. Further, the crew is able to tolerate seeing more light because of drinking the water. In fact, the water seems like drinkable light, as if the life-giving energy of the sun were poured into the sea. The farther the *Dawn Treader* has sailed from Ramandu's island, the brighter everything has become, but the crew is able to see more light than they had ever seen before because of the water. This is important because the sun actually grows larger as they near the eastern limits of the world, and its brightness could otherwise be blinding.

The growing size of the sun is significant for what it tells about the structure of Narnia's world and what it tells about

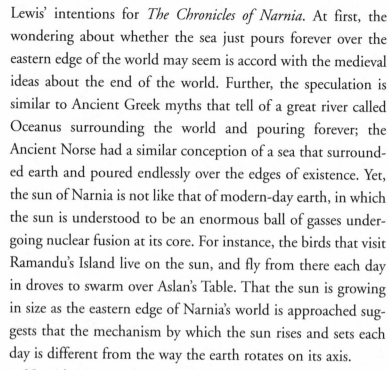

Lewis' intentions for *The Chronicles of Narnia*. At first, the wondering about whether the sea just pours forever over the eastern edge of the world may seem is accord with the medieval ideas about the end of the world. Further, the speculation is similar to Ancient Greek myths that tell of a great river called Oceanus surrounding the world and pouring forever; the Ancient Norse had a similar conception of a sea that surrounded earth and poured endlessly over the edges of existence. Yet, the sun of Narnia is not like that of modern-day earth, in which the sun is understood to be an enormous ball of gasses undergoing nuclear fusion at its core. For instance, the birds that visit Ramandu's Island live on the sun, and fly from there each day in droves to swarm over Aslan's Table. That the sun is growing in size as the eastern edge of Narnia's world is approached suggests that the mechanism by which the sun rises and sets each day is different from the way the earth rotates on its axis.

Narnia's sun must be much closer to the world of Narnia at its eastern edge than when high up in the sky for it to look bigger. Further, this implies that it actually is the sun that moves, not Narnia's world. Eventually, the *Dawn Treader* approaches the Silver Sea covered in lilies (symbols of Christ) and the Last Wave, which is perpetually at its peak without ever breaking. Narnia's world seems to have an eastern edge. This notion is emphasized by the children being able to walk south along the edge.

Lewis does not tell about the western part of Narnia's world, although he mentions in *The Last Battle* that there were many unusual creatures living beyond Narnia's Western Mountains, but it is possible that the world has a western, as well as an eastern edge. Perhaps it, too, ends at Aslan's Country. In any case, what experiences in *The Voyage of the "Dawn Treader"* all add up to is Aslan having created a world very different from that of earth, but it also implies that Narnia's world is not even in the same universe as that of earth. This would explain why the stars seem different; it would also explain why magic works differently in Narnia than on earth—there are different physical laws. Further, it means that the entire universe of Narnia was created solely for the sake of Narnia's world; everything focuses on it. This implies that Lewis wished to view the earth in a similar way, as the focus of creation. This would seem to be contradicted by Lewis's science fiction novels of the Perelandra series, in which Mars and Venus are inhabited, and in fact, Lewis thought that the universe could have other worlds created by God. But I use the phrase *wished to view* because Lewis wanted modern people to recover the sense of the pre-eminence of God that medieval Christians had. In *The Voyage of the "Dawn Treader,"* he presents a world in which that pre-eminence is embodied in a medieval society and a world that actually is the center of its universe, much as many medieval and Renaissance Christians saw the earth. This may be a passion for a more primitive way of life than the modern world offers, but Lewis had seen firsthand too much of how "progress" had developed efficient ways of killing people in droves. I doubt that he would have given up his modern comforts, and especially not the modern medicine that helped keep his wife alive years after her cancer was first diagnosed. He also was not naive enough to think more primitive societies are somehow more benevolent, but he did think that if people regained a sense that God's attention is focused on earth and on them, then they would feel more secure in a modern world that measures life impersonally.

— Chapter 16: The Very End of the World —

The *Dawn Treader* sails a sea covered in white lilies. This is a sign that those on the ship cannot reasonably be expected to understand; the lilies are there for Lewis' readers, who may recognize the lily as a symbol for Christ, and a sign that Aslan's Country would be near.

As he concludes the tale, the narrator (Lewis) hints that Lucy told him the story of her adventures on the *"Dawn Treader,"* remarking that the children had a mystical experience that Edmund and Eustace would not talk about afterwards, an experience that would break your heart, although Lucy said it was not sad. This would suggest that *The Voyage of the "Dawn Treader"* is a remarkable chronicle told to the narrator by Lucy, Edmund, and Eustace. This is probably why Lewis' novels about Narnia are called *The Chronicles,* because this brief passage suggests that the narrator recorded stories that were told to him by those who had the experience, which would make him a chronicler, or someone who records events.

The mystical experience came from a breeze blowing for a couple of seconds from the east that flowed over the Last Wave. "It brought both a smell and a sound, a musical sound." If Aslan's Country is east of the Last Wave (and *The Silver Chair* confirms that it is), then the breeze probably carried hints of Paradise, a place of glorious beauty and the promise of being with Aslan forever. When Lucy and Edmund learn that they will never return to Narnia's world, they are very sad, with Lucy saying that they are unhappy that they will never see Aslan again. He reminds them that He is in earth's as well as Narnia's

466

world. They have the smell and the sound of Aslan's Country to remember as the promise of being with Him. The smell may be the Spirit of Aslan (the Holy Spirit) and the musical sound may be His Voice (in *The Magician's Nephew*, Aslan sang the world into being).

Lucy, Edmund, and Eustace wade from their stranded boat, southward with the Last Wave to their left. Reepicheep paddles his coracle up and over the wave, toward land that is surely Aslan's Country. As they walk, the children undergo an experience similar to what Peter, Susan, Edmund, and Lucy experienced when they walked back through the wardrobe after having been kings and queens in Narnia for many year: They feel younger, but not as strong as they were only minutes earlier.

They see a fire and approach it. There is Something so brightly white that they could hardly look at It: It was a Lamb. The closer they get to Aslan's Country the more Christ and Aslan seem to merge. The Lamb is a symbol of Christ; its brightness is attributable to its being Christ, but such brightness is shared by Aslan. When they ask whether they are walking toward Aslan's Country, the Lamb says, "Not for you . . . For you [the three children] the door into Aslan's country is from your own world." This is a foreshadowing of the train wreck in *The Last Battle*, as well as Eustace's entry into Narnia in *The Silver Chair*. In that novel, he steps from earth into Aslan's Country, and from there he is blown across the sea to Narnia. So he enters Aslan's Country from his own world, implying Aslan's Country (heaven) is the same place for both earth and the world of Narnia and that therefore they share heaven in common.

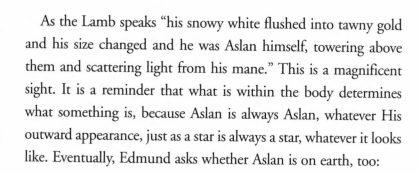

As the Lamb speaks "his snowy white flushed into tawny gold and his size changed and he was Aslan himself, towering above them and scattering light from his mane." This is a magnificent sight. It is a reminder that what is within the body determines what something is, because Aslan is always Aslan, whatever His outward appearance, just as a star is always a star, whatever it looks like. Eventually, Edmund asks whether Aslan is on earth, too:

> "I am," said Aslan. "But there I have another name. You must learn to know me by that name. This was the very reason why you were brought to Narnia, that by knowing me here for a little, you may know me better there [earth]."

This is about as close as Lewis comes in *The Chronicles of Narnia* to making a statement of purpose, that through the account of Aslan in *The Voyage of the "Dawn Treader"* and the other novels people may come to know His Other Incarnation (Christ) better.

VOCABULARY FOR *THE VOYAGE OF THE "DAWN TREADER"*

CHAPTER 1: THE PICTURE IN THE BEDROOM
balmier: crazier

assonance: In poetry *assonance* is a partial rhyme in which vowel sounds correspond but consonant sounds do not, such as "lake" and "fate"; Eustace's verse is very poorly done.

Isle of Wight: a large island in the ocean just south of England

cinema: motion picture; movie

flagon: a vessel that holds wine or other alcoholic beverages, having a spout and a large handle for pouring into smaller vessels such as cups

CHAPTER 2: ON BOARD THE 'DAWN TREADER'

by her rig: by her arrangement of masts and sails

lodge a disposition: make a formal complaint

cogs: heavy wooden ships

dromonds: large ships propelled by sails and oars; large galleys

carracks: a merchant ship of Renaissance Europe similar to a galleon

swank: swaggering

bulwarks: the parts of the ship's sides that rise higher than the upper deck

forecastle: the part of the ship's upper deck that is at the bow

poltroon: a low-life coward

CHAPTER 3: THE LONE ISLANDS

carrion: dead flesh

fief: estate

CHAPTER 4: WHAT CASPIAN DID THERE

postern: a small gate

vagabonds: homeless beggars

bilious: bad tempered, gassy, the color of bile

such a drug: such an unwanted commodity

victualled: supplied with food

fortnight: two weeks; fourteen days

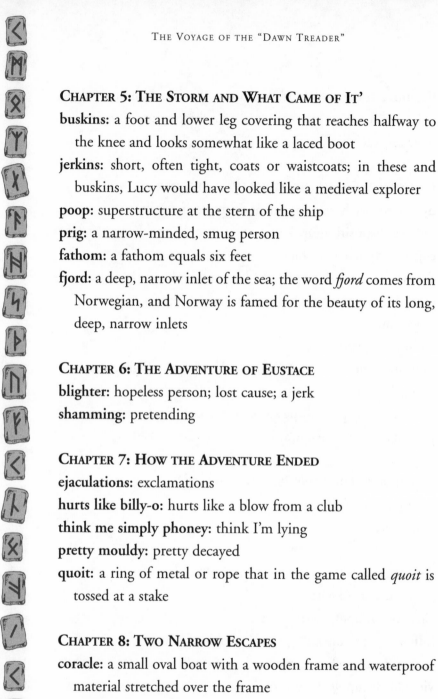

Chapter 5: The Storm and What Came of It'

buskins: a foot and lower leg covering that reaches halfway to the knee and looks somewhat like a laced boot

jerkins: short, often tight, coats or waistcoats; in these and buskins, Lucy would have looked like a medieval explorer

poop: superstructure at the stern of the ship

prig: a narrow-minded, smug person

fathom: a fathom equals six feet

fjord: a deep, narrow inlet of the sea; the word *fjord* comes from Norwegian, and Norway is famed for the beauty of its long, deep, narrow inlets

Chapter 6: The Adventure of Eustace

blighter: hopeless person; lost cause; a jerk

shamming: pretending

Chapter 7: How the Adventure Ended

ejaculations: exclamations

hurts like billy-o: hurts like a blow from a club

think me simply phoney: think I'm lying

pretty mouldy: pretty decayed

quoit: a ring of metal or rope that in the game called *quoit* is tossed at a stake

Chapter 8: Two Narrow Escapes

coracle: a small oval boat with a wooden frame and waterproof material stretched over the frame

vermilions: bright reds

baccy: tobacco

CHAPTER 9: THE ISLAND OF THE VOICES

parley: negotiate

all of a muck sweat: covered in sticky, filthy sweat

CHAPTER 10: THE MAGICIAN'S BOOK

red currants: small sour fruit that look like berries

curds: semi-solids from milk

mead: honey wine

as they did poor Bottom: this is a reference to a character in
Shakespeare's *A Midsummer Night's Dream*

CHAPTER 11: THE DUFFLEPUDS MADE HAPPY

astrolabes: an instrument for measuring the altitude of the sun,
moon, and stars

orreries: models of the solar system; one of these for Narnia's
world would be very interesting to see

chronoscopes: used for measuring small amounts of time

poesimeters: Lewis is probably having fun with words, here. A
poesimeter probably measures the rhythm of poetry

choriambuses: A *choriamb* is a form of poetic rhythm

odolinds: surveyor's instruments for measuring horizontal and
vertical angles with a telescope

monopod: one foot

CHAPTER 12: THE DARK ISLAND

rowlocks: oarlocks

albatross: a seabird with large, narrow wings noted for its forays far
over oceans; in sailing lore, it is usually a symbol of good fortune

boon: favor

CHAPTER 13: THE THREE SLEEPERS
luminous: full of light

CHAPTER 15: THE WONDERS OF THE LAST SEA
cutting: a passage cut through high ground
pinnacles: small spires
minarets: slender towers with balconies
domes: a hemispherical, or half of a sphere, roof
kraken: a sea monster
keel-hauled: a very nasty punishment in which someone is
    dragged under the keel of a ship

CHAPTER 16: THE VERY END OF THE WORLD
pledged: toasted

REFERENCES TO THE BIBLE IN
THE VOYAGE OF THE "DAWN TREADER"

The passage from *The Voyage of the "Dawn Treader"* is first
quoted, followed by the relevant passage in the Bible. A transliteration of the 1611 edition of the King James version of the
Bible is used for the Biblical quotations. Comments then follow.

– Chapter 7: "How the Adventure Ended" –

1. "'Well—he [Aslan] knows me,' said Edmund."

> **I Corinthians 13:12:** "For now we see through a glass,
> darkly: but then face to face: now I know in part, but then
> shall I know even as also I am known."

Comments: As yet, Edmund only sees Aslan "through a glasse, darkely"; you may remember the difficulty he had in even seeing Aslan at first in *Prince Caspian.* On the other hand, Aslan knows him as the phrase "I am knowen" implies. Note the emphasis on meeting Aslan "face to face" in *The Chronicles of Narnia* and its mention in this passage from I Corinthians; at the end of the world in *The Last Battle,* everyone from the world of Narnia meets Aslan face to face, just as Paul says he will someday meet the Lord face to face.

— Chapter 12: "The Dark Island" —

2. "and with the voice a delicious smell breathed in her [Lucy's] face."

> **John 20:22:** "And when He said this, He breathed on them, and said to them, 'Receive you the Holy Ghost.'"

Comments: Lewis alludes to this verse from John several times in *The Chronicles of Narnia.* The "delicious smell breathed in her face" represents the Holy Spirit and Lucy's strong bond with Aslan.

— Chapter 14: "The Beginning of the End of the World" —

3. "But Lucy, looking out from between the wings of the birds that covered her, saw one bird fly to the Old Man [Ramandu] with something in its beak that looked like a little fruit, unless

it was a little live coal, which it might have been, for it was too bright to look at."

> **Isaiah 6:6-7:** "Then flew one of the Seraphims to me, having a live-coal in his hand, *which* he had taken with the tongs from off the altar. / And he laid *it* on my mouth, and said, 'Loe, this has touched your lips, and your iniquity is taken away, and your sin purged.'"

Comments: In Isaiah 6:5, Isaiah bemoans being "a man of unclean lips," meaning a sinner and possibly a liar. The giving of the "fruit" or "live coal" to Ramandu may represent his veracity: That is, he tells the truth, even about his being a retired star, and he is trustworthy.

4. "He's [Ramandu is] a *retired* star."

> **Revelation 9:1:** "And the fifth Angel sounded, and I saw a star fall from heaven to the earth: and to him was given the key of the bottomless pit."

Comments: Perhaps this passage from Revelation was part of the inspiration for Lewis to make Narnia's stars living beings.

— Chapter 16: "The Very End of the World" —

5. "'Come and have breakfast,' said the Lamb in its sweet milky voice."

John 21:12: "Jesus said to them, "Come, and dine." And none of His disciples dared ask Him, 'Who are you?' knowing It was the Lord."

Comments: Just as Jesus' disciples recognize Him when He invites them to eat, we recognize the Lamb as a symbol of Christ, as well as a form assumed by Aslan.

DISCUSSION QUESTIONS AND PROJECTS FOR THE VOYAGE OF THE "DAWN TREADER"

— Overview —

1. Why would Lord Drinian and the ship's crew remain faithful to Caspian X throughout their dangerous journey?

2. How do the Dufflepuds have fun?

3. What do you think the beautiful story from the magician's book is about? What are the clues? How do you explain them?

4. Coriakin serves Lucy and the others one o'clock tea. What is one o'clock tea in England? What is served?

5. What are the traditions about seafaring and albatrosses? Why would Aslan choose an albatross to send to the *Dawn Treader* to lead it out of the Darkness?

6. Why would the daughter of a star marry a human? What would make Caspian attractive to her?

7. Why do Lucy, Edmund, and Eustace not row their boat back to the *Dawn Treader*?

8. Why won't Aslan let the children enter Aslan's Country from Narnia's world?

9. What is meant by saying that the stars of earth's universe are only outwardly balls of hot gases?

10. The are many opportunities for making drawings of scenes, from the old dying dragon to the sea people. Draw a scene from *The Voyage of the "Dawn Treader"* making it as close as you can to Lewis' description. You will probably have to add details of your own to make your picture complete.

11. In each of His appearances in *The Voyage of the "Dawn Treader,"* Aslan teaches something. What does He teach in each instance?

12. What are the stages of Eustace's growth during *The Voyage of the "Dawn Treader"*?

13. What does Caspian X achieve during the voyage? Are these accomplishments worth the trip? (Remember, a crewman died.)

14. For someone being punished, Coriakin seems very friendly and quite happy to see Aslan. Why would this be?

Chapter 1: The Picture in the Bedroom

1. Why would Lewis introduce such a spoiled, unpleasant person as Eustace into *The Chronicles of Narnia*?

2. How well does Lewis capture the spirit of adventure in this, the opening chapter on *The Voyage of the "Dawn Treader"*?

Chapter 2: On Board the 'Dawn Treader'

1. Are there any hints as to why Lucy, Edmund, and Eustace would be brought into Narnia's world for this adventure?

2. Why does Caspian think it is safe for him to leave Narnia on what may be a long expedition?

Chapter 3: The Lone Islands

1. Is Caspian's escape from slavery too easy?

2. If Lord Bern considers slavery to be "vile," why has he purchased Caspian? Does he own any slaves?

Chapter 4: What Caspian Did There

1. What are the evils of Gumpas' government?

2. What does Caspian do to end the evils in the Lone Islands?

Chapter 5: The Storm and What Came of It

1. Why not just give up on Eustace at this point?

2. How does Eustace's experience of adventure in this chapter differ from how Lucy experiences it?

CHAPTER 6: THE ADVENTURE OF EUSTACE

1. Why does the dragon look so forlorn?

2. What is the significance of Eustace turning into a dragon?

3. Why don't the people on the beach panic when Eustace (now a dragon) lands between them and their ship?

CHAPTER 7: HOW THE ADVENTURE ENDED

1. What do you suppose happened to Lord Octesian?

2. Why does Lord Octesian's arm-ring remain on the island? What does that signify?

3. Why does Aslan have Eustace, as a dragon, bathe?

4. What are signs that Eustace is growing, becoming a fuller, richer person?

CHAPTER 8: TWO NARROW ESCAPES

1. How does the battle with the Sea Serpent further develop the crew's character?

2. Why do Caspian and Edmund argue about the pool?

3. Why do those at the pool all agree to keep its existence secret?

CHAPTER 9: THE ISLAND OF THE VOICES

1. When you first hear the thumping, what do you think it is?"

2. What do the voices seem to have in mind?

Chapter 10: The Magician's Book
1. Why must Lucy go upstairs and work the visibility spell?

2. What does she learn from reading the magic book? What do we readers learn from her reading the magic book?

3. What mistake does Lucy make when she listens in on the two girls on a train?

Chapter 11: The Dufflepuds Made Happy
1. What does Aslan mean when he says, "I call all times soon"?

2. Why would the Dufflepuds speak badly of Coriakin?

3. What explanation does Coriakin offer for Aslan's sudden comings and goings?

Chapter 12: The Dark Island
1. Why would the island where dreams come true be surrounded by darkness?

2. Why does the crew automatically think of dreams they would like to have come true rather than their nightmares?

3. Why does it take an appeal to Aslan to free the *Dawn Treader* from the Darkness? Would the ship have been stranded in the Darkness without His help?

CHAPTER 13: THE THREE SLEEPERS

1. The girl says the Knife of Stone "was brought here to be kept in honour while the world lasts." Why would the knife the White Witch used to kill Aslan at the Stone Table in Narnia "be kept in honour"?

2. Why is Aslan's Table set with food? What does this suggest about Aslan?

CHAPTER 14: THE BEGINNING OF THE END OF THE WORLD

1. It is one of the mysteries of the world of Narnia that the sun looks bigger the farther east one travels. What other signs are there that the *Dawn Treader* is close the end of the world?

2. Why not just gather up the sleeping lords, put them in the *Dawn Treader* and take them away?

CHAPTER 15: THE WONDERS OF THE LAST SEA

1. Why do the sea people live in shallow water?

2. What do the signs of sweet water and bright light mean?

CHAPTER 16: THE VERY END OF THE WORLD

1. Does Reepicheep bodily enter heaven (Aslan's Country)?

2. "But there [on earth] I have another name," says Aslan. What name would that be?

3. What does the transformation of the Lamb into Aslan tell about Aslan's nature?

CHAPTER 14

THE SILVER
CHAIR

OVERVIEW

The Silver Chair begins with a depiction of school as a home of horrors, typical of Lewis' views on how not to run a school; introduces a character new to *The Chronicles of Narnia*, Jill Pole; and then thrusts her and Eustace Scrubb quickly into the action. *The Silver Chair* provides a first look at Aslan's Country from the inside. It is forested, mild, and very high.

A serpent has stolen Caspian X's son Rilian, heir to Narnia's throne, and Aslan has summoned the children to go on a quest to find the prince. Their adventure is a good one to read about, although it is very hard on the children. Through barren lands, bitter cold, snow, and hostile giants, the children and their companion Puddleglum try to follow Aslan's signs. They discover a previously unknown Underworld, as well as a plot to force Narnia to submit to the rule of an evil witch.

THE GEOGRAPHY OF *THE SILVER CHAIR*

The Silver Chair provides the only close look at the lands north of Narnia in *The Chronicles of Narnia*, but the novel begins in England at Experiment House, a supposedly progressive school for children. Jill Pole hides behind the school gym because a gang of bullies, encouraged by those who run the school, have decided to beat her up. There, Eustace Scrubb bumps into her and is quick to sympathize with her plight, showing that he has indeed been changed by his experiences in *The Voyage of the "Dawn Treader."* Nearby is a door in a wall that apparently rings the school. When Jill and Eustace call for

Aslan's help, the gang of bullies find them, but Jill and Eustace flee through the doorway and find themselves in an unexpected land. This land is part of Aslan's Country.

To the west is the edge of an enormously high cliff; when one looks past it, one is looking in the opposite direction from which the voyagers on the *Dawn Treader* would have looked. In an effort to show off and to treat Eustace as inferior to her because he is afraid of heights, Jill manages to fling Eustace over the cliff's edge, but instead of falling to his death, Eustace flies away westward.

To the south of where the two children were standing when Eustace fell is a forest. Jill wanders through it, unaware that she is being called. She finds a river flowing east to west, beside which is a huge, fearsome Lion. Because she is desperately thirsty, Jill ventures forth, but is afraid to pass the Lion, Who tells her that the only way to reach the river is through Him. When she finally drinks, she is refreshed in spirit, because she has been spiritually thirsty, and the river represents the spiritual fulfillment that only Aslan and the Emperor-over-sea can offer.

Jill is blown by Aslan across the Eastern Sea, probably passing over the route taken by the *Dawn Treader* in *The Voyage of the "Dawn Treader."* She lands near Eustace, just across the water from Cair Paravel, which King Caspian the Navigator has restored to glory. This must be at the mouth of the Great River. Later, Jill and Eustace are carried by owls to an ancient ruin of a tower that is along the river, so they must have flown west because near Cair Paravel, the Great River flows east.

The youngsters are carried to the north to Puddleglum, who

chair

RUINED CITY

STEEP SLOPE

CAPTURED BY WARDEN OF THE MARCHES

CAVERN

the underworld

CAVE

FATHER TIME

CAVES

Legend

1 Hole where travelers enter
2 Steep slope where Jill, Eustace and Puddleglum fall
3 Enormous cavern with sleeping animals
4 The travelers board an open boat propelled by oars
5 The travelers' boat docks here
6 Jill, Eustace, Rilian and Puddleglum try to escape through the city
7 The travelers meet Golg as the city begins to crumble
8 Race to beat rising water
9 Where the army was to gather

GREAT UNDERGROUND SEA

EXIT TO NARNIA

PORT

QUEEN'S PALACE

BISM CHASM OF FIRE

ESCAPE THROUGH CITY

lives in a marsh near Narnia's northeastern border. Puddleglum is a Marsh-wiggle, and Marsh-wiggles treasure their privacy, so the marsh is divided up into squares of land separated from each other by a grid of marshy water. On each square is a "wigwam," a conical hut with a low doorway (even though Marsh-wiggles have unusually long legs). A typical day for a Marsh-wiggle is to sit beside the water and fish for eels while contemplating the seriousness of life.

Puddleglum and the children hike north to a very high, frightening cliff, but they manage to find a route down. The land they enter is Ettinsmoor (meaning "giants' land"), a nation of somewhat slow-witted and evil giants. The one time the Ettinsmoor giants are seen, they don't seem to have much intellectual substance for their bulk. They stand along a cliff and throw rocks at piles of stone for amusement. They do not even notice the three travelers who pass in front of them. This dull-witted behavior suggests that some other giants may have built the great, ancient bridge that the travelers cross on their way north.

Ettinsmoor is a land of stone and dirt, and looks like a cool desert. North of it, the land shows more vegetation, although it is uncomfortably cold. Following an ancient road northward, Jill, Eustace, and Puddleglum meet the woman in green and the knight in black armor amid low, rocky hills. The farther north they go, the more bitter the weather. When they climb great stone steps onto a plateau, they are buffeted by harsh winds, frozen by falling snow, and the land is dark. It is no wonder that they do not realize that they have entered the ruins of a huge city that was built by ancient giants, apparently long forgotten.

The city of Harfang is on a hill to the north of the ruined city, and it has high walls that apparently run together all along the rim. There are several doors in the walls that lead into homes, but the travelers arrive at the main gate. The interior of Harfang has many large open spaces, as one would reasonably expect for a city inhabited by giants. In addition to homes, there is a palace in Harfang, and it is there that the travelers rest; in its kitchen they discover the recipes for cooking humans and Marsh-wiggles, and from there they find a door leading to the outside.

When they finally heed one of Aslan's signs, Jill, Eustace, and Puddleglum slide down a steep rocky slope and are captured by Earthmen (people who live underground, although "earth man" is sometimes a reference to a Dwarf). The travelers are taken through a string of caverns, in a straight line; because they will emerge in Narnia at the end of *The Silver Chair,* it is likely that they are being taken due south. Jill has a fear of closed-in places, and has a hard time forcing herself to squeeze through the cracks that lead to the first caverns.

The travelers are in Underworld (also called Underland), a land ruled by a witch. One of the wonders they encounter is a huge cavern filled with sleeping animals. Like the three sleeping lords on Ramandu's island in *The Voyage of the "Dawn Treader,"* these animals have been asleep for a very long time but are not dead. The Warden tells the travelers that it is said the animals will awaken at the end of the world. The cavern also has unusual plants, including spongy, treelike ones. They pass a sleeping, gigantic man, Father Time, who may once have been a king. In *The Last Battle,* Aslan will summon Father Time to blow the horn that signals the cataclysmic end of Narnia.

Eventually, the travelers come to the edge of a great sea, in a cavern so wide that its edges cannot be seen in the faint illumination given off by the lamps of the boat they board. The sea has much traffic, as if there is much business to be done along its shores. At its far southern edge is a large city, populated by quiet, gloomy Earthmen. Its shore is lined with quays, with many boats. As the travelers are led into the city, they climb higher, passing many busy Earthmen in the streets. The Queen of Underworld's palace is high into the city.

After killing the serpent queen, Prince Rilian and the others go to a stable out back and rescue his horse. They then work their way east past crumbling buildings and frantic Earthmen. The underground sea is rising, and they can see lamps going out as the water covers them. Across a bridge up to the east is the staging area for the army the Queen of Underworld planned to use to invade Narnia. This is a big area, and after water covered it, Narnians would go inside to boat on it. Jill is the first to poke her head out of a hillside and to see Narnians dancing.

THEMES AND CHARACTERS

Jill Pole is a particularly interesting character. Whereas earlier figures Edmund and Eustace are victimizers when they are first introduced, Jill is a victim. Yet, she is in her own way almost as big a problem as the boys. Chased about the school grounds and bullied cruelly, she begins as a sympathetic character. Eustace, now much improved over what he had been, befriends her and even tells her about Narnia, thereby showing some trust in her. But this turns around when the two call for Aslan, rush through a doorway in a wall, and step into Aslan's Country. Jill treats Eustace with contempt because he does not wish to step to the edge of the top of a very high cliff; she even shows off by stepping to the edge, just to show how superior to him she is. In so doing, she very nearly falls, and when Eustace tries to pull her back, she flings him (probably unintentional) over the cliff. This all makes Jill a very complex character right at the beginning of the novel, and *The Silver Chair* is in part a story of how she learns to manage her impulsiveness and self-centeredness.

Like Jill, Eustace still has much to learn. In *The Voyage of the "Dawn Treader,"* he underwent a transformation with the help of Aslan, but he still has far to go before he ceases to cause problems. He likes to show off his knowledge and is prone to interrupting other people's stories with displays of how smart he thinks he is. Even so, he is more up for adventure than Jill; once in Narnia, physical strength and courage become what they were when he left Narnia's world at the end of *The Voyage of the "Dawn Treader."*

Adding comic relief, as well as some good sense, is Puddleglum, a Marsh-wiggle from the northern marshes of Narnia. A serious-minded fellow, he faces each hardship as something only to be expected. His stubborn allegiance to Aslan is crucial in the effort to free Rilian, especially when the Queen of Underworld tries to enchant the children and him.

The Queen of Underworld is an interesting figure. She is a woman who wears a green kirtle; the green is meant to remind readers of the serpent that she can transform into. Before the beginning of *The Silver Chair*, she has already murdered Rilian's mother, the star child of Ramandu in *The Voyage of the "Dawn*

Treader." She has kidnapped Rilian, and for ten years Narnians have searched for him without success. Her serpent form suggests the serpent in the Garden of Eden that tempted Eve and Adam, which suggests her connection with original evil, which in the world of Narnia is the White Witch. Symbolically, she is either Satan or Satan's disciple.

A JAPANESE TALE OF UNDERWORLD

The Japanese and Chinese share many tales of Underworld, a place that exists underground and under the floor of the Pacific Ocean. It can sometimes be entered through mountain caverns on the mainland, but is more often entered through caves on a mysterious Pacific island that glows red, or through an opening in the ocean floor. Traditionally, a dragon rules Underworld, living in a magnificent palace. In the tales from Japan and China, people often visit Underworld by accident, especially castaways on the mysterious, glowing red island. Other people visit Underworld deliberately, out of curiosity, a desire to pay homage to the ruler of Underworld, or to retrieve a magical item from Underworld. The story I am going to tell you is an ancient folk tale from Japan, and it has significant points of resemblance to the Underworld of *The Silver Chair*.

This is a tale of the Kusanagi Sword, a weapon of great power that terrifies enemies and can defeat entire armies. Even so, it does not always bring success. For instance, it was wielded by Antoku, a boy who was for a brief time emperor of Japan. When his forces were defeated in a naval battle, at the urging of his grandmother, Antoku leaped from his ship and drowned rather than surrender to his enemies. He took the Kusanagi Sword with him, and it disappeared into the depths of the sea, close to the coast of Japan, but no one realized that he had taken the sword to the battle. Everyone assumed that it was still stored in a temple near Kyoto, the imperial city of Japan.

Many years later, the Emperor Go was attacked by a great army that landed on the shores of Japan and killed many of his subjects. The war was a desperate one, because the enemy was clever and skilled; their strength overwhelmed the emperor's defenders. Thus, Go called for the Kusanagi Sword to be brought to him, so that he could wield it in a desperate battle to save himself and his empire. But the sword was not in its temple.

The emperor ordered soothsayers, monks, and priests to use their rituals to ask spirits to tell them where the sword was. They failed, except, perhaps, for one case, for an ancestor of the emperor came to him in a dream and told him that the sword was beneath the ocean, in the home of the ruler of Underworld. To recover the sword, someone would have to enter Underworld and take it away. One possible entrance was off the western coast, and two pearl divers, both girls, were charged with the task of finding the entry to Underworld and of retrieving the sword. Thus, the fate of thousands of men in battle, of an empire, and of the emperor came to rest in the hands of two commoners who had nothing to recommend them but their courage and their swimming skills.

Among monks and priests, incense and chanting, the girls paddled in a boat to sea and dove, looking for the entry that the emperor's dream said would be there. This was the very area where Emperor Antoku had committed suicide ages ago.

After much diving and paddling about, taking a whole day, they found a cave and swam into it. They found breathable air and were able to stand and walk, but it was dark, and they stumbled and hurt their bare feet several times. Eventually they entered a huge cavern, the ceiling of which was blue and from which the sun of Underworld illuminated a land filled with trees. These were not trees like those of the world above. Their fruit were sapphires and emeralds that grew in clusters, like grapes. Serpents guarded the trees and kept the girls from touching the fruit-gems.

The girls passed the trees unharmed, for the serpents were only interested in them if they reached for the fruit. Beyond the forest was a city, the imperial city of the emperor of Underworld. It had golden walls and tall towers made out of the many kinds of stone and coral found in the ocean. Menacing guards, clad in magnificent armor, threatened the girls when they approached the gates of the city. Because the guards wore warlike masks, it was impossible to tell whether they were human or not.

"Who are you?" someone behind a gate asked. He was an old man who was curious about the strange girls.

He asked the girls why they wanted to enter the city, and when they told him, he said they could not enter without the appropriate magic. The girls had to go back above the sea and acquire charms from priests. They did as they were told (they must have been very strong, because walking long distances and then swimming from the bottom of the sea to the surface and then back again would be exhausting).

Each carried a magical charm that was inscribed with sacred texts, and they showed these to the city's guards, who let them through one of the gates.

The streets were paved in silver, gems, and pearls. The buildings were brightly decorated and gilded. It took some time to find the Emperor of Underworld's palace, and once the girls did, they found the doors of the palace protected by invisible beings, perhaps demons, perhaps men, perhaps women. But the girls crept around the palace, and climbing a tree, they found an open window.

When they peered through the window, they saw a large green serpent. They were amazed to see a boy asleep amid the serpent's coils. A sword lay by the serpent's head. The serpent was the Emperor of Underworld, and he was no fool. He quickly realized that there were girls at his window. He demanded to know what they wanted.

They told them that they had come for the Kusanagi Sword.

He declared that the sword belonged to him, that a dragon had stolen it and then lost it to a Japanese warrior, from whom it passed to the Japanese emperor. The war in which the boy Antoku had committed suicide had been engineered by the serpent's agents; the boy's grandmother was actually a serpent (or a dragon) who had taken on the form of a woman, and it was she who had persuaded Antoku to jump while carrying the mighty sword. The boy in his coils was that very boy, who had been thought to have died many years before. The sword, he insisted, was his to keep. Emperor Go and the fate of Japan were not of interest to him.

Possibly by magic, but I like to think by cleverness, the girls found an entry into the palace. They were daring and courageous, because they had to contend with invisible guards and

with a big serpent who could easily kill them. Quietly they crept through the palace to the throne room, where the serpent slept with the boy amid his coils. I doubt that they could have done anything to free the boy, who was asleep the whole time. But they were able to lift the sword and carry it away.

It had taken them a few days to find and spirit away the Kusanagi Sword, but they hauled it to the surface of the ocean in time for Emperor Go to use it in battle. With the sword, he was able slay many of his enemies and defeat them in a crucial battle. He then put it in a secure place in a temple so that he and his successors might be able to find it to defend themselves and Japan.

There are important similarities between this Japanese myth and *The Silver Chair*. The trees that grow gems are like the gems Golg says grow in Bism, beneath the world of Narnia's Underworld. The trek of the pearl divers is paralleled by that of Puddleglum, Jill, and Eustace. The ocean that the girls swim through to reach the cave has its representation in the great underground sea that Puddleglum, Jill, and Eustace cross. The grandmother who is actually a serpent or dragon who has taken the form of a woman is like the Queen of Underworld, who can take the form of a serpent or of a woman. That the emperor is a serpent is particularly interesting, because in most Japanese tales of Underworld, the emperor is a dragon. He does not seem to be as evil as is the Queen of Underworld, a green serpent too, in *The Silver Chair,* but he is just as menacing. On the other hand, he seems dragonish (as Lewis said of Eustace's thoughts in *The Voyage of the "Dawn Treader"*) in his possessiveness and love of his treasure.

The boy in the serpent's coils has his analog in Prince Rilian, who is metaphorically in the coils of the wicked queen. I do not know what would have happened had the girls tried to free the boy, but I suspect the serpent emperor would have been as angry and dangerous as the serpent queen.

Had Lewis read this tale? I do not know, although the parallels are enough to make me think that he may have. On the other hand, his was a fertile imagination, and the details about gems growing like fruit, a royal young man a prisoner, and an evil serpent as ruler may have come solely from his mind. Certainly the serpent queen may have her origins in the Bible. After all, her invasion of the garden with the fountain in it and her seduction of Prince Rilian there have antecedents in Genesis and the Fall.

CHAPTER-BY-CHAPTER DEVELOPMENT OF THEMES AND CHARACTERS IN *THE SILVER CHAIR*

— Chapter 1: Behind the Gym —

Jill Pole hides behind the gym of Experiment House, a school that supposedly reflects advanced learning techniques, but actually only fosters bullying and violence. It is a place where good books are not read, and the children are even discouraged from reading them. When Eustace wants to swear to Jill that he is telling truth, he stumbles by "I swear" to "by everything." Lewis notes that in an earlier time, Eustace would have sworn by the Bible, but Bibles were not encouraged at Experiment House.

Experiment House is a despicable place where those who run it do not exercise their authority to stop the evils perpetrated by bullies and thugs, using the excuse that Experiment House is a supposedly advanced school where the shackles of morality are not imposed on children. The students are actually lazy and mean spirited, and judging by the principal, they are without any sense of morality. This makes Experiment House a kind of hell, where evil rules, and any mention of God is forbidden.

Eustace and Jill call to Aslan, are chased up a slope, open a door in a wall, and step into another world filled with grass, bright light, blue skies and flying jewels. One of the signs of Aslan's Country is its brightness; when the *Dawn Treader* neared it, light increased in brightness. In *The Last Battle*, bright, vivid colors are typical of Aslan's Country.

Aslan soon makes His appearance. Having nearly killed Eustace by her showing off, Jill is surprised by a very large animal that comes to the cliff edge and blows. The dark speck that flies away in the distance is probably Eustace. Thirsty, Jill wanders into a nearby wood looking for water and she is surprised by the figure of a lion.

– Chapter 2: Jill Is Given a Task –

A very thirsty Jill finds a stream, but there is a huge lion beside it. "There is no other stream," Aslan tells her, meaning that there is only one source of spiritual fulfillment. To drink from the stream to quench her craving, Jill must pass the fearsome Lion. Eventually, she gives in and her spiritual awakening begins. Being thirsty is a common metaphor for yearning to know God; it is common to all people, even to those who do not know why they thirst. In *The Last Battle,* Emeth has sought the Calormene false god Tash in order to satisfy his thirst, but his thirst is eventually quenched by Aslan, Who he unknowingly actually sought. Aslan tells Jill that she would not have called to Him unless He had been calling to her.

This chapter introduces the undercurrent of comedy that follows Jill's adventures. Lewis views Christ as being happy and emotional. Aslan also has a sense of humor. You may remember that in *The Lion, the Witch and the Wardrobe,* Aslan was cheerful and playful after His resurrection. But Aslan can also be tough and demanding. He commands Jill to seek this lost prince and not to abandon her search until she has found him, died in the attempt, or returned to earth. This is not a contradiction. In following Aslan's commands, characters in *The Chronicles of Narnia* find wonders, amazement, and joy.

Aslan gives Jill four signs to follow: First, Eustace will meet a friend as soon as he enters Narnia and he must greet that friend at once. If he does, this friend will help them. It is interesting that Aslan tells Jill what will happen if Eustace greets his old friend; Aslan is usually not forthcoming with such details. Jill's adventure will soon go awry because she fails to tell Eustace about the first sign until it is too late for Eustace to greet Caspian X. It is typical in *The Chronicles of Narnia* for characters to fail to follow one or more of Aslan's signs. For example, in *Prince Caspian,* Lucy fails to follow Aslan when she sees Him on a mountain path at the river gorge. It may be frustrating to never know what would have happened if one had done as Aslan wished, but there is comfort in *The Chronicles of Narnia*

that people get second chances. It is possible to fail to do as Aslan wishes in one instance, yet still fulfill Aslan's commands. Failure to take heed of the first sign costs Eustace and Jill the help of Caspian and makes their journey very difficult and uncomfortable, but as long as they stick to their quest, they can still succeed.

Aslan's second command is for Jill to undertake a journey to the ruined city of ancient giants. Had they heeded Aslan's first command to greet Caspian, they could have marched north with his army, but now they must go alone. This sets up their acquaintance with the wonderful Puddleglum, who is worth an army of soldiers when he defies the Queen's magic and hangs on to his faith in Aslan.

Aslan tells them that the third sign will be writing on a stone in the ruined city, and that they must follow the instructions on the stone. However, it is not easy for them to see this third sign because they are standing on it. Aslan also tells them that the lost prince will be the first person who asks them to do something in Aslan's name. This last sign is crucial; those who take oaths in Aslan's name tend to love Him. In Underworld, dominated by a witch, someone asking for anything in Aslan's name would stand out. Characters in *The Lion, the Witch and the Wardrobe* sometimes have trouble following Aslan's signs, mostly because of faint hearts or of forgetfulness. Jill will have her troubles.

— Chapter 3: The Sailing of the King —

Eustace is shocked by the age of Caspian, who had been young in *The Voyage of the "Dawn Treader"*; he sees a "doddering old man" and finds the sight "frightful." He is not used to the time being different in Narnia than in England. He misses Aslan's first sign: "If you'd only listened to me when I tried to tell you, we'd be all right," Jill insists. Eustace shoots back, "Yes, and if you hadn't played the fool on the edge of that cliff and jolly nearly murdered me—all right, I said *murder*, and I'll say it again as often as I like, so keep your hair on—we'd have come together and both known what to do." The quest is hardly begun when Aslan's first sign is blown, and the two questers are bickering, already. Given his behavior at the beginning of *The Voyage of the "Dawn Treader,"* bickering is an improvement for Eustace, who had been far too antisocial for even a good bicker, but it does not bode well for a quest in which they could die. Caspian has sailed to the eastern islands, where Aslan has reportedly been seen, and there is no chance of catching him.

— Chapter 4: A Parliament of Owls —

"A Parliament of Owls" is Lewis' play on a medieval literary work titled "A Parliament of Fowls" by Geoffrey Chaucer. In it, a council of birds try to figure out the rights and wrongs of a dispute over love. It is played for comedy, but its undercurrent is an inquiry into the nature of love.

At the gathering of owls in *The Silver Chair,* Glimfeather explains that thirty champions, have at one time or another set out to look for the lost Prince, and none of them has ever returned. Thus King Caspian ordered that no more Narnians go in quest of his son, for fear of their perishing. Trumpkin, in charge while Caspian is gone (as he was in *The Voyage of the*

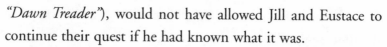

"Dawn Treader"), would not have allowed Jill and Eustace to continue their quest if he had known what it was.

The Parliament of Owls is a noisy gathering, with "Tu-whoo! Tu-whoo" a common noise. It is one of the owls who lays out the story of the death of the Queen and the loss of her son. He notes that the serpent was "great, shining, and as green as poison," an important image that should stick with us as we read *The Silver Chair*. This serpent killed the Queen. Prince Rilian searched fruitlessly for the serpent so that he might kill it. Apparently no one thinks of it as anything more than a snake. Lord Drinian calls it a "witless brute." Even so, Rilian continually returns to the fountain where his mother was killed.

Eventually he discovers something special and allows Lord Drinian to ride with him to see it. It is an apparition of a woman, "And she was tall and great, shining, and wrapped in a thin garment as green as poison." The thin garment sounds like the serpent's skin; her tallness recalls the White Witch.

— Chapter 5: Puddleglum —

Eustace does not seem to be tiring, even after a night among the owls and a flight on an owl's back (talking owls are bigger than ordinary owls). Similar to what Peter, Susan, Edmund, and Lucy experienced before him, he is rejuvenated by the Narnian air. He and Jill find the Marsh-wiggles living somewhat like monks, each to a small square of land with a hut on it. Fishing seems to be their specialty. Although the March-wiggles live in a marsh, it is fresh and clean. Puddleglum seems a typical Marsh-wiggle, although perhaps a bit too cheerful.

Puddleglum has somewhat sunken cheeks on a long, narrow face, and he wears a high, pointed hat with a wide flat brim. Each strand of his hair is flat rather than round. He has very long legs that make him taller than most people. His arms are also very long and he has webbed fingers and toes suitable for marshland habitation. From his solemn expression "you could see at once that he took a serious view of life." This odd character, one of the best-drawn companions in *The Chronicles of Narnia,* will supply more merriment than his solemn face and serious speaking would imply. Although an unimposing figure, he will turn out to have much courage.

— Chapter 6: The Wild Waste Lands of the North —

Before now, Lewis has not provided much of a view of the land north of Narnia, although he has mentioned that giants live there. It is quite a sight when Jill, Eustace, and Puddleglum arrive at its southern edge. Looking down a long slope ending in cliffs, they see beyond high mountains, dark precipices, stony valleys, deep ravines, and rivers flowing out of gorges to plunge sullenly into black depths. The trio of travelers must traverse a daunting land where danger could be anywhere. The precipices and ravines make it seem as if the land itself were determined to prevent their surviving long enough to reach the ruined city of ancient giants.

Jill and Eustace are pretty good at handling the travails of crossing Ettinsmoor and avoiding the notice of the stupid giants who live there. But they and Puddleglum eventually meet

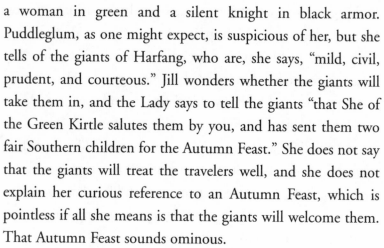

a woman in green and a silent knight in black armor. Puddleglum, as one might expect, is suspicious of her, but she tells of the giants of Harfang, who are, she says, "mild, civil, prudent, and courteous." Jill wonders whether the giants will take them in, and the Lady says to tell the giants "that She of the Green Kirtle salutes them by you, and has sent them two fair Southern children for the Autumn Feast." She does not say that the giants will treat the travelers well, and she does not explain her curious reference to an Autumn Feast, which is pointless if all she means is that the giants will welcome them. That Autumn Feast sounds ominous.

Why don't the children and Puddleglum notice that she is in green and is an imposing figure, like the woman Lord Drinian saw? Perhaps they were too tired to think well, or perhaps they are enchanted. We shall learn later that enchantment is something the Lady does well. In any case, the children's behavior becomes very bad: "And though you might have expected that the idea of having a good time at Harfang would have made them more cheerful, it really made them more sorry for themselves and more grumpy and snappy with each other and with Puddleglum." There is something to be said in favor of Puddleglum's grim demeanor; he does not allow the prospect of beds and baths to make him cranky, and he manages to put up with Jill and Eustace's bickering. Distracted by her somewhat selfish hope for comfort in Harfang, and bitter about her having to suffer through a difficult trek (her own fault for missing the first of Aslan's signs), it is about here that Jill begins to forget the remaining signs that Aslan had given her.

— Chapter 7: The Hill of the Strange Trenches —

Something of an understatement is "There is no denying it was a beast of a day." Jill, Eustace, and Puddleglum, a very patient fellow, find themselves on a plateau littered with huge stones. They do not realize that they have entered the City Ruinous. When they scale a series of four-foot high ledges, it seems plain that they are climbing giant stairs, because Lewis points out, that the stones around them are "squarish," but they do not notice. Had they been mindful of Aslan's signs, they might have been mentally prepared to recognize that the great square stones were building blocks for a giant city. So preoccupied are they by their bickering and their yearning for good food and warm beds that Aslan slips out of their minds.

Everybody is wet and cold, and they are in an autumn snow storm, so they have the excuse of being at less than their best and probably are not alert enough to notice anything odd about the passageways or trenches that cross the floor. Later, Eustace will berate himself for having missed their significance while he was in one. Had he been mindful of Aslan's signs, he might have realized that he was standing in a letter of the message Aslan had wanted them to follow, but he may be too hard on himself; understanding the meaning of the trenches would be very difficult in a snow storm.

— Chapter 8: The House of Harfang —

Harfang seems to be all that She of the Green Kirtle claimed it was. There are baths, beds, and more children's toys than Jill

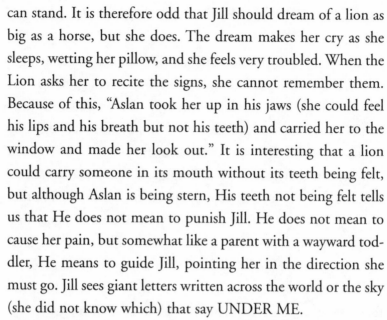

can stand. It is therefore odd that Jill should dream of a lion as big as a horse, but she does. The dream makes her cry as she sleeps, wetting her pillow, and she feels very troubled. When the Lion asks her to recite the signs, she cannot remember them. Because of this, "Aslan took her up in his jaws (she could feel his lips and his breath but not his teeth) and carried her to the window and made her look out." It is interesting that a lion could carry someone in its mouth without its teeth being felt, but although Aslan is being stern, His teeth not being felt tells us that He does not mean to punish Jill. He does not mean to cause her pain, but somewhat like a parent with a wayward toddler, He means to guide Jill, pointing her in the direction she must go. Jill sees giant letters written across the world or the sky (she did not know which) that say UNDER ME.

This seems to be more than a run-of-the-mill dream; it carries a message. The dream's message is fulfilled in the morning when Jill, Eustace, and Puddleglum look out her bedroom window and see, below them, spread out like a map, the ruins of a gigantic city. (This is followed by an excellent description of the city and how Jill had reacted to it when she had crossed through it in the snow storm.) What Jill sees carved into the pavement of the ruined city are the words UNDER ME. In this passage Lewis brilliantly conjures up great antiquity and much mystery. Phrases such as "their fragments lay at their bases like felled trees of monstrous stone" are striking in their ability to create both an image and a feeling about the image.

Their discovery creates problems, although they will not know how big their problems really are until the next chapter. "Aslan's instructions always work: there are no exceptions,"

Puddleglum declares, which means that however odd UNDER ME seems, they must figure out a way to go back to the ruined city and find a way under it.

— Chapter 9: How they Discovered Something Worth Knowing —

This chapter is an example of Lewis' skill at writing comedy while at the same time getting some serious business done. The comedy enlivens the narrative by adding variety to the tone and subject matter. Jill shows one of a child's survival skills by putting on a charming show that endears her to the adult. She has curls that fall to her shoulders and that fall just right when she cocks her head. She is wonderful with the giants, playing the role of cute, sweet, empty-headed little girl, asking seemingly innocent questions and learning about Harfang. Lewis deepens Jill's characterization by having her pretend to be empty headed, seemingly a shallow girl who gets what she wants by behaving brainlessly. She is deepened because she shows how she can hold two very different thoughts at once: She must think of being cute and adorable while simultaneously thinking about everything she hears and sees, very seriously trying to find her way out of a what seems like a trap. Eventually, her efforts will make the difference between life and death for her and her companions. American author F. Scott Fitzgerald once said that a sign of genius is the ability to hold two contradictory thoughts in one's mind at the same time. This qualifies Jill as a genius, and by extension, Lewis, as well.

For his part, Puddleglum discovers a distressing fact at lunch:

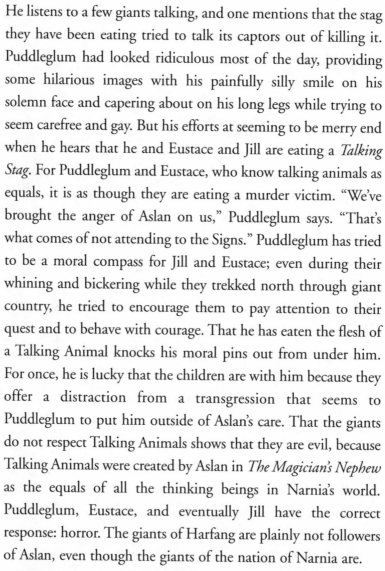

He listens to a few giants talking, and one mentions that the stag they have been eating tried to talk its captors out of killing it. Puddleglum had looked ridiculous most of the day, providing some hilarious images with his painfully silly smile on his solemn face and capering about on his long legs while trying to seem carefree and gay. But his efforts at seeming to be merry end when he hears that he and Eustace and Jill are eating a *Talking Stag*. For Puddleglum and Eustace, who know talking animals as equals, it is as though they are eating a murder victim. "We've brought the anger of Aslan on us," Puddleglum says. "That's what comes of not attending to the Signs." Puddleglum has tried to be a moral compass for Jill and Eustace; even during their whining and bickering while they trekked north through giant country, he tried to encourage them to pay attention to their quest and to behave with courage. That he has eaten the flesh of a Talking Animal knocks his moral pins out from under him. For once, he is lucky that the children are with him because they offer a distraction from a transgression that seems to Puddleglum to put him outside of Aslan's care. That the giants do not respect Talking Animals shows that they are evil, because Talking Animals were created by Aslan in *The Magician's Nephew* as the equals of all the thinking beings in Narnia's world. Puddleglum, Eustace, and eventually Jill have the correct response: horror. The giants of Harfang are plainly not followers of Aslan, even though the giants of the nation of Narnia are.

Matters worsen when Jill discovers a cookbook open to recipes for cooking humans for the Autumn Feast. That people who would eat Talking Stags would also eat humans seems logical, but it is still unnerving to find a recipe in which one is the meal. This gives the true meaning of the woman in green's words to the travelers in Chapter 6, for the travelers to say that they have been sent to Harfang for the Autumn Feast. Puddleglum had been right to be suspicious of her.

Jill and the others find a scullery door that opens to the outside of Harfang. Apparently, the giants of Harfang have little to fear, and their fortresslike city has dozens of windows opening to outside world, as well as doors. The three travelers manage to sneak out of Harfang, but are soon spotted. Hunting dogs are sent after them: Jill feels like a hunted animal, perhaps the way the Talking Stag felt. "UNDER ME" was the sign Aslan meant them to look for, and with dogs at their heels they climb into a hole by the stairway of the ruined city. From the world of the sun, with its dangers, the travelers crawl into a world without sunlight.

— Chapter 10: Travels Without the Sun —

To emphasize how desperate the situation is for the travelers, Lewis has them slide down a very steep, very long slope. When they reach its bottom, they are about a mile beneath the surface, and the slope is too steep and slippery to climb. Thus, Jill, Eustace, and Puddleglum have no choice but to face the dangers of the darkness (Puddleglum has lost his tools for making fire). This is a good way to create tension in a narrative: place characters in an unpredictable situation that they cannot avoid. After they have rested for a long time, they hear a soft, mournful voice. One might expect that hearing the voice would make the travelers happy, but the voice identifies itself as the Warden of the Marches of Underland and says that he is accompanied by a hundred armed Earthmen. In *The Silver Chair,* "Earthmen" does not mean people from planet earth. Instead, they are people who live underground in Narnia's world. Lewis also uses "Earthmen" to describe Dwarfs, because Dwarfs love to dig into the ground. He serves the Queen of the Deep Realm (also called the Queen of Underland and, most often, the Queen of Underworld), and he declares that the Queen's will is not to be questioned but obeyed. (This may be an allusion to *She* by H. Rider Haggard, in which a queen is referred to as "She who must be obeyed.") It may be good for the travelers that the queen had not ordered that strangers be put to death the moment they are found, but it will seem to be in her character in *The Silver Chair,* where she is shown to be a manipulator, someone who prefers to control her victims rather than just kill them.

When finally some light is provided, the travelers see a wide variety of shapes and sizes of people, and "every face in the whole hundred was as sad as a face could be." Their sad looks seem different from Puddleglum's solemn face; theirs is an unhappiness that seems to occupy every inch of their bodies. Good Puddleglum tries to keep Jill's spirits up by observing that at least it doesn't rain underground, but the sadness of the Earthmen suggests that something worse than rain may be found in Underworld. Even so the words of Puddleglum deepen his character, as do his actions throughout this chapter, because he turns out to be affectionate, as well as intrepid. Eustace, too, deepens. For instance, when Jill in claustrophobic terror refuses to slip into a narrow crack between caverns, he thoughtfully suggests that she take hold of Puddleglum and him, giving her comforting people to hold on to. Still, he is still the sharp-tongued youngster of *The Voyage of the "Dawn Treader,"* noting that Jill should now know how he felt at the edge of the cliff in Aslan's Country. The complex point Lewis makes here is that fear is universal, that people vary in their fears but everyone has them. Like Jill, Puddleglum is afraid of the dark, but he yields to necessity and perseveres. In Jill's case, she needs help, not criticism, and when she gets help, she overcomes her fear, at least for the period it takes her to crawl through a very tight, utterly dark crack in stone. Friends should help someone overcome fear, not make fun of it or pretend, as Jill had at the cliff, that it makes someone inferior. Jill seems to learn most of this lesson in this chapter, because near the novel's end, she and her companions face another narrow space in the ground, and only she is small enough to crawl through it. She swallows her fear and does what she must.

Puddleglum points out that they are at least back on the right track. Aslan's sign told them to go under the Ruined City, and that's where they are. They are following His instructions again. There is much to distract them from the signs, because Underworld is full of strange sights. For instance, there are spongy plants that are not trees but grow like them; there is a cavern full of sleeping animals who, the Warden says, may sleep until the end of the world before awaking; and they see a giant old man, asleep, who is Father Time. The Warden tells them that Father Time has "sunk down into the Deep Realm and lies dreaming of all the things that are done in the Upper World." He may awaken at the end of the world. Father Time will figure importantly in *The Last Battle.*

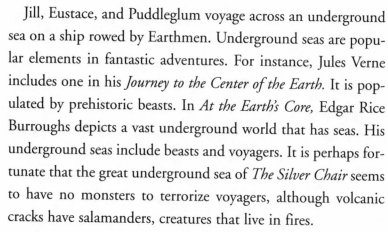

Jill, Eustace, and Puddleglum voyage across an underground sea on a ship rowed by Earthmen. Underground seas are popular elements in fantastic adventures. For instance, Jules Verne includes one in his *Journey to the Center of the Earth.* It is populated by prehistoric beasts. In *At the Earth's Core,* Edgar Rice Burroughs depicts a vast underground world that has seas. His underground seas include beasts and voyagers. It is perhaps fortunate that the great underground sea of *The Silver Chair* seems to have no monsters to terrorize voyagers, although volcanic cracks have salamanders, creatures that live in fires.

After a long time, heading south on the sea, they reach a dock. There, they see dark figures of Earthmen bustling about in a great city of homes, businesses, and temples, yet there are few lights and almost no sound other than footfalls and low-voiced mutterings. The Earthmen do not need as much light as the travelers do; their silence may mean dedication to their tasks, or it may reflect a deep inner sadness that discourages speaking to each other. In any case, they are all business, no fun.

The travelers are escorted to a large building, where they are handed over to an Earthman named Mullugutherum, who quickly decides to put them in prison to await the queen, who is away. They are saved from this by someone upstairs, who orders that they be brought to him: "A young man with fair hair rose to greet them. He was handsome and looked both bold and kind, though there was something about his face that didn't seem quite right." He turns out to be the Black Knight who had been riding with She of the Green Kirtle, which is bad news. But the young man insists that She is good; he also remarks that the Queen is of divine race, and knows neither age nor death. Could this be an incarnation of the White Witch, who had eaten fruit from the tree of life in *The Magician's Nephew*? Perhaps it is true that the White Witch is not dead but transformed.

By now, readers may have guessed who the young man is, but Jill is unsure, because his face has an odd twist to it, and the young man laughs too readily and spouts nonsense. The only moment in which he is human in his behavior is when Eustace points out that the queen's planned invasion of a country in Overworld would be bad for those invaded; briefly, the young man seems troubled by the thought. Yet, it is as if he were drugged or, as can happen in Narnia's world, he were enchanted. There is a clue that the travelers and readers can latch onto if they pay close attention. The young man sees to the comfort of his guests and feeds them. In this behavior, he is not a villain, but seems to be kind at heart.

— Chapter 11: In the Dark Castle —

The young man explains that he has a curious affliction: Every night he loses his mind. Further, he cannot remember anything about his life before he entered this Dark World. By now we should have strong impression that the young man is actually Prince Rilian. "I wonder what game that witch is really playing with this young fool," Puddleglum thinks. The game is deep, for the Queen plans to use him to seize Narnia's throne.

The children and Puddleglum hide in the young man's quarters while Earthmen tie him down; when the travelers return, the Earthmen having left, "The knight [young man] was seated in a curious silver chair, to which he was bound by his ankles,

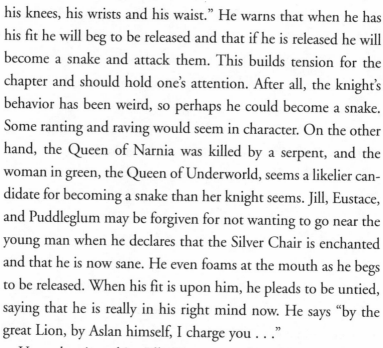

his knees, his wrists and his waist." He warns that when he has his fit he will beg to be released and that if he is released he will become a snake and attack them. This builds tension for the chapter and should hold one's attention. After all, the knight's behavior has been weird, so perhaps he could become a snake. Some ranting and raving would seem in character. On the other hand, the Queen of Narnia was killed by a serpent, and the woman in green, the Queen of Underworld, seems a likelier candidate for becoming a snake than her knight seems. Jill, Eustace, and Puddleglum may be forgiven for not wanting to go near the young man when he declares that the Silver Chair is enchanted and that he is now sane. He even foams at the mouth as he begs to be released. When his fit is upon him, he pleads to be untied, saying that he is really in his right mind now. He says "by the great Lion, by Aslan himself, I charge you . . ."

Upon hearing this, Jill, Eustace, and Puddleglum have a dilemma, and so do we readers. Aslan's last sign was someone asking for something in His name, and the raving young man tied to the silver chair has done just that, but who would go over to a raving maniac and untie him? They are afraid that he will turn into a snake and kill them. It is easy to say to oneself that if one heard the sign of Aslan, that one would do what Aslan commanded, which in this case is to do what the person swearing in Aslan's name says to do, but life does not work that way. Jill, Eustace, and Puddleglum reasonably wonder whether the swearing by Aslan is just a coincidence, that the real sign is to come later: that a completely crazed young man should say it could be only part of his ravings.

This is a moral and intellectual dilemma that I believe Lewis means for you and me to ponder. That is why the scene is long and the dithering of the travelers builds suspense. All of their reasons for not responding to the sign are good ones, and they are persuasive. When on the spot, with only minutes to decide, with life and death in the balance, exactly what should be done? What would a smart person do? Lewis strings along the scene until one answer survives all the doubts: Do what Aslan says to do, even if you die because of it. That is a tough idea, but from Aslan's view, "death" is a concept hardly worth considering; those who serve Him live forever.

After being freed, the knight still seems to be crazed, because he grabs his sword (a scary moment because he could chop up Jill, Eustace, and Puddleglum), and he hacks apart the silver chair. He then declares, "I am Rilian, prince of Narnia." It is what the travelers may have hoped for, but it does not mean that they are safe. There are the guards to contend with, and Rilian still may not be himself.

— Chapter 12: The Queen of Underland —

This is a momentous chapter not only in *The Silver Chair* but for *The Chronicles of Narnia* as a whole. The Queen, a witch, tries to overcome the travelers and Rilian with a spell. She tries to persuade them that the Overworld had never existed, that they had only dreamed of it, much like earthly atheists would insist that there is no God and no heaven, that they are no more than imaginary. She tries to make them have strictly materialistic views of life, where what cannot be seen cannot exist. She speaks like a condescending adult instructing children, annoyingly twisting their words and mocking them for having silly imaginations.

Puddleglum stubbornly keeps faith with Aslan, even while being nearly overcome; he stamps his foot in the witch's fire: "There is nothing like a good shock of pain for dissolving certain kinds of magic." The Queen is very angry at this, but Puddleglum continues to argue, saying that even if they had only imagined the world above, it was more important than the world they inhabited now.

This is one of the most important passages in all of *The Chronicles of Narnia*. The Queen's argument is for atheism; it is a denial of all the good things in life, from stars to trees. It is an utterly dreary view that makes life hardly worthwhile. Remember how all the Earthmen look sad and go about their business quietly and unhappily? This is because they are forced to live in the Queen's miserable excuse for a world. The Queen tries to put Puddleglum and the others into a position that some of the ungrateful Dwarfs will be in when inside the stable in *The Last Battle*; a beautiful feast is placed before them and they see nothing but darkness and misery. Puddleglum's point is that the dark world of the Queen is worthless without the wonders of Aslan's world, dream or not.

Another aspect of Puddleglum's reasoning is its support for the use of the imagination. When Lewis was a little boy, he and his brother made up magical countries in which they and their toys had wonderful adventures. To Lewis, this free exercise of one's imagination was part of intellectual and spiritual growth. Fantasies such as *The Chronicles of Narnia* invite people to exercise their imaginations and thereby to learn new ways of thinking, and perhaps most important, to look at life from new angles. By looking at life in new ways, people will touch on truths that cannot be explained in strictly material ways. This is one of the foundations of mythologies, and it is essential to *The Chronicles of Narnia*, which is, after being entertaining, a way of seeing supernatural truths from new angles. It is a way to see Aslan (Christ). When Puddleglum declares that the sun and the stars may not exist, as the queen claims, then he still prefers them as figments of his imaginations over her miserable world, Puddleglum is touching on one of the reasons mythologies have survived: They offer something more than a strictly materialistic existence; in fact, they give meaning to life. In the case of the queen by sarcastically and condescendingly denying the existence of the sun and stars, she is denying what people have actually experienced. To deny the existence of the sun and stars would be to deny part of themselves for Jill, Eustace, Puddleglum, and Rilian; like the sun and stars, Puddleglum implies, Aslan (Christ) is a part of their experience, and like the sun and stars, He brightens life, brings warmth in the cold, brings sight in the dark.

Puddleglum adds that "I'm on Aslan's side even if there isn't any Aslan to lead it." In Lewis' view, the responsibility to do good does not end with a lack of religious belief; it remains a responsibility. Further, Puddleglum expresses an idea that will reach its fullest expression in Emeth in *The Last Battle*; that is, that people have within them a yearning for good that is independent of religious belief. Those that follow this yearning, as Puddleglum insists on doing, automatically search for Aslan (Christ) even if they do not believe in Aslan. The witch wants them to lead dark lives, but Puddleglum resolutely stands his ground, saying, "But four babies playing a game can make a play-world which licks your real world hollow. That's why I'm going to stand by the play world." Here, Puddleglum makes a profound statement of faith, and with this statement, Lewis suggests the bleakness of lives without faith: Their world is too dark, and it misses too much of the real world.

— Chapter 13: Underland Without the Queen —

With the death of the Queen of Underworld, her magic seems to have ended with her life, and her magical works begin falling apart. Although he refuses to wear his black armor again, Rilian fetches his shield in case he and his companions need to fight their way past the Earthmen. His shield has undergone a miraculous transformation; it was entirely black and without markings. Now, it is silver with a rampant red Lion, Aslan. "This," says Rilian, "signifies that Aslan will be our good lord." This is a reference to High King Peter's shield given to him by Father Christmas in *The Lion, the Witch and the Wardrobe,* and like that shield, it refers to Ephesians 6:16 and "the shield of Faith, with which you shall be able to quench all the fiery darts of the wicked." Rilian's shield is symbolic of his faith, and it is a reminder that is was the faith of Puddleglum and the others that prevented the Queen of Underworld's enchantment from working on them. Their faith was indeed a shield against her wickedness.

Although the Earthmen do not know that the Queen is dead, they and the Underworld seem thrown into chaos. Rilian takes charge (probably because he is a prince) of the travelers, and they try to find their way out without attracting attention to themselves. It turns out that they may have reason to fear the Earthmen, but not the reason they think. Far from being angry, the Earthmen are delighted when Rilian says the Queen is dead. The Earthmen are dangerous only if they think Rilian is the Queen's friend. Their sad faces are explained in the next chapter.

— Chapter 14: The Bottom of the World —

It turns out that the Earthmen dislike Overworld because it is too high for them. The possibility of emerging from the ground into sunlight to fight a war is a miserable prospect. The thought of not having a roof over their heads terrifies them. As much as Jill, Eustace, Puddleglum, and Rilian preferred the open air, the Earthmen preferred the confines of the underground. In fact, Golg sounds agoraphobic (afraid of open spaces), which may make one wonder whether he and the other Earthmen would have been up to battling an enemy above ground.

The Really Deep Land, Bism, sounds like an amazing place. Imagine being able to drink gems! Rilian shows the adventuresome, valiant side of his nature by seriously wondering whether being able to visit Bism is a chance that is too good to miss. He is probably right to choose not to go, because the chasm between Underworld and the Really Deep Land eventually closes. Aslan might have provided a way out to the Overworld, but then again, He might not have.

The trek upward is a harrowing one and Puddleglum wonders whether they have waited too long to climb up the path toward the Overworld. Certainly, having lights vanish as he and the others climb must be somewhat unnerving.

– Chapter 15: The Disappearance of Jill –

When Jill eventually works her way to a hole in the ground, she shows that she has become much more responsible than she was at the beginning of *The Silver Chair*. At the start, she carelessly played with Eustace's life at the edge of a cliff, just to show off and to put Eustace down, but now she readily climbs into a narrow dark place, even though she is frightened by such places, as she was when she had to crawl through a crack in stone in at the beginning of her adventures in Underworld. She is rewarded by seeing the Great Snow Dance of Dwarfs, fauns, and dryads—quite a sight as they dance in rhythm, with snowballs flying between dancers but never *at* dancers. The dance is a dazzling sight, not only a celebration of the season but of life.

The travelers not only have emerged into the upper world, but have come out in the heart of Narnia. The fullness of the witch's scheme is revealed, here. The land she intended to conquer and rule was none other than Narnia! Rilian, the son of Caspian X, would have had a strong claim to the throne, and she could have ruled Narnia through him as his queen and with him under her enchantment. Perhaps she would have begun another winter without Christmas; perhaps she overestimated her abilities, because the Earthmen feared the outside with no roof and might have been unable to help her hold onto power.

Jill's shouts for help are eventually heard by the dancers, and then follows one of the happiest scenes in *The Chronicles of*

Narnia. Upon discovering Jill, the Narnians dissolve into chaos as they all try to help rescue her. The Bears and Owls try to supervise; fauns and others bring hot drinks; and the Moles and Dwarfs, who love to dig, dig merrily away at the hole where Jill is trapped. This is a sharp shift in perspective; the travelers have spent most of *The Silver Chair* in hostile lands, with danger everywhere. When Jill overcomes her fears and climbs up into Narnia, there is much relief as the danger melts away. This is the Narnia of Caspian the Navigator, not the Narnia of the usurper Miraz, and the people think in terms of cooperation rather than war. The life of Caspian is a tragedy, with his wife murdered and his son lost for over ten years, but for Narnia, he has been glorious—hence dancing celebrations and eagerness to help, free them from fear. This is a strong contrast to the fear that ruled Underworld.

— Chapter 16: The Healing of Harms —

When Jill and Eustace return to Aslan's country, they look in a stream to find King Caspian, dead, with the "water flowing over him like liquid glass." It is a surprising sight, for Caspian had just been an old man who had died moments after seeing his son. This is a marvelous image, and a sad one: even Aslan weeps. Eustace, Jill notes, weeps like an adult, not a child. She has noticed "that people don't seem to have any particular ages on that mountain." This foreshadows the depiction of Peter, Edmund, Lucy, Digory, Polly, Eustace, and Jill in Aslan's Country in *The Last Battle,* because the mountain in *The Silver Chair* is in Aslan's Country. In *The Silver Chair,* it shows Aslan's life-giving power at work, and it is a cause for joy.

Aslan tells Eustace that Caspian X has died but not to despair. He says that most people have died, even Aslan Himself, but that in Aslan's Country death is only the ending to the prelude to the first chapter of life. Caspian has been rejuvenated and is among friends, after a hard life in which he had to curb his personal desires and submit to the duties Aslan had entrusted to him. Remember how angry he was that he could not go with Reepicheep to Aslan's Country in *The Voyage of the "Dawn Treader"*? He is there, now, and he discovers something special about Aslan's Country: When Caspian asks Aslan whether it is wrong for him to want "one glimpse of *their* world," Aslan tells him, "You cannot want wrong things any more now, that you have died, my son." This is one of the rewards of Aslan's Country: a true heart that does not mislead. This idea recurs in *The Last Battle,* where Aslan's Country is a place where whatever a person wants, it is right. Further, it turns out that one can visit any world from Aslan's Country, which means that Caspian can glimpse earth.

There is a satisfying completeness to the conclusion of *The Silver Chair.* The cruel children of Experiment House are whacked soundly with the flat end of swords; the evil director of Experiment House is replaced by someone with common sense; Rilian buries his father, Caspian the Navigator, and then rules well. Narnia "was happy in his days, though Puddleglum (whose foot was as good as new in three weeks) often pointed out that bright mornings brought on wet afternoons, and that you couldn't expect good times to last." It is comforting to realize during the awful events of *The Last Battle* that the good times in fact lasted for many generations before the time of King Tirian, as Lewis takes pains to point out in the concluding novel of *The Chronicles of Narnia*. As for Underworld, it is under a vast sea, but Narnians enjoy going in through the hole that had been dug to let Jill and her companions free and sail to and fro in ships, telling each other stories of the cities that lie fathoms deep below.

VOCABULARY FOR *THE SILVER CHAIR*

CHAPTER 1: BEHIND THE GYM
Lor: Lord
hols: holidays
blithering: talking nonsense

CHAPTER 2: JILL IS GIVEN A TASK
aeroplane: airplane

CHAPTER 4: A PARLIAMENT OF OWLS
crumpets: a soft bread that is baked on a griddle
maying, not hunting: gathering flowers
stung: bit
worm: serpent or dragon

CHAPTER 5: PUDDLEGLUM
bobance: perhaps bouncy spirits
sparring: arguing

CHAPTER 6: THE WILD WASTE LANDS OF THE NORTH
cock-shies: throwing at a target
lammed: walloped; hit with great force

cairn: a pile of stones

Stonehenge: a ruin of immense stones on England's Salisbury Plain; erected before recorded history, Stonehenge probably had a religious significance

balustrade: a rail supported by posts along the side of a staircase

device: an image used as an heraldic symbol; for instance, the red lion on High King Peter's shield would be called a *device*

banneret: a small banner that a knight would use to identify himself to others

thither: towards there

burgh: town

tarry: linger

kirtle: a long woman's dress

CHAPTER 7: THE HILL OF THE STRANGE TRENCHES

funked it: yielded to fright

portcullis: an armored grille that drops down to block the gateway to a fortress

pluck: courage

cheek: impudence

puttees: strips of fabric wound around the lower leg

goggled: stared wide eyed

salt-celler: salt shaker

pattering: light, barely audible steps

CHAPTER 8: THE HOUSE OF HARFANG

possets: hot sweetened milk mixed with wine

comfits: candies

caraways: probably sweets made with caraway seeds

poppet: darling

cock-a-leekie soup: chicken and leek soup

gasometer: a device for measuring gasses such as natural gas

frolicsome: frisky, playful

caper: a playful leap

beagling: hunting with dogs

gamesome: merry and playful

CHAPTER 9: HOW THEY DISCOVERED SOMETHING WORTH KNOWING

prattled: talked aimlessly

She made love to everyone: praised everyone endearingly

scullery: a room beside the kitchen where dishes are washed and similar tasked performed

fidget: nervous, random movement of one's body

hooters: honkers of automobile horns

pottered: puttered

blamey: damned

Mallard: wild duck

shingle: coarse gravel

CHAPTER 10: TRAVELS WITHOUT THE SUN

drowsy: sleepy

bulwarks: the parts of the ship's sides that rise higher than the upper deck

footmen: men employed to watch the door

strait prison: strictly imprisoned

coil: disturbance

nosegay: a bundle of flowers

CHAPTER 11: IN THE DARK CASTLE
fie: an exclamation of distaste for something
sap: a fool
chamberlain: the manager of the household of a monarch or noble

CHAPTER 12: THE QUEEN OF UNDERLAND
blub: cry

CHAPTER 13: UNDERLAND WITHOUT THE QUEEN
sirrah: a medieval expression of contempt

CHAPTER 14: THE BOTTOM OF THE WORLD
squib: a short comical writing
salamander: from European folklore, a giant lizard that likes fire

CHAPTER 15: THE DISAPPEARANCE OF JILL
victuals: food

CHAPTER 16: THE HEALING OF HARMS
humbug: fraud
the ship was warped in: the ship was pulled in with ropes attached to pilings

REFERENCES TO THE BIBLE IN
THE SILVER CHAIR

The passage from *The Silver Chair* is first quoted, followed by the relevant passage in the Bible. A transliteration of the 1611 edition of the King James version of the Bible is used for the Biblical quotations. Comments then follow.

— Chapter 2: "Jill Is Given a Task" —

1. "If you are thirsty, you may drink."

2. "If you are thirsty, come and drink."

> **John 7:37:** "In the last day, that great day of the feast, Jesus stood, and cried, saying, 'If any man thirsts, let him come to me and drink.'"

Comments: Aslan twice invites Jill to drink from His stream; she is a stubborn person and hesitates even though she is extremely thirsty. She does not realize it, but she is thirsting for the Lord; when she finally drinks, she is exceptionally refreshed. This is because by drinking the water she has received the Holy Spirit, which is explained by John in 7:39. When Aslan says, "There is no other stream," he means that there is only one source of spiritual fulfillment. Taken as a whole, Chapter 2 is an example of Aslan's mercy; through self-centered behavior, Jill has nearly killed Eustace, who was saved only by Aslan's grace, yet Aslan offers her redemption and forgiveness.

3. "I [Aslan] have swallowed up girls and boys, women and men, kings and emperors, cities and realms."

> **Psalm 21:9:** "You shall make them as a fiery oven in the time of your anger: the Lord shall swallow them up in His wrath, and the fire shall devour them."

Comments: The Biblical passage refers to the Lord swallowing up the enemies of King David. In *The Silver Chair,* Aslan's remark is a reminder that Aslan is dangerous, and it is a warning to Jill. Throughout *The Chronicles of Narnia,* Lewis drops reminders such as this passage that Aslan is powerful and even warlike, that He is willing, even eager, to fight evil people.

4. "There is no other stream."

> **Revelation 22:1:** "And he showed me a pure river of water of life, clear as Crystal, proceeding out of the throne of God, and of the Lamb."

Comments: The river from which Jill drinks is this river, of which there is only one because there is only one flowing from God's throne. Its water is powerful, offering healing of the spirit.

5. "Do so no more."

> **John 8:11:** "She said, 'No man, Lord.' And Jesus said to her, 'Neither do I condemn you: Go, and sin no more.'"

Comments: John tells of a woman accused of adultery who was brought to Jesus; those who brought her wanted to stone her to death according to law (what Lewis might call Deep Magic in *The Chronicles of Narnia*). When Jesus said, "Hee that is without sinne among you, let him first cast a stone at her," the crowd dispersed, leaving only Jesus and the woman. Drawing on the Deeper Magic that predates the world, Aslan forgives Jill as Jesus forgives the woman. In Jill's case, she almost killed someone because she wanted to show off and to show how cowardly he was; she was wrong on both counts, but she shows that she understands what she did, thus Aslan says, "Do so no more," and so far as He is concerned, the matter is closed.

6. "You [Jill] would not have called to me [Aslan] unless I had been calling to you."

> **Revelation 17:14:** "These shall make war with the Lamb, and the Lamb shall overcome them: For He is Lord of Lords, and King of kings, and they that are with Him, are called, and chosen, and faithful."

Comments: Aslan makes the point that He called Jill. She has been chosen for a mission in service of Aslan, and she will be faithful.

7. "But, first, remember, remember, remember the signs."

> **Deuteronomy 6:6-8:** "And these words which I command you this day, shall be in your heart. / And you shall teach them diligently to your children, and shall talk of them when you sit in your house, and when you walk by the way, and when you lie down, and when you rise up. / And you shall bind them for a sign on your hand, and they shall be as frontlets between your eyes."

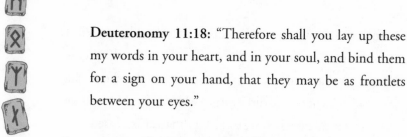

Deuteronomy 11:18: "Therefore shall you lay up these my words in your heart, and in your soul, and bind them for a sign on your hand, that they may be as frontlets between your eyes."

Comments: Aslan has given Jill signs to follow and has admonished her to follow them carefully. At first, Jill recites the signs to herself, especially at bedtime ("when you lie down"); she is diligent in following Aslan's commands. Eventually, she becomes neglectful, failing to "bind them for a sign on your hand." When she does that, she and Eustace and Puddleglum leave the path Aslan wants them to follow.

— Chapter 13: "Underland Without the Queen" —

8. "'Look friend,' he [Rilian] said, holding out the shield towards them. 'An hour ago it was black and without device; and now, this.' The shield had turned bright as silver, and on it, redder than blood or cherries, was the figure of the Lion."

Romans 13:12: "The night is far spent, the day is at hand: let us therefore cast off the works of darkness, and let us put on the armor of light."

Comments: Rilian has "cast off the works of darkness." His shield shines once again and the symbol of Aslan, a source of light, has become visible on it.

9. "This signifies that Aslan will be our good lord, whether he means us to live or die."

> **Romans 14:8:** "For whether we live, we live to the Lord: and whether we die, we die to the Lord: whether we live therefore or die, we are the Lord's."

Comments: This indicates that Rilian is in a courageous frame of mind and that he has fully recovered his senses after being freed from the witch's enchantment. Further, he is putting his life in the care of Aslan.

10. "and you [Jill] must commend yourself to the Lion."

> **Psalm 31:5:** "Into your hand I commit my spirit: you have redeemed me, O Lord God of truth."

> **Luke 23:46:** "And when Jesus had cried with a loud voice, He said, "Father, into your hands I commend my spirit": And having said, thus, He gave up the ghost."

Comments: Rilian reminds Jill to place herself in Aslan's care when they face deadly danger. In so doing, she would be following Jesus' example in Luke and Aslan's example in *The Lion, the Witch and the Wardrobe,* in which Aslan trusted Himself to the Deeper Magic of His Father.

— Chapter 14: "The Bottom of the World" —

11. "Whether we live or die Aslan will be our good lord."

> **Romans 14:8:** "For whether we live, we live to the Lord: and whether we die, we die to the Lord: whether we live therefore or die, we are the Lord's."

Comments: This repetition of an idea from Chapter 13 emphasizes how Rilian, Jill, Eustace, and Puddleglum are intent on doing Aslan's (Christ's) work and have, after several missteps, stepped firmly into the path Aslan wishes them to follow. This passage may be mistaken for *fatalism,* which it is not. Instead, it is courage, an expression of willingness to do what is right even at the cost of their lives, even though none of them intend to be killed.

— Chapter 16: "The Healing of Harms" —

12. "And there came out a great drop of blood, redder than all redness that you have ever seen or imagined."

> **I John 1:7:** "But if we walk in the light, as He is in the light, we have fellowship one with another, and the blood of Jesus Christ His Sin cleanses us from all sin."

Comments: Aslan's blood cleanses Caspian X and revives him in Aslan's Country (Heaven).

13. "as soon as it [the switch] was in her hand it turned into a fine new riding crop."

> **Exodus 4:4:** "And the Lord said to Moses, "Put forth your hand, and take it by the tail": And he put forth his hand, and caught it, and it became a rod in his hand:"

Comments: Moses' experience is more dramatic, but both he and Jill participate in a miracle of transformation.

14. "and turned his [Aslan's] golden back to England, and his lordly face towards his own lands."

> **Exodus 33:23:** "And I will take away My hand, and you shall see My back parts: but My face shall not be seen."

Comments: Even when he blesses Moses in Exodus, the Lord keeps His back to him; even while Aslan creates a miracle for Jill and Eustace, He keeps His back to them.

DISCUSSION QUESTIONS AND PROJECTS FOR *THE SILVER CHAIR*

— Overview —

1. Lewis often mentions bad books and right books in *The Chronicles of Narnia*. What books is he talking about? Does he ever explain the differences?

2. Why does Jill not write down Aslan's signs sometime during her quest?

3. From what you know from *Prince Caspian*, *The Voyage of the "Dawn Treader,"* and *The Silver Chair*, has Caspian X had a good life or a bad one?

4. In what ways does She of the Green Kirtle interfere with the quest for Rilian by Jill, Eustace, and Puddleglum by telling them about Harfang?

5. Rilian is excited by what Golg tells him of the Really Deep Land, and he sounds a bit like Reepicheep in his wondering whether he ought to go there. Write a story about Rilian, Jill, Eustace, or Puddleglum having an adventure in the Really Deep Land.

6. Chapter 16 mentions "the nine names of Aslan." How many of these names can you find in *The Chronicles of Narnia*? What are they? Why wouldn't Lewis just tell what they are?

7. "They [the cruel children] shall see only my back," says Aslan. Why only His back? Take a look at the Biblical reference number 14 (Exodus 33:23) for *The Silver Chair* for a clue.

8. Aslan tells Eustace, "He [Caspian X] has died. Most people have, you know. Even I have. There are very few who haven't." In *The Chronicles of Narnia*, who are the characters who do not seem to die by the end of *The Last Battle*? What makes you think so?

9. The Underworld city in which Rilian has lived for ten years is a shadowy, mysterious place. Draw or paint a depiction of it, or build a model of it. How would it look different from Overworld cities?

10. Is Caspian X's death sad or happy in *The Silver Chair*?

11. Why would Aslan help people who ignore His signs?

CHAPTER 1: BEHIND THE GYM

1. Why would adults allow bullying to continue without let up in a school?

2. By the end of this chapter, Jill seems to be a contradictory personality. What aspects of her character have evolved?

CHAPTER 2: JILL IS GIVEN A TASK

1. Why is Jill as thirsty as she is?

2. Why does she undertake Aslan's quest without question?

CHAPTER 3: THE SAILING OF THE KING

1. Who is at fault for missing Aslan's first sign?

2. Why don't Eustace and Jill tell someone besides Glimfeather about their quest?

CHAPTER 4: A PARLIAMENT OF OWLS

1. Why won't an owl accompany Jill and Eustace on their quest?

2. Why do the characters in *The Silver Chair* not figure out what we readers can see, that the serpent and the woman in green are likely to be related?

CHAPTER 5: PUDDLEGLUM

1. Why would Eustace be stronger in Narnia than he is on earth?

2. What sort of companion do you expect Puddleglum to be after reading Lewis' description of him?

CHAPTER 6: THE WILD WASTE LANDS OF THE NORTH

1. Why would Jill and Eustace actually behave worse than they had been after hearing of a place ahead of them that might give them some civilized comforts?

2. How does Puddleglum prove his value as a member of the quest in this chapter?

CHAPTER 7: THE HILL OF THE STRANGE TRENCHES

1. How well does each member of the party handle the adventure among the stones? Is the conduct admirable or not?

2. Do Jill, Eustace, and Puddleglum have good reasons for not noticing the significance of the ruins?

CHAPTER 8: THE HOUSE OF HARFANG

1. Lewis says that Jill did not remember that she had dreamed at all when she woke up the morning after she dreamed of Aslan and the big letters UNDER ME. What would be the point of

giving someone a dream with a message in it if she is not going to remember the dream?

2. Why does Jill say "Oh, how perfectly dreadful!" when she looks out of her bedroom window at the ruined city?

Chapter 9: How they Discovered Something Worth Knowing

1. What techniques does Jill use to convince the giants of Harfang that she is an empty-headed innocent child? Are any of these techniques familiar to you?

2. Why would Puddleglum and Eustace be horrified at eating venison from a Talking Stag? Why would Jill not be horrified?

Chapter 10: Travels Without the Sun

1. Why does Puddleglum try to find good things to say about the travelers' journey in the Underworld?

2. What is Lewis suggesting when he says that the young man was handsome and looked "both bold and kind, though there was something about his face that didn't seem quite right"?

Chapter 11: In the Dark Castle

1. Why don't Jill, Eustace, and Puddleglum realize the young man is Prince Rilian before he is tied to the silver chair?

2. How much of the Queen's plans for Rilian have you learned by the end of this chapter?

3. Why do the children and Puddleglum hesitate to release the young man even though he has invoked Aslan's name.

CHAPTER 12: THE QUEEN OF UNDERLAND

1. Why does Puddleglum step in the fire?

2. What does Puddleglum mean when he says he prefers the game to the witch's reality?

3. How do Jill, Eustace, Puddleglum, and Rilian overcome the witch's spell?

4. Why do Jill, Eustace, Puddleglum, and Rilian almost believe the nonsense the witch is telling them?

CHAPTER 13: UNDERLAND WITHOUT THE QUEEN

1. What is happening in Underworld as the travelers and Rilian try to escape? Why would this be happening?

2. Are the travelers wise to let go of the Earthman after he proclaims Rilian a friend?

CHAPTER 14: THE BOTTOM OF THE WORLD

1. What would have happened if Rilian had gone with Golg to the Really Deep Land?

2. What does the Great Snow Dance tell about how the Narnians get along with each other?

3. Would the witch's scheme have worked if she could have gotten Rilian to lead a war of the Earthmen against Narnia?

CHAPTER 15: THE DISAPPEARANCE OF JILL

1. What is best thing, to the travelers, about emerging into Narnia?

2. How does Jill's handling of her climb to the hole tell about how much she has grown since the beginning of *The Silver Chair*?

CHAPTER 16: THE HEALING OF HARMS

1. What does Lewis mean by "it is the stupidest children who are most childish and stupidest grown-ups who are most grown-up"?

2. Why don't people seem to have any particular ages on that mountain?

3. Caspian X is dead, yet he is alive. How is this possible?

CHAPTER 15

THE LAST
BATTLE

OVERVIEW

The Last Battle is a controversial book, especially because Susan Pevensie is no longer a friend of Narnia. This novel is tough to write about and it is tough to think about. Having provided a depiction of how Aslan (Christ) might create a world other than earth in *The Magician's Nephew,* Lewis, here, provides an account of how a world other than earth might die. He draws heavily on the Bible for inspiration, including vivid depictions of events that are prophesies for earth's ending.

In the last days of Narnia, evil masquerades as good, and good and evil become so confused that some people give up trying to tell the difference. Lies overrule truth; good people are murdered and enslaved, Narnia is invaded and conquered by Calormen, and all that stands between Narnia and utter destruction is a king, a unicorn, Eustace, Jill, and a few true-hearted followers who defy the lies that they have heard by giving their lives to Aslan. Matters have never been so bleak before in Narnia; the White Witch's winter without Christmas is not so horrifying in comparison. How will King Tirian and his friends defeat the evil that has come to live in Narnia?

Eschatology is the study of death and for Christianity, the study of the end of the world, and it is an important part of *The Last Battle.* Characters speculate on what may happen after their deaths; the situation for King Tirian and his followers is very grim, and they are well aware that they are likely to die at the hands of the enemies of Narnia and Aslan. Jewel the Unicorn says that there is an afterlife, but others are not so sure, because Aslan has not made an appearance in Narnia for a long time and

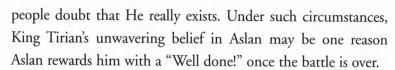

people doubt that He really exists. Under such circumstances, King Tirian's unwavering belief in Aslan may be one reason Aslan rewards him with a "Well done!" once the battle is over.

Other characters reject the supernatural. Rishda, the Calormene commander, is certain that Tash and Aslan do not exist. He tells lies about each, confident that there will be no reckoning from either. The ungrateful Dwarfs foolishly decide that if Shift the Ape and Rishda are lying about Tash and Aslan, then King Tirian and others must also be lying about Aslan; this is illogical, but it suits their prejudices. Further, their atheism stems from their being blinded by their own personal desires. When they declare "Dwarfs for the Dwarfs," they reveal their own selfishness and their refusal to look at good and evil rationally. They fail to understand that by declaring themselves to be in favor of only themselves they lose any possibility of objectivity toward moral and religious issues. This makes it difficult (but not impossible, for one of them finds his way into Aslan's Country) for them to recognize their own salvation and probably impossible to act in a way that is sensible.

The door to the stable represents death, and it is through death that truth is found. Lewis draws on Christian theology and particularly the book of Revelations, which says that the world we know will be destroyed but will be replaced by a better one. He roughly follows Biblical accounts of how earth will end, condensing events a bit. For instance, instead of seven angels with seven horns as is found in Revelations chapter 8, he provides only Father Time and his one horn.

Like death, the stable's door appears dark and frightening when viewed from the outside. When people are tossed inside the stable and do not return, it appears as if what is beyond the door is a final end to life. Yet, most of those who pass through the door discover wonders on the other side. For those who have passed through the door (that is, they have died), the door is a curiosity. It is possible to walk around it, yet it is possible to look through it and see Narnia.

Just as the end of earth is supposed to bring with it a final judgment, the end of the world of Narnia brings with it a calling up of all humans and Talking Beasts and other sentient beings who are divided by how they regard Aslan (Christ). Those who love Him pass through the door and into a land of wonders; the others pass into Aslan's shadow. Important to note, here, is that even unbelievers can enter heaven. Lewis indicates that Aslan's love is for everyone, and he makes a point of having a worshipper of a false god, Emeth, and an atheist Dwarf admitted to Aslan's Country. When Aslan explains to Emeth why he has been admitted to Aslan's Country, the underlying idea is that what is in a person's heart is essential for salvation.

Other interesting aspects of eschatology are the timelessness of Aslan's country, the absence of fear, and having all desires be good desires. Christian eschatology says that the end of the earth will bring with it the end of time. For someone who has lived only in a world governed by time, this can be a difficult concept to visualize. Lewis expresses it first in his descriptions of the Pevensies and their companions just beyond the door in Aslan's Country; they seem young and grownup at the same time. Further, he draws on the concept of a place without time to explain the passage of judgment on millions of beings who seem to flow to the door quickly yet slowly. Each being is given its turn, yet no time seems to pass. It seems impossible for so many beings to pass though the door, yet they do so, and to observers, the passage simultaneously took much time and little time.

Lucy discovers that she can do anything she wants without fear in Aslan's country. When Eustace hears her point this out, he tries to be afraid, but he cannot. Freed from the limitations of fear, a particular problem for Eustace, who spent much of *The Voyage of the "Dawn Treader"* being afraid, people can do what they please. Neither death nor injury is possible. Further, Peter notes that they are in a land where whatever a person wants is good. He and the others may eat freely from the trees of life, because in Aslan's Country all desires are good ones, including the desire to eat whatever fruits are found there.

To all this, Lewis adds his own analogy to help explain how life-after-death may be wonderful. He calls the now destroyed world of Narnia a mere prelude to a great book, implying that life on earth is only a prelude, too. What lies beyond the stable door (death) is chapter one of the great book. When the new arrivals discover that in the heart of Aslan's country there are a multitude of worlds, including earth, attached as if spokes on a wheel, they see the potential for unending adventure. In *The Last Battle,* the next life is one filled with joy, pleasure, beauty beyond anything experienced in the first life, and activity. People have much to do, and they do it while surrounded by and filled with the Father's good grace.

THE GEOGRAPHY OF *THE LAST BATTLE*

The events of *The Last Battle* take place in a fairly limited area in the northwestern region of the Great River. On the eastern edge of the Western Mountains is the Great Waterfall, which pours into the Cauldron Pool, beside which Shift the Ape and Puzzle live. Water flows out of the Cauldron Pool to become the Great River, which flows southeast until it merges with the River Rush; thereafter the river flows in a more easterly direction.

In the mountains to the west of the Great Waterfall, a hunter kills a lion and skins it. Perhaps by accident, the hunter drops the skin in the river that flows to the waterfall, and Shift the Ape, sees it drop into the Cauldron Pool. Shift lives on the northern side of the pool; to the southeast is the village of Chippingford, where Shift often sends Puzzle to pick up goods.

Beyond Chippingford, the river flows through the Lantern Waste, where the lamp that was planted in *The Magician's Nephew* stands and where Lucy first stepped into Narnia. In the Lantern Waste, near to the river, is the stable that Shift and Rishda Tarkaan pretend that Aslan occupies. The stable is among Talking Trees, many of which are chopped down, lashed together into rafts and then floated downriver, as King Tirian sees when a Water Rat floats past him. These trees are sentient beings, and chopping them down is murder. This is why Tirian and Jewel are so furious when they learn of the felled trees.

A generation before Tirian's time, a Narnian king erected a series of tall stone towers in meadows through the Lantern Waste in order to defend against bandits who would raid Narnia from the northwest. It is in one of these towers that Tirian and his companions find supplies for their resistance against the Calormenes and the Calormenes' Narnian allies.

GREAT WATERFALL

APE'S HUT

CAULDRON POOL

CHIPPING FORD VILLAGE

the end o

the Lo

STABLE

FIRE

WHERE THE LAST BATTLE
IS FOUGHT

1

2

3

4

5

6

LANTERN
WASTE

WESTERN MOUNTAINS

Legend

1 Hyads and dryads are first murdered
2 Where the ungrateful dwarfs are freed
3 King Tirian and his companions bathe
4 Tower where King Tirian, the Unicorn,
   the children and the Dwarf stay
5 Tash's route
6 King Tirian and the Unicorn's vacation
   Lodge
7 Where Roonwit is murdered

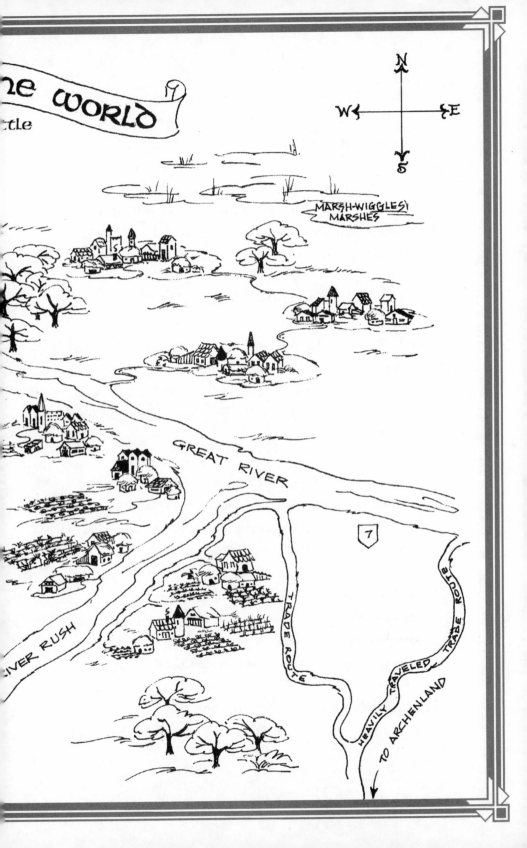

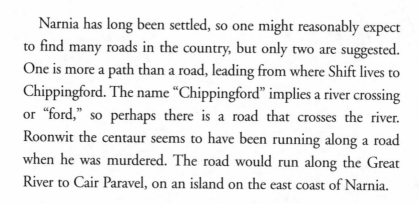

Narnia has long been settled, so one might reasonably expect to find many roads in the country, but only two are suggested. One is more a path than a road, leading from where Shift lives to Chippingford. The name "Chippingford" implies a river crossing or "ford," so perhaps there is a road that crosses the river. Roonwit the centaur seems to have been running along a road when he was murdered. The road would run along the Great River to Cair Paravel, on an island on the east coast of Narnia.

THEMES AND CHARACTERS

"And of course the Ape and Puzzle, just before the last Judgement (in the *Last Battle*) are like the coming of Antichrist before the end of our world," Lewis tells Patricia. (C. S. Lewis, *Letters to Children*, 1985, p. 93.) For this, Lewis may have drawn on II Peter 2:1-3:

> But there were false prophets also among the people, even as there shall be false teachers among you, who secretly shall bring in damnable heresies, even denying the Lord that brought them, and bring on themselves swift destruction. / And many shall follow their pernicious ways, by reason of whom the way of truth shall be evil spoken of: / And through covetousness shall they with false word, make merchandise of you, whose judgment now of a long time does not linger, and their damnation does not slumber.

The false prophets seem to be Shift the Ape, Rishda Tarkaan, and Ginger the Cat. Each one of them finds out what serving evil actually means when the demon Tash comes when he is called. Their heresies include insisting that Aslan and Tash are the same, and that an angry Aslan would do the evil of Tash. Many Narnians in their audience "follow their pernicious wayes," confused by what they hear and what they think they see. Shift and Rishda are notably covetous, desiring to own what others have, with Shift eventually eating and drinking himself into near oblivion, and with Shift and Rishda making "marchandise" (*merchandise*) of Narnians by selling them into slavery. As for their judgment and damnation, the novel draws its own conclusion.

CHAPTER-BY-CHAPTER DEVELOPMENT OF THEMES AND CHARACTERS IN *THE LAST BATTLE*

— Chapter 1: By Caldron Pool —

The Last Battle begins with the tone of a fairy tale: "In the last days of Narnia, far up to the west beyond Lantern Waste and close beside the great waterfall, there lived an Ape." Only later do events suggest that the ape, whose name is Shift, has apparently been devised a conspiracy for many years. In this chapter, he bullies and bosses Puzzle, a donkey who admits that Shift is much smarter than he. He often fetches food from a nearby village for Shift, who seems to spend his time lazing about. However, there is more to Shift than laziness; when he sees a lion's skin wash over the waterfall near his home, he instantly recognizes an opportunity.

– Chapter 2: The Rashness of the King –

King Tirian, last king of Narnia, is a strong young man who has fought well in war. His companion is Jewel, a unicorn who is also a skilled warrior. The characterization of Jewel may have been inspired by Isaiah 34:7:

> And the Unicorns shall come down with them, and the bullocks with the bulls, and their land shall be soaked with blood, and their dust made fat with fatness.

This verse is part of Isaiah's prophesy of God's dealing with the enemies of His people (those who love Him). Later in *The Last Battle,* Jewel will prove to be the embodiment of this apocalyptic vision, because he is a fearsome warrior.

Tirian has heard of Aslan's having returned to Narnia. For him, it is a matter for much excitement. His friend is cautious, saying that it is too good to be true. Where Tirian is quick to act, without thinking, sometimes, Jewel is calmer. Roonwit the Centaur dampens Tirian's spirits, telling the king that the stars never lie, but Men and Beasts do. "If Aslan were really coming to Narnia," he says, "the sky would have foretold it." If he were really coming, all the most gracious stars would have assembled in his honor. In *Prince Caspian,* Narnia's Centaurs are very learned and can read the planets and stars well; also, the stars of Narnia's universe are shining living beings who probably would assemble in Aslan's honor if He reappeared. Thus, one of the major difficulties Tirian will face in *The Last Battle* is that Aslan has not been seen in Narnia for a long time. In this, the Narnia of *The Last Battle* somewhat parallels the modern world: Those who argue that there is no Aslan (Christ) point out that He has not been seen in Narnia (on earth) for a long time. "Seeing is believing" some Dwarfs will say. But that is a backwards argument; just because someone has not been seen does not mean he or she does not exist.

– Chapter 3: The Ape in Its Glory –

The Narnians assembled at the stable (or barn) seem incredibly gullible. Shift gives them clear signs that he does not serve Aslan. For instance, he declares, "Anything you want to say to him [Aslan] will be passed on through me: if I think it's worth bothering him about." Everyone has always been able to talk to Aslan; the need of a go-between is nonsense. Some critics believe that this is an attack on the papacy of Roman Catholicism, because the Pope is an intercessor with God on behalf of worshippers. Although Lewis believed that anyone can talk to God directly, he did not associate the Pope with evil, which Shift plainly is. Lewis saw good in the Roman Catholic church, even if he did not agree with every one of its doctrines. Lewis would have forthrightly rejected notions that the institution of the papacy was itself a source of evil. His concept of mere Christianity links all Christians who share basic beliefs.

Instead, in this passage in *The Last Battle,* Lewis is criticizing a concept: that not all people can talk to God. Lewis' own personal experiences taught him that anyone can talk to God, even an atheist such as he was. In the Bible, there is the example of Paul, a persecutor of Christians and seemingly among the last people Christ would speak to, yet Christ did speak to him. Paul became a great man of God. This is where the evil of Shift's assertion lies: To deny a person direct access to Christ is to imply that his or her salvation depends not on himself, and not on Christ, either, but on another person. It is an outright denial of Christ's interest in the lives of people; indeed, it implies that Christ is remote from His people and does not care for them. Throughout *The Chronicles of Narnia,* Aslan is shown as taking a personal interest in everyone, and He emphasizes the responsibility of individual people to choose to live good lives. Shift slanders Aslan/Christ when he declares himself the arbiter of what Aslan will hear or not hear; he invites his audience to surrender their responsibility for moral behavior to him and he commits heresy by denying Aslan's deep interest in the lives of all people.

Another sign that Shift does not serve Aslan is his declaration that he is a man and not an ape. Shift, most certainly an ape, seems to be repeating what the green witch tried to do to Jill, Eustace, Puddleglum, and Rilian in *The Silver Chair* by persuading people to believe what obviously is not true. In the witch's case, she uses magic on her victims; Shift relies on his audacity and the fear of his audience. Even so, he plainly lies when he declares himself anything other than an Ape, and from there it is not hard to realize that his association with Aslan is a fake, too. Further, he uses double talk: "True freedom means doing what I tell you," Shift insists. And there is the crowning lie, the absolute verification that he lies: "Tash is only another name for Aslan." It is with this assertion that he seals his own doom: "Sorrow to those that call evil 'good,' and good 'evil,' that put darkness for light, and light for darkness, that put bitter for sweet, and sweet for bitter" (Isaiah 5:20).

Shift's co-conspirator is Rishda Tarkaan (Tarkaan is an honorary Calormene title for nobles). The presence of the Calormenes is evidence that Shift has long communicated with Calormen. The soldiers have sneaked into Narnia, disguised as merchants, a process that would probably take months. An opportunist, Ginger, a cat, joins the conspiracy.

— Chapter 4: What Happened That Night —

Tirian is a young, energetic man used to leadership in combat and among friends, but he is going to have to behave more wisely than he has if he hopes to defy the conspiracy of Shift and the Calormenes. At last, he reaches the right conclusion, and for a right reason when he recognizes that the Ape's assertion that Tash and Aslan are the same is a lie. Some friendly Talking Animals feed him, but they are afraid to free him. Their instincts are good because they realize that tying up Tirian is wrong, but they do not go where their good instincts should lead them: that Tirian is good and Shift and the fake Aslan are bad.

It is interesting to watch Tirian struggle to apply his mind to the problems he has. These problems seem overwhelming, as if he has no hope of defeating his enemies. But he recognizes that his enemies are also the enemies of Narnia, and he falls back on his faith. He remembers how Aslan has called upon children to help the ancient kings of Narnia (it has been two hundred years since Rilian's reign). He appears before Peter, Lucy, Edmund, Eustace, Jill, Digory (now old), and Polly (old, as well), the seven friends of Narnia. Tirian wanted to say that he was Tirian of Narnia, in great need of help, but he has no voice and cannot cry for help. He wakes from the vision, and "That waking was about the worst moment he had ever had in his life."

This is a way that Lewis builds suspense. The only situation that may have appeared as hopeless as that in which Tirian finds himself was when Aslan was killed on the Stone Table in *The Lion, the Witch and the Wardrobe*. This meeting of Tirian and the seven friends, as frustrating as it may be, implies that help from the children of earth may come and, as in the past, help to defeat great evil. Perhaps Tirian's plight is not utterly lost.

— Chapter 5: How Help Came to the King —

The train Eustace and Jill are riding comes to a jerking halt in the station as they arrive in Narnia. This foreshadows revelations at the end of *The Last Battle*. To Tirian, the response to his plea for help seems swift: "But his misery did not last long. Almost at once there came a bump, and then a second bump, and two children were standing before him." They free him, thus beginning the last adventures of earth children in Narnia. They are to face horrors that no others have endured.

Although this is primarily a transition chapter, that is a chapter that explains what has gone before and sets forth the situation for the chapters that follow, it makes some interesting points about the characters. Perhaps most interesting is Tirian's reaction to the coming of the children. Back in *Prince Caspian*, Trumpkin was unhappy to see four children instead of four adult warriors when he met the Pevensie children. He wanted to find warriors to lead the Old Narnians in battle against their Telmarine overlords. Even High King Peter had trouble being taken seriously by the Narnians. Yet, in this chapter, Tirian is not at all dismayed to have two children pop out of thin air. Apparently, the descendants of King Rilian, Tirian's seventh royal ancestor counting back, emphasized that the helpers from earth had come in the form of children. Thus, for Tirian, there is happiness at seeing Jill and Eustace, and he treats them respectfully, not as inferiors. Further, he is glad to have his faith in Aslan visibly supported by the presence of the children who had rescued King Rilian two hundred years before. He delights in the presence of the children, and all in all, he sounds like a man children would like to have around.

Eustace is still sharp tongued and prone to interrupting people while they talk, but he is thoughtful, too. He produces the six sandwiches he had been carrying with him on the train and gives them to Tirian, who must be very hungry. How much Eustace has matured! Jill herself shows much more confidence than she had at the start of *The Silver Chair*. She has a great spirit of adventure and is eager to help the king. She has learned to be modest, something that was a problem Aslan said she should correct, and she understates her skill with the bow and arrow, even though she has been practicing with Eustace on earth. Her tendency to act rather than talk will annoy Tirian a bit when she takes off on her own without his permission, but overall it will serve Tirian and the forces of good well to have her taking action when it is needed. Eustace's own cool head and confidence in Aslan will be a steadying influence on his companions. King Tirian's own buoyant personality and confidence in the courage of his companions will help him to endure the humiliation of losing a kingdom and the horrors of his subjects being enslaved and murdered.

Isaiah 22:8: "And he has taken away the covering of Judah, and you looked in that day to the armor of the house of the forest" might be a possible inspiration for Tirian leading his party to one of the three towers built for defense against bandits, where the children find armor and other supplies, there. It *is* in a forest. Further, Isaiah mentions the "house of the forest" as a place for arming oneself for battle against the forces of evil. In the tower, Tirian finds weapons, armor, and other supplies.

– Chapter 6: A Good Night's Work –

The children have much to offer Tirian's cause, as the king had hoped. Tirian is pleasantly surprised at the strength of the children who have also grown. We have seen these effects before, especially in *Prince Caspian*; all the Pevensies recovered their Narnian skills and grew stronger as their adventure progressed. In particular, Peter had regained enough of his past Narnian strength to fight the usurper Miraz, a grown man, in hand-to-hand combat. Further, Eustace himself has had the experience before: In *The Silver Chair,* he recovers the strength and skill he had gained in *The Voyage of the "Dawn Treader,"* sailing with Caspian X to the End of the World. It is the Narnian air that has this effect on visitors from earth; those from earth who revisit Narnia slowly regain the strength and skills they had before returning to earth. In *The Last Battle,* Eustace recovers his sword-fighting skills, and Jill puts to use some of what she had learned in *The Silver Chair* by moving silently through bushes. She is crucial to the freeing of Jewel and Puzzle.

And what about Puzzle? He has been presented as Aslan Himself, without much protest. But when Tirian moves to lop off the Ass's head, Jill declares, "He didn't know any better. And he's very sorry. He's a nice donkey. His name's Puzzle. And I've got my arms around his neck." It seems that those skills she put to use fooling the Harfang giants into thinking she was cute and sweet in *The Silver Chair* are still with her. Tirian says to her that she is the bravest of all his subjects, but also the most disobedient, but he lets the donkey live. Forgiveness is highly valued by Aslan, and Tirian's forgiving Puzzle is not only a sign of his being a follower of Aslan but serves to distinguish him from the evildoers, showing that there is a plain difference between Tirian and Shift and his co-conspirators. Eventually, Aslan Himself forgives Puzzle, who is in Aslan's Country after the end of the world.

— Chapter 7: Mainly about Dwarfs —

"*The light is dawning, the lie broken,*" declares Tirian, and in the other novels of *The Chronicles of Narnia* this would be cause for celebration, but *The Last Battle* remains dark, with evil subverting the truth. The Dwarfs don't care to hear any more stories. Even though Tirian has just freed them from going to a life of slavery on Calormen, the Dwarfs show no gratitude. The effect of the lies of Shift and Rishda has been to make them not believe in any deity, Aslan or otherwise. Evil is served by people not

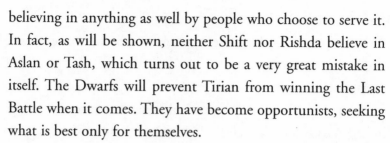

believing in anything as well by people who choose to serve it. In fact, as will be shown, neither Shift nor Rishda believe in Aslan or Tash, which turns out to be a very great mistake in itself. The Dwarfs will prevent Tirian from winning the Last Battle when it comes. They have become opportunists, seeking what is best only for themselves.

Not all the Dwarfs have become disbelievers. Poggin the Dwarf sneaks away from the group and joins Aslan; he has the good sense and strength of character to separate truth from lies. He is proof that not all Dwarfs are only for themselves. Indeed, he indicates that like humans, Dwarfs are capable of much good as well as much evil. Poggin is also courageous and strong, making him a welcome addition to Tirian's party. Still, the betrayal by the other Dwarfs of Poggin's party is a heavy blow. If they choose to support Tirian, they could make the difference between success and failure in battle, but by choosing to support no one but themselves, they serve the cause of evil. In the case of the Calormenes, the Narnians who choose not to support either side make it easier for them to defeat resistance. But the evil conspirators have problems of their own, for Shift's excesses have caught up with him; he is lost in overindulgence of food and drink and is unable to do more than what he is told to do. Once the clever instigator of a plot to overthrow the government of Narnia and to drive the faith in Aslan from the land, he is no longer able to contribute to the planning of Narnia's death. He has fallen prey to his own deviltry, and he has been overwhelmed by his own greed and self-indulgence. The Calormenes are likely to have little use for him once they are securely in power.

— Chapter 8: What News the Eagle Brought —

A sign that the events Jill, Eustace, Tirian, and the others are experiencing may truly be the beginning of the end of all things is also one of Lewis' eeriest passages. King Tirian and the others see something "gliding" slowly in the trees beyond the clearing. The word *gliding* suggests that whatever it is, it is not walking or running like ordinary creatures; its slow movement suggests something moving with difficulty or with unconcern, even at the presence of Tirian's group. At first they thought it was smoke because it was grey and transparent, but it did not smell like smoke and it did not billow or curl. Although ghostly figures who glide very slowly provide much of the suspense in gothic tales, Lewis wants to create a unique image that avoids the clichés of ghost stories. He accomplishes this through details; the thing we see is hazy, not quite solid because we can see through it. Lewis then turns the image of smoke back on itself by noting that it did not smell like smoke but of death. Adding the sense of smell to the image is a fine touch; in so doing, Lewis not only expands the sensory response to the thing, but creates a contradiction: the apparition looks like one thing but is another. This becomes important later when Tash appears in the stable.

The thing is a gathering of monstrous contradictions: Not only can one see through it, but it's shape is manlike although it is a bird. Further, it has four arms, all raised high and facing northward, the general direction of the stable. The arms seem humanlike, but their fingers are curved talons. Its posture is menacing, with its fingers-like-talons poised high, as if ready to

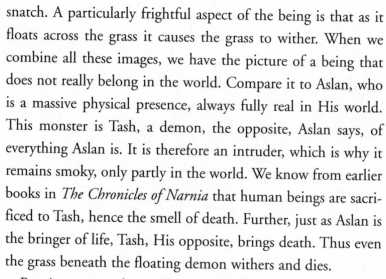

snatch. A particularly frightful aspect of the being is that as it floats across the grass it causes the grass to wither. When we combine all these images, we have the picture of a being that does not really belong in the world. Compare it to Aslan, who is a massive physical presence, always fully real in His world. This monster is Tash, a demon, the opposite, Aslan says, of everything Aslan is. It is therefore an intruder, which is why it remains smoky, only partly in the world. We know from earlier books in *The Chronicles of Narnia* that human beings are sacrificed to Tash, hence the smell of death. Further, just as Aslan is the bringer of life, Tash, His opposite, brings death. Thus even the grass beneath the floating demon withers and dies.

Poggin sums up the implications for Shift when he notes that the Ape called for Tash even though he did not believe in Tash. One of Lewis' theological principles is his belief in a literal supernatural world that is active around us all. Angels are, to him, facts. When Poggin tells Shift that people shouldn't call for demons unless they really mean what they say, he may be speaking for Lewis himself. To Lewis, calling on evil spirits was no game, and nothing to play with: Evil can have an actual effect on people.

If one knows what is to come in *The Last Battle*, then Jill's belief that her world will end someday but that Aslan's will not shows her resilience and the positive outlook that she learned from her experiences in *The Silver Chair*, but it seems out of place in the nightmare that has become Narnia. Roonwit may be speaking as a prophet when he says to Farsight, an eagle, that "all worlds draw to an end," but Jewel seems to offer a fuller view of Aslan's creation when he says, "except Aslan's own country." Jill stubbornly sticks to her hope when she says that she hopes the end of this world is millions of years away. What she will learn is that the world will live on in Aslan's Country; as Jewel's remark suggests, nothing ends in Aslan's Country.

— Chapter 9: The Great Meeting —

Eustace has grown considerably in spirit and integrity during his adventures in Narnia's world, but he can still be irritating, especially when his matter-of-factness dampens the others' excitement. While Jill tells Tirian that she and Eustace will stick with him throughout his fight (she learned about doing so even if it meant dying in *The Silver Chair*), Eustace points out the obvious: that they have no way of going back to earth, anyway. Even when fighting a lost cause, Eustace remains Eustace, trying to sound too smart.

Jill has become a noble spirit, saying that she'd rather be killed fighting for Narnia than grow old at home. There is an undercurrent of courage to Eustace, too, when he talks about dying, "Well when that awful jerk came—the one that seemed to throw us into Narnia—I thought it *was* the beginning of a railway accident." This foreshadows what is to come, perhaps softening the blow when the truth is known.

— Chapter 10: Who Will Go into the Stable? —

Events become confused in this chapter because even the conspirators Shift, Rishda, and Ginger lose track of what is going on. What had been a catastrophe for Narnia is becoming

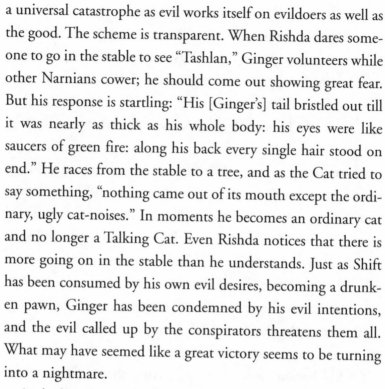

a universal catastrophe as evil works itself on evildoers as well as the good. The scheme is transparent. When Rishda dares someone to go in the stable to see "Tashlan," Ginger volunteers while other Narnians cower; he should come out showing great fear. But his response is startling: "His [Ginger's] tail bristled out till it was nearly as thick as his whole body: his eyes were like saucers of green fire: along his back every single hair stood on end." He races from the stable to a tree, and as the Cat tried to say something, "nothing came out of its mouth except the ordinary, ugly cat-noises." In moments he becomes an ordinary cat and no longer a Talking Cat. Even Rishda notices that there is more going on in the stable than he understands. Just as Shift has been consumed by his own evil desires, becoming a drunken pawn, Ginger has been condemned by his evil intentions, and the evil called up by the conspirators threatens them all. What may have seemed like a great victory seems to be turning into a nightmare.

At the beginning of the world Aslan had turned the beasts of Narnia into Talking Beasts and warned them that if they weren't good they might one day be transformed again and be like the poor witless animals one meets in other countries. What the Narnians fail to remember was what conduct would result in a Talking Animal becoming an ordinary animal, "'And now it is coming upon us,' they moaned, almost mindlessly." Ginger has suffered the fate of loss of his mind, brought on by his own deviousness, but the response of his audience seems more distressing. They do not take action to save their own souls, merely moaning and leaving matters up to Shift, Rishda, and "Tashlan."

The Narnians know the sign of a Talking Animal turned dumb

animal, but they fail to understand the wrong that has prompted Ginger's transformation. They call upon "Lord Shift" to intercede with Aslan on their behalf, failing to recognize that Shift does not speak and never has spoken for Aslan. You may remember that among Jill's transgressions in *The Silver Chair* was her failure to remember Aslan's signs and act upon them when she found them. When she and her companions followed Aslan's signs, they accomplished good works; failure to follow Aslan's signs resulted in unnecessary danger. In this chapter of *The Last Battle,* the Narnians see an important sign but fail to understand and act upon it. In *The Magician's Nephew,* Aslan is plain-spoken on the matter: If a Talking Beast behaves like a wild animal, it will lose its power of speech and become an ordinary beast. A lesson in this occurs in *Prince Caspian* when the schoolboys become pigs. Thus, the sign in this chapter means that Ginger has behaved like a dumb animal; it does not represent some horrifying Aslan hiding away in the stable. The proper action to take would be to defy Ginger's allies, not to beg Shift to intervene with Aslan for them.

— Chapter 11: The Pace Quickens —

Tirian acts quickly; he grabs Shift and flings him into the stable, and Poggin slams the door: "But as the Dwarf banged the door shut again, a blinding greenish-blue light shone out from the inside of the Stable, the earth shook, and there was a strange noise—a clucking and screaming as if it was the hoarse voice of some monstrous bird." Although most of those at the stable have not seen Tash making its way into Narnia, we readers and

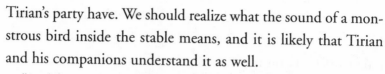

Tirian's party have. We should realize what the sound of a monstrous bird inside the stable means, and it is likely that Tirian and his companions understand it as well.

"And from what Farsight saw there [Rishda's face] he knew at once that Rishda was just as surprised, and nearly as frightened, as everyone else. 'There goes one,' thought Farsight, 'who had called on gods he does not believe in. How will it be with him if they have really come?'" Lewis seems to have been of the opinion that calling on false gods is dangerous even in real life. He believed that evil could have its way with people foolish enough to dabble in the occult.

In a novel of horrors, one of the most horrible comes when the Talking Horses rush to Tirian's aid. The Dwarfs, who are excellent archers, shoot the horses and not one reaches the King. This is inexcusably evil, even though the Dwarfs suggest that they are neutral. Later they will fire on the Calormenes, only to discover that their armor is resistant to arrows. They don't care which side wins—evil or good—and they kill for no reason nor from any convictions. They jeer at Eustace and tell him he can't take them in. This is proof that these Dwarfs are fools. They have understood nothing of what they have seen and experienced, and in their effort to be fooled by no one, they have fooled themselves.

— Chapter 12: Through the Stable Door —

The group of Dwarfs, only recently enslaved by Calormenes and freed by Tirian, have become opportunists: They want Narnia for their own and they look for opportunities to seize power. This aspect of the battle can be confusing, because one moment the Dwarfs seem to help the Calormenes and another they seem to help Tirian's side; in so doing they aid evil in its victory. Their immorality, however much they pretend otherwise, can land them only on the side of evil.

Tirian has deepened quickly, considering he has had little time to think about the meaning of events. For example, he says that the stable door is a 'grim door,' more like a mouth than a portal. This sounds less like the rash man that began the novel and more like a man who sees under the reality of events. It turns out that the door is a kind of mouth, at least for Shift, who was swallowed by Tash.

After a valiant fight, Tirian's companions are killed or forced through the Stable door. Eventually, Tirian in spite of his remarkable fighting, is edged into the door. "Come in and meet Tash yourself!" cries Tirian, pulling Rishda by the belt back into the stable with him. Tash seizes Rishda: "Begone, Monster, and take your lawful prey to your own place: in the name of Aslan and Aslan's great Father, the Emperor-over-sea," says someone, probably High King Peter, who stands near Tirian. The phrase "lawful prey" has come up before, in reference to Edmund in *The Lion, the Witch and the Wardrobe*. In that case, Edmund was a traitor whose evil deeds made him the White Witch's; Rishda had called upon evil, and evil came, making him evil's possession.

Tirian is in the presence of the miraculous. He sees seven kings and queens, each dressed in their finest clothes and armor. Jill has been transformed: she now looks cool and fresh. Tirian is a bit embarrassed to be in the company of such eminent people while looking beaten up, dirty, and sweaty, but he too has

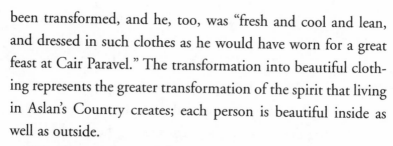

been transformed, and he, too, was "fresh and cool and lean, and dressed in such clothes as he would have worn for a great feast at Cair Paravel." The transformation into beautiful clothing represents the greater transformation of the spirit that living in Aslan's Country creates; each person is beautiful inside as well as outside.

Tirian has some trouble with Jill's age. At first he thought she looked older, but then she didn't, and he could never decide her age. This passage echoes the impression Caspian X makes in Aslan's Country at the end of *The Silver Chair*. Apparently, in Aslan's Country age does not matter much; people seem to be whatever is best for them.

As he is introduced to each king and queen, Tirian asks High King Peter where Queen Susan is and Peter's answer is mysterious and controversial. Peter answers gravely that Susan is no longer a friend of Narnia. Elsewhere, Lewis explains that Susan still lives in England and may eventually find her way into Aslan's Country. Within *The Chronicles of Narnia* Lewis has steadily shown Susan trying to be too adult and becoming condescending toward her brothers and sister, but her being no longer a friend of Narnia is sad. Susan has become devoted to being an adult, and in the process has lost herself to looking good for others while neglecting her spiritual life. You may recall how she behaved and spoke in *Prince Caspian*: For instance, she spoke to Lucy as if she were a little girl, sounding somewhat like the Queen of Underworld sounded in *The Silver Chair* when she tells Jill, Eustace, Puddleglum, and Rilian that there is no Overworld, nor sun and no stars. Later in *Prince Caspian*, she admits that she knew in her heart that Lucy was telling the truth but that she had suppressed it. By the time of *The Last Battle,* Susan has thoroughly suppressed her spiritual life and denies its existence. She speaks condescendingly to her brothers and sisters about how charming it is of them to continue to pretend that Narnia exists. According to Peter, she has lost herself in the pursuit of being an adult. She has lost her childlike faith.

— Chapter 13: How the Dwarfs Refused to Be Taken In —

Tirian thought that they were inside the thatched stable, but the reality of the stable requires a leap in understanding and imagination for Tirian. Like the door in *Prince Caspian,* the stable door seems to stand free in an open field. "In reality they stood on grass, the deep blue sky was overhead, and the air which blew gently on their faces was that of a day in early summer." For Lewis, summer was associated with happy times and freedom; it was a period without school. Looking from the outside, the stable was twelve feet long and six feet wide, but once inside there is a whole other world.

Peter's observation that the stable is bigger inside than outside is an allusion to the birth of Christ in a stable; as the Son of God, He was much larger than the whole world; the spiritual renewal He represented was for all people, a scope vastly larger than His stable. The group wonders whether they are allowed to eat the fruit from the trees that are growing on the inside of the stable. This is a reasonable concern; after all, there has been forbidden fruit both on earth and Narnia's world (*The*

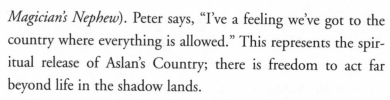

Magician's Nephew). Peter says, "I've a feeling we've got to the country where everything is allowed." This represents the spiritual release of Aslan's Country; there is freedom to act far beyond life in the shadow lands.

The Dwarfs who have been tossed into the stable behave oddly. People around them are enjoying themselves and wandering about a beautiful land, but the Dwarfs sit huddled together. Aslan growls at them but they say, "They won't take *us* in again!" To make a point, "Aslan raised his head and shook his mane. Instantly a glorious feast appeared on the Dwarfs' knees: pies and tongues and pigeons and trifles and ices, and each Dwarf had a goblet of good wine in his right hand," but the Dwarfs are unsatisfied. Aslan's Country is all around them, as can be plainly seen, but Lewis says that some people refuse to see the obvious; this was his opinion of atheists and agnostics.

The Dwarfs are strict materialists and refuse to look beyond the surface of anything. They declare that this makes them smart, but it causes them to miss most of what is actually going on and they refuse to let Aslan help them. Still, they have made it into the stable. Perhaps enlightenment will come. Plainly, Aslan is willing to welcome them into His Country.

– Chapter 14: Night Falls on Narnia –

Father Time from *The Silver Chair* is awakened by Aslan's roar. He raises his horn and blows on it and amazing phenomena occur rapidly, one upon another. The stars fall, the sun and moon shift out of their usual paths, "And at last, out of the shadow of the trees, racing up the hill for dear life, by thousands and by millions, came all kinds of creatures—Talking Beasts, Dwarfs, Satyrs, Fauns, Giants, Calormenes, men from Archenland, Monopods, and strange unearthly things from the remote islands or the unknown Western lands":

> But as they came right up to Aslan one or other of two things happened to each of them. They all looked straight in his face: I don't think they had any choice about that. And when some looked, the expression of their faces changed terribly—it was fear and hatred: except that, on the faces of Talking Beasts, the fear and hatred lasted only for a fraction of a second. You could see that they suddenly ceased to be *Talking* Beasts. They were just ordinary animals. And all the creatures who looked at Aslan in that way swerved to their right, his left, and disappeared into his huge black shadow, which (as you have heard) streamed away to the left of the doorway. The children never saw them again. I don't know what became of them. But the others looked in the face of Aslan and loved him, though some of them were very frightened at the same time. And all these came in at the Door, on Aslan's right. There were some queer specimens among them. Eustace even recognized one of those very Dwarfs who had helped to shoot the Horses.

This elegant passage relates Lewis' conception of the judgment of the peoples of Narnia's world. It is breathtaking in its scope, yet direct and clear. As the case of Emeth will illustrate

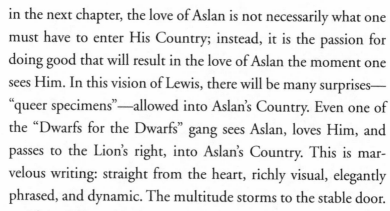

in the next chapter, the love of Aslan is not necessarily what one must have to enter His Country; instead, it is the passion for doing good that will result in the love of Aslan the moment one sees Him. In this vision of Lewis, there will be many surprises—"queer specimens"—allowed into Aslan's Country. Even one of the "Dwarfs for the Dwarfs" gang sees Aslan, loves Him, and passes to the Lion's right, into Aslan's Country. This is marvelous writing: straight from the heart, richly visual, elegantly phrased, and dynamic. The multitude storms to the stable door.

After all this, the Dragons and Giant Lizards tear apart the forests on Narnia, killing every living thing, and eventually dying themselves. The world dies. "The giant [Father Time] threw his horn into the sea. Then he stretched out one arm—very black it looked, and thousands of miles long—across the sky till his hand reached the Sun. He took the Sun and squeezed it in his hand as you would squeeze an orange. And instantly there was total darkness." This image is breathtaking, tragic and glorious at the same time. Aslan tells Peter to shut the door; Peter takes a key of gold and locks it.

His locking the door and keeping the key may be based on the Christian tradition that the Apostle Peter is keeper of the gates to heaven. In Matthew 16:19, Jesus Christ says to Peter, "And I will give to you the keys of the kingdom of heaven, and whatever you shall bind on earth, shall be bound in heaven; whatever you shall loose on earth, shall be loosed in heaven." This passage is the source of the tradition of Peter keeping the gates; in *The Last Battle*, High King Peter is the keeper of the key to the door from the shadow-land Narnia to Aslan's Country.

Peter and the others "find themselves in warm daylight, the

blue sky above them, flowers at their feet, and laughter in Aslan's eyes." Lucy feels the events more deeply than the others, and weeps for Narnia, but there is laughter in Aslan's eyes.

— Chapter 15: Further Up and Further In —

Lewis believed that Christianity is the one true myth of all the world's myths because Christ's resurrection is an historical fact, much as Aslan's resurrection in *The Lion, the Witch and the Wardrobe* is a fact in Narnian history. He also saw Christianity as an *inclusive* religion—that it is for every person. In the story of Emeth's experiences in Aslan's Country, he shows some of how his views would apply to people who did not worship Aslan, but were good people anyway. This would tie in with his belief that other myths could have spiritual aspects and values that would echo some of Christianity, even though they are not *true* myths. This reflects a positive attitude on Lewis' part; as is the case with Emeth, people have the capacity to seek that which is good without necessarily knowing what is good. In Lewis' view, God is more intent on including than excluding. Christianity is for all people, even if not all people realize it.

Emeth tells his story in the Calormene style that Aravis used for her story in *The Horse and His Boy*. When he sees the wonderful land inside the stable, he looks for Tash, but he finds instead a great Lion. Emeth has reason to be frightened by what he sees; in *The Horse and His Boy*, we learn that Calormenes are taught that Aslan is a demon who will do them harm. But Emeth is courageous, and he manages to give us a fine description of Aslan in full glory in His Country:

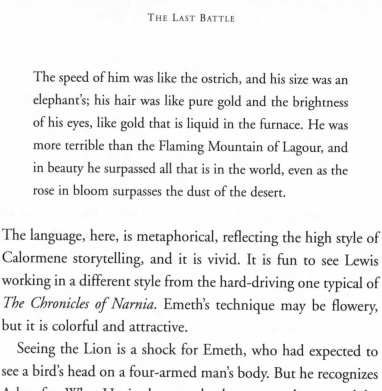

The speed of him was like the ostrich, and his size was an elephant's; his hair was like pure gold and the brightness of his eyes, like gold that is liquid in the furnace. He was more terrible than the Flaming Mountain of Lagour, and in beauty he surpassed all that is in the world, even as the rose in bloom surpasses the dust of the desert.

The language, here, is metaphorical, reflecting the high style of Calormene storytelling, and it is vivid. It is fun to see Lewis working in a different style from the hard-driving one typical of *The Chronicles of Narnia*. Emeth's technique may be flowery, but it is colorful and attractive.

Seeing the Lion is a shock for Emeth, who had expected to see a bird's head on a four-armed man's body. But he recognizes Aslan for Who He is, because he has a true heart, and he laments that Aslan knows that he has served Tash and not Him. That Emeth recognizes and understands his mistake is remarkable, but events reveal that those who try to do what is right will smile on Aslan, even if they, like Emeth or the redeemed ungrateful Dwarf, have not realized in life Who Aslan is. Showing his courageous nature, Emeth recognizes that it is better to have seen the Lion and die than never to have seen Him at all. This echoes the idea of the inside of the stable being bigger than its outside; the spiritual gift from Aslan is greater than all the world. Emeth reveals a stouthearted frame of mind; he is honest with himself and sees reality plainly when reality is there for him to see it. He is about to learn about Aslan's character.

Aslan speaks a remarkable passage in which He tells Emeth that those who do good in Tash's name do so for Him, but those who do evil in Aslan's name do so for Tash. It is an important idea of Lewis that Christ belongs to everyone, that His ministry was for every human being who ever lived or would ever live. This created a profound problem: What about those people who have never heard of Christ? Some theologians have proposed *limbo,* a place of nonbeing for the souls of people who never had the choice of worshipping Christ. This seems to have been insufficient for Lewis, who was convinced that God means to give everyone a chance to share in His Kingdom. In this chapter of *The Last Battle,* Lewis explains through the voice of Aslan that if someone keeps his oath for the oath's sake, even if it is an oath to Tash, Aslan will reward him. Conversely, if someone says that he has performed an act of cruelty in Aslan's name, then he is Tash's servant. These two opposites explain about evils done in the name of good, even in the name of God, as well as what happens to good people who do not recognize the true God while they live in the shadow-lands. According to Revelation 20:12, the dead shall be judged "according to their works," and it appears that Emeth has been judged on that basis. Do good, and God has it within Him to be merciful; do evil in His name, and there is only the long shadow. (This varies from Revelation 20:11-15, which says that "death and hell" will be "cast into the lake of fire" and that "whosoeuer was not found written in the booke of life" would likewise be cast into the lake, but I think the point made by Lewis is the same.)

Underlying this passage is another of Lewis' principles: personal responsibility. He believed in a personal God; someone whom any person could talk to anytime, anyplace, directly. Such a personal relationship implies some personal responsibility. Remember how the multitudes of the world of Narnia either passed through the stable door or turned into Aslan's shadow according to how they regarded Him? Their individual responses determined each of their fates. In the case of Emeth, his response determined his fate.

Emeth, who has tried to live up to a warrior's code of honor, has actually sought Aslan whenever he sought to do good, no matter in whose name he did it. Aslan's great heart loves all who do good, so Aslan's Country is open to all people, regardless of where they live or what they have been taught.

Emeth tells Aslan that he had been seeking Tash all of his life. Emeth has felt something missing in his life, and has long sought to fill it; he unknowingly was seeking the spiritual fulfillment only Aslan can give even though it was in the misguided search for Tash, and so he has therefore sought Aslan without realizing it. Emeth has found Aslan, huge and noble. Emeth notes that Aslan breathed on him, giving him the gift of the Holy Spirit. As has happened with other characters in *The Chronicles of Narnia,* Emeth is strengthened by the breath.

The story of Emeth (Hebrew for *faithful*) may reflect Lewis' personal spiritual experiences. During the years that he advocated atheism, he studied the mythological traditions of cultures other than his own, and partly through this study, as well as his spiritual experiences, he came first to believe in God and second to believe Jesus is the Son of God. Like Emeth, he may have been seeking Christ all along, without realizing it. Emeth had been seeking his heart's greatest desire, Aslan, for his whole life.

This does not mean that Lewis thinks any religion may lead to heaven; when he calls Christianity the one "true myth," he means among other things that Christianity is the one true religion. Remember in *The Silver Chair,* when Aslan says to Jill that she and Eustace would not have called to Him if He had not called to them first? Emeth's case is another illustration of Aslan's calling; He calls Emeth "beloved," and shows that He is aware of all that Emeth has done. He knows that Emeth has been seeking Him all his life; it is as though Aslan has called and Emeth has answered the call. In no way does Aslan or Lewis suggest that by being true to Tash, Emeth has earned his way into Aslan's Country (heaven). When Emeth asks whether Aslan and the demon Tash are the same as Shift and Rabadash Tarkaan claimed, Aslan responds "wrathfully," because He and Tash are opposites, and worshiping anything other than Him is wrong. Emeth's true heart has led him to Aslan, but his worship of Tash is plainly a mistake, one that Aslan has chosen to forgive.

The Kings and Queens, the dogs, and the others discover a special quality about the part of Aslan's Country that they are crossing. Edmund notices that Aslan's Country looks like Narnia, especially the mountains that look like the mountains to the west of Narnia. All soon realize that they are in a place like Narnia, only brighter, deeper, better: all objects and living things are richer in color and depth of meaning. Lewis seems to be a bit mystical, here, but he is trying to convey an important idea—that in Aslan's Country the spiritual significance of each of God's creations is fully visible. Digory asserts that the Narnia they had seen die was not the true Narnia because it had a beginning and an end, implying that Aslan's Country has neither beginning nor end—that's its two or three versions of Narnia (each successively richer than the others) will last forever. "It was only a shadow or copy of something in Aslan's real world," Digory asserts. That is, earth and the world of Narnia outside of Aslan's Country both are shadow-lands, pale copies of the true worlds of Aslan's Country.

— Chapter 16: Farewell to Shadow-Lands —

All that is good about the world of Narnia is preserved in Aslan's Country. When the Pevensies see the earth of Aslan's Country, they see Professor Kirke's country house, even though it had been demolished in the shadow-earth. It was good, and it was therefore preserved by Aslan. Thus, the presence of Tashbaan in Aslan's Country may confuse some readers; Lucy sees "the great city of Tashbaan." The "Tash" of Tashbaan refers to Tash, a demon who embodies the opposite of Aslan. There, human beings were sacrificed on alters to Tash and a poisonous system of government ruled there for over a thousand years. These facts would seem to disqualify Tashbaan, even all of Calormen, from Aslan's Country. On the other hand, Tashbaan had beautiful gardens and palaces. Further, in *The Horse and His Boy*, Tashbaan was home to a friend of Aravis who helped her when Aravis needed her. That Tashbaan could be home to such people implies that there was good as well as evil in Calormen, and the good people and the good aspects of Calormen are preserved in Aslan's Country.

Aslan has not been this playful since His resurrection in *The Lion, the Witch and the Wardrobe*. He urges everyone to go deeper and deeper into His country. No one gets tired. They can swim up waterfalls. And when they seem to reach the end of Aslan's country, it seems to start all over again, only even more wonder-ful than before. "The further up and further in you go, the bigger everything gets. The inside is larger than the outside," Tumnus tells Lucy. Yes, Mr. Tumnus is there. The redoubtable Reepicheep is there. King Frank is there. Even the Pevensies' mother and father are there. "'There *was* a real railway accident,' said Aslan softly. 'Your father and mother and all of you are—as you used to call it in the Shadow-Lands—dead.'" This is a dicey passage; having all the Pevensies (except Susan) killed in a train wreck is bound to be saddening. But from the perspective of Aslan (and Lewis, too), death is only a passage from the half-life of the shadow-lands into the full, rich life of Aslan's Country (Heaven). Death is a release and it is a waking up from the shadow-lands that are only pale copies of the real, rich lands of Aslan's country. The best adventures are only beginning after death: "But for them it was only the beginning of the real story. All their life in this world and all their adventures in Narnia had only been the cover and the title page: now at last they were beginning Chapter One of the Great Story, which no one on earth has read: which goes on for ever: in which every chapter is better than the one before." This is a very appealing metaphor. The idea is that the life in the shadow-lands—our own earth, for instance— is only a prelude to the real life in the real world that people pass into when they die. There, the really good life begins.

VOCABULARY FOR *THE LAST BATTLE*

CHAPTER 1: BY CALDRON POOL
panniers: a pair of baskets carried on each side of a pack animal
fell archers: lethal archers who aim to kill

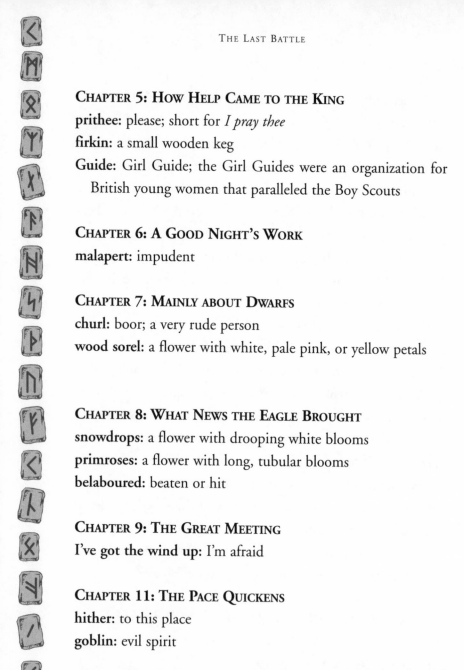

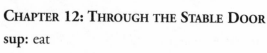

CHAPTER 5: HOW HELP CAME TO THE KING

prithee: please; short for *I pray thee*

firkin: a small wooden keg

Guide: Girl Guide; the Girl Guides were an organization for British young women that paralleled the Boy Scouts

CHAPTER 6: A GOOD NIGHT'S WORK

malapert: impudent

CHAPTER 7: MAINLY ABOUT DWARFS

churl: boor; a very rude person

wood sorel: a flower with white, pale pink, or yellow petals

CHAPTER 8: WHAT NEWS THE EAGLE BROUGHT

snowdrops: a flower with drooping white blooms

primroses: a flower with long, tubular blooms

belaboured: beaten or hit

CHAPTER 9: THE GREAT MEETING

I've got the wind up: I'm afraid

CHAPTER 11: THE PACE QUICKENS

hither: to this place

goblin: evil spirit

CHAPTER 12: THROUGH THE STABLE DOOR

sup: eat

CHAPTER 13: HOW THE DWARFS REFUSED TO BE TAKEN IN
a hack at rugger: to strike or kick an opponent's arms or legs in
   Rugby
It's like your sauce!: you are being impudent or rude
trifles: a desert of sponge cake, jam, wine, macaroons, custard,
   and cream

CHAPTER 15: FURTHER UP AND FURTHER IN
hovel: a shed

REFERENCES TO THE BIBLE IN
THE LAST BATTLE

The passage from *The Last Battle* is first quoted, followed by
the relevant passage in the Bible. A transliteration of the 1611
edition of the King James version of the Bible is used for the
Biblical quotations. Comments then follow.

– Chapter 1: By Caldron Pool –

1. "At that moment there came a great thunderclap right overhead and the ground trembled with a small earthquake."

> **Psalms 77:18:** "The voice of Your thunder *was* in the
> heavens: the lightning lighted the world, the earth trem-
> bled and shook."

> **Mark 13:8:** "For nation shall rise against nation, and king-
> dom against kingdom: and there shall be earthquakes in

many different places, and there shall be famines, and troubles: these are the beginnings of sorrows."

Comments: The motifs of thunder and earthquakes in *The Last Battle* are reminders of Aslan's power and interest in the world. When all seems utterly miserable in *The Chronicles of Narnia*, people recall Aslan's earthshaking deeds. Mark's prophecy for earth begins to be fulfilled in Narnia, as well.

— Chapter 3: The Ape in Its Glory —

2. "Tash is only another name for Aslan." [Says Shift.]

> **Isaiah 5:20:** "Woe to those that call evil good, and good evil, that put darkness for light, and light for darkness, that put bitter for sweet, and sweet for bitter."

Comments: For Shift, Rishda, and Ginger, who pretend that Tash (evil) and Aslan (good) are the same, going so far as to coin the name *Tashlan* for the both of them, the woe is to be unambiguous. Shift is eaten by Tash, Rishda is carried away as Tash's "lawful prey," and Ginger becomes a dumb beast, losing both speech and the ability to reason.

— Chapter 7: Mainly about Dwarfs —

3. "We've no more use for stories about Aslan."

4. "The Dwarfs are for the Dwarfs."

II Peter 3:3: "Knowing this first, that there shall come in the last days scoffers, walking after their own lusts,"

Comments: This particular group of Dwarfs (remember, there are others like Poggin who remain faithful) fills the role of "scoffers." Their repeated declaration that "The Dwarfs are for the Dwarfs" is reminiscent of "walking after their own lusts," because they choose to follow their own immediate desires.

— Chapter 10: Who Will Go into the Stable? —

5. "Come on, Monkey, show us what's in the stable, seeing is believing."

> **John 20:25:** "The other disciples therefore said to him, 'We have seen the Lord.' But he said to them, "'Except I shall see in His hands the print of the nails, and put my finger into the print of the nails, and thrust my hand into His side, I will not believe.'"

Comments: In each case, the expression of doubt eventually results in a confirmation of the existence of Aslan and Christ.

6. "But courage, child [Jill]: we are all between the paws of the true Aslan."

> **Deuteronomy 33:27:** "The eternal God is *your* refuge, and underneath are the everlasting arms: and He shall thrust out the enemy from before you, and shall say, "'Destroy *them*."

Comment: King Tirian reminds Jill that they are between God's "everlasting arms" (or Aslan's "paws"). Like Rilian in *The Silver Chair*, Tirian adopts a courageous frame of mind and trusts himself to Aslan's care.

— Chapter 11: The Pace Quickens —

7. "'Go and drink your own medicine, Shift!' said Tirian and hurled the Ape through into the darkness. But as the Dwarf [Poggin] banged the door shut again, a blinding greenish-blue light shone out from the inside of the Stable, the earth shook, and there was a strange noise a clucking and screaming as if it was the hoarse voice of some monstrous bird."

> **II Peter 2:12:** "But these, as natural brute beasts made to be taken and destroyed speak evil of the things that they do not understand, *and* shall utterly perish in their own corruption."

Comments: Shift has spoken much evil about Aslan, about Whom he knows very little. He has also invited Tash to Narnia. Thus, when he is tossed into the stable, he is sent to the very corruption he called upon. Later, it is revealed that Tash swallowed him.

8. "But Dwarfs jeered back at Eustace. 'That was a surprise for you, little boy, eh? Thought we were on *your* side, did you? No fear. We don't want any Talking Horses. We don't want you to win any more than the other gang. You can't take *us* in. The Dwarfs are for the Dwarfs.'"

Jude 18: "*How* that they told you there should be mockers in the last time, who should walk after their own ungodly lusts."

Comments: The Dwarfs are not only mockers, they indeed "walk after their ungodly lusts," because by now it is clear that they hope to take advantage of the war between the Calormenes and Tirian to seize power for themselves.

9. "You can't take *us* in."

Isaiah 5:21: "Woe unto them that are wise in their own eyes, and prudent in their own sight."

Comments: These Dwarfs plainly think that they are both wise and prudent, determined as they are to be "practical." This makes them fools, and they suffer a loss of spiritual life because of it.

— Chapter 12: Through the Stable Door —

10. "Begone, Monster, and take your lawful prey to your own place: in the name of Aslan and Aslan's great Father, the Emperor-over-sea."

Isaiah 30:22: "You shall defile also the covering of your graven [carved] images of silver, and the ornament of your molten images of gold: you shall cast them away as a menstrous cloth, you shall say to it, 'Get you away.'"

Comments: Like the "graven images," Tash is a false deity. It is probably High King Peter who tells him to leave.

11. "Tirian suddenly felt awkward about coming among these people with the blood and dust and sweat of a battle still on him. Next moment he realised that he was not in that state at all. He was fresh and cool and clean, and dressed in such clothes as he would have worn for a great feast at Cair Paravel."

> **I Corinthians 15:51:** "Behold, I show you a mystery: we shall not all sleep, but we shall all be changed."

Comments: In I Corinthians, Paul writes about the change into a spiritual body; Tirian has undergone such a transformation, and he is cleansed of blood, dust, and sweat because he has been cleansed of his sins.

12. "Here are lovely fruit trees."

> **Revelation 22:2:** "In the middle of the street of it, and of either side of the river, *was there* the tree of life, which bare twelve manner of fruits, and yielded her fruit every month: and the leaves of the tree were for healing of the nations."

Comments: The fruit trees in Aslan's Country bear several different colors of fruit, but all the fruits are delicious. Lewis places these trees just beyond the entrance to Aslan's Country, and all are invited to eat from them. You may recall that in

The Magician's Nephew eating of the fruit was by Aslan's invitation, only.

— Chapter 13: How the Dwarfs Refused to Be Taken In —

13. "In our world too, a Stable once had something inside it that was bigger than our whole world."

> **Luke 2:7:** "And she [Mary] brought out her first born Son, and wrapped Him in swaddling clothes, and laid Him in a manger, because there was no room for them in the Inn.

Comments: The sentence from *The Last Battle* is an allusion to Christ's having been in a manger. The stable is symbolic of Christ's humility and His connection with ordinary people, animals, and all creatures.

14. "Well done, last of the kings of Narnia who stood firm at the darkest hour."

> **Matthew 25:21 and Matthew 25:23:** "His Lord said to him, 'Well done, you good and faithful servant, you have been faithful over a few things, I will make you ruler over many things: enter you into the joy of your lord.'"

Comments: Both passages in Matthew are addressed to servants who in their lord's absence took their talents and multiplied them. This is what Tirian has been doing throughout *The Last*

Battle: He has been expanding his view of possibilities and has used all the talents he has to resist evil until death. Like the lord in Matthew, Aslan greets Tirian with "Well done" as He welcomes Tirian into Aslan's Country. It may be significant that Tirian does not die, but enters Aslan's Country bodily.

15. "He [Aslan] came close to the Dwarfs and gave a low growl: low, but it set all the air shaking. But the Dwarfs said to one another, 'Hear that? That's the gang at the other end of the Stable. Trying to frighten us.'"

> **Revelation 3:20**: "Behold, I stand at the door, and knock: if any man hear my voice, and open the door, I will come in to him, and will eat with him, and he with me."

Comments: The Dwarfs hear Aslan's voice but refuse to open the door to their thoughts to let Him in. Aslan even offers them a feast, inviting them to eat with Him. This is this an allusion to Holy Communion.

16. "They [the Dwarfs] will not let us help them. They have chosen cunning instead of belief. Their prison is only in their own minds, yet they are in that prison; and so afraid of being taken in that they can not be taken out." (Aslan)

> **I Corinthians 2:14**: "But the natural man does not receive the things of the Spirit of God, for they are foolishness to him: neither can he know *them*, because they are spiritually discerned."

Comments: These particular Dwarfs have been fond of being "practical," a word Lewis sometimes uses to depict the attitude of atheists and evildoers. These Dwarfs have chosen to live only in the physical world, making them "naturall" men; they refuse to discern the spiritual aspect of life.

— Chapter 14: Night Falls on Narnia —

17. "Immediately the sky became full of shooting stars. Even one shooting star is a fine thing to see; but these were dozens, and then scores, and then hundreds, till it was like silver rain: and it went on and on."

> **Matthew 23:29:** "Immediately after the tribulation of those days, shall the Sun be darkened, and the Moon shall not give her light, and the stars shall fall from heaven, and the powers of the heavens shall be shaken."

> **Mark 13:25:** "And the Stars of heaven shall fall, and the powers that *are* in heaven shall be shaken."

> **Revelation 6:13:** "And the stars of heaven fell to the earth, even as a fig tree casts her untimely figs when she is shaken of a mighty wind."

Comments: As is prophesied for earth, the stars of Narnia fall. Narnia's stars are living beings who fall to Narnia and then are brought into Aslan's Country.

18. "Especially, one couldn't say how long it had taken. Sometimes it seemed to have lasted only a few minutes, but at others it felt as if it might have gone on for years."

> **II Peter 3:8:** "But (beloved) be not ignorant of this one thing, that one day is with the Lord as a thousand years, and a thousand years as one day."

Comments: This is an expression of the timelessness of Aslan's Country and the ending of time as we think of it at the end of the world. In *The Last Battle,* Father Time's blowing of the horn puts an end to timekeeping in a worldly sense; in Aslan's Country, time means little.

19. "They all looked straight in his [Aslan's] face; I don't think they had any choice about that. And when some looked, the expression of their faces changed terribly—it was fear and hatred: except that, on the faces of Talking Beasts, the fear and hatred lasted only for a fraction of a second. You could see that they suddenly ceased to be *Talking* Beasts. They were just ordinary animals. And all the creatures who looked at Aslan in that way swerved away to their right, his left, and disappeared into his huge black shadow, which (as you have heard) streamed away to the left of the doorway. The children never saw them again. I don't know what became of them. But the others looked in the face of Aslan and loved him, though some of them were very frightened at the same time. And all these came in at the Door, in on Aslan's right."

Revelation 22:11-15: "He that is unjust, let him be unjust still: and he that is righteous, let him be righteous still: and he that is holy, let him be holy still. / And behold, I come quickly, and my reward is with me, to give every man according as his work shall be. / I am Alpha and Omega, the beginning and the end, the first and the last. / Blessed are they that do his commandments, that they may have right to the tree of life, and may enter in through the gates into the city. / For without *are* dogs, and sorcerers, and whoremongers, and murderers, and idolaters, and whosoever loves and tells a lie."

Comments: In the passage from *The Last Battle*, Lewis envisions how the separating of souls—evil to one side, good to the other—might look. The essence of each Talking Beast, Dwarf, and human being is revealed by his or her looking at Aslan's face, and they part company accordingly. Note that "they who do his commandments . . . have right to the tree of life" and that the fruit trees are immediately available to those who pass through the Door and enter Aslan's Country.

20. "Eustace even recognized one of those very Dwarfs who had helped to shoot the Horses. But he had no time to wonder about that sort of thing (and anyway it was no business of his) for a great joy put everything else out of his head."

John 21:22: "Jesus said to him [Peter], 'If I so will that he wait until I come, what is that to you?'"

Comments: When He says—"what is that to you?"—Christ tells Peter that His choice ("will") is "no business of his." Aslan's choosing the Dwarf who had helped to shoot the horses is His "will" and should not be questioned.

21. "Then the Moon came up, quite in her wrong position, very close to the sun, and she also looked red."

> **Joel 2:31:** "The Sun shall be turned into darkness, and the Moon into blood, before the great and the terrible day of the Lord come."

> **Revelation 6:12:** "And I beheld when he had opened the sixth seal, and low, there was a great earthquake, and the Sun became black as sackcloth of hair, and the Moon became as blood."

Comments: Narnia's "terrible day" has come; this is a prelude to the darkness that will engulf Narnia's world.

— Chapter 15: "Further Up and Further In" —

22. "For always since I was a boy, I have served Tash and my great desire was to know more of him and, if it might be, to look upon his face."

> **Psalms 27:8:** "*When you said, 'Seek you my face,'* my heart said to You, 'Your face, Lord, will I seek.'"

Comments: This has the potential for being a troubling passage in *The Last Battle,* because Tash is an evil demon, and Psalms 27 refers to the Lord, but Aslan explains that when Emeth sought to do good, he in fact, without knowing it, sought Aslan, not Tash. This helps explain why Emeth took joy in seeing Aslan the moment he saw Him. He knew the face of Aslan was the face for which he had searched.

23. "and resolved to look upon the face of Tash, though he should slay me."

Job 13:15: "Although he slay me, yet will I trust in Him: but I will maintain my own ways before Him."

Comments: In each case, this is an expression of faith. Job goes on to explain, "He also *shall* be my salvation" (Job 13:16). As he speaks in *The Last Battle,* Emeth already realizes that he actually sought Aslan, not Tash.

24. "The new one [Narnia] was a deeper country: every rock and flower and blade of grass looked as if it meant more."

II Peter 3:13: "Nevertheless we, according to His promise, look for new heavens, and a new earth, where dwells righteousness."

Comments: The children and their companions discover that they are in the new world, and righteousness—all that is good—is there.

25. "Faster and faster they raced, but no one got hot or tired or out of breath."

> **Isaiah 40:31**: "But they that wait on the Lord, shall mount up with wings as Eagles, they shall run and not be weary, *and* they shall walk, and not faint."

Comments: Aslan has called to Lucy and the others to follow Him "further up, and further in," and when they do as He says, they find themselves capable of amazing feats of strength, speed, and endurance; they even swim up a waterfall.

— Chapter 16: "Farewell to Shadow-Lands" —

26. "But that was not the real Narnia. That had a beginning and an end. It was only a shadow or copy of something in Aslan's real world."

> **Revelation 21:1**: "And I saw a new heaven, and a new earth: for the first heaven, and the first earth were passed away, and there was no more sea."

Comments: Narnia passes away the way earth will pass away, but there will be a new world in which to live.

27. "Have you noticed one can't feel afraid, even if one wants to?"

> **I John 4:18**: "There is no fear in love, but perfect love casts out fear: because fear has torment: he that fears, is not made perfect in love."

Comments: As is usually the case, Lucy understands what is happening before anyone else (except Aslan). They are in a land of God's perfect love, and His love has cast out their fear.

DISCUSSION QUESTIONS AND PROJECTS FOR *THE LAST BATTLE*

— Overview —

1. Lewis begins *The Last Battle* with "In the last days of Narnia." Does this increase or decrease your interest in the novel?

2. Dwarfs chant "The Dwarfs are for the Dwarfs" often in *The Last Battle*. What does this mean? What does the Dwarfs being for the Dwarfs get the Dwarfs?

3. What has happened to Jill and Eustace that makes them strong when facing their own deaths?

4. Should Susan be allowed to join the other kings and queens in Aslan's Country? Why is she not there at the end of *The Last Battle*?

5. Aslan says to Lucy, "I will show you both what I can, and what I cannot, do," when He tries to communicate with the Dwarfs in the stable. What is there that Aslan cannot do? Why can He not do it?

6. What does Aslan mean when He refers to Father Time, saying, "While he lay dreaming his name was Time. Now that he is awake he will have a new one"?

7. Does Lewis offer a satisfactory answer to what happens to good people who do not believe in Christ after they die?

8. Is it bothersome that Aslan welcomes equally into His world those who believed in Him and those who did not? Should there be special privileges for those who kept the faith?

9. What is important about the stable and the garden both being larger inside than they are outside?

10. Why would Tashbaan be included in Aslan's Country?

CHAPTER 1: BY CALDRON POOL

1. Does Lewis tell you enough about Shift and Puzzle in this Chapter? What else would you like to know about them before Chapter 2?

2. What is significant about the location of Shift's home?

CHAPTER 2: THE RASHNESS OF THE KING

1. What does the Dryad's death signify to Tirian? What does it say about the forest?

2. Why does Tirian head toward the troubles rather than going with Roonwit to rally his army?

CHAPTER 3: THE APE IN ITS GLORY

1. After what he has witnessed, is King Tirian too hard on himself for killing the Calormenes who were tormenting the Talking Horses, who are, after all, the king's subjects?

2. Why would Tirian be willing to submit to any sort of god, even Aslan, that supposedly condones, even orders, the enslavement of the king's own Narnians? Shouldn't he know that those works of evil cannot be Aslan's?

CHAPTER 4: WHAT HAPPENED THAT NIGHT

1. Puzzle in the lion's skin is a pitiful sight, even in shadows, and Shift is such an utter liar, so how is it that Narnians actually think the donkey is Aslan? What does this tell about state of faith in Narnia?

2. Why do Narnians submit to the brutal treatment of the Calormenes?

3. Why don't the Talking Animals who feed Tirian free him? They seem to be good, so why are they confused about what is right?

CHAPTER 5: HOW HELP CAME TO THE KING

1. Jill and Eustace each bring special qualities to the aid of King Tirian. What do you anticipate they will be able to do for him in later chapters?

2. Why do Eustace and Jill readily take orders from Tirian?

CHAPTER 6: A GOOD NIGHT'S WORK

1. "'If she were a boy,' said Tirian, 'she'd be whipped for disobeying orders.'" What does he mean by this? If it were not dark, would the others see him frowning or smiling?

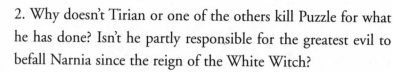
2. Why doesn't Tirian or one of the others kill Puzzle for what he has done? Isn't he partly responsible for the greatest evil to befall Narnia since the reign of the White Witch?

3. Is Puzzle's excuse "I only did what I was told" a good one?

CHAPTER 7: MAINLY ABOUT DWARFS

1. "*The light is dawning, the lie broken*" is a great line. Why does it not inspire the newly freed Dwarfs? Why does it instead fizzle?

2. Why does Poggin sneak away from the group of Dwarfs rather than openly declaring his allegiance to King Tirian and Aslan?

CHAPTER 8: WHAT NEWS THE EAGLE BROUGHT

1. Jill says, "*Our* world is going to have an end some day. Perhaps this one won't." Is this line intended to build suspense, to encourage us readers to think that somehow Tirian and Narnia will triumph, or to tell us about Jill herself?

2. If Tirian believes "Narnia is no more," then why does he continue to fight?

CHAPTER 9: THE GREAT MEETING

1. The Narnians at the stable are afraid. What difficulties does this present to Tirian?

2. What signs are there in this chapter that Jill and Eustace are continuing to grow as characters? How credible is their growth?

Chapter 10: Who Will Go into the Stable?

1. What seems to be the scheme behind Ginger going into the stable? Why would Rishda and others be surprised by Ginger's reaction to their scheme?

2. Why do the Beasts wail, "Spare us, Lord Shift, stand between us and Aslan, you must always go in and speak to him for us. We daren't, we daren't"?

Chapter 11: The Pace Quickens

1. When Tirian calls Narnians to his side, why do some say, "We daren't . . . Tashlan would be angry. Shield us from Tashlan"?

2. Why do the Dwarfs murder the horses?

Chapter 12: Through the Stable Door

1. How do the Dwarfs' seeking their own self-interest actually serve evil?

2. What makes Rishda Tash's lawful prey?

3. Why can Tirian not tell Jill's age?

4. Did Tirian die when he passed through the door of the stable?

Chapter 13: How the Dwarfs Refused to Be Taken In

1. Why can the Dwarfs in the stable not see the marvels that others see? What does their behavior suggest about real intelligence vs. conceit?

2. What does Peter mean when he says, "I've a feeling we've got to the country where everything is allowed"?

CHAPTER 14: NIGHT FALLS ON NARNIA

1. Is it right to mourn for Narnia as Tirian suggests, or should the characters rejoice at being in Aslan's Country?

2. Why is it Peter who carries the key of gold that locks the stable door?

3. Why does Peter say to the Dogs of the Calormene, "Whether he meets us in peace or war, he shall be welcome"?

CHAPTER 15: FURTHER UP AND FURTHER IN

1. Why is Puzzle permitted to enter Aslan's Country?

2. What does Digory mean when he says that the Narnia he and the others had known "was not the real Narnia. That had a beginning and an end. It was only a shadow or copy of something in Aslan's real world"?

3. What does Emeth's story tell about who is welcome in Aslan's Country?

CHAPTER 16: "FAREWELL TO SHADOW-LANDS"

1. Why does Aslan call our world and the old Narnian world "Shadow-Lands"?

2. Should Lucy be sad or happy that she has died?

3. What does Lewis mean by "Chapter One of the Great Story"?

SECTION IV

CONCLUSION,
BIBLIOGRAPHY,
INTERNET RESOURCES

CONCLUSION

— *The Chronicles of Narnia* as Entertainment —

The Chronicles of Narnia are magnificently entertaining works written by a master storyteller at the height of his powers, and they have been enjoyed by millions, possibly hundreds of millions, of people of many different faiths. A belief in God or a belief in Christianity is not necessary for the enjoyment of the novels. Lewis said that he put entertaining first and all else second when he wrote the Narnian books, and it is true.

Do not think that this source book, long though it may be, entirely conveys the experience of reading the novels themselves. There is no substitute for reading what Lewis actually wrote. Besides, reading the novels is one of the great experiences one can have. Children and adults love these books enough to read all of them and to read them more than once. They are the sort of books young readers will take to bed with them, to read when they are supposed to be sleeping, and they are treasures that youngsters like to keep close at hand. Some adults such as I also like to keep these novels close at hand, as I have done for decades.

The Chronicles of Narnia are written with such passion and ingeniousness that they are entertaining even if you know everything that will happen in them. Few novels can be read and reread with as much pleasure and profit as *The Chronicles of Narnia*.

One of the reasons the novels are entertaining is the way they are told. Lewis chose to structure the Narnian novels as high adventures, epic in scope. Just read the first chapters of each novel, and right away the main characters are plunged into mysterious worlds that are full of menace. Then note how by the end of the third chapter the conflict has become grand in scale: The survival of entire nations, sometimes the entire world is jeopardized, and the children from earth are vital to good defeating evil. This is a classic structure found in mythologies and folk tales, and it not only makes for fast-paced, exciting reading, but also creates a sense of being part of a grand adventure. In addition, Lewis takes advantage of the writing of fantasy; he can have danger pop up anyplace (it's magic!), and the danger can be amazing. Exotic settings are also common in mythologies and folk tales, and *The Chronicles of Narnia* are full of settings such as Dark Island where real dreams come true in *The Voyage of the "Dawn Treader,"* Tashbaan with its tier upon tier of palaces and lush gardens in *The Horse and His Boy,* and Narnia itself, where even some trees can talk and even dance. These are novels to lose oneself in.

— *The Chronicles of Narnia* as Literature —

The Chronicles of Narnia are proof that great literature can be entertaining literature. I use the word *great* advisedly. Taken as a whole, the seven volumes of *The Chronicles of Narnia* are great literature. One of their best attractions is their depth, which sometimes seems to go on forever, and which helps to account for their enduring popularity. Never have the novels been out of print since they were first published, and they are likely to stay in print far into the future. Longevity is one of the classic tests

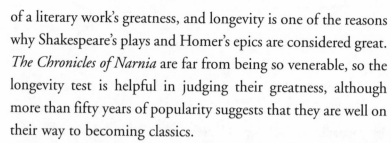

of a literary work's greatness, and longevity is one of the reasons why Shakespeare's plays and Homer's epics are considered great. *The Chronicles of Narnia* are far from being so venerable, so the longevity test is helpful in judging their greatness, although more than fifty years of popularity suggests that they are well on their way to becoming classics.

Characterization is one of the outstanding aspects of *The Chronicles of Narnia,* and the characters are one of the reasons the novels are popular, as well as one of the reasons for arguing for their greatness. As an exercise, you might try writing down everything you know about High King Peter, King Edmund, Queen Lucy, or Queen Susan. You will find that you know what they like to eat, how each one talks, how each one feels about the others, and even their fears, their hopes, and their wishes. We know that Peter is serious and that he leads by example. Edmund is prone to making aphorisms such as when there is a wasp in the room, he would like to keep it sight (pertaining to a dragon having landed on the beach near him in *The Voyage of the "Dawn Treader"*). Lucy is thoughtful, courageous, and spiritually strong. Susan is prone to making fun of children, is anxious that she not appear to be childlike, and is beautiful—so beautiful that Lucy is envious of her and how she makes herself the center of attention. You could make a long list of what you know about each character; it is possible for one to know more about the characters in *The Chronicles of Narnia* than one knows about the person sitting five days a week at a desk next to you.

Throughout this book, I have endeavored to show how Lewis' vigorous prose style enhances the experience of reading *The Chronicles of Narnia*. His mastery of prose style is wonderful; take note of how he shifts tone and phrasing for Aravis' telling her story in the High Calormene style. It is elaborate and ornate, like something from the *Arabian Knights,* and markedly different from the style of most of the narrative of the Narnian books. His descriptive powers are notable, from making Tashbaan come alive in *The Horse and His Boy* in all of its hustle and bustle and beauty to a feast at Aslan's Table near the End of the World in *The Voyage of the "Dawn Treader."* His achievement in describing Aslan's Country at the end of *The Last Battle* is extraordinary and one of the great achievements of literature written in English. Describing Heaven has been a challenge for centuries, but Lewis creates a full picture of Aslan's Country (Heaven) with its mysteries intact, but even so, alive and active. The main plot of *The Last Battle* ends early, with Tirian being pushed into the Stable, marking the victory of the forces of evil over the forces of good, yet the narrative still commands attention and still entertains, primarily with description.

Making Aslan's Country come alive is a great achievement, but not unique in *The Chronicles of Narnia.* You may have noticed the many maps provided in this book that indicate the richness of the places in *The Chronicles of Narnia.* Mountains, forests, deserts, islands, and may other sorts of places are part of a detailed world. Lewis builds his places with descriptions of seasonal changes, color of the soil, even how the air smells. Further, his places are not static. Regardless of his distaste for Darwinism, he was a well-read man who understood that geography changes as time passes. For example, in *Prince Caspian,* the Great River has formed a delta which at first confuses the Pevensie children because when they were kings and queens in *The Lion, the Witch*

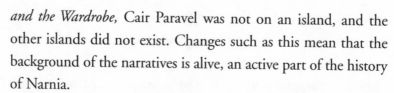

and the Wardrobe, Cair Paravel was not on an island, and the other islands did not exist. Changes such as this mean that the background of the narratives is alive, an active part of the history of Narnia.

Much of this source book has been devoted to the themes of the novels, and you may have noticed that they can be complex. Even though the novels seem to be straightforward accounts of conflicts between good and evil, there is much depth beneath the surface. His plots involve fundamental aspects of the human condition such as war, sorrow, and pleasure, and his characters find that such matters are not easy to understand or define. Yet, Lewis offers honest accounts of how people might behave when dealing with weighty matters such as a brother who is a traitor to his own brother and sisters, a young woman who betrays a servant in order to escape a loveless marriage, and whether to punish or give a second chance to enemies who have done great harm. Central to this is Aslan's own sacrifice, the ultimate giving of a second chance to Edmund, who had caused much evil.

In brief, for characterization, prose style, descriptive power, and extraordinary thematic depth, *The Chronicles of Narnia,* taken as if it were a single literary work, qualifies as great literature and should rank high among modern literary achievements. It is my contention that *The Chronicles of Narnia* should be considered as a complete literary work, not seven novels set in the same imaginary world. First of all, the Narnian books have a clear beginning, with the creation of the world, and a clear ending, with the destruction of the world. Further, they are not only linked by continuing characters such as Lucy and

Eustace, but they are linked by Aslan. It is Aslan Who makes the seven novels cohesive. Each novel is an account of Aslan's relationship to His creation and His people, and each novel advances by adding details to Aslan's work in Narnia's world.

— Lewis' Moral Views and The Chronicles of Narnia —

One of the elements that runs through all of *The Chronicles of Narnia* is strong, stern morality. Aslan expects His followers to adhere to a moral code. The code does not allow for lying. One would think that Shasta in *The Horse and His Boy* would have a good excuse for being untruthful while in the quarters of the Narnians in Tashbaan. After all, he has known little but cruelty from adults and therefore is suspicious of them. Letting the Narnians think he is someone else without telling them the truth stems from a very cautious nature in Shasta. Yet, Aslan reprimands Shasta, as does King Edmund, who additionally reprimands Shasta for listening in on a conversation that was none of his business. Likewise, Lucy is reprimanded by Aslan for magically listening in on a conversation not meant for her in *The Voyage of the "Dawn Treader."* Eavesdropping on other people is a violation of their privacy and seems to be against the moral code of *The Chronicles of Narnia*.

I say "seems" because there are instances of eavesdropping for which people are not reprimanded. For example, one important instance is Puddleglum listening to the conversation among giants who are eating together. He learns that they are eating the flesh of a Talking Stag, a very important bit of information,

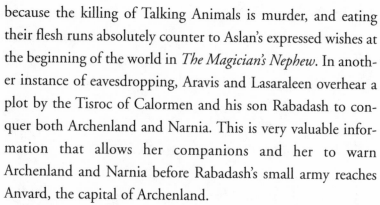

because the killing of Talking Animals is murder, and eating their flesh runs absolutely counter to Aslan's expressed wishes at the beginning of the world in *The Magician's Nephew*. In another instance of eavesdropping, Aravis and Lasaraleen overhear a plot by the Tisroc of Calormen and his son Rabadash to conquer both Archenland and Narnia. This is very valuable information that allows her companions and her to warn Archenland and Narnia before Rabadash's small army reaches Anvard, the capital of Archenland.

Is there a double standard at work in *The Chronicles of Narnia* in which it is okay to listen in on the conversations of bad people but not good people? If this were so, it would be hard to be true to Aslan's insisting that His followers not eavesdrop, because it would be hard to tell ahead of time whether one is listening in on evildoers or good people. In the case of Puddleglum listening in on a conversation in a dining commons, people in such a public place must allow for the possibility that they will be overheard by everyone in the dining area. On the other hand, the conversation of the Tisroc, Rabadash, and the Grand Vizier is unmistakably meant to be private, and it is hard to distinguish their plotting from the plotting of the Narnians in Tashbaan. Yet, without Aravis overhearing the Calormene scheme to conquer two countries, both Archenland and Narnia might be lost (although I believe Rabadash would have been overmatched in a battle against High King Peter). Remember the orders Rabadash gave his troops? He told them to kill every male in Anvard, even babies, and to divvy up the women among themselves. Aravis helps prevent a terrible atrocity, which is made possible only by eavesdropping. Further, had she declared her presence, as King Edmund thinks Shasta should have done, she and Lasaraleen would have been murdered on the spot.

Lewis' presentation of the morality of listening in on other people may be muddy, but his view on the proper treatment of people is emphatic. For instance, in *The Horse and His Boy*, Aravis' back is painfully clawed by the Lion that chases her to the Hermit. Aslan later reveals that this Lion was He, and the clawing was for the whipping Aravis' servant received after Aravis escaped from her. This is straightforward incidence of Aravis being punished for not following the Golden Rule: Do to others as you would have them do to you. The cuts on Aravis' back are slight; Aslan could have done worse had He wanted to do so, but He does only what is needed as a lesson to Aravis.

A good deal of the Narnian code of honor involves following the Golden Rule. For example, when Eustace grabs Reepicheep's tale in *The Voyage of the "Dawn Treader"* and whirls the Mouse around, the talk afterward is seriously about a duel between Reepicheep and Eustace to settle Eustace's cruelty toward the Mouse. His apology, although reluctant, marks the beginning of learning to treat others as he wants them to treat him, which in this case is with respect. Indeed, cruelty is the most frequent violation of the Golden Rule, and it is regularly punished, from the cruel teacher in Beruna in *Prince Caspian* to Uncle Andrew in *The Magician's Nephew*. The Golden Rule underlines the first days of Narnia's World, during which Aslan decreed that all Talking Animals and other people be treated fairly and as equals. This idea is part of the fabric of Narnian society and may explain why Narnia has hundreds of years of

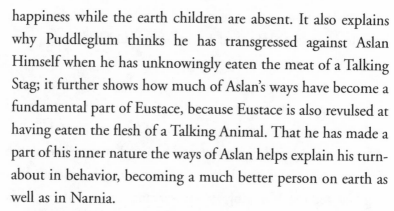

happiness while the earth children are absent. It also explains why Puddleglum thinks he has transgressed against Aslan Himself when he has unknowingly eaten the meat of a Talking Stag; it further shows how much of Aslan's ways have become a fundamental part of Eustace, because Eustace is also revulsed at having eaten the flesh of a Talking Animal. That he has made a part of his inner nature the ways of Aslan helps explain his turnabout in behavior, becoming a much better person on earth as well as in Narnia.

Following the Golden Rule is a sign that someone is good, as is the case with Mr. Tumnus in *The Lion, the Witch and the Wardrobe,* who chooses not to turn Lucy in to the secret police of the White Witch, even though it may cost him his life. In the case of Coriakin on the Island of the Dufflepuds in *The Voyage of the "Dawn Treader,"* doing good to others seems to be the magician's penance for his misdeed when he was a star in the firmament. This is a clue for what he may have done wrong; perhaps he treated someone very badly and must treat the Dufflepuds with courtesy and forbearance because he failed to treat others that way, before.

Another aspect of the morality of *The Chronicles of Narnia,* is violence. Lewis explained that violence was an important part of fairy tales, and that children wanted definitive results for evil and good characters; the wicked should be punished and the good rewarded. I would take Lewis' idea somewhat further and assert that adults by-and-large like definitive endings, too, even though experience has taught them that good people often suffer while wicked people enjoy themselves. *The Chronicles of Narnia* are like very long fairy tales in their use of magic and depiction of exotic characters, and the violence in them reflects Lewis' view that his young readers can understand the reasons for the violence. In addition, he believed that in real life, good people need to take action against evil, even violent action. He viewed both World War I and World War II as conflicts in which moral people and good nations fought evil.

In the case of *The Chronicles of Narnia*, there is little doubt of who is right and who is wrong. The evil of Jadis is evident in *The Magician's Nephew* the moment she remarks that every last person in her world should be ready to die for her. Guilty of genocide on a worldwide scale, she has no remorse. After many years of murder and cruelty, she eventually meets her end in battle in *The Lion, the Witch and the Wardrobe*. Her death seems appropriate. Another example of evil is Rabadash, who orders his troops to kill noncombatants, including day-old babies. His fate is ironic: He is forced to be a peacemaker instead of a rampaging killer. It is of special interest that it is Aslan who gives Rabadash a second chance in the courtyard in front of the gates to Anvard, because the people there believe that execution is suited to Rabadash's deeds.

The quality of mercy is another aspect of moral behavior often associated with Aslan, and good characters can be identified by their being merciful to people who deserve no mercy. This is not to say that Aslan was other than a stern figure. The witches—Jadis in *The Lion, the Witch and the Wardrobe* and the Queen of Underworld in *The Silver Chair*—die for their evil, as do the usurper Miraz and his henchmen in *Prince Caspian*. Further, *The Last Battle* features the definitive reward of good and the permanent separation of good from evil at the end of the world when the dead of Narnia's world rise and meet Aslan at the door to Aslan's Country. There is something satisfying about this absolute ending to the world.

Even so, Aslan is merciful to those who repent or who have been misled but try to be good anyway—remember, both the Calormene warrior Emeth and at least one of the ungrateful Dwarfs are allowed into heaven. Coupled with mercy is an admiration for intelligence. For example, King Caspian is extraordinarily merciful in *The Voyage of the "Dawn Treader."* At the Lone Islands he allows the slavers who kidnaped him to go free, but without their slaves. He had good reason to execute them. Additionally, he allows Governor Gumpas to live after discovering the evil Gumpas has encouraged with the bureaucratic excuses of economics and other abstractions that have nothing to do with the actual welfare of the people of the islands. He used his intelligence and diplomatic skills to secure a just government for the Lone Islands and to put an end to slavery. Just imagine what Rabadash would have done in the same situation.

— The Bible and *The Chronicles of Narnia* —

The Chronicles of Narnia can be read and enjoyed without any understanding of the Biblical sources for some of its events, although young readers tend to catch on to Aslan and His relationship to Christ. The arrival of Father Christmas in *The Lion, the Witch and the Wardrobe* is a giveaway of the Christian themes of the novel. Even so, Lewis wrote to entertain, not to preach. That his passionate interest in Christianity should find expression in *The Chronicles of Narnia* is as natural as his love of Norse Mythology which shapes the characters and locales for his adventures set in Narnia's world. Even so, anyone may love the books for their adventures, characters, and conflicts.

It is important for understanding the Biblical themes of *The Chronicles of Narnia* to keep in mind that Lewis regarded Christianity as a mythology, but as a mythology that is *true*—the only true myth. Thus, Aslan Himself is a representation of Christ as how He might appear in another world. Since it is Aslan Who appears in every Narnian book, religious themes are inevitably part of every book. Lewis also had an ambitious desire to give his audience a remythologizing of Christianity, a series of books that represent the essential elements of Christianity. Thus, he emphasizes the highly personal nature of Aslan. For instance, His sacrifice of His own life to save another life focuses tightly on Edmund. The cosmic aspect of His resurrection is pointed out when Aslan says that death is running backwards after He has revived, but its emotional meaning is rooted in Edmund, the fallen Son of Adam.

Lewis' references to the Bible in *The Chronicles of Narnia* are usually not as obvious as the ones to Christ's sacrifice and resurrection. They are scattered through his tales of adventure and add depth to the events he describes. For example, when Prince Rilian's shield changes from black to silver with a red rampant lion on it, the events that led to his being freed take on meaning larger than just plot devices. The shield indicates a connection to Aslan, showing that a spiritual battle has been won as well as a physical one. When Rilian struck off the head of the serpent, the transformation of the shield indicates a victory against primal evil, against evil that defies Aslan's Father.

In addition to inspiring spiritual ideas in *The Chronicles of*

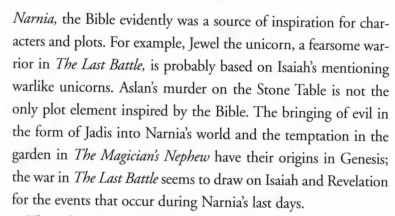

Narnia, the Bible evidently was a source of inspiration for characters and plots. For example, Jewel the unicorn, a fearsome warrior in *The Last Battle,* is probably based on Isaiah's mentioning warlike unicorns. Aslan's murder on the Stone Table is not the only plot element inspired by the Bible. The bringing of evil in the form of Jadis into Narnia's world and the temptation in the garden in *The Magician's Nephew* have their origins in Genesis; the war in *The Last Battle* seems to draw on Isaiah and Revelation for the events that occur during Narnia's last days.

The references to the Bible add much depth to the action in the Narnian novels. For example, the voyage undertaken in *The Voyage of the "Dawn Treader"* becomes a spiritual passage as well as an adventurous one. Reepicheep's paddling over the Last Wave to Aslan's Country has a deep poignancy not only because the Chief Mouse is a well-developed character, but because he is realizing a goal that is part of his heart. He will fulfill a spiritual hope; he will be with Aslan. As another example, the Biblical aspects of *The Silver Chair* make the quest of Jill and Eustace not just a rescue mission, as exciting as that would be by itself, but a journey of personal discovery. In following, as well as not following, Aslan's sign, Jill and Eustace learn of the hardships of making spiritual journeys, and the challenges involved in trying to come closer to Aslan. For instance, their petty bickering caused them both to forget to look for the signs. Less focus on their personal wants and more focus on helping each other would not only make the journey's hardships easier to bear, but might leave them clearheaded enough to pay attention to why they are out struggling. They need to grow spiritually, so that they can remember that Aslan had a purpose in sending them on their quest.

BIBLIOGRAPHY

Resources For Young Readers

Bingham, Derick. *C. S. Lewis: The Storyteller*. Tain, Ross-shire, Scotland: Christian Focus, 1999. This is a slightly fictionalized account of Lewis' life. Its details are accurate, and it is engagingly written.

Coren, Michael. *The Man Who Created Narnia: The Story of C. S. Lewis*. Grand Rapids: William B. Eerdmans, 1994. This book is excellent in its explanation of Lewis' personality, and it does so as plainly and well as any of the biographies for adults. Coren's treatment is free of cant and easily read. Although the title might suggest an emphasis on *The Chronicles of Narnia*, Coren's book actually covers the whole of Lewis' life fairly evenly, creating a well-rounded picture of the man. The many photographs are excellent.

Gormley, Beatrice. *C. S. Lewis: Christian and Storyteller*. Grand Rapids: Eerdmans, 1998. As the title may suggest, this is a spiritual biography of Lewis, tracing his development as a Christian writer. Some of the passages will challenge younger readers of *The Chronicles of Narnia*, but many readers will find Gormley's account helpful for understanding the kind of man who invented Narnia.

Gresham, Douglas. *The Narnia Cookbook: Foods from C. S. Lewis' The Chronicles of Narnia*. New York: HarperCollins, 1998. This book is much fun and includes essays from "Stewed

Eel" to "Gooseberry Fool." The favorite recipes of Narnia are explained. This book includes a section "A Word about Safety" that is valuable. Young chefs probably should be supervised by an adult while attempting recipes such as "Rhubarb Fool" that may require the use of appliances. Most of what one needs to know to reconstruct homey meals such as the Beavers serve in *The Lion, the Witch and the Wardrobe* to banquets like that on Ramandu's island in *The Voyage of the "Dawn Treader."*

Lewis, C. S. *Letters to Children.* Edited by Lyle W. Dorsett and Marjorie Lamp Mead. New York: Touchstone (Simon & Schuster), 1985. Lewis made it a habit to wake up early everyday and read and reply to letters he had received. Upon the publication of the Narnia books, he received hundreds, maybe thousands, of letters from young people. In this gathering of some of the letters, Lewis tells about what he hoped to achieve with the books, how they were written, and how young people might write stories of their own.

The Narnia Trivia Book. New York: Harper Trophy (HarperCollins), 1999. This is a charming book of questions and answers that may inspire readers to look closely at the texts of *The Chronicles of Narnia*. A typical question is: "Who is the old man Jill and Eustace see getting on the ship?" for *The Silver Chair.*

Sibley, Brian. *The Land of Narnia.* New York: Harper Trophy (HarperCollins), 1989. Sibley finds the beginnings of Narnia in Lewis' childhood fantasies and includes some early drawings of "Animal-Land." This book offers an interesting account of Lewis' imagination at work. It includes new illustrations by Pauline Baynes, who was Lewis' original choice to illustrate the Narnian books.

Swift, Catherine. *C. S. Lewis.* Minneapolis: Bethany House, 1989. This small book traces Lewis' spiritual journey through atheism to Christianity, making Lewis' life an example of how someone can recognize Christ in his life. This biography is meant to be inspiration rather then analytical.

Wellman, Sam. *C. S. Lewis: Author of Mere Christianity.* Uhrichsville, OH: Barbour, 1996. Wellman emphasizes how Lewis sought a focus on Jesus that would unite Christians of very diverse backgrounds through faith.

Resources for Adults

Duriez, Colin. *The C. S. Lewis Encyclopedia: A Complete Guide to His Life, Thought, and Writings.* Wheaton, IL: Crossway Books (Good News), 2000. This is a list with notes of the people in Lewis' life, Lewis' publications, and the significant characters in Lewis' fiction. Its strength is in Lewis' writings for adults, but it is a handy, easy-to-read reference.

Ford, Paul F. *Companion to Narnia.* New York: HarperCollins, fourth edition 1994 (first edition 1980). Although difficult to find, this is a fine resource for details about *The Chronicles of Narnia* and is the best single companion guide.

Hooper, Walter. *C. S. Lewis: Companion and Guide.* New York: HarperCollins, 1996. Hooper has devoted nearly all of his life to the study of Lewis and was trusted by Lewis himself. In this huge book, Hooper discusses the background for nearly every publication of Lewis', from poetry to theology. This is not for the casual reader, but for someone serious enough to spend many hours gleaning details of the backgrounds for Lewis' work. For that serious reader, this is a wonderful reference.

Lindskoog, Kathryn. *Journey into Narnia*. Pasadena, CA: Hope, 1998. Offers background information on the concepts in *The Chronicles of Narnia*.

Schultz, Jeffrey D. and John G. West Jr., editors. *The C. S. Lewis Readers' Encyclopedia*. Grand Rapids: Zondervan (HarperCollins), 1998. This book has a biography of Lewis followed by an alphabetical listing of people, places, things, and concepts. It is particularly good at explaining concepts of nature and magic. The entries were written by forty-three people. This is a good book, but for references on Narnia one probably should use it in conjunction with Ford's *Companion to Narnia*.

Wilson, A. N. *C.S. Lewis: A Biography*. London: Collins, 1990. This is the best biography of Lewis. It is a psychoanalytical biography, which Wilson acknowledges Lewis would have disliked, preferring that an author's work be considered apart from his state of mind. According to Wilson, Lewis failed to come to terms with his grief over his mother's premature death, and that his relationships with women were influenced by a desire to recover his lost mother. Wilson does a good job of clearing away the legendary version of Lewis to find the real, robust man.

Major Works by C. S. Lewis

Spirits in Bondage, 1919 (poem written as Clive Hamilton)

The Pilgrim's Regress: An Allegorical Apology for Christianity, Reason and Romanticism, 1933 (autobiographical allegory)

The Allegory of Love: A Study in Medieval Tradition, 1936 (criticism)

Out of the Silent Planet, 1938

The Problem of Pain, 1940

The Screwtape Letters, 1942 (theology)

Perelandra, 1943

That Hideous Strength, 1945

The Lion, the Witch, and the Wardrobe, 1950

Prince Caspian, 1951

Mere Christianity, 1952 (theology)

The Voyage of the 'Dawn Treader', 1952

The Silver Chair, 1953

The Horse and His Boy, 1954

The Magician's Nephew, 1955

Surprised by Joy, 1955 (autobiography)

The Last Battle, 1956

Till We Have Faces: A Myth Retold, 1956

A Grief Observed, 1961 (autobiography)

Letters to Malcolm, 1962 (theology)

INTERNET RESOURCES

Narnian Web Sites

Army of Aslan

http://www. geocities.com/Area51/Vault/9451

In addition to providing background information on Lewis and *The Chronicles of Narnia*, this site has some wonderful art based on the novels.

Danielle's Narnia Page.

http://www.geocities.com/RainForest/Andes/6712

This has pictures and maps, as well as information on the characters of *The Chronicles of Narnia*.

#narnia

http://narnia.freeservers.com

This is a chat site for *The Chronicles of Narnia* and the Bible.

"Official" web site

http://www.narnia.com

This site is run by HarperCollins Publishers Ltd. It offers a brief guide to Narnia's world.

C. S. Lewis Web Sites

An Annotated Bibliography to C. S. Lewis: Till We Have Faces: a myth retold

http://ivory.trentu.ca/www/cl/materials/lewis-bib.html

The bibliography is focused on the one book, but it is remarkable scholarship by H. Lesfloris and I. C. Storey.

The Bible and C. S. Lewis
http://members.aol.com/thompsonja/cslewis.htm
This is a resource for Lewis's use of the Bible, and it offers notes on upcoming events and links.

C. S. Lewis: 20th-Century Christian Knight
http://ic.net/~erasmus/RAZ26.HTML
A good collection of photographs sets this site apart, and it offers details on Lewis's thought.

C. S. Lewis & Public Life
http://www.discovery.org/lewis/
This is the web site of the C. S. Lewis Institute, and it provides many good, in-depth papers and articles about Lewis.

C. S. Lewis and Related Authors
http://www.tayloru.edu/upland/programs/lewis/
Lewis's life and work, as well as the relation of his work to the works of other writers are the focus of this site.

C. S. Lewis (and the Inklings)
http://personal.bgsu.edu/~edwards/lewis.html
A special aspect of this site is its tips for youngsters researching Lewis.

C. S. Lewis Campfire Chat
http://www.killdevilhill.com/c.s.lewischat/wwwboard.html
This is a chat site, including live chats, focusing on Christian issues, particularly in popular culture.

C S Lewis Centenary Group
http://dnausers.d-n-a.net/cslewis/
This offers historical background for Lewis.

C. S. Lewis Directory of Hyperlinks
http://www.rwf2000.com/CH/cslewis.htm
This site offers reflective thoughts on Lewis as well as links.

C. S. Lewis Foundation
http://www.cslewis.org/
This is a wide-ranging site about Lewis, his influence, and influences on him.

C. S. Lewis Institute
http://www.cslewisinstitute.org/
This elaborate site offers courses on Lewis, background information, and links. The Institute is a Christain proselytizing organization.

C. S. Lewis Lecture Hall
http://mobydicks.com/lecture/CSLewishall/wwwboard.html
Run by Western Canon University, this is a chat room with links to additional chat rooms. The expectation is that those chatting will focus on Lewis.
The C. S. Lewis Society: A Resource for your Ministry

http://www.apologetics.org/societies/fellowship.html
To be found here are links, news of events, and a biographical
sketch.

Into the Wardrobe: The C. S. Lewis Web Site
http://cslewis.drzeus.net/
An impressive gathering of material related to Lewis, this site
emphasizes literature.

The Lewis Legacy Online
http://www.discovery.org/lewis/lewislegacy.html
This has many essays by scholars about aspects of Lewis's works,
with some focusing on allegations by some scholars that some
posthumous publications attributed to Lewis are fraudulent.

Memphis C. S. Lewis Society
http://www.narnia.org/
This is a good place to look for links to other sites.

INDEX

ABOUT KIRK H. BEETZ

Kirk H. Beetz holds two bachelor's degrees from the University of California, Davis, in English literature and in creative writing, a master's degree in English literature, and a Ph.D. in Victorian and Renaissance literature and English drama. He has published full-length works on John Ruskin, Wilkie Collins, Algernon Charles Swinburne, and Alfred Tennyson and hundreds of critical analyses on modern and young adult writers. From 1991-1999 he served as project editor for *Beacham's Guide to Literature for Young Adults* and *Beacham's Encyclopedia of Popular Fiction*, and was co-editor of *Beacham's Guide to International Endangered Species*. He lives with his wife, Suzanne Munich, in Davis, California and can be reached by e-mail at www.BeachamPub.com.